HISTORICAL DICTIONARIES OF INTELLIGENCE AND COUNTERINTELLIGENCE

Jon Woronoff, Series Editor

1. *British Intelligence*, by Nigel West, 2005.
2. *United States Intelligence*, by Michael A. Turner, 2006.
3. *Israeli Intelligence*, by Ephraim Kahana, 2006.
4. *International Intelligence*, by Nigel West, 2006.
5. *Russian and Soviet Intelligence*, by Robert W. Pringle, 2006.
6. *Cold War Counterintelligence*, by Nigel West, 2007.
7. *World War II Intelligence*, by Nigel West, 2008.
8. *Sexspionage*, by Nigel West, 2009.
9. *Air Intelligence*, by Glenmore S. Trenear-Harvey, 2009.
10. *Middle Eastern Intelligence*, by Ephraim Kahana and Muhammad Suwaed, 2009.

Historical Dictionary of Middle Eastern Intelligence

Ephraim Kahana
Muhammad Suwaed

*Historical Dictionaries of Intelligence and
Counterintelligence, No. 10*

The Scarecrow Press, Inc.
Lanham, Maryland • Toronto • Plymouth, UK
2009

SCARECROW PRESS, INC.

Published in the United States of America
by Scarecrow Press, Inc.
A wholly owned subsidiary of
The Rowman & Littlefield Publishing Group, Inc.
4501 Forbes Boulevard, Suite 200, Lanham, Maryland 20706
www.scarecrowpress.com

Estover Road
Plymouth PL6 7PY
United Kingdom

British Library Cataloguing in Publication Information Available

Library of Congress Cataloging-in-Publication Data

Kahana, Ephraim.
  Historical dictionary of Middle Eastern intelligence / Ephraim Kahana,
Muhammad Suwaed.
     p. cm. — (Historical dictionaries of intelligence and counterintelligence ;
no. 10)
  Includes bibliographical references.
  ISBN 978-0-8108-5953-1 (cloth : alk. paper) — ISBN 978-0-8108-6302-6
(eBook)
  1. Military intelligence–Middle East–History–Dictionaries. 2. Intelligence
service–Middle East–History–Dictionaries. 3. Espionage–Middle East–History–
Dictionaries. I. Suwaed, Muhammad. II. Title.
  UB251.M53K34 2009
  327.1256003–dc22   2008049302

⊗™ The paper used in this publication meets the minimum requirements of
American National Standard for Information Sciences—Permanence of
Paper for Printed Library Materials, ANSI/NISO Z39.48-1992.
Manufactured in the United States of America.

Contents

Editor's Foreword

Given the rivalries and suspicions prevailing in the Middle East, it is not surprising that most of these states are very concerned about espionage and infiltration. Without much ado, therefore, they engage in spying and subversion of their neighbors, whether enemies or—theoretically at least—friends. The result is an impressively busy intelligence industry, proportionately larger and more extensive than in most other regions, and this in both times of war and peace. Moreover, since most of the states are—to varying degrees—autocratic, they are often more concerned about keeping track of what their own citizens are doing than what external enemies are up to. To this must be added the increasing threat of terrorism; like most of the rest of the world, Middle Eastern states worry about attacks from both internal and external terrorist organizations, which also engage in various forms of espionage. This naturally adds to the importance of the intelligence agencies, and sometimes gives them exceptional clout in running the countries—indeed, occasionally to the extent of being a threat to even the most insidious regime. But the story does not quite end here since the Middle East has also been involved in international politics, especially during the two world wars and the Cold War, which means that outside powers have also engaged in massive espionage to keep track of what is going on there.

Since intelligence has been such an important matter for so long, it is not surprising that there is much to say about it in this latest addition to the series of Historical Dictionaries of Intelligence and Counterintelligence. Yet, considering the depths of secrecy that prevail even about the most ordinary things, and the limited information generally available, this book has been harder to compile than others. So it has taken some time to fill this gap in the series. A good place to start in this volume is the chronology, which traces the role of intelligence over the years—indeed, decades and sometimes centuries. The overall situation is summed up in the introduction. But the most significant material is provided in the dictionary section, which includes, among other things, entries not only on the intelligence situation of all the main players and most of the minor ones but also specific aspects thereof, such as involvement in the various wars or in fighting terrorism. Other entries focus on specific intelligence agencies, their directors, and notable cases of espionage. The list of acronyms is particularly important in this book, simply to identify the players; their names in Arabic or other languages can be found in the entries. The bibliography directs readers to other sources that, alas, are far fewer than one would have hoped, but not surprisingly so.

This *Historical Dictionary of Middle Eastern Intelligence* was written by Ephraim Kahana and Muhammad Suwaed. Both of these scholars presently teach at Western Galilee College in Israel, and Dr. Kahana has also taught at the University of Haifa and the Israeli Technion. Dr. Kahana specializes in international relations and, more specifically, intelligence and national security issues, on which he has lectured and written extensively. He recently published the *Historical Dictionary of Israeli Intelligence* in this series. Dr. Suwaed deals with the national security of Arab states, among other things, and has also published extensively. Between them, they cover most of the region and can show not only what has been happening in each country but also—and more importantly—how the various states in the region relate to one another. That is no mean feat given the constantly changing situation in Middle Eastern countries, most of which are not known for being very open on their activities, and most particularly not those related to intelligence.

Jon Woronoff
Series Editor

Preface

Historical research of intelligence organizations and communities is a relatively new field, due to restricted access to archives and a lack of alternative sources. As a result, the historiography of intelligence is often focused on a limited time period or region. This dictionary is based on a wide variety of records and documents from intelligence and counterintelligence organizations whose operations spanned the closing quarter of the 19th century until the beginning of the 21st century in various parts of the Middle East. Defining the boundaries of the Middle East itself is not an easy task. Traditionally, the Middle East has been defined as the region extending from Morocco and Mauritania on the Atlantic Ocean to the states on the Persian Gulf. This vast area includes a number of Arab countries as well as three non-Arab countries: Iran, Israel, and Turkey. After the terror attack of 11 September 2001, the definition of the Middle East was extended even further eastward to include Afghanistan and Pakistan.

This dictionary is a tool to familiarize the reader with the historical background of important events and key organizations involved in all aspects of intelligence gathering and analysis, as well as the biographies of key players who have had an influence on the current situation in the Middle East. The dictionary addresses intelligence issues in the region from ancient history and the Middle Ages through modern times, covering the decline of the Ottoman Empire, intelligence activity in the Middle East during and between the two world wars, and the interplay between colonial and local intelligence and counterintelligence agencies of the period. It also presents the relatively new fundamentalist terrorist organizations that have had a significant impact on international relations and on the structure and deployment of intelligence, counterintelligence, and other security organs in the Middle East today.

Acknowledgments

Writing a dictionary like this cannot be done alone. Many helped in this mission and all deserve my gratitude. First and foremost, I would like to thank Richard R. Valcourt, editor in chief of the *Journal of Intelligence and Counterintelligence*, who recommended me to Jon Woronoff, the editor of the series of Historical Dictionaries of Intelligence and Counterintelligence. I am grateful to Jon Woronoff for asking me to write this dictionary on Middle Eastern intelligence.

I would also like to thank Western Galilee College and especially the library staff for their kind assistance in locating the proper references. A special thanks go to Zahava Santo, director of the library, and Tamar Israeli, the library's information specialist, who helped with the technical side of preparing the bibliography.

To Muhammad Suwaed, who agreed to take part and assist me in writing the dictionary, I owe a deep debt of gratitude. Special recognition is due to Dr. Suwaed for his contribution of material to many interesting entries, particularly intelligence in ancient Islam.

Many thanks are also due to Jon Woronoff for his useful corrections and suggestions throughout the course of my writing. I would also like to thank April Snider of Scarecrow Press for her technical assistance in the layout of the book.

Last, but of course not least, I would like to thank my family, who had to live with the fact that so much of my time over the past year was devoted to bringing the book to completion.—Ephraim Kahana

I wish to express my thanks to the Western Galilee and the Jordan Valley Academic Colleges for the encouragement and financial support provided to me during the period I was engaged in writing of this book.

I also wish to express thanks to Dr. Jon Woronoff for approaching Dr. Kahana and myself regarding the writing of this book.

And finally, I wish to thank my family who bore with me during the period I was engaged in writing this book. I hope the book will be an appropriate compensation for their patience and understanding.
—Suwaed Muhammad

Acronyms and Abbreviations

ACPSS	Ahram Center for Political and Strategic Studies
AFI	Air Force Intelligence (Syria)
AHC	Arab Higher Committee
AIC	Anti-Imperialism Center/Al-Mathaba
AIOC	Anglo–Iranian Oil Company
AIS	Islamic Salvation Army (Algeria)
ALN	Armée de Libération Nationale (Algeria)
AMIA	Argentine Israelite Mutual Association
ANO	Abu Nidal Organization
ANP	Armée Nationale Populaire (Algeria)
APC	Armored Personnel Carriers
ARAMCO	Arabian–American Oil Company
ATI	Agence Tunisienne d'Internet (Tunisian Internet Agency)
AWACS	Airborne Warning and Control System
BCCI	Bank of Credit and Commerce International
BDA	Battle Damage Assessment
BDF	Bahrain Defense Force
BND	Bundesnachrichtendienst/Federal Intelligence Service (Germany)
BTWC	Biological and Toxin Weapons Convention
CBME	Combined Bureau Middle East
CIA	Central Intelligence Agency (United States)
CPA	Coalition Provisional Authority (Iraq)
CTC	Counterterrorist Center (United States)
CTC/SO	Counterterrorist Center Special Operations (United States)
CTU	144th Counterterrorist Unit (Sudan)
CW	Chemical Warfare

DCI	Director of the Central Intelligence Agency (DCI)
DGDS	Delégation Générale de Documentation et Sûreté Générale/Delegation for Documentation and Security (Algeria)
DGMI	Directorate of General Military Intelligence/al-Istikhbarat al-Askariyya (Iraq)
DGS	Directorate of General Security/al-Amn al-Amm (Iraq)
DGSN	Direction Générale de la Sûreté Nationale/General Office of National Security (Morocco)
DIA	Defense Intelligence Agency (United States)
DMI	Director of Military Intelligence
DRG	Diversionnye Rrazvedyvatelnye Gruppy/Sabotage–Intelligence Groups (Soviet Union)
DSDE	Director of Security for the Defense Establishment/Memuneh Al Habitahon Be'Maarekhet Ha'Bitahon (Israel)
DST	Direction de la Surveillance du Territoire/Territory Security Directorate (Morocco)
EAF	Egyptian Air Force
EEF	Egyptian Expeditionary Force
EIJ	Egyptian Islamic Jihad
ESD	External Security Department (Syria)
ESO	External Security Organization (Libya)
EUSC	European Union Satellite Centre
FBI	Federal Bureau of Investigation (United States)
FIA	Federal Investigation Agency (Pakistan)
FIBE	Faisal Islamic Bank of Egypt
FIS	Front Islamique du Salut/Islamic Salvation Front (Algeria)
FRE	Former Regime Elements (Iraq)
FSU	Former Soviet Union
GAF	German Air Force
GCC	Gulf Cooperation Council
GDSSI	General Directorate for State Security Investigations/Mubahath el-Dawla (Egypt)

GI	General Intelligence/Mukhabarat al-Amma/Palestinian National Authority
GIA	Groupe Islamique Armé/Armed Islamic Group (Algeria)
GIB	Guide's Intelligence Bureau/Maktab Maaloumat al-Kaed (Libya)
GID	General Intelligence Department/Dairat al-Mukhabarat al-Ammah (Jordan)
GID	General Intelligence Directorate (Syria)
GIS	General Intelligence Service/Jihaz al-Mukhabarat al-Amma (Egypt)
GIS	General Intelligence Service/Mudiriyat al-Amn al-Amma (Palestinian National Authority)
GMT	GeoMiliTech
GSD	General Security Directorate/Sûreté générale (Lebanon)
GSS	General Security Service (Palestinian National Authority)
GWAPS	Gulf War Air Power Survey
HM	Hizb ul-Mujahidin
HPG	People's Defense Force
HUMINT	Human Intelligence
IAEA	International Atomic Energy Agency
IAEC	Iraq Atomic Energy Commission
IAF	Israeli Air Force
IAI	Israel Aerospace Industries
IB	Intelligence Bureau (Pakistan)
IC	Intelligence Community
IDF	Israel Defense Forces
IED	Improvised Explosive Devices
IG	Islamic Group/Gamaya Islamiya (Egypt)
IIS	Iraqi Intelligence Service
IMEMO	Institute of World Economy and International Relations (Russia)
INIS	Iraqi National Intelligence Service
IRG	Iranian Islamic Revolutionary Guard/Sepáh e Pásdárán e Enqeláb e Eslámi
ISA	Israeli Security Agency

ISD	Internal Security Department (Syria)
ISFC	Internal Security Forces Command (Syria)
ISI	Directorate for Interservices Intelligence (Pakistan)
JCIB	Joint Counter Intelligence Bureau (Pakistan)
JIB	Joint Intelligence Bureau (Pakistan)
JIM	Joint Intelligence Miscellaneous (Pakistan)
JIN	Joint Intelligence (Pakistan)
JIX	Joint Intelligence X (Pakistan)
JSIB	Joint Signal Intelligence Bureau (Pakistan)
JSO	Jamahiriya Security Organization/Haiat amn al Jamahiriya (Libya)
JTF	Joint Task Force (United States)
KGB	Komitet Gosudarstvennoy Bezopasnosti/Committee for State Security (Soviet Union)
LAKAM	Lishka Le'Ksharim Madaiim/Bureau of Scientific Liaison (Israel)
LAP	Literature and Publications
LIS	Laser Isotope Separation
LIS	Libyan Intelligence Service/Istikhbarat al Askariya
LF	Lebanese Forces
MAGTF	Marine Air-Ground Task Force (United States)
MALMAB	Memuneh Al Habitahon Be'Maarekhet Ha'Bitahon/Director of Security for the Defense Establishment (Israel)
MEH	Milli Emniyet Hizmeti/National Security Service (Turkey)
MEIC	Middle East Intelligence Centre in Cairo
MEK	Mujahedeen-e Khalq
MI	Military Intelligence
MIC	Military Industrial Commission (Iraq)
MIM	Mudafaa-i Milliye/National Defense (Turkey)
MIT	Milli Istihbarat Teskilati/National Intelligence Organization (Turkey)
MOIS	Ministry of Intelligence and Security/Vezarat-e Ettela'at va Amniat-e Keshvar (VEVAK) (Iran)

MTR	Materials Test Reactor
NALT	Northern Afghanistan Liaison Team
NATO	North Atlantic Treaty Organization
NBC	Nuclear, Biological and Chemical Weapons
NCR	National Council of Resistance (Iran)
NESO	North East Students Organization (Pakistan)
NGA	National Geospatial-Intelligence Agency (United States)
NIE	National Intelligence Estimate (United States
NILI	Netzah Yisrael Lo Yeshaker ("the Everlasting of Israel will not lie"; 1 Sam 15:29)
NOC	Nonofficial Cover
NPT	Nuclear Nonproliferation Treaty
NSA	National Security Agency
NSCN	National Security Council of Nagaland (Pakistan)
NSF	National Security Forces (Sudan)
NUMEC	Nuclear Materials and Equipment Corporation
OIF	Operation Iraqi Freedom
ORTAG	Organisation, Revisions und Treuhand AG (Germany)
OSCINT	Open Sources Intelligence
PFLP	Popular Front for the Liberation of Palestine
PG	Presidential Guard (Syria)
PIJ	Palestinian Islamic Jihad
PKK	Partiya Karkerên Kurdistan/Kurdistan Worker's Party
PLO	Palestinian Liberation Organization
PNA	Palestinian National Authority
PSD	Political Security Directorate (Syria)
PSF	Preventative Security Force (Palestinian National Authority)
RAF	Royal Air Force (Great Britain)
RAO	Royal Army of Oman
ROP	Royal Oman Police
SAF	Sultan's Armed Forces (Oman)
SAS	Special Air Service (Great Britain)
SAVAK	Sazeman-i Ettelaat va Amniyat-i Keshvar/National Organization for Intelligence and Security (Iran)

SAVAMA	Sazman-e Ettela'at va Amniat-e Melli-e Iran/Ministry of Intelligence and National Security (MOIS)
SDECE	Service de Documentation Extérieure et de Contre-Espionnage (France)
SF	Special Forces (Syria)
SHAI	Sherut Yedioth/Information Service (Israel)
SIBAT	Siyua Bithoni/Security Support (Israel)
SICRI	Supreme Council for Islamic Revolution in Iraq
SIGINT	Signals Intelligence
SIME	British Security Intelligence Middle East
SIS	Secret Intelligence Service (Great Britain)
SITREP	Situation Report (United States)
SOART	Special Operations Aviation Regiment (United States)
SOS	Save Our Souls
SPF	Special Police Force (Sudan)
SPLA	Sudan People's Liberation Army
SPLM	Sudan People's Liberation Movement
SSF	Special Security Force/al-Amn al-Khass (Palestinian National Authority)
SSO	Special Service Officers (Great Britain)
SSO	Special Security Organization/al-Amn al-Khas (Iraq)
SSO	State Security Organization (Sudan)
SSTL	Surrey Satellite Technology Ltd. (Great Britain)
SVR	Sluzhba Vneshnei Razvedki/Foreign Intelligence Service (Russia)
SWS	Special Wireless Section
TAPLINE	Trans-Arabian Pipe Line
THB	Turkish Hizballah
UAE	United Arab Emirates
UAR	United Arab Republic
ULFA	United Liberation Front of Assam (Pakistan)
ULFOSS	United Liberation Front of Seven Sisters (Pakistan)
UN	United Nations
UNSC	United Nations Security Council

UNSCOM	United Nations Special Commission on Iraq
USAFE	United States Air Forces in Europe
USCENTCOM	United States Central Command
USFP	Union Socialiste des Forces Populaires/Socialist Union of Popular Forces (Morocco)
VARASH	Va'adat Rashei Hasherutim/Committee of Directors of the Intelligence Services (Israel)
VEVAK	Vezarat-e Ettela'at va Amniat-e Keshvar/Ministry of Intelligence and Security (MOIS) (Iran)
WMD	Weapon of Mass Destruction
WTO	World Trade Organization

Chronology

1479 BCE   The battle of Megiddo I takes place. King Tuthmose III of Egypt moves troops against the king of Kadesh in Palestine. The intelligence of Egypt about the Canaanite forces is wrong.

610 to 613 CE   Prophet Muhammad sets up an intelligence apparatus to protect the newly established religion (Islam).

1914   The first Turkish intelligence organization is established in 1914 under the name of Teskilat-i Mahsusa (Special Organization) to undertake important missions and carry out military and paramilitary activities during World War I.

1915   NILI, the Jewish espionage ring in the Ottoman Palestine network, is established. **28 January:** The First Suez Offensive starts. **3 February:** The First Suez Canal Offensive ends with an Ottoman withdrawal. **April:** The battle of Gallipoli starts.

1916   The Arab Bureau is established in Cairo as a central agency in charge of Arab issues in the Middle East, particularly for dealing with propaganda. Great Britain establishes a wireless intelligence unit to be deployed at various sites in Egypt and Cyprus. **January:** The battle of Gallipoli ends. **June:** The Arab revolt led by Hussein Bin Ali, the sheriff of Mecca and Benin, starts against the Ottoman Empire. **6 June:** The first issue of the *Arab Bulletin* is published. The bulletin describes political viewpoints and thoughts of the Arab Bureau. **3 August:** The battle of Romani starts.

1917   **26 March:** The battle of Gaza starts. **May:** Colonel Richard Henry Meinertzhagen joins General Edmond H. Allenby's Intelligence Section in Cairo, Egypt. **October:** NILI is captured by the Turks. **30 October:** The British army launches a surprise attack on Beersheba and a simultaneous attack on Gaza, Palestine.

1918   The Turkish Karakol Cemiyeti (Police Guild) is established, replacing the Teskilat-i Mahsusa (Special Organization). **19 September:** The battle of Megiddo II starts. **21 September:** The battle of Megiddo II end; the superiority of Great Britain's Egyptian Expeditionary Force and achievements of the air force against the Ottoman Empire's forces are attributed to good intelligence.

1920   The Turkish Askeri Polis Teskilati (Military Police Organization) is founded.

1921   The Transjordan Frontier Force is formed as a regular army. Lebanon's General Security Directorate (GSD)/Sureté Générale is established. **May:** Mudafaa-i Milliye (MIM)/National Defense is founded by the Turkish Grand National Assembly in order to fill the intelligence vacuum left by the Askeri Polis Teskilaty.

1923   The Transjordan Frontier Force is renamed the Arab Legion. **5 October:** The Turkish Mudafaa-i Milliye (MIM) is dissolved.

1925   **25 July:** The Great Syrian Revolt (also known as the Druze Revolt) starts.

1927   **6 January:** The first intelligence organization of the Republic of Turkey is established under the name Milli Emniyet Hizmeti (MEH)/National Security Service.

1932   Aziz Bek's book *Syria and Lebanon during the World War: Intelligence and Espionage in the Ottoman Empire* is published.

1936   The second edition of Aziz Bek's book *Intelligence and Espionage in Syria, Lebanon, and Palestine during the World War* is published. **April:** The Great Arab Revolt starts in Palestine.

1939   John Bagot Glubb, known as Glubb Pasha, becomes the Arab Legion's commander and transforms it into the best trained Arab army. **June:** Great Britain establishes the Middle East Intelligence Centre (MEIC) in Cairo for coordinating and furnishing intelligence. **13 September:** Sidi Barrani battle, the Italian offensive against the British, starts.

1940   **November:** The Combined Bureau Middle East (CBME) is created as a center for cryptanalytic activity. **December:** The Camilla Plan, designed to deceive the Italian forces in eastern Africa into thinking that Somaliland was being targeted in an upcoming attack, is started.

1941   **January:** Great Britain's A Force unit, dedicated to counterintelligence and deception operations, is established by Archibald Percival Wavell, commander of the British forces in North Africa. **February:** Camilla Plan ends. **28 March:** A Force is officially established as a national brigade of the British Special Air Service; Jasper Maskelyne, assigned to A Force, is involved in an elaborate operation to divert German bombers from the port of Alexandria by setting up a fake harbor in a nearby bay.

1942   Operation Salaam is a covert operation under the command of László Almásy to insert two German agents deep into British-held Egypt. **26 May:** The battle of Gazala starts in North Africa around the port of Tobruk, Libya. **21 June:** Battle of Gazala ends. **23 October:** Operation Bertram, which marked a significant turning point in the Western Desert Campaign of World War II, starts. **3 November:** Operation Bertram ends. **8 November:** Operation Torch, aimed to gain control of North Africa through simultaneous landings at Casablanca, Oran, and Algiers, is launched by the United States, British, and Free French forces.

1945   Lebanon's General Security Directorate (GSD)/Sureté Générale is placed under the authority of the minister of the interior, with headquarters in Beirut.

1948   The Israeli intelligence community is established.

1949   Science Corps C, a special unit of the Israel Defense Force's Science Corps, begins a two-year geological survey of the Negev Desert to discover uranium reserves. **13 December:** The Israeli Secret Intelligence Service, Mossad Le'Modi'in Ule'Tafkidim Meyuhadim, is established.

1952   The Israeli Atomic Energy Commission is established.

1953   TPAJAX launched; it is a covert operation jointly carried out by the United States and Britain to overthrow the elected Iranian Prime Minister Muhammad Mossadeq and his cabinet and to bring to power Muhammad Reza Pahlavi as the shah of Iran.

1955 A Force is officially established as a national brigade for the British Special Air Service.

1956 John Bagot Glubb (Glubb Pasha) retires from the position of commander of the Arab Legion. Yevgeni Primakov becomes a correspondent in the Middle East for the State Committee for Television and Radio. Operation Rainbow, the deception operation to make Arab countries believe that the United States and Great Britain were working on developing alternative sources of energy, takes place. **13 June:** Colonel Mustafa Hafez, the commander of Egyptian intelligence in Gaza, is assassinated by an explosive device hidden in a book handed to him by an Egyptian double agent. **29 October:** Operation Musketeer starts.

1957 Great Britain's intelligence begins its involvement in Oman to assist Qaboos bin Said to become Oman's ruler. The Iranian intelligence Sazeman-e Ettelaat va Amniyat-e Keshvar/Organization for Intelligence and National Security (SAVAK) is founded; General Taimour Bakhtiar is the founder and first director SAVAK. Al Fatah, a Palestinian group, is founded in exile by Yassir Arafat. Salah Nasr Al-Nogomy is appointed director of the Egyptian General Directorate for State Security Investigations (GDSSI)/Mubahath al-Dawla. **3 October:** France and Israel conclude an agreement for the construction of a 24-megawatt research reactor at Dimona in the Negev Desert.

1958 The Trident Network for collecting intelligence about the Egyptian government comes into being at the initiative of the Israeli Mossad under Isser Harel, with the cooperation of the intelligence communities of Turkey and Iran. Zakareia Mohy El-Dien is assigned the establishment of the first Egyptian intelligence apparatus.

1959 Iran purchases a research nuclear reactor from the United States. Gaby Lahoud joins the Lebanese intelligence agencies. Yevgeni Primakov joins the Russian Committee for State Security, KGB.

1960 **13 February:** The first French nuclear weapons test takes place in Algeria.

1961 General Taimour Bakhtiar is dismissed from SAVAK.

1964 Captain Hilmi defects to Israel flying his Soviet-made Yak trainer aircraft. The Jordanian intelligence (General Intelligence Directorate [GID] /Dairat al Mukhabarat), is established. Gaby Lahoud is appointed head of Lebanon's intelligence agency under President Charles Helou.

1965 **25 Feburary:** Farhan Attassi (U.S. citizen) is hanged as a spy in Damascus, Syria. **July:** The Turkish Milli Emniyet Hizmeti (MEH)/National Security Service is dissolved. **30 October:** Mehdi Ben-Barka, former tutor of King Hassan and former Moroccan agent, is abducted in Paris.

1967 Cooperation between Israel and South Africa on nuclear technology seems to have started. The Popular Front for the Liberation of Palestine (PFLP), a Marxist-Leninist group, is founded by George Habash. Salah Nasr Al-Nogomy ends the position of director of the Egyptian General Directorate for State Security Investigations (GDSS). **5 June:** The Israel Defense Forces launches the Six-Day War. **8 June:** The Israeli Air Force (IAF) attacks the intelligence ship USS *Liberty* while the ship is in international waters off the town of El Arish in the Sinai Desert.

1968 The Al-Ahram Center for Political and Strategic Studies (ACPSS) is established in Cairo, Egypt. The Central Intelligence Agency concludes that Israel has started producing nuclear weapons.

1969 **Spring:** Marwan Ashraf contacts the Israeli Embassy in London and suggests handing over official Egyptian state documents; he becomes a walk-in agent.

1970 Great Britain's Special Air Service (SAS) becomes involved in Oman to support the regime of the sultan of Oman.

1971 The Bern Club (the International Counterterrorist Intelligence Network), known by its codename "Kilowatt," is formed.

1972 Lieutenant General Samih Asfourah joins Jordan's Mukhabarat/ General Intelligence Department (GID). The Bank of Credit and Commerce International (BCCI) is founded in Pakistan.

1973 **23 April:** Iran ratifies the Biological Weapons Convention.

1974 The Abu Nidal Organization (ANO) is established by Sabri al-Banna, also known as Abu Nidal, as a breakaway from the Palestinian

Liberation Organization (PLO). The Kurdistan Workers' Party (PKK) is founded by Abdullah Öcalan as a Marxist–Leninist organization.

1976 The Arab Satellite Communications Organization (ARABSAT) is founded as the satellite telecommunications organization of the Arab League. Imad Fayes Mugniyah joins Yasser Arafat's Security Force-17. The Muslim Brotherhood Revolt begins in Syria as a response to President Hafez al-Assad's approval of a new, secular constitution for Syria.

1977 The BCCI develops a plan to infiltrate the U.S. banking system by secretly purchasing U.S. banks. The Hizb-i-Islami Gulbuddin (HIG) is founded. **22 September:** Israel may have played a part in a nuclear weapons test in the Indian Ocean.

1978 **27 November:** The Kurdistan Workers' Party (PKK) adapted its name.

1979 The Popular Front for the Liberation of Palestine-Special Command (PFLP-SC) is formed.

1980 **24 April:** Operation Eagle Claw (known also as Operation Evening Light), the U.S. military operation to rescue 53 American diplomat hostages from the U.S. Embassy in Tehran, is launched by Delta Force and fails. The Iran–Iraq war starts.

1981 Colonel Driss Basri is appointed Morocco's interior minister. **7 June:** Operation Opera, the Israeli Air Force bombing of the Iraqi nuclear reactor Tammuz-1, takes place. **6 October:** President Anwar Sadat is assassinated.

1982 The Algerian Commissariat for New Energy (Commissariat aux Énergies Nouvelles) is established to develop nuclear energy, solar energy, and other potential sources of power. Colonel Ghazi Kanaan ends his position as the head of Syrian intelligence in Homs and is appointed commander of Syrian intelligence in Lebanon.

1984 Ali Fallahian is recruited to the Iranian Intelligence and Security Ministry (MOIS).

1985 The first issue of the *Arab Strategic Report* is published by the al-Ahram Center for Political and Strategic Studies (ACPSS). The CIA discovers that the First American Bank, which BCCI had secretly purchased, is being used as a corrupt criminal enterprise with extensive involvement in money laundering.

1986   15 April: Operation El Dorado Canyon (the codename for the joint U.S. air and navy bombing against Libya) is launched.

1987   Operation Eager Glacier begins and continues through 1988. **July:** Operation Earnest Will is launched by the United States to provide military protection for Kuwaiti oil tankers from Iraqi and Iranian attacks during the Tanker War phase of the Iran–Iraq War (1980–1988). It lasts until December 1988. Earnest Will overlaps with Operation Prime Chance, a largely secret effort to stop Iranian forces from attacking gulf shipping.

1988   6 April: Abu Jihad (Khalil el-Wazir), a senior member of the PLO, is assassinated in Tunisia by Israeli elite unit commandos of Sayeret Matkal. **18 April:** Operation Praying Mantis is carried out by U.S. naval forces in retaliation for the Iranian mining of a U.S. warship.

1989   The Iranian Supreme National Security Council is created in accordance with Article 176. The Hizb ul-Mujahidin (HM) is formed.

1990   22 March: Gerald Bull, who allegedly assisted the Iraqi regime of Sadam Hussein to build a powerful cannon, is shot dead from close range at the entrance to his home.

1991   Operation Rockingham, the codeword for Britain's involvement in inspections in Iraq following the war in Kuwait, takes place. Colonel Driss Basri is dismissed by King Muhammad Ben al-Hassan VI from his position of interior minister of Morocco. The BCCI becomes the focus of the world's worst financial scandal and collapses. **17 January:** Operation Desert Storm, the U.S.-led coalition, launches air attacks against Iraqi targets.

1992   The Armed Islamic Group (GIA) initiated its first violent action in Algeria. **February:** Under U.S. pressures, Algeria accepts the International Atomic Energy Agency (IAEA) safeguards.

1993   Omar Suleiman is appointed by President Husni Mubarak as the director of Egyptian intelligence.

1994   The Palestinian National Authority General Intelligence Service (GIS)/Mudiriyat al-Amn al-Amma is established; Amin Fawzi al-Hindi becomes chief of the GIS with the rank of general. **18 July:** A car bomb attack is perpetrated on the Jewish community's Argentine Israelite Mutual Association (AMIA) building in Buenos Aires, Argentina, killing 200 people and injuring 250 others.

1995 January: Algeria joins the Nuclear Nonproliferation Treaty (NPT).

1996 The Egyptian satellite company NileSat is established for the purpose of operating satellites and their associated ground control station and other facilities. **5 January:** Yahya Ayash, a member of Hamas and known as "the engineer," is killed, allegedly by the Israeli Security Agency (ISA).

1998 August: The Iran–Iraq War ends.

1999 Ruhollah Hosseinian is appointed Iranian deputy minister of intelligence. **15 February:** Abdullah Öcalan, the leader and founder of the Kurdistan Workers' Party (PKK), is captured by the Mossad.

2000 February: Operation Great Bahman is begun by the Mujahedeen-e Khalq (MEK), launching a dozen attacks against Iran.

2001 13 June: The Tenet Plan to bring the security organizations of Israel and the Palestinian National Authority to reaffirm their commitments to a cease-fire in line with the security agreements forged at Sharm al-Sheikh in October 2000 goes into force. **11 September:** Al Qaeda hijackers intentionally crash two airliners into the World Trade Center in New York and a third airliner into the Pentagon, Washington, D.C., killing thousands of people. A fourth airliner crashes into a field in Pennsylvania.

2002 3 January: The *Karine-A,* loaded with weapons for the Palestinian National Authority, is captured by the Israeli navy. Abu Nidal is assassinated in Baghdad, Iraq.

2003 17 March: Operation Iraqi Freedom starts. **18 March:** Operation Liberty Shield, the set of special measures to prevent terrorist attacks, is launched by the U.S. Homeland Security Department. **December:** Libya agrees to give up its research programs for biological and chemical weapons and to allow unconditional inspection and verification by American and British inspectors.

2004   March: The new Iraqi National Intelligence Service (INIS) is established.

2005   The Palestinian National Authority Intelligence Law is adopted. Amin Fawzi al-Hindi resigns from the position of chief of the GIS. **5 July:** Lieutenant-General Samih Asfourah is appointed director of the Jordanian GID. **October:** Sina 1, the first Iranian intelligence satellite, is launched. **12 October:** Major General Ghazi Kanaan is killed by a gunshot in his office in Damascus. **December:** Lieutenant General Samih Asfourah resigns from the GID and is replaced by Major General Mohamed al-Zahabi.

2006   September: Charki Draiss is appointed the new chief the Morocco's National Security General Directorate (DGSN). General Hamidou Laanigri is appointed general inspector of Morocco's Auxiliary Forces. **November:** Ali Reza Askari is appointed member of the Iranian Strategic Defense Planning Commission set up by Ali Khamenei. Fatah al-Islam, the Syrian-backed Palestinian group based in Lebanon, is established.

2007   Muhammad Hussein Akhtari is appointed deputy head of the Iranian international department in Ali Khamenei (the supreme leader's) office. **February:** Tehran authorities issue a confirmation statement claiming that Ali Reza Askari has been abducted by a Western intelligence agency and taken to an unknown country in northern Europe. **27 June:** Marwan Ashraf dies after falling off the balcony of his fifth-floor apartment in London. **6 September:** The Israeli Air Force targets Syria, bombing what it claims to be nuclear facilities allegedly obtained from North Korea.

2008   12 February: Hizballah's senior intelligence officer Imad Mughniyah is killed in a car bomb in Damascus, Syria, allegedly by Mossad agents.

Introduction

INTELLIGENCE AND
COUNTERINTELLIGENCE THROUGH HISTORY

Ancient Times

The Middle East is a region of early civilizations and has always been a geographical crossroads between contesting forces and civilizations. Thus, whenever there is a conflict or a clash of interests, intelligence gathering plays a crucial role for all parties involved. Records and archeological findings indicate that intelligence has been an important issue ever since the appearance of kingdoms and empires and played a part in their rivalry for resources and influence. For example, Egyptian hieroglyphs and papyri reveal the presence of spies to uncover disloyal subjects and to locate tribes for slave trade operations. There is also abundant evidence from the texts of ancient civilizations, including Moses' and Joshua's spies of the Old Testament. There is evidence from the Assyrian texts in Mesopotamia showing that spies were sent out in advance of the invasion or conquest of foreign countries. Likewise, the ancient Greeks and Romans used to gather information about foreign militaries via merchants, sailors, and other travelers, as well as send trained agents who were well versed in a given country's language and culture prior to launching every military campaign.

The large Roman governmental bureaucracy established one of the earliest civilian intelligence agencies. The Roman Empire displayed a genuine penchant to engage in political espionage, and spying was regularly practiced in domestic politics against political rivals and other internal threats.

The Middle Ages

Byzantium followed the governmental bureaucracy of the Roman Empire and formed an intelligence apparatus. The decline of the Byzantine Empire in the seventh century and the surge of Islam from the East caused a radical change in the area and brought new players to the arena that changed the nature of its dynamics. The Prophet Muhammad was very careful about preaching the new religion and used secretive measures that included the gathering of intelligence to locate and identify enemy agents living in Muslim communities. The next radical change occurred with the arrival of the Crusaders, who used spies and saboteurs to promote their cause, with torture and extortion applied as a major component of the Inquisition. The Crusades continued for nearly four centuries, draining the military and intelligence resources of most of the European monarchs.

The Renaissance

The Ottoman Empire ruled most of the Mediterranean basin for almost four centuries, from the 16th century until the beginning of the 20th century. Although it employed intelligence and counterintelligence organizations in order to maintain its domain, the empire did not develop modern intelligence organizations until the end of the 18th century, when conflicting European powers arrived in the Middle East and challenged Ottoman domination of the area. During the 19th century, the Ottoman Empire was a declining power, and France and Great Britain appeared as new players on the scene. Ottoman agents created spy networks in order to infiltrate communities suspected of dual loyalty and to monitor every move of its enemies.

World War I

Common interest in the Balkans generated an alliance between the Ottoman and the Austro–Hungarian Empires. One of the major civilian projects of that alliance was the building of the Hijaz railway, which drew Austro–Hungarian diplomats, travelers, and explorers to the Middle East, some of whom were used as intelligence agents. The new partners brought together by the railway project were the Austrians and the

Germans. German experts of all sorts became involved in various construction and restoration projects throughout the empire, supervising the building of roads, bridges, and railways. By the beginning of the 20th century, these European powers had become major players in all political and military events that took place in the Middle East and the surrounding countries. There were other new players in the region as well, including the Italians who occupied Ethiopia and later Libya, establishing power bases on the shores of the Red Sea and North Africa.

Toward the beginning of World War I, the Middle East became a center for numerous intelligence activities. The British already had spy networks all over the region in an attempt to secure their hold in the area, including Egypt, Sudan, Cyprus, Palestine, Arabia, Mesopotamia, and the Persian Gulf. The French also had interests in the Middle East, but they concentrated on two major areas: North Africa and greater Syria. For centuries, since the time of the Crusaders, France had cultivated diverse contacts with the Catholic communities in the Middle East. By World War I, they were already in Algeria and worked hard to spread their cultural influence in neighboring Morocco and Tunis. They built schools and hospitals, using the wide foundation of the Catholic Church's institutions and human resources. They built a new educational network to cater to the needs of French settlers in North Africa. They used the same methods in Egypt, Palestine, Syria, and Lebanon. In fact, at the beginning of the 20th century, a significant proportion of the young local elite had received a French education and cultural inclinations. The Ottomans were aware of the French espionage networks, and when the war began, they arrested some leaders of the Catholic communities, especially in Syria and Lebanon.

British intelligence promoted insurgency and encouraged rebellious movements of local nations within the boundaries of the Ottoman Empire. The Arab revolt against the Ottomans was led by Hussein bin-Ali, then sheriff of Mecca and Benin, in June 1916. Britain financed the revolt and provided the rebels with weapons. The revolt was not a success story, but the British made contacts that proved to be very useful at a later stage.

Between the Two World Wars

At the conclusion of World War I, the Ottoman Empire was dismantled and a new era began under the leadership of Ataturk. Previous territories of the empire were divided among the victorious nations, who drew new maps and divided the area according to their interests and prewar agreements. This new situation led to the flourishing of intertwined colonial and local organizations in the area. It also brought to the scene resistance movements of all types, including terrorist organizations. This phenomenon had a significant impact on the development and structure of intelligence, counterintelligence, and other security organizations in the Middle East. Various newly formed countries, including Iraq, Iran, and Turkey, were undergoing territorial and administrative changes and established their own intelligence and counterintelligence organizations.

In the 1930s, the British became the major power in the Middle East, following a treaty that gave Great Britain the right to station troops on Egyptian soil in order to protect the Suez Canal. The Royal Navy moved its Mediterranean Fleet headquarters from Malta to Alexandria, and in June 1939, Great Britain established the Middle East Intelligence Centre (MEIC) in Cairo for coordinating all intelligence activities. As the war progressed and the Middle East arena expanded, the British had to create new departments and new branches assigned to cope with new developments.

France's intelligence in Syria and Lebanon faced a worse situation. The newly created Syria was a conglomerate of different ethnic groups, some of which resented being subjects of a Christian nation and preached that the French were the new Crusaders. Some wanted independence, while others supported the idea of a Pan-Arab kingdom. France did not cope well with the insurgents and was too concerned about the welfare of the Christian communities to notice the needs of other ethnic and religious groups. In 1925, it had to subdue the Great Syrian Revolt, also known as the Druze Revolution. It lost control of the borders and could not prevent huge waves of immigration from the poor Syrian mountains to the neighboring countries where jobs were available. Thus, it was forced to reorganize its intelligence services and change its structure.

This unstable situation gave rise to some new intelligence factors with the approach of World War II. An important new player was the Jewish Agency, the official leadership of the Jews in Palestine. The Jewish Agency maintained its intelligence branch, the SHAI (Information Services), with three different intelligence organizations: one was spying on the British in order to anticipate their anti-Jewish moves and to circumvent their various restrictions, another was gathering information about the intentions of the hostile Arabs, and the third was attempting to monitor the persecution of Jews abroad. This Jewish intelligence apparatus had some limited cooperation with British Intelligence, but as the objectives of the organizations were different, cooperation was not consistent or regulated. Information was occasionally shared, especially during the 1936 Great Arab Revolt in Palestine, but more on an informal basis than through official channels. It is also alleged that the Axis powers funded the Great Arab Revolt, which took place in Palestine in 1936, but there is no record proving these allegations.

World War II

Early in World War II, Great Britain's intelligence in Egypt and Sudan created in November 1940 the Combined Bureau Middle East (CBME). In addition to the pressing needs of military intelligence and counterintelligence to meet the threat of the Axis powers, Great Britain had to maintain additional intelligence units connected to the police in order to monitor the activities of local organizations of various ethnic groups, some of which were directed against the ruling British. They watched specifically for connections between local factors and external powers, such as the Soviet Union and Nazi Germany.

Germany was preparing to seize world domination. The Italian and German armies invaded and occupied many countries on the southern shores of the Mediterranean. In 1941, there was a coup attempt in Iraq, allegedly funded and supported by German and Italian intelligence. After a series of previous coups that had started in October 1936, this coup was in great part the initiative of the grand mufti of Jerusalem, Haj Amin al-Husseini.

Turkey remained neutral throughout World War II and became a haven for spies. It was the site of meetings, contacts, negotiations, plots, and conspiracies, with all parties involved trying to gather information, spread disinformation, and anticipate or prevent future moves of their opponents. Everybody was watching everybody else, as a function of operations of the war. These activities were intensified by the addition of new players, as every country that was occupied during the war had a government in exile employing its own agents and operating its own spy network.

The United States played a major role during World War II in the western Mediterranean, and also had economic interests in the Middle East. Toward the end of the war, the United States decided it no longer wanted to rely on British Intelligence and instead created its own network in the area. When the war ended, the United States had its own military fleet in the Mediterranean, maintained military forces in southern Europe, and was negotiating harbor services with Turkey and Greece.

Cold War Intelligence

Soon after the end of World War II, the international atmosphere changed dramatically. The domination of the European powers ended, colonialism was no longer tolerated, and new borders were carved out in the Middle East. The fact that the leadership in some of these newly independent countries did not reflect the choices of all their inhabitants led to the oppression of minority groups, the escalation of local conflicts into wars, and the proliferation of subversive groups. Thus, in addition to civil and military intelligence and counterintelligence organizations, these countries had to build internal security organizations and establish antisubversion campaigns.

The intelligence activity patterns of the colonial era often continued during the initial years of the independent Middle Eastern states. The former colonial powers established arrangements for the training of local intelligence agencies. Glubb Pasha, the British intelligence officer, trained the Arab Legion. Thus military and civilian intelligence personnel in Jordan and many of the gulf countries were trained in Great Britain. France, on the other hand, assisted in forming the intelligence agencies for Morocco and Tunisia. The United States and Israel assisted in forming the Iranian intelligence Sazeman-e Ettela'at va Amniyat-e Keshvar (SAVAK)/ National Intelligence and Security Organization.

The withdrawal of the French from Syria and Lebanon resulted in several internal conflicts. Although Syria was comprised of several rival ethnic groups, it was consolidated into a sovereign state after the feudal regime was ousted by a military coup. From the day it became an independent entity, Syria was afflicted by subversive groups that operated in various countries in the region, including Turkey, Lebanon, Israel, Yemen, Saudi Arabia, and Iraq. Prior to its independence in 1945, Syrian intelligence agencies had been responsible only for internal security and counterespionage. However, after independence the mission of these services was expanded by the Ba'ath party leadership to target opposition groups in Lebanon and simultaneously to gather intelligence against Israel, Turkey, and Jordan. Likewise, in Lebanon, ethnic conflict and rivalry have consistently caused unrest, internal disputes, political assassinations, and destruction.

The British withdrawal from Palestine in 1948 and the events that ensued gave birth to the state of Israel, leaving an Arab minority in its borders, while Jordan took over the West Bank and Egypt occupied the Gaza Strip. The new state of Israel already had budding intelligence, counterintelligence, and security services. The secretive units and agencies during the time of the British mandate now became official state institutions. The SHAI (Information Services), an organization that was gathering all sorts of information abroad, became the Israeli Military Intelligence and later the Mossad, which conducted covert operations, and the Israeli Security Agency (ISA) evolved into a competent organization. Soon after the establishment of the state of Israeli, the foreign intelligence of the Israeli Foreign Ministry was engaged in tracing Nazis in hiding and Arab terrorists. The ongoing internal and external Arab threat gave rise to the ISA, which works closely with the Israel Defense Forces (IDF) and with the Israeli police.

The two major superpowers replaced Great Britain and France in the Middle East, with the United States allying itself with Israel and the Soviet Union supporting the new regimes in Syria and Egypt.

Following Egypt's revolution of 1952, the Central Intelligence Agency (CIA) assisted in restructuring the Egyptian intelligence apparatus. However, after the 1956 Suez Canal crisis, President Gamal Abdel Nasser turned to the Soviet Union for military and economic aid. Nasser saw Egypt as the natural leader of the Arabic world and did his best to achieve this goal. He built up a huge army and internal intelligence, trained by Soviet instructors, and changed the structure and objectives of his civilian and military intelligence.

In Egypt and other Middle Eastern countries like Jordan and Lebanon, fighting fundamentalism has been a constant struggle. Terrorist groups have become a burden to these governments and people, and their presence has led to additional conflicts. However, regimes that have always promoted terror—like those in Syria, Iraq, and Iran—have managed to channel much of this fervor against their own enemies and have provided these groups with bases, aid, funds, and support, using them for their own purposes when convenient. In contrast to the Western intelligence communities that have traditionally emphasized the formation of intelligence communities with the ability to cope with international threats, the Soviet Union trained intelligence officers mainly for missions of domestic threats, especially for surveillance—and most frequently the intimidation of the regime's own populations—both at home and abroad.

By the 1960s, the Soviet Union and East Germany had begun to play important advisory and training roles in Iraq, Syria, the former People's Democratic Republic of Yemen, and Libya. The Cold War's players were right in the midst of the petroleum-rich Middle East.

Rival and overlapping services were created to check authority and autonomy, and the result was factionalism. Some rulers—those of Syria and Iraq provide examples—appointed close relatives to key intelligence posts. For instance, in Syria, Rifat al-Asad, the brother of President Hafez al-Asad, was head of Syria's intelligence service and was linked to the Red Knights.

Post–Cold War Intelligence

As soon as the Cold War was over and the globalization process began, terrorism also became a global phenomenon. Thus, fundamentalism is no longer restricted to the region of its origin. On the one hand, this new situation creates a global threat but on the other facilitates more cooperation and sharing of information in order to overcome this threat. The intelligence communities of Western countries as well as the Israeli intelligence community also have to deal with the development and use of weapons of mass destruction, which are sometimes camouflaged as energy sources for civilian purposes, even though they can be adapted to generate nuclear weapons.

The U.S. intelligence community became a major player in the Middle East long before the end of the Cold War. In fact, it began its involvement soon after World War II, when oil became a prized commodity. Until Operation Desert Storm in 1991, the U.S. intelligence community relied mainly on its cooperation and good contacts with the Israeli Mossad. After Desert Storm, cooperation with several Arab countries in the region, such as Jordan, also increased.

After the 11 September 2001 terrorist attacks on the United States, the attitude of the world against terror changed with the realization that, as terrorism had become a global phenomenon, it required a global solution. This new situation led to further cooperation and exchange of information between various states, some of which had previously considered themselves to be rivals. For example, Libya voluntarily cancelled its nonconventional weaponry plans in order to become part of the general struggle against terror, and Sudan refused further haven to international terrorists and became an ally of the West in tracking and restricting terrorist movements.

The new threats of terrorism and the use of nonconventional weaponry have required the development of relevant intelligence and surveillance units, employing new methods of intelligence gathering and verification to anticipate such threats or take measures to remove or prevent them. Such measures were taken by Israel against the site of the Iraqi nuclear reactor in June 1981 in Operation Opera and against the Syrian site that may or may not have been the foundation of a nuclear reactor on 6 September 2007. The other rogue country that is openly developing its nuclear capabilities is Iran, which stopped pretending that its nuclear program was designed for civilian use only. The Western intelligence community has attempted to supervise and restrict this project and even threatens sanctions to stop the process, but thus far to no avail. The only country that has used chemical weapons in warfare in the Middle East until now is Iraq; however, the facilities used to produce these chemicals have been dismantled or completely destroyed.

THE CHALLENGE OF FACING THE FUTURE OF INTELLIGENCE

The current high-tech revolution has changed the nature of intelligence gathering and, accordingly, the structure and budgeting of the intelligence communities. Modern agents have state-of-the-art audiovisual devices for bugging, hacking into computers, changing data, planting disinformation for the opposition, and creating forgeries. Spy satellites roam the sky, taking pictures and transmitting data. Modern intelligence uses the mass media and various communication technologies not only to provide information but also to deceive the enemy with disinformation and propaganda. These advanced techniques are not exclusive to large wealthy countries. Several countries in the Middle East, including Israel, Egypt, Turkey, Iran, and the United Arab Emirates, have developed various research centers and local military communication and high-tech equipment, with decrypting technologies as well as facilities for launching satellites of their own. There are also some very rich countries in the region that can simply buy advanced military and communication equipment, attract high-salary experts to work for them, and fund laboratories and industries in other countries.

However, even though intelligence activities in the Middle East may have undergone a technological revolution, the problems in the region remain complex and the solutions are as elusive as ever.

THE DICTIONARY

– A –

A FORCE. In January 1941, **Archibald Percival Wavell**, commander of the British forces in North Africa, created a unit called A Force that was dedicated to counterintelligence and deception operations. By this stage, deception was playing a major part in the war effort with such successfully completed operations as **Operation Compass** (June 1940), which was designed to deceive the Axis forces in North Africa, and the **Camilla Plan** (December 1940), which was designed to deceive Benito Mussolini's forces in the horn of Africa. By the end of 1941, A Force was well established and continued its operations under Brigadier **Dudley Clarke**, who replaced General Wavell. The tasks of A Force were eventually expanded beyond purely military aims. For example, the rapid German advance into Russia in August 1941 caused concern in Great Britain for the safety of Turkey, which served as the main venue for A Force deception military operations. Thus, a team of double agents was formed by A Force in Cairo, Egypt, in anticipation of a possible breach in Turkey's neutrality. *See also* MASKELYNE, JASPER.

AANSAR AL-ISLAM. AAnsar al-Islam (AI; also known as Partisans of Islam, Helpers of Islam, and Supporters of Islam) was formed in December 2001 and numbers between 700 and 1,000 members from central and northern Iraq. It is a radical Islamist group of Iraqi Kurds and Arabs who have vowed to establish an independent Islamic state in Iraq. Closely allied with **al Qaeda**, some of its members trained in al Qaeda camps in Afghanistan and the group provided a safe haven to al Qaeda fighters prior to **Operation Iraqi Freedom** (OIF). Since OIF, AAnsar-al-Islam has been one of the leading groups engaged in anticoalition attacks.

AAnsar al-Islam has primarily fought against one of the two main Kurdish political factions—the Patriotic Union of Kurdistan (PUK)—and has mounted ambushes and attacks in PUK areas. AI members have been implicated in assassinations and assassination attempts against PUK officials and work closely with both al Qaeda operatives and associates in Abu Musab al-Zarqawi's network. Before OIF, some AI members claimed to have produced cyanide-based toxins, ricin, and alfatoxin.

In the lead-up to the 2003 invasion of Iraq, U.S. Secretary of State Colin Powell told the United Nations Security Council in February that Iraq housed an agent in the most senior levels of the radical organization AAnsar al-Islam, which controlled that corner of Iraq. In 2000, the agent offered al Qaeda safe haven in the region; after al Qaeda was swept from Afghanistan, some of its members accepted this safe haven. Since that time, some have maintained that Saddam Hussein had links to AAnsar al-Islam, while others argue he infiltrated the group for intelligence-gathering purposes but did not actively assist the group. The general consensus of experts, as well as the conclusion of the intelligence community and the Senate Select Committee on Intelligence, was that Saddam infiltrated the group, but the two parties remained hostile to each other and did not establish a collaborative relationship. The 2006 U.S. Senate Intelligence report questioned where and how AAnsar al-Islam received chemical and biological know-how, including ricin, botulinum, and possibly cyanide and equipment.

ABBAS, TAHA. Born in Tikrit, General Taha Abbas al-Ahbabi was appointed by Saddam Hussein as the commander of the **Iraqi Directorate of General Security** (DGS) in 1996. He served in this position for only one year and was replaced by **Tahir Jalil al-Habbush** in 1997. The exact reason for replacing him after such a short tenure is still in question. Abbas had previously served as the head of the Iraqi Military Security Service (MSS). *See also* IRAQI DIRECTORATE OF GENERAL MILITARY INTELLIGENCE; IRAQI INTELLIGENCE; IRAQI SPECIAL SECURITY ORGANIZATION.

ABD AL-MUNIM, MUHAMMAD. Muhammad Abd al-Munim al-Azmirli was an Egyptian chemist who immigrated to Iraq. He served as a technical and scientific consultant for the Explosive Section of the Iraqi Intelligence Service (IIS) from 1980–1987. In 1988, he was appointed as director of the section reporting directly to the IIS director. *See also* IRAQI DIRECTORATE OF GENERAL MILITARY INTELLIGENCE; IRAQI DIRECTORATE OF GENERAL SECURITY; IRAQI INTELLIGENCE; IRAQI SPECIAL SECURITY ORGANIZATION.

ABDULLAH I (1882–1951). King as-Sayyid Abdullah bin al-Hussein, also known as King as-Sayyid Abdullah I, was the Hashemite ruler of Transjordan after its creation by Great Britain in 1921. In the 1930s, the relationship between Great Britain and the king became stronger, and when the financial crisis increased in Transjordan in 1932–1934, Emir Abdullah secretly applied to the **Jewish Agency in Palestine** to invest in Transjordan by buying land for Jewish settlement. At the same time, Abdullah and the Zionist movement began exchanging intelligence information. The Information Service (Sherut Yedioth; SHAI) of the Hagana (the intelligence unit of the Jewish Agency) gave Abdullah the nickname "Meir." Abdullah provided the SHAI's agents with information regarding the Arab world and in return he got from the SHAI information about his political rival in Palestine, the Mufti Hajj Amin al-Husseini. The mufti wanted to establish an independent Palestinian country, and therefore he opposed the king's political ambition to annex Palestine to Transjordan. Abdullah became king in 1946 when Transjordan gained formal independence. King Abdullah was driven by a long-standing ambition to make himself the master of Greater Syria, which included Transjordan, Syria, Lebanon, and Palestine. However, his ambition was a direct threat to Egypt's leadership in the Arab world. The rulers of Syria and Lebanon also viewed King Abdullah as a threat to the independence of their countries and suspected him of collaborating with Israel.

The Jewish Agency in Jerusalem had always attempted to cultivate friendly relations with Abdullah bin al-Hussein, who was one of the moderate Arab leaders. This resulted in the development of special relations between the Jewish community in Palestine and King Abdullah, who became an immensely valuable ally of the Jewish Agency. Abdullah and his aides and agents were a source of information about the other Arab countries involved in the Palestine problem. The king was also on the payroll of the Jewish Agency for providing them with information.

On 17 November 1947, as the conflict over Palestine entered the crucial stage, the contacts between the Jewish side and King Abdullah intensified. Abdullah held a secret meeting with Golda Meir (Myerson) as the representative of the Jewish Agency. The two leaders discussed the resolution to the partition of Palestine, which was then before the United Nations. The king told Golda Meir that he would take over the Arab part of Palestine, as he would not permit another Arab state to be set up, and that he would then conclude a treaty with the Jewish state. The two leaders reached a preliminary agreement to coordinate their diplomatic and military strategies in order to prevent the other Arab states from intervening directly in Palestine.

On 29 November, the UN adopted its resolution in favor of dividing the area of the British mandate into two states, one Jewish and one Arab. In return for Abdullah's promise not to enter the area assigned by the UN to the Jewish state, the Jewish Agency agreed to the annexation by Transjordan of most of the area earmarked for the Arab state. Precise borders were not drawn and Jerusalem was not even discussed, as under the UN plan it was to remain a separate entity under international control. Despite the Jewish Agency's efforts to commit King Abdullah to a written agreement, one was never drawn up. However, an understanding was reached between King Abdullah and the Jewish Agency in which Abdullah agreed that he would not prevent the establishment of the state of Israel, and the newly established state would agree to the conquest of the Arab part of Palestine by Abdullah, though it would not help him.

From a political point of view, the Syrians saw King Abdullah as their principal enemy and felt compelled to intervene, if only to prevent him from tipping the balance of power in the region against them. There was a wide belief that King Abdullah had made a deal with the Jewish Agency for the **Arab Legion** to invade Syria, though the agreement was never put into writing. This situation pushed the Arab governments, with Syria at their head, to the brink of war.

Indeed, the new prime minister of the newly established state of Israel, David Ben Gurion, had a "grand plan" for the conduct of the war. He reached a tacit understanding with King Abdullah, allowing the latter to move into the territories west of the Jordan River, which had been allotted by the 1947 UN Partition Plan to the Arab Palestinian state. This plan was not revealed either to the Israeli cabinet or to the military command, who wished to conquer the West Bank territories. As such, the military objectives contradicted the political and diplomatic considerations of Ben Gurion's grand plan. Ben Gurion's decision to prevent a military incursion was in accordance with Golda Meir's agreement with King Abdullah, as it was concluded on 17 November 1947.

On 20 July 1951, while visiting al-Aqsa Mosque in Jerusalem, King Abdullah was assassinated by a Palestinian extremist so as to prevent the old king from reaching a separate peace agreement with Israel. The gunman fired three fatal bullets into the king's head and chest. Abdullah's grandson, Hussein bin-Talal (king of Jordan from 1953 to 1999) was at his side and grappled with the assailant until he was shot himself. A medal that had been pinned to Hussein's chest at his grandfather's insistence deflected the bullet and saved his life. *See also* JEWISH AGENCY IN EGYPT; JEWISH AGENCY IN SYRIA; JORDANIAN INTELLIGENCE.

ABU JIHAD (1935–1988). The nom de guerre of Khalil el-Wazir. He was born in the mandate of Palestine, and after the establishment of the state of Israel in 1948 he fled with his parents to Egypt, where he spent his youth. In 1954, he was arrested in Egypt for laying mines in the Gaza Strip. The next year, he infiltrated Israel from the Egyptian border and attacked Israeli water installations. In 1959, he met Yasser Arafat and joined his group. Abu Jihad became one of the Palestinian Liberation Organization (PLO) leaders, and after the Peace of Galilee operation in 1982, he fled with Arafat to Tunisia. The entire **Israeli intelligence** community—the **Mossad**, the Israeli Security Agency, and Military Intelligence—kept close watch on his movements. He was described by the Israeli intelligence community as highly intelligent, with a keen analytical mind, and a good organizer. Abu Jihad was likewise known to Israeli intelligence as the great conciliator in the PLO between Arafat and his violent rivals. In 1988, the Israeli inner cabinet (the 10 leading ministers out of the full cabinet of 25 ministers), in a no-vote procedure, resolved to have Abu Jihad assassinated in Tunisia, nearly 1,500 miles (2,400 kilometers) away from Israel. The immediate reason for the decision was to raise the morale of Israelis in the difficult days of the Palestinian uprising in the late 1980s. In a brilliantly planned mission, one of the most elaborate ever, based on excellent intelligence, Abu Jihad was assassinated on 6 April.

Because of Tunisia's long distance from Israel, it was decided to use the Israel Air Force's Boeing 707 and a flying command post. Major General Ehud Barak, then deputy chief of the General Staff, commanded the entire operation from that aircraft, which was equipped with a highly sophisticated communications systems somewhat similar to the American AWACS (Airborne Warning and Control System) platform, to serve as a link between the commanders and the Israeli troops on the ground in Tunisia. Alongside Barak on board the Boeing was the deputy head of the Mossad's operations branch. The airplane cruised on a civilian flight path between Sicily and Tunisia, and its pilots were in constant contact with Italian air traffic control. The controllers had neither the time nor the interest to ask the pilots too many questions. To them, the Boeing seemed to be a charter flight of El Al Israel Airlines. Seven Mossad operatives, using fake Lebanese passports and speaking the right Arabic dialect, had prepared the way on the ground. They had hired three vehicles and driven eight Israeli commandos to the target. These men, belonging to the elite Sayeret Matkal unit of the Israel Defense Forces, had landed in rubber dinghies launched from a ship anchored a safe distance offshore. The commandos were in three teams: one handled the on-site security; they killed Abu Jihad's driver who drove him to his villa near the Sidi Boussaid neighborhood of Tunis. Another team operated jamming equipment to disrupt telephone calls near the villa. The third team was assigned to the target himself. They forced open the front door of the villa, shot a Tunisian guard using pistols with silencers, and then spotted Abu Jihad at the top of the stairs and shot him.

The details of this episode were published in the Israeli press soon after the assassination. Officially, however, Israel has never admitted responsibility for the assassination of Abu Jihad. Still, the fingerprints on the entire operation are those of Israel.

ABU NIDAL ORGANIZATION (ANO). The Abu Nidal Organization was established in 1974 by Sabri al-Banna, also known as Abu Nidal or "Father of Struggle," as a branch the Palestinian Liberation Organization (PLO). Also known as **al-Fatah** Revolutionary Council, Arab Revolutionary Council, Arab Revolutionary Brigades, Black September, and the Revolutionary Organization of Socialist Muslims, the ANO consists of a few hundred members plus a limited overseas support structure made up of various functional commissions, including political, military, and financial committees. In November 2002, Abu Nidal died in Baghdad; the new leadership of the organization is unclear.

The ANO is an international terrorist organization par excellence, having carried out terrorist attacks in 20 countries and killing or injuring almost 900 persons. In the 1980s, the ANO began working and cooperating with Iraqi intelligence. Targets include the United States, Great Britain, France, Israel, moderate Palestinians, the PLO, and various Arab countries. Major attacks included the Rome and Vienna airports in December 1985, the Neve Shalom Synagogue in Istanbul, the Pan Am Flight 73 hijacking in Karachi in September 1986, and the City of Poros day-excursion ship attack in Greece in July 1988. The ANO is also suspected of assassinating PLO Deputy Chief Abu Iyad and PLO Security Chief Abu Hul in Tunis in January 1991 as well as a Jordanian diplomat in Lebanon in January 1994, and has been linked to the killing of the PLO representative there. The group has not staged a major attack against Western targets since the late 1980s.

As an extremely paranoid leader, Abu Nidal subjected his followers to endless security checks. Members of the ANO spied on one another, and the slightest deviation from routine was punished, often by death. Penetrating the ANO has become an almost impossible mission. The Central Intelligence Agency's (CIA) Duane Clarridge wisely decided that penetration could not succeed; therefore, he decided to destroy it from the outside. Clarridge and his associates were able to assemble an amazingly complete picture of the Abu Nidal gang and wage psychological warfare against the followers. Clarridge repeatedly approached his sources and offered to pay them to work for the United States; this resulted in the sources publicly exposing the names of Abu Nidal's commercial intermediaries and bankers. All this took a terrible toll on the ANO, which retaliated. Those gunned down got merciful deaths compared to those who were subjected to the ghastly tortures of Abu Nidal; victims were routinely buried alive, fed through a tube lodged in their mouths, and finally executed by a single bullet fired through the feeding tube. Still others had their sexual organs placed in skillets full of boiling oil.

In December 1998, the ANO relocated to Iraq, where the group currently maintains a presence; it also has an operational presence in Lebanon, including several Palestinian refugee camps. In 1999, Libyan authorities shut down the ANO's operations in Libya, and Egyptian authorities soon followed suit. However, the ANO succeeded in operating over a wide area, including the Middle East, Asia, and Europe. The ANO is financially supported—including efforts related to safe havens, training, logistics assistance, and financial aid—by Iraq, Libya, and Syria (until 1987) in addition to close support for selected operations. However, financial problems and internal disorganization have reduced the group's activities and capabilities, and the organization is no longer active.

Abu Nidal was a force to be reckoned with, and his organization reached as far as the United States. His American sleeper network was discovered by the CIA—surfacing in one of the most spectacular events in the late 1980s—and put on round-the-clock surveillance by the Federal Bureau of Investigation (FBI). In the 1980s, one of the ANO agents—a Palestinian who had moved from the West Bank to St. Louis, Missouri, where he raised three daughters—inadvertently exposed the FBI operation. Having grown up in the United States, the agent's daughters had the usual headstrong independence of young American women and often rebelled against their severe father. One started dating a black man, which drove her father into a frenzy. One night, her father stabbed her to death. The entire scene was recorded by FBI bugging devices, and the tape was presented to local prosecutors, thereby wrecking the FBI operation while documenting the presence of the ANO in the United States. *See also* ABU NIDAL'S ASSASSINATION.

ABU NIDAL'S ASSASSINATION. In the early 1970s and again in the 1990s, Iraq hosted the headquarters of the **Abu Nidal Organization** (ANO), one of the most active Palestinian terrorist organizations, responsible for killing some 300 people. Its leader, Sabri al-Banna, whose nickname was Abu Nidal or "Father of Struggle," was found murdered in his apartment in Baghdad on 19 August 2002 together with two of his top operatives. This had followed a long struggle with British intelligence services, the MI5 and MI6, which reached across all of Europe, the subcontinent of India, the Middle East, and the Persian Gulf. Sometimes Abu Nidal operated in cooperation with other intelligence organizations from Syria, Iraq, Libya, Yemen, or Sudan, and sometimes he operated by himself.

The animosity that Abu Nidal held for British intelligence services was shared in common by the **Iraqi intelligence** organizations and the Iraqi ruler Saddam Hussein. Saddam Hussein and Abu Nidal both perceived British intelligence operations in the Middle East—and especially their relationships with Yasser Arafat and the leaders of the Palestinian movement—as an obstacle to taking control of the Palestinian movement.

British Prime Minister Tony Blair was hoping that the war in Iraq would not only increase military cooperation between the United States and Great Britain but would also bring back the status that the British spy system had enjoyed during the period of the Cold War. He instructed the leaders of British intelligence services to prepare a sting operation that would prove to Washington that the British have the only intelligence body capable of penetrating deeply into the heart of the Iraqi intelligence apparatus. Leaders of the British MI5 and MI6 thought that the war with Iraq would set the background and provide the right conditions for finally taking down Abu Nidal.

In formulating the sting operation, the British found ways to "plant" clues and bits of information showing that Abu Nidal and his men had agreed, for a large sum of a few million dollars, to cooperate with American intelligence agencies and pass them intelligence information about the goings-on of Saddam Hussein's family, the hiding places of the Iraqi ruler, details about the Iraqi Army movements, and preparations for the war. Since no spy organization, and especially a man as sophisticated and cautious in intelligence matters as Saddam Hussein, would operate on the basis of rumors alone, British intelligence services had to make sure that the ruler of Iraq would be shown actual evidence to verify the information about Abu Nidal's cooperation with the Americans. Saddam Hussein took the bait that the British sent that indicated an American connection with Abu Nidal, and the British sting operation was a success.

On 19 August 2002, the news broke from Baghdad that Abu Nidal and two leaders of his operation had been murdered in his apartment by unknown assassins. Two days later, on 21 August, the head of Iraqi intelligence, Tahr Habush, appeared before journalists in Baghdad and presented them with the shocking photos taken in Abu Nidal's apartment by Iraqi intelligence in order to prove that the terrorist had committed suicide and was not murdered. Habush told the journalists that Iraqi intelligence had not known until a short while earlier that Abu Nidal was even in Baghdad and that when they found out, they sent a few Iraqi security men to check the apartment where he was staying. Allegedly, when Iraqi intelligence operatives entered the apartment, Abu Nidal realized that he was caught, took out his gun, put it in his mouth and shot himself.

ABU RAJAB, TAREQ (1946–). Brigadier General Tareq Abu Rajab has been acting head of the Palestinian National Authority's (PNA) General Intelligence Service (GIS; Mudiriyat al-Amn al-Amma) since the resignation of **Amin Fawzi al-Hindi** in July 2004. On 20 May 2006, Tareq Abu Rajab was seriously injured by gunmen firing from two moving cars as he drove to his office at GIS headquarters in Gaza City. Two of Abu Rajab's bodyguards were killed and another wounded in what appeared to be a carefully planned attack. The attack came just before a Palestinian parliamentary committee was due to present a report that was expected to call for urgent reforms in order to help end the worst internal unrest since the Palestinians had gained some self-rule in 1994. *See also* PALESTINIAN NATIONAL AUTHORITY (PNA) INTELLIGENCE.

AHRAM CENTER FOR POLITICAL AND STRATEGIC STUDIES, AL- (ACPSS). The Al-Ahram Center for Political and Strategic Studies is an Egyptian center, located in Cairo, that was established in 1968 within the framework of the al-Ahram Foundation, for the study of Zionism and Israeli society. The center has evolved over time, particularly since 1972, when its research scope was extended to incorporate studies of international and strategic issues. It is now engaged in the research of international political issues that have a bearing on the Middle East in general and the Arab–Israeli conflict in particular. The center has a special unit that concentrates on various aspects of Egyptian society.

The aim of the center is to provide an intellectual, investigative vision of a vast range of relevant issues, and its research activities are independent of external influence and intervention. It emphasizes freedom of speech and interpretation of its scholars and researchers in order to maintain their objective approach and scientific research. The target audience of the research conducted by the ACPSS includes political leaders, policymakers, legislators, political organizations, political parties, national governments, military units, policy analysts and researchers, academia, media and journalists, and the general public.

At the time of writing, the ACPSS is headed by Abdel Moneim Said. Said is assisted by a council of experts consisting of the deputy director, assistant directors, the heads of various research units, and other experts invited by the center. The current staff of the ACPSS is comprised of 34 members, including 19 experts in various political and strategic topics, eight researchers, and seven administrative personnel. The ACPSS cooperates with organizations and research institutions all over the world through the exchange of publications and information on topics of mutual interest. In addition, the center receives a number of visitors from abroad, including academic staff, prominent scholars, representatives of press and publishing agencies and the media, as well as members of diplomatic missions in Cairo. Although the ACPSS is considered an academic institute, in fact it performs intelligence analysis. It is also known for its annual *Arab Bulletin Report*.

AKHTARI, MUHAMMAD HUSSEIN. As of 2007, Akhtari is the deputy head of the Iranian international department in the office of Supreme Leader Ali Khamenei. He was formerly the president of the Revolutionary Court in the province of Mazandaran, where he issued hundreds of execution orders. He also served for over eight years (1988–1997) as Iran's ambassador to Syria, where he entertained close relations with the **Hizballah**. In this capacity, he planned terrorist actions in the region as well as in Europe, including the assassinations of Iranian opposition members abroad. *See also* IRANIAN INTELLIGENCE.

ALGERIAN INTELLIGENCE. On 5 July 1962, Algeria gained its independence from France. Since then the Algerian Army has maintained huge influence over Algeria's politics since its independence from France in 1962. After the coup d'état of 19 June 1965 against President Ben Bella, Houari Boumédiène took the position as president with the official title of Algeria's chairman of the Revolutionary Council. He served in this position until 12 December 1965. Under Boumédiène, open criticism of the regime was not permitted, and violators were subject to arrest and severe punishment. The Armée de Libération Nationale (ALN), also known as the Front de Libération Nationale (FLN), was defined as representing all legitimate political tendencies, while relegating all other political organizations to an illegal status.

The General Delegation for Documentation and Security (DGDS; Delégation Générale de Documentation et Sûreté) is the civilian Algerian intelligence apparatus for conducting foreign intelligence and counterintelligence surveillance. However, the Armée Nationale Populaire (ANP), known as Military Security (Sûreté Militaire), is the principal and most effective intelligence service in the country, with its abundant documentation on the leadership and organization of the radical Islamist groups. During the difficult process of uniting "external" and "internal" FLN personnel, some of whom were of questionable loyalty, Military Security became the dominant security service in the 1970s, responsible to the head of state for monitoring and maintaining files on all potential sources of opposition to the national leadership. The DGDS conducts foreign intelligence and countering of internal subversion and has successfully infiltrated Islamist groups and monitored opposition movements by employing paid informers. However, the DGDS is theoretically bound by legal restrictions, whereas Military Security is less circumscribed in its operations and remains the senior intelligence body concerned with internal security.

Immediately after assuming power, Boumédiène started to rely heavily on the security forces, particularly the intelligence service of the ANP, to maintain strict surveillance within and beyond the national boundaries on people whose ideologies were considered questionable. In response to a failed coup attempt by Chief of Staff Tahar Zbiri at the end of 1967, Boumédiène dissolved the general staff and solidified his control over the ANP by personally assuming many staff responsibilities. He excluded the ANP leadership from day-to-day policymaking but remained close to the army commanders whose support he needed to maintain political control.

Several groups—mostly former internal leaders and politically motivated enemies of Boumédiène—sought to preserve the Algerian armed forces' guerrilla traditions and strongly opposed the creation of a strong, centralized military power under Boumédiène's control. By contrast, according to Boumédiène's philosophy, the security of a modern state required a well-equipped armed force that was trained and organized along conventional lines. The brief border war with Morocco in 1976, in which the conventional Moroccan Army proved to be superior to the ANP, underscored the need to convert the ANP into a unified modern army. The external forces were better organized, equipped, and trained and were not fractured by local loyalties (known as *wilaya*). Boumédiène vigorously undertook to reduce, consolidate, reorganize, and train the ANP's various elements. He purged most of the headstrong former guerrilla commanders while retaining professionals of the external army, as well as about 250 officers and noncommissioned officers (NCOs) with experience in the French Army.

Boumédiène never considered himself a military professional, and he and his top aides never appeared publicly in uniform. He asserted that as a socialist state, Algeria was not the instrument of a military regime or an officer caste. Nonetheless, the ANP was the best-organized and best-managed institution in the country, and many technically competent and experienced military personnel entered ministries and parastatal (partly government owned and partly privately owned) corporations as part of the national economic elite.

After Boumédiène was incapacitated by a fatal illness in late 1978, the Council of the Revolution assumed day-to-day political power on an interim basis. Closely identified with the Boumédiène government, this was the country's supreme governing body through which the ANP exercised its influence. The council was comprised largely of military men with wartime or postwar service, many of whom served on the ANP general staff or as commanders of military regions. One member of the council was Chadli Benjedid, who was the nation's senior military officer and was viewed as the ANP's candidate to replace Boumédiène. He became president when the FLN

Party Congress became deadlocked over two more prominent candidates.

During the 1980s, Benjedid took a number of measures to reorganize the military high command to enhance the ANP's efficiency and military effectiveness. Benjedid's Council of Ministers included strong ANP representation, with military men consistently making up half the membership of the FLN Political Bureau. The ANP's favorable image was badly tarnished by the ruthless way in which it suppressed the strikes and riots of the 1988 "Black October." Troops deployed in the center of Algiers and other cities fired indiscriminately, with little regard for civilian casualties. Reacting to criticism by human rights activists at home and abroad, Benjedid purged a number of military commanders and appointed younger, more professional officers with personal loyalty to him. Soon thereafter, all senior army officers resigned from the FLN Central Committee so as to formally, if not actually, distance themselves from civilian politics.

As the threat of Islamic militancy became more acute, the power of the army reemerged as the primary defense against religiously inspired violence. The role of the armed forces was legitimated by a four-month state of emergency declared after the May–June 1991 rioting. The military high command felt that the government's political liberalization measures and its lax attitude toward the Islamic threat were mistaken. Benjedid was forced to resign as president when the first round of national election results of 26 December 1991 resulted in an overwhelming victory for Algeria's Islamic Salvation Front (Front Islamique du Salut; FIS), which was the central player in the militant opposition to the regime.

Under the constitution, the president is supreme commander of all the armed forces and is responsible for national defense. The head of state can turn for advice on national security matters to the High Security Council, which—along with the Council of Ministers—is required to give its consent to the declaration of a state of emergency in the event that the country faces imminent danger to its institutions, its independence, or its territorial integrity. The High Security Council must also be heard prior to a declaration of war by the president. The Security Council's members include the prime minister, the minister of national defense, the chief of staff of the armed forces, the minister of the interior (an army officer), and the minister of justice.

Upon Benjedid's resignation, the High Security Council assembled to cancel the second round of the general election and created a five-member interim governing body, the High Council of State, to exercise interim presidential powers.

The council's only military representative was the minister of defense, Major General Khaled Nezzar, who was seen as the strong man of the regime. The military exerted strong influence on the interim government; troops and armored vehicles were deployed in the cities, military checkpoints were set up, and gatherings at mosques for political purposes were prohibited. The regime declared a one-year state of emergency, banned the FIS, and arrested thousands of its supporters. Convinced that the stability of the nation was at stake, the army clearly intended to crush the FIS. The militants resorted to terrorist attacks; the June 1992 assassination of Boudiaf, one of the original founders of the group that became the FLN, hardened the attitude of the military. Nezzar vowed that the army would wage war against the Islamic extremists until their total eradication was achieved. After the Algerian government nullified the likely victory of the Islamic Salvation Front during the 1991 legislative elections, numerous Algerian Islamists and especially the Armed Islamic Group (Groupe Islamique Armé; GIA) began a series of violent, armed attacks against the government and against foreigners in the country. Several of the Algerian security and intelligence agencies have succeeded in penetrating the GIA.

As 1992 drew to a close, the suppression of the Islamic political movement by the ANP and police appeared to be outwardly effective, though individual acts of violence continued. Senior commanders asserted that the cohesion of the army was unaffected by desertions and arms thefts by sympathizers in the military. The military leaders maintained that they deemed it necessary to intervene only for reasons of heading off anarchy. Although the armed forces could have assumed power directly during the turmoil of 1992, they refrained from doing so. They continued to profess their intention of returning to their basic mission of providing for the defense and territorial integrity of the nation.

Both Military Security and the DGDS were implicated in the brutal treatment of detainees to obtain confessions or extract information on clandestine political activists, especially after the riots of October

1988. Government officials have acknowledged that individual cases of improper behavior by security forces did occur but stressed that torture and human rights abuses were not sanctioned and that evidence of it would be investigated. In September 1990, Benjedid announced the dissolution of the DGDS after criticism of its repressive role in the 1988 riots. The dissolution coincided with other government reforms to remove barriers to individual liberties. Informed sources believed, however, that this action did not represent an end to domestic intelligence operations but rather a transfer of DGDS functions to other Algerian intelligence and security agencies. These agencies include the Coordinating Directorate of Territorial Security, an Antiterrorist Detachment, and a working group of the High Council of State dealing with security matters, whose precise functions and jurisdictions are very fluid.

Abdelaziz Bouteflika was elected president in 1999 and continued to use intensively Algerian intelligence in the war against terror. The Algerian Department for Information and Security (DRS) continued systematically to hold suspects in secret places of detention, and their families received no information about their whereabouts, sometimes for months. While held by the DRS, detainees have no contact with the outside world, and there are persistent reports of torture and other ill treatment of people who are thought to have information about terrorism.

ALGERIAN NUCLEAR WEAPONS PROGRAM. The first French nuclear weapons tests were conducted in Algeria between 1960 and 1965. The first test took place on 13 February 1960 at Reggan. A total of 14 nuclear weapons tests, four atmospheric and 10 underground, were conducted at two Algerian locations.

The Algerian government established the Commissariat for New Energy (Commissariat aux Énergies Nouvelles) in 1982 to develop nuclear energy, solar energy, and other potential sources of power. Whereas solar power proved to have considerable potential, particularly in desert locations, their nuclear development program was a cause for concern, and allegations by the West declared that it could be used for military purposes. Algeria was thought to want nuclear weapons to counter a perceived threat from the radical regime of Libya's Colonel Muammar Qaddafi.

It is reported that secret agreements were signed by Algeria with China and Argentina at the beginning of the 1980s to produce weapons-grade plutonium. Under a secret 1983 agreement, the Chinese government provided a nuclear reactor to Algeria that, along with a related research facility, could form the central component of a weapons program. In 1984, Algeria purchased 150 tons of uranium concentrate from Niger. It was also reported that Iraq had sent scientists and some uranium to Algeria. In addition, Algeria has uranium deposits of its own in the southeastern part of the country. Algeria now operates two nuclear reactors: one in the capital of Algiers, supplied by Argentina, and a second at Ain Oussera, supplied by the Chinese. Discussions were held with Argentina about supplying Algeria with a larger reactor, but these discussions ultimately led nowhere.

The collapse of world oil prices in 1986 plunged Algeria into a severe recession. Several years later, the country became embroiled in political turmoil, and violent demonstrations broke out in many cities. During this period of uncertain transition, many Algerians became alienated by what they felt was the unwelcome encroachment of secular, or Western, values. On 10 April 1991, the Algerian government expelled the British military attaché, William Cross, who had been found taking pictures near the Es Salam nuclear reactor. In addition to Algeria's severe economic situation, strong pressures from the United States led Algeria to accept International Atomic Energy Agency (IAEA) safeguards in February 1992. However, the Algerian government continues to maintain that both of its nuclear reactors are being used strictly for civilian purposes. The U.S. intelligence community was divided in regard to Algeria's real nuclear intentions. In January 1995, Algeria joined the Nuclear Nonproliferation Treaty (NPT) and agreed to inspections by the IAEA of its nuclear facilities. *See also* ALGERIAN INTELLIGENCE.

ALI YUNESI, HOJATOLESLAM (1955–). Hojatoleslam Ali Yunesi served as the Iranian minister for intelligence and security, Vezarat-e Ettela'at va Amniat-e Keshvar (VEVAK), from February 1999 until 2005; he was replaced by **Hojatoleslam Gholam-Hussein Mohseni-Ejei**. Yunesi studied in a Qum seminary. Because of his political activism, he was imprisoned by the monarchy several times, until he left for military training in Palestinian and Lebanese camps. After the revolution, Yunesi held a number of positions in the judicial area. His background in intelligence work includes service as representative of the Iranian armed forces deputy commander-in-chief to the Military Intelligence Department. Yunesi worked with **Muhammad Muhammadi-Reyshahri** in creating the Intelligence and Security Ministry (MOIS). Ali Yunesi also served as a member of the MOIS committee for investigating the 1998–1999 murders of Iranian intellectuals and oppositionists. *See also* IRANIAN INTELLIGENCE.

ALLAM, FOUAD. Fouad Allam served as the head of the Egyptian security service for 20 years. Following Anwar **Sadat's assassination** in 1981, General Allam and the new president, Hosni Mubarak, waged a campaign against radical Islam through unlawful arrests, detention without trial, and torture to force confessions. Such actions had not been taken since the days of former Egyptian president Gamal Abdel Nasser in the 1950s and 1960s. Thousands of suspected terrorists were rounded up and jailed, including Sheikh Omar Abdel Rahman, who was later convicted of conspiring to blow up the World Trade Center, and Ayman al-Zawahiri, one of Osama bin-Laden's two top aides. *See also* EGYPTIAN INTELLIGENCE; NASSER'S ASSASSINATION ATTEMPTS.

ALMÁSY, LÁSZLÓ (1895–1951). Born into a noble family in the Austrian–Hungarian monarchy, Count László Almásy was a Hungarian aristocrat, pilot, and soldier. The lead character of *The English Patient* was based on his life. During **World War I**, he served with the Austro–Hungarian Imperial and Royal Aviation Troops. After the war, Almásy became a researcher and explorer in the Sahara Desert and was given the nickname Abu Ramla (Father of the Sands) by his Bedouin friends. In the following years, Almásy led archeological and ethnographical expeditions with the German ethnographer Leo Frobenius; he also worked in Egypt as a flying instructor.

After the outbreak of **World War II**, Almásy returned to Hungary under suspicion by the British that he was a spy for the Italians—and vice versa. As a Hungarian reserve officer, he was assigned as a captain to the Afrika Korps. The Abwehr, the German military intelligence service, recruited him in Budapest. In 1941–1942, he worked with the German troops of Field Marshal Erwin Rommel and led military missions using his desert experience. One of these missions was **Operation Salaam**, which aimed to infiltrate enemy territory with two German spies. This was not a covert operation, and Almásy and his team wore German uniforms. Almásy delivered the German Abwehr agents **Johannes Eppler** and Peter Stanstede to Cairo in the same way.

The details of Almásy's role in World War II are unclear. He received the Iron Cross from Rommel for delivering spies, and he was promoted to the rank of major. He was, however, never a spy or a Nazi. After the end of the desert war, Almásy relocated to Turkey, where he became involved in a plan to cause an Egyptian revolt that never materialized. He then returned to Budapest where, with his contacts from the Roman Catholic Church, he helped save the lives of several Jewish families at a time when Jews were being sent to concentration camps.

After the war, Almásy was arrested in Hungary and ended up in a Soviet prison. When the communists took control of Hungary, Almásy was tried for treason in the Communist People's Court. He was eventually acquitted, but he escaped the country into British-occupied Austria, reputedly with the aid of British intelligence. He was chased by a KGB "hit squad" and captured on the way to Cairo. British intelligence bribed Hungarian communist officials to enable Almásy's release. He returned to Egypt at the invitation of King Farouk and became technical director of the newly established Desert Institute. He became ill in 1951 during his visit to Austria and died of dysentery in a hospital in Salzburg, where he was buried.

AMER, ABDEL HAKIM (1919–1967). Abdel Hakim Amer was recruited into the Egyptian Army in 1939 and served in the 1948 Arab–Israeli War. He took part in the 1952 revolution and played a key role in the military coup that overthrew King Farouk. In 1956, Amer was appointed commander in chief of the joint military command established by Egypt and Syria. He commanded the Egyptian Army during the 1956 **Suez crisis** and the North **Yemen Civil War** during the early 1960s. After Egypt's defeat by Israel in the **Six Days' War** of June 1967, Amer's distinguished military career came to a sudden end and he was forced into early retirement; Field Marshal Amer had been responsible for the failure of **Egyptian intelligence**

on the eve of the Six Days' War when he discounted Israel's military capability. In August of that year, Amer, along with over 50 Egyptian military officers and two former ministers, was arrested for allegedly plotting a coup to overthrow Gamal Abdel Nasser. In September 1967, Amer was approached in his jail cell by high-ranking Egyptian officers and was given a choice to remain there and stand trial for treason, which would inevitably have ended with his conviction and execution, or die an honorable death by taking poison. He chose the second option. Six-Day War

AMERICAN HOSTAGES IN IRAN. *See* OPERATION EAGLE CLAW.

ANCIENT AND MEDIEVAL INTELLIGENCE IN THE MIDDLE EAST. Historical and literary accounts of spies and acts of espionage appear in some of the world's earliest recorded histories. Egyptian hieroglyphs and papyri reveal the presence of court spies and extensive military and slave trade operations. Early Egyptian pharaohs employed agents to uncover disloyal subjects and to locate tribes that could be conquered and enslaved. From 1,000 BCE onward, Egyptian espionage operations focused on foreign intelligence about the political and military strength of rivals Greece and Rome.

Egyptian spies made significant contributions to the communication tools of espionage. The ancient civilizations of Egypt, Greece, and Rome employed literate subjects in their civil services, and many spies dealt with written communications. The use of written messages necessitated the development of codes, disguised writing, trick inks, and hidden compartments in clothing. Egyptian spies were the first to develop the extensive use of poisons, including toxins derived from plants and snakes, to carry out assassinations or acts of sabotage.

In the Middle East, and later Byzantium, the large Roman governmental bureaucracy established one of the earliest civilian intelligence agencies. Civilian agents of espionage gathered information about foreign militaries and economic practices from traders, merchants, sailors, and other businessmen. The Roman Empire displayed a penchant for the practice of political espionage. In order to conquer North Africa and northern Europe, spies were used in both foreign and domestic political operations to gauge the political climate of the empire and surrounding lands by eavesdropping in the forum or in public market spaces. Several ancient accounts, especially those of the first century CE, mention the presence of a secret police force, the *frumentarii*.

In 1095, Pope Urban II called for the first Crusade, a military campaign to recapture Jerusalem and the Holy Lands from Muslim and Byzantine rule. The Church amassed several large armies and employed spies to report on defenses surrounding Constantinople and Jerusalem. Special intelligence agents also infiltrated prisons to free captured crusaders or sabotage rival palaces, mosques, and military defenses. The Crusades continued for nearly four centuries, draining the military and intelligence resources of most of the European monarchs. The Crusades also changed the focus of espionage and intelligence work within Europe, with espionage becoming an essential component of the Inquisition. *See also* BATTLE OF MEGIDDO I; EARLY ISLAMIC INTELLIGENCE; EGYPTIAN INTELLIGENCE.

ARAB BULLETIN. During World War I, the **Arab Bureau in Cairo** published a newsletter about the Middle East, describing the political viewpoints and thoughts of the small Arab Bureau, the group that organized the **Arab Revolt** (1916–1918) led by Sharif Hussein, the emir of Mecca. The idea for the bulletin was introduced by **Thomas Edward Lawrence**, a junior member of the Arab Bureau. The newsletter was first published under the name of *Arab Bureau Summaries* and only later as the *Arab Bulletin*. The first edition came out on 6 June 1916 and continued to be published until the end of 1918. It was published in the Arab Bureau offices of the Savoy Hotel in Cairo and was classified as top secret. Each newsletter was printed in 26 copies for a limited distribution, including the high-level British personnel in Egypt and Sudan, and the War and Navy Offices in London. The newsletters included confidential background information on the Arab and Muslim world, and one of the topics largely discussed was the Arab Revolt.

ARAB BUREAU IN CAIRO. The Arab Bureau was established in Cairo in 1916 as a central agency in charge of Arab issues in the Middle East, particularly for dealing with propaganda. The bureau allowed the expansion of control by British Egypt over the Arab world, with Cairo as the center for the establishment of British policy in the Middle East. The bureau was organized by Sir Mark Sykes, a Middle Eastern issues specialist appointed personally by Lord Horatio Kitchener, the minister of war, together with **Gilbert Clayton**, head of British intelligence in Cairo. During the years 1915–1916, the British began to focus in an organized way on the use that Great Britain could make of Arab leaders in dealing with the Middle East. After the de Bunsen Committee, led by Sir Mark Sykes, submitted its report on the postwar Middle East, the British government sent Sykes to Egypt, the Persian Gulf, Mesopotamia, and India in order to discuss the committee's recommendations with the high-level officials in the area.

Using input from local leaders, the committee agreed to Sykes's proposition for a general bureau, not as a separate body but only as a department of British intelligence in Cairo. Thus, instead of building a central agency that would be in charge of a general policy, as proposed by Sykes, the different government bureaus continued to set and carry out their own policies, independent of each other and sometimes even contradicting each other. Kitchener did not want the reins taken from his hands, and the Foreign Ministry accepted his authority. Sykes continued to determine policy only as Kitchener's representative and not by his own merits as the head of an independent agency. *See also ARAB BULLETIN*; BELL, GERTRUDE MARGARET LOWTHIAN; BRITISH INTELLIGENCE IN EGYPT AND SUDAN; BRITISH INTELLIGENCE IN MESOPOTAMIA.

ARAB LEGION. The Arab Legion (al-Jaysh al-Arabī), also known as the Transjordan Frontier Force, was the regular army of Transjordan and then Jordan. In 1921, the Hashemite Emir **Abdullah I** of Transjordan formed the Transjordan Frontier Force as a police force to keep order among the tribes of Transjordan and to guard the important Jerusalem–Amman road. The name was changed to the Arab Legion in 1923.

In 1939, John Bagot Glubb, better known as **Glubb Pasha**, became the legion's commander and transformed it into a well-trained Arab army. He served in this position until 1956. During **World War II**, the Arab Legion took part in the British war effort against pro-Axis forces in the Middle East theater. By then, the force had grown to 1,600 men. The legion was also the most successful of the Arab armies during the 1948–1949 Israeli War of Independence. There was considerable embarrassment from the British government that British officers were employed in the legion during the conflict, and one British member of Parliament called for Glubb Pasha to be imprisoned for serving in a foreign army without the king's permission.

Until 1948, Transjordan had never faced an external threat and thus had no need for a system that would provide it with military intelligence. The Arab Legion received intelligence from the British army, which was responsible for Jordan's security in case of war. The British decision to evacuate Palestine and the establishment of the state of Israel forced the Arab Legion to establish a combat intelligence unit. This intelligence unit was built according to the British model and received assistance from the British. The Arab Legion's intelligence section was a subsection of the Department of Operations, and the intelligence unit was comprised of subunits attached to each of the legion's battalions for gathering information and conducting research. The intelligence subunits of each division conducted specific investigations on officers, units, targets, and forces of the Israeli Army. If the collected intelligence received was considered of great importance, it was passed upward to the commander in chief in Amman and, in some cases, discussed at the political level of the state.

There was a strong tie between British intelligence and the budding Jordanian intelligence. The British shared information with the Jordanians about the newly established state of Israel and preparations for the war. However, the intelligence that the British passed on to the Jordanians was generally limited to information that could serve British interests in the region. When the Arab Legion was deployed in their major base of Shunna prior to the invasion of Israel, the officers received booklets prepared by Jordanian intelligence containing basic information about the target country and the expected battlefield.

Jordanian military intelligence gathered information by several methods, such as OSCINT (open sources) from the Israeli press and radio broadcasts, as well as Israel Defense Forces (IDF) communications. Listening to IDF communications proved to be problematic, however, due to the lack of Hebrew-speaking agents. Attempts by

Jordanian intelligence to recruit Hebrew-speaking agents were not successful, and their failure to do so caused the Arab Legion serious difficulties throughout the 1948–1949 War of Independence. The IDF made it even more difficult by adopting the method of flooding the transmissions.

The Arab Legion's intelligence also conducted observations and reconnaissance, the importance of which was evident in the first battle at Latrun on 25 May 1948. When the Arab observation post reported the movements of the IDF prior to the attack, the legion blockaded the Jerusalem highway. The efficiency of the legion's intelligence and the results of their cooperation with the British were also demonstrated by the successful attack they conducted on Gush Etzion, during which they avoided the minefields and bypassed the fortifications prepared by the IDF. The attack was preplanned by the British, who gathered the information and passed it over to the Jordanians. On 28 May 1948, they conquered the Jewish Quarter of Jerusalem's Old City, expelled the Jews who lived there, and took part in the destruction of the synagogues therein. The legion also secured the West Bank for Transjordan.

The Arab Legion's counterintelligence was aimed at thwarting Israeli efforts to obtain information about Jordan and the Arab Legion through document supervision, communication security, facility guarding, and the use of codes and ciphering. Soldiers were under strict orders not to speak with civilians in order to prevent information from leaking out. However, protecting the Hashemite regime of Jordan from inner opposing factors was considered a higher priority, and most of the effort of this section of the intelligence mechanism was directed to that cause. Although the Arab Legion received some information from collaborators throughout the 1948–1949 War of Independence, the Arab Legion did not have spies in Israel. Perhaps this was due to the fact that it did not need spies there, as it received information on a regular basis from the British army units that had remained in the newly established state of Israel. *See also* JORDANIAN INTELLIGENCE.

ARAB REVOLT (1916). The Arab Revolt was led by Hussein bin-Ali, who was Mecca and Benin's sharif, in June 1916 against the Ottoman Empire, which was at war with Great Britain and its allies at the time.

Before the revolt, letters were exchanged between Hussein and Sir Henry McMahon, the British high commissioner in Egypt, in which the sharif was promised support for an Arab state after winning the war. Britain financed the revolt and provided weapons to the rebels. Britain also brought experts to the guerilla war, led by Colonel **T. E. Lawrence**. The rebels recruited a Bedouin army from the northern region of the Arabian Peninsula, especially from the Hijaz area. According to various reports, Hussein expected from 100,000 to 250,000 Arab soldiers to join them. However, the Arab Revolt that Hussein hoped for never occurred. He did not have a compulsory army, and different estimates of his forces ranged from 30,000–70,000 desert fighters. The few non-Hijaz Arab officers who joined the revolt were either war captives or exiles who already lived in the territories under British rule.

The majority of the revolt's activity consisted of sabotaging the Hijaz railroad, the Turkish provision line to Hijaz. In the Arab world outside of Hijaz and the neighboring tribes, support of the revolt was not evident. Although Hussein always presented himself to the British as the Arab nation's spokesman, it seems that he did not have the full support of any Arab organization. According to reports, the British realized from the beginning of the revolt that they had made the wrong choice when they gambled on Hussein. About three months after Hussein announced his revolt, the British War Bureau advised the government that the Arab world was not joining the cause. Clearly, Hussein could not stand alone against the Turks.

Immediately after the revolt in Hijaz began in early June, Lawrence reported to the Arab Bureau that there were problems with Hussein's soldiers caused by divisive arguments every time tribal gatherings were held. After all, they were not true soldiers but rather untrained tribal people, and it was difficult to keep them united without money and food rations. The Turks understood this and bided their time, waiting with confidence for the tribal disagreements to quickly split the opposition.

The **Arab Bureau in Cairo** was very disappointed with Hussein's performance, and the British began to see that Hussein was far from being the leader of a new Arab state. A year after Hussein declared the Arab Revolt, **David George Hogarth**, manager of the Arab Bureau, reported that the Arab Revolt had not lived up to expectations and was viewed as a failure. The financial, political, and military investment made by Britain in Hussein's revolt had not paid off. However, by 1918 British officials were suggesting the merits of making it look as if Hussein had not failed so as to protect Britain's reputation and prevent Muslims everywhere from perceiving the British part in the revolt suspiciously or loathingly. *See also* BRITISH INTELLIGENCE IN EGYPT AND SUDAN; HIJAZ OPERATION; WORLD WAR I.

ARAB SPIES IN THE OTTOMAN SERVICE. Turkish espionage and counterespionage played an important part in **World War I**. Networks of spies, collaborators, and informants were set up in all the Middle Eastern territories under Ottoman rule. When Ahmed Jamal Pasha, the Ottoman ruler of Syria, began to take action against Lebanese leaders, he recruited spies and informants to collect information about every Lebanese dignitary in Beirut. He charged those arrested with incitement and anti-Turkish expressions or activities and sent letters of accusation to the military courts. Some of the information and the accusations were true, or partially so, but there were also cases in which the accusations were made up and witnesses were paid for their fabricated testimonies in court. *See also* TURKISH INTELLIGENCE.

ARAB STRATEGIC REPORT. The *Arab Strategic Report* is the regular annual report published by the **al-Ahram Center for Political and Strategic Studies** (ACPSS) since 1985. The main aim of the report is to create an Arab perspective for strategic research according to the principles set by the center. The *Arab Strategic Report* is published in order to provide a substantial basis for debate and strategic thinking in political and intellectual circles on various issues within the Arab world and countries considered as Third World. The annual report is subdivided into three sections: the larger international and regional perspective; the Arab regional perspective; and the local Egyptian perspective. Since 1997, the report has been focusing on the research and assessments of basic developments of the year from the perspective of Arab interests and to visualizing future horizons. The *Arab Strategic Report* is considered an intelligence assessment tool.

ARAFAT, MOUSSA (1941–). Moussa Arafat was born in Jaffa, Palestine, to a mother from Jerusalem and a father from Gaza. The family moved to Gaza after the 1948 Israeli War of Independence. Arafat started law school at Cairo University but failed to graduate. In 1965 he was arrested by the Egyptian police for subversive activities, and later he attended a university in Yugoslavia and obtained a master's degree in military studies.

Moussa Arafat was considered as a key member of **al-Fatah**, which is a major secular Palestinian political party and the largest organization in the Palestine Liberation Organization (PLO). Moussa Arafat was always close to his brother Yasser Arafat, the PLO leader and chairman. In 1967, Moussa Arafat took an active part in the battles against Israel on the Syrian front. He also participated in the battle of Karameh in Jordan in 1968. He was arrested by the Jordanian police during the events of September 1970 (known as Black September) in which the Palestinians conducted an uprising in Jordan after which the PLO leadership was deported to Lebanon. He continued his activities in Lebanon until the Palestinians were deported from Lebanon as a result of the 1982 Lebanon War I. Moussa Arafat settled in Tunis and was appointed deputy head of the military intelligence of the PLO. After the 1993 Oslo Accord and the establishment of the Palestinian National Authority (PNA), Moussa Arafat was engaged in the construction of the Palestinian military intelligence organization in Gaza and the West Bank and commanded the organization until he was appointed by his brother Yasser as the commander of the National Security Forces of the PNA.

Moussa Arafat carried this job in addition to his job as chief of the PNA military intelligence. In 2005, when Mahmoud Abbas (also known as Abu Mazen) succeeded Yasser Arafat, he dismissed Moussa Arafat. *See also* PALESTINIAN NATIONAL AUTHORITY INTELLIGENCE.

ARMED ISLAMIC GROUP/GROUPEMENT ISLAMIQUE ARMÉ (GIA). The Armed Islamic Group is an Islamic extremist group aiming to overthrow the secular Algerian regime and replace it with an Islamic state. The GIA began its violent activity in 1992 after Algiers annulled the victory of the Islamic Salvation Front—the largest Islamic opposition party—in the first round of legislative elections in

December 1991. Precise numbers remain unknown, although it probably has fewer than 100 members. The GIA frequently attacks civilians and government workers. Since 1992, it has conducted a terrorist campaign of civilian massacres, sometimes wiping out entire villages in its area of operation, although the group's dwindling numbers have caused a decrease in the number of attacks. Since announcing its campaign against foreigners living in Algeria in 1993, the GIA has killed more than 100 expatriate men and women—mostly Europeans—in the country. The group uses assassinations and bombings, including car bombs, and is known to favor kidnapping victims and slitting their throats. In December 1994, the GIA hijacked an Air France flight to Algiers; in 2002, a French court sentenced two GIA members to life imprisonment for conducting a series of bombings in France in 1995.

In 1995, a member of a cell of the al Qaeda–linked GIA in Brussels, known by the pseudonym Omar Nasiri, stole money from a more senior member of the cell. Not knowing what to do and being unhappy about the way the cell used his mother's house, he contacted the French Direction Générale de la Sécurité Extérieure (DGSE), which gave him money to repay what he stole and made him an informer. Nasiri's task in the cell was to purchase weapons and ammunition, as well as smuggling explosives into North Africa before a bombing there. After being recruited by French intelligence, Nasiri provided information about the cell's members, associates passing through, and weapons smuggling to the GIA and to AAnsar al-Islam. The cell and other parts of the network were raided in March 1995 by the Belgian authorities and some members were jailed. Nasiri subsequently penetrated al Qaeda's camps in Afghanistan, met some of its top commanders, and reported on them to French and the British intelligence.

Nasiri, who used to take the explosives hidden in a car for a GIA cell in Belgium, informed his contacts in DGSE about the trip beforehand but was reluctant to provide the French with updates about his progress while on route to Tangiers, Morocco, where he was expected to give the car and explosives to another operative. Within a short period after Nasiri started his smuggling activity, a car bomb was detonated in Algiers, killing over 40 people. Nasiri commented that he did not know if the explosives that he transported in his car were used for that blast.

The Algerian government manipulated the GIA from its creation in 1991. The newly appointed GIA leader in 1994, Djamal Zitouni, was allegedly planted by the Algerian government as a mole in the GIA. In fact, Zitouni was an agent of **Algerian intelligence**. Prior to Zitouni taking over, the GIA tried to limit civilian casualties, but Zitouni launched many attacks on civilian targets, attacked other Islamist militant groups such as the rival Islamic Salvation Army (AIS), and launched a series of attacks inside France. Zitouni was responsible for the killing of many of the genuine Islamists within the GIA. These controversial tactics caused the GIA to slowly lose popular support and the group split into many dissident factions.

ASFOURA, SAMIH (1948–). Born in Mafraq, Jordan, Lieutenant General Samih Asfoura holds a bachelor's degree in law and was a practicing attorney until he joined the Jordanian Mukhabarat (General Intelligence Department; GID) in 1972. Asfoura, who was serving as the assistant to the director, was appointed on 5 July 2005 to be director of the GID as a replacement for Lieutenant General **Saad Kheir**. However, shortly after he entered his new position as director of the GID, Asfoura resigned in December 2005 and was replaced by Major General **Mohammad Dahabi**, most probably as a result of the November 2005 terrorist bombing in a hotel in Amman. *See also* JORDANIAN INTELLIGENCE.

ASHRAF, MARWAN (1944–2007). Marwan Ashraf was married to the third daughter of former Egyptian president Gamal Abdel Nasser. He was also President Nasser's liaison to the intelligence services and part of the inner circle of leaders who determined Egypt's future. In the spring of 1969, Marwan Ashraf came to London, ostensibly to consult a doctor about a stomach ailment. He chose to be examined by a doctor whose offices had been used previously for a covert meeting between King Hussein of Jordan and the general director of the Israeli prime minister's office. Along with his X-rays, Marwan Ashraf handed the doctor a file full of official Egyptian state documents and asked that they be delivered to the Israeli embassy in London.

Upon inspection of the documents, the **Mossad**, the **Israeli intelligence** service, determined that they were genuine. Although they considered it a risk to deal with a volunteer who might be a double agent spreading disinformation, it was decided that the risk was worth taking in this case. Three days after meeting with the doctor, Marwan Ashraf was contacted by the Mossad as he walked through Harrods, the London department store. That was the day his operational life as a spy began. From the start, Ashraf delivered many top-secret Egyptian documents, which formed the basis for what became known as "the Concept" among Israel's political and military leaders. The Concept held that until Egypt possessed missiles and long-range bombers and until the Arab states united in a genuine coalition, a new war with Israel would not take place.

Running Ashraf's operations grew into a small industry. A safe house was purchased in London for face-to-face meetings with his agent and often with Zvi Zamir, the director of the Mossad. The house was wired to record every conversation, and a special team of clerks transcribed the tapes for submission to Israeli Prime Minister Golda Meir, the chief of staff of the Israel Defense Forces (IDF), and other top Israeli officials. Marwan received $50,000 at each meeting, but this was only a minor expense compared to the estimated $20 million spent over the first four years of Marwan Ashraf's operational life. He was given various codenames, including "Angel," "Babylon," and, most frequently, "the In-Law."

In April 1973, the In-Law sent a flash message to the Mossad using the word "radish," which was the code for an imminent war. Zvi Zamir flew from Israel to the London safe house to meet with the In-Law, who revealed that Egypt and Syria were planning to launch a surprise attack on 15 May 1973. Consequently, Israel called up tens of thousands of reservists and deployed additional brigades and support equipment both in the Sinai and the north. The alert dragged on for three months and cost $35 million, but it turned out to be a false alarm.

Six months later, on 5 October 1973, the In-Law sent another flash message with the code word "radish." Zvi Zamir was awakened at 2:30 A.M. with the news and took the first flight to London. After speaking with the In-Law at the safe house, Zamir phoned an aide on the morning of Yom Kippur, the holiest day on the Jewish religious calendar, to report that the Egyptians and Syrians were planning a simultaneous attack on both fronts at sunset. It was reported that Syria was amassing tanks and missiles in the north and that Egypt was conducting military maneuvers near the Suez Canal. Despite those reports, Major General Eli (Eliyahu) Zeira, the director of the Israeli Military Intelligence (MI), announced at an Israeli cabinet meeting later that day that a coordinated attack by Egypt and Syria was still an extremely low probability. The In-Law's warning was not considered persuasive, as the last time he had promised war would break out, nothing had happened and the response had been very costly. Moshe Dayan, the minister of defense, argued that the warning did not provide enough of a basis to mobilize a whole army.

Nevertheless, it was decided that at 4 P.M. on Yom Kippur eve, 6 October 1973, two hours before the In-Law said the attack would be launched, armored brigades would move into position along the Suez Canal. Until then, there would be only three tanks in position to hold off any invasion. At 2 P.M. on 6 October 1973, the Arab armies attacked, with Egypt crossing the Suez Canal from the south and Syrian tanks charging from the north. Their armies overwhelmed the surprised and unprepared state of Israel, but Israel's outnumbered forces fought back and recovered their key positions. With the help of airlifts of weapons and supplies from the United States, Israel won the war before the month's end.

Despite their final victory, the **Yom Kippur War** was an Israeli intelligence disaster. Decades later, the Mossad and the MI continued to argue over who was to blame. Major General Eli Zeira lost his job as head of the MI and spent years sifting through the events leading up to the attacks. He concluded that Israel had been deliberately and artfully misled and that the In-Law had been a double agent from the start. However, the Mossad formed a special committee to examine the In-Law's role and reached the conclusion that Marwan Ashraf was not, in fact, a double agent.

Still, Eli Zeira was not convinced and he began to talk to journalists and academic scholars about his theory, indicating that Marwan Ashraf was the top Egyptian source for the Israeli Mossad on the eve of the Yom Kippur War. Not long after the leak, Zvi Zamir called General Zeira a "traitor" for divulging Marwan Ashraf's identity. He petitioned the Israeli attorney general for an investigation. Although there was no official inquiry, Eli Zeira was sued for slander. The Israeli Supreme Court ruled in arbitration that Zeira had in fact revealed Marwan Ashraf's identity.

Marwan Ashraf retired and moved to Great Britain in the late 1970s to work in business. On 27 June 2007, Ashraf died after falling off the balcony of his fifth-floor apartment in London. His body was repatriated to Egypt on 30 June 2007. The burial ceremony on 1 July 2007 in Cairo was attended by Gamal Mubarak, the president's son and possible successor, and **Omar Suleiman**, the head of the **Egyptian intelligence** service. Beyond the unexplained cause of his death, the mystery behind Marwan Ashraf's life was further complicated when President Hosni Mubarak referred to Ashraf as "a patriot" in response to reporters' questions. He credited Ashraf with carrying out patriotic acts that could not yet be revealed, according to Egypt's official Middle East News Agency. Egypt's highest-ranking imam, Sheik Muhammad Seyed Tantawi, led the prayers over the coffin, which was covered with an Egyptian flag.

Marwan Ashraf was apparently writing a book about the war at the time of his death, but neither British Scotland Yard nor other intelligence agencies have been successful in locating the manuscript. As Scotland Yard investigates the suspicious fall to determine whether any of several intelligence services played a role in his death, the debate continues over whether Marwan Ashraf was a well-connected and resourceful Israeli spy or a brilliantly manipulative Egyptian double agent. Ashraf's death also brought a new and chilling significance to the long-running legal battle in Israel involving the unauthorized leak of his name to journalists. Zvi Zamir commented to the newspaper *Haaretz* that he had no doubt that reports published about Marwan Ashraf in Israel had caused his death, and he again called on the attorney general to indict former Israeli MI director Eli Zeira. Despite all the speculation, one thing is certain: Marwan Ashraf was the most effective spy in the history of the Middle East.

ASKARI, ALI-REZA (1944–). A retired two-star general of the Iranian Islamic Revolutionary Guard (IRG) and former deputy defense minister, Askari joined the IRG at its very start in 1979. He was an associate of Mostafa Chamran, a naturalized U.S. citizen of Iranian origin who returned to Iran when the mullahs seized power in 1979 and helped found the IRG. When Chamran was appointed defense minister two years later, Askari became one of his advisers.

Askari was in charge of a program to train foreign Islamist militants as part of Tehran's strategy of "exporting" the Khomeinist revolution. In 1982–1983, Askari, along with Ayatollah **Ali-Akbar Mohatashami-Pur**, founded the Lebanese branch of **Hizballah** and helped set up its first military units. The two men supervised the 1983 suicide attacks on the U.S. embassy and the U.S. Marine barracks in Beirut, which killed more than 300 Americans, including 241 Marines. Askari served as commander of the IRG corps in Lebanon, which controlled Hizballah's armed units in the late 1980s and 1990s. He was a central figure in the Western hostage taking that was prevalent during Lebanon's long civil war, including the 1984 kidnapping of Central Intelligence Agency (CIA) station chief Lieutenant Colonel William F. Buckley.

In November 2006, Askari was appointed as a member of the Iranian Strategic Defense Planning Commission set up by Ali Khamenei. In that capacity, he often traveled abroad to negotiate arms deals. He was also involved in Iran's controversial nuclear program, which, although presented as a civilian project, is known to be controlled by the IRG.

Askari disappeared following a military mission to Damascus, when he stopped over in Turkey on his way back to Tehran on 7 February 2007. The goal of the Iranian mission was to lay the foundations for a Syrian armament industry, licensed to manufacture Iranian-designed weapons. The 30 or so experts who had accompanied Askari on the trip remained in Syria to work out the technical details. According to some reports, Askari had stopped over in Istanbul to meet with an unidentified Syrian arms dealer who lives in Paris.

After initially denying reports of Askari's disappearance, Tehran authorities eventually issued a confirmation statement in late February 2007, claiming that the missing general had been abducted by a Western intelligence agency and taken to an unknown country in northern Europe. Iranian Foreign Minister Manouchehr Mottaki was quoted as saying that Iran would take all the necessary steps to solve the case, including asking Turkey to investigate Askari's disappearance.

Foreign Ministry sources in Tehran, however, said that Askari might have defected, possibly to the United States, where he has relatives.

Indeed, Iran is rife with rumors about the case, including claims that Askari was transferred to Romania, where he was debriefed by the Americans, and that he had documents with him, mostly related to Iran's military purchases abroad. Some reports in the Iranian and Arab media suggest that the Israeli secret service **Mossad** and the American CIA are behind Askari's disappearance.

Israel has denied involvement in the general's disappearance. However, according to speculation by the London *Daily Telegraph*, Askari could have been abducted by Israel in order to shed light on the whereabouts of missing Israel Air Force Lieutenant Colonel Ron Arad, who might have been held at one point by Iran. Askari was involved in a deal to transfer Arad to Tehran after his capture by the Lebanese Hizballah in 1986.

Whether he defected or was abducted, Askari is regarded as a big catch with a wealth of information about the activities of the IRG and its elite arm, the Quds corps, which controls Arab and Turkish radical groups financed by Tehran. The most important information Askari could provide to the West is in connection with **terrorism**, particularly Hizballah's network in Lebanon and the **Iranian nuclear weapons program**. *See also* IRANIAN INTELLIGENCE.

ATTASSI AFFAIR. The Attassi affair involved a naturalized U.S. citizen, Farhan Attassi, who was hanged as a spy in Damascus on 23 February 1965 at the age of 37. On the same day, Attassi's cousin and alleged accomplice in spying for the United States, Syrian Lieutenant Colonel Abdel Muin Hakemi, was shot in the courtyard of a Damascus army barracks. The Syrians charged that Attassi had obtained from Hakemi 11 shells of a new Soviet antiaircraft gun of the Syrian armed forces and had handed them over to Walter Snowdon, second secretary of the U.S. embassy in Damascus. Snowdon was subsequently expelled from Syria, and Washington denied the spy charges, but not very convincingly. Instead, the United States objected to Syria's brutal treatment and torture of Attassi before he went on trial, which included beating, brainwashing, and starvation. U.S. officials were not allowed to see him in jail, he was not provided with legal counsel, and only carefully edited portions of his secret trial were televised.

Attassi's hanging was used as a warning to all agents of imperialism, capitalism, and Zionism and as a protest against the alleged American policy of sabotage in Syria. Attassi was dressed in the white robe customary for a condemned criminal and bore a large poster stating the verdict. His limp body was on display for seven hours in al Marjah Square for curious onlookers to see before it was cut down and taken away for burial.

AYASH, YAHYA (1966–1996). Born near Nablus, Ayash studied electrical engineering at Bir Zeit University near Ramallah and joined **Hamas** shortly afterward. He is best known in the world as "the Engineer." During a 24-month campaign of terror beginning on 6 April 1994, Ayash killed 130 Israelis and wounded nearly 500. His first car bomb, detonated by a suicide bomber, killed eight people and wounded 30. A week later a man destroyed a crowded bus with 50 pounds of explosives strapped to his body. More bombings, all masterminded by the Engineer, followed with dreadful regularity. As the carnage in the streets of Israeli cities mounted, the Engineer became the most wanted man in modern Israeli history, resulting in one of the largest manhunts ever. The search involved the British Secret Service (MI5), the Royal Jordanian Special Forces, the U.S. Federal Bureau of Investigation (FBI), and the New York City Police Department. In charge of catching Ayash was the Israeli Security Agency (ISA), the most elite of Israel's secret services. On one occasion in the manhunt, Ayash escaped detection by disguising himself as an old Arab woman; on another, he donned the garb of an Orthodox Jewish student. As the search wore on and the killings continued, Ayash became revered by masses of Palestinians.

Finally, the ISA succeeded in finding an operative who agreed to give Ayash a booby-trapped cell phone. The operative had been told only that through the cell phone the ISA would be able to monitor Ayash's conversations. In fact, the ISA planted 1.7 ounces of explosives in the device. On 5 January 1996, the cell phone was detonated after Ayash answered a call made on it and his voice was confirmed. Yahya Ayash was killed. More than 100,000 Palestinians attended his funeral. *See also* ISRAELI INTELLIGENCE.

– B –

BAD BUSINESS. *See* LAVON AFFAIR.

BAHRAINI INTERNAL SECURITY. After more than 150 years of British presence and protection, Bahrain gained full independence on 15 August 1971. As in other Persian Gulf States, the Bahraini ruling family keeps a tight hold on important positions in the national security structure. The Bahrain Defense Force (BDF) is principally dedicated to the maintenance of internal security and the protection of the shores of the Bahrain archipelago. Nevertheless, with the rise of tensions in the Persian Gulf, the force has nearly tripled in size since 1984 and has added significantly to its inventory of modern armaments. In addition to the usual police functions, the mission of the Bahraini national police force is to prevent sectarian violence and terrorist actions.

Bahrain has a high proportion of native Shi'ite, possibly 65 to 70 percent of the population. Two clandestine political groups with ties to Iran are active in Bahrain. The Islamic Front for the Liberation of Bahrain, which was responsible for the 1981 coup attempt, consists of militant Shi'ite promoting violent revolution. The Islamic Call Party, which also has ties to Iran, is more moderate, calling for social and economic reforms. Two secular leftist groups with ties to Arab regimes and Arab nationalist organizations are the Popular Front for the Liberation of Bahrain and the National Front for the Liberation of Bahrain, though their influence appears to be on the decline in recent years.

The agencies of the Ministry of Interior, the police force, and the Security and Intelligence Service (SIS) maintain strict control over political activities. It is thought that their operations are extensive and highly effective. Detention and arrest can result from any actions construed as antiregime activity, including membership in illegal organizations, antigovernment demonstrations, possession or circulation of subversive writings, or preaching sermons of a radical or extreme Islamist tone. Prisoners charged with security offenses are tried directly by the Supreme Court of Appeal, serving as the Security Court. The procedural guarantees of the penal code do not apply, with proceedings conducted in secret and without the right to judicial appeal.

BAKHTIAR, TAIMOUR (?–1970). General Taimour Bakhtiar was the founder and first director of the Iranian National Organization for Intelligence and Security (Sazeman-i Ettelaat va Amniyat-i Keshvar), known by its Farsi acronym SAVAK. During his tenure as director of SAVAK beginning in 1957, relations between Israel and Iran improved significantly.

In September 1957, Bakhtiar met secretly in Paris with **Mossad** case officer Ya'acov Caroz. Caroz served in France under the cover of political councilor in the Israeli embassy. This meeting gave a vital boost to relations between the two countries in general and between the two intelligence communities in particular. Isser Harel and Prime Minister Golda Meir extended these relations; Harel and Bakhtiar had a close personal friendship.

The main Israeli goal in these ties with Iran was to encourage pro-Israeli and anti-Arab views among Iranian government officials. Relations with Iran were just one part of the comprehensive **Periphery Doctrine**. Bakhtiar also maintained contact with the Central Intelligence Agency.

Bakhtiar was dismissed in 1961, allegedly for organizing a coup; he was assassinated in 1970 under mysterious circumstances, probably at the shah's direct order. However, the unique relations between the Mossad and SAVAK remained in force until the Islamic revolution in Iran in 1979. *See also* IRANIAN INTELLIGENCE.

BANK OF CREDIT AND COMMERCE INTERNATIONAL (BCCI). The Bank of Credit and Commerce International (BCCI) was a major international bank founded in Pakistan in 1972. At its peak, it operated in 78 countries, had over 400 branches, and claimed assets of $25 billion. BCCI catered to notorious dictators and terrorists, including Iraqi dictator Saddam Hussein, the heads of the Medellin cocaine cartel, and the Palestinian terrorist group **Abu Nidal Organization** (ANO). According to the U.S. Central Intelligence Agency (CIA), it also did business with those who went on to lead **al Qaeda**. BCCI went beyond merely offering financial assistance with its operation of a global intelligence unit and a Mafia-like enforcement squad.

Unlike an ordinary bank, BCCI was made up of multiple layers of entities related to one another through an impenetrable series of holding companies, affiliates, subsidiaries, banks-within-banks, insider dealings, and nominee relationships. By fracturing corporate structure, record keeping, regulatory review, and audits, the complex BCCI network was able to evade ordinary legal restrictions on the movement of capital and goods as a matter of daily practice and routine. As a vehicle that was essentially free of government control, BCCI provided an ideal mechanism for conducting illicit activity by officials of many of the governments whose laws BCCI was breaking.

BCCI's fraudulent activities involved billions of dollars in money laundering throughout Europe, Africa, Asia, and the Americas; support of **terrorism**, arms trafficking, and the sale of nuclear technologies; prostitution and narcotics rings; income tax evasion; bribery of officials; smuggling; illegal immigration; illicit purchases of banks and real estate; and a wide range of financial crimes, including handling of the banking transactions related to the Pakistani nuclear program and the Iran–Contra illegal arms deals.

In 1977, BCCI developed a plan to infiltrate the U.S. banking system by secretly purchasing U.S. banks while opening branch offices of BCCI throughout the United States and eventually merging the institutions. BCCI had significant difficulties implementing this strategy due to regulatory barriers in the United States designed to ensure accountability. Despite these barriers, which delayed BCCI's entry, BCCI was ultimately successful in acquiring four banks, operating in seven states and the District of Colombia. The techniques used by BCCI that were essential to its success in the United States had been previously perfected in its acquisition of banks in Europe and a number of Third World countries. These included purchasing banks through nominees and arranging to have its activities shielded by prestigious lawyers, accountants, and public relations firms. Collusion with nominees included the heads of state of several foreign emirates as well as key political and intelligence figures in the Middle East.

By early 1985, the CIA knew that First American Bank, which BCCI had secretly purchased, was being used as a corrupt criminal enterprise with extensive involvement in money laundering. However, despite the agency's knowledge of many critical aspects of the bank's operations, structure, personnel, and history, there were also wide gaps in the CIA's reported knowledge about BCCI. A congressional investigation of the CIA's handling of BCCI revealed that information provided by the agency was either untrue or incomplete and that a "full" account of its knowledge of BCCI was not provided until almost a year after the initial request for information.

In 1991, BCCI became the focus of one of the world's worst financial scandals. Members of Abu Dhabi's ruling family appeared to be the owner of record of almost one quarter of BCCI's total shares, with an unknown but substantial percentage of their shares acquired through nominee arrangements on a risk-free basis, either with guaranteed rates of return, buy-back arrangements, or both. Interests were also held in BCCI by rulers of the three other gulf sheikdoms in the United Arab Emirates. In April 1990, Abu Dhabi's royal family was told in detail about BCCI's fraud by top BCCI officials, though together they continued to conceal information from the auditors.

From April 1990 through July 1991, Abu Dhabi tried to save BCCI through a massive restructuring. As part of the restructuring process, Abu Dhabi agreed to take responsibility for BCCI's losses, while Price Waterhouse agreed to certify BCCI's books for another year. Abu Dhabi, Price Waterhouse, the Bank of England, and BCCI agreed to keep all information concerning BCCI's fraudulent activities secret from the bank's one million depositors, as well as from U.S. regulators and law enforcement, in order to prevent a run on the bank.

However, after the Federal Reserve was advised by the New York district attorney of possible nominee arrangements involving BCCI and First American Bank, Abu Dhabi did provide the Federal Reserve with limited access to selected BCCI documents, ending in the closure of BCCI on 5 July 1991. Yet Abu Dhabi has since failed to provide further documents and witnesses to U.S. law enforcement authorities and Congress—despite repeated promises to do so—thus preventing access to vital information necessary for an investigation of BCCI's global crimes. The proposed agreement between Abu Dhabi and BCCI's liquidators to settle their claims against one another contains provisions that could have the consequence of permitting Abu Dhabi to cover up any wrongdoing it may have had in connection with BCCI. *See also* FAISAL ISLAMIC BANK OF EGYPT; IRANGATE AFFAIR.

BASRI, DRISS (1938–). Colonel Driss Basri served as interior minister of Morocco from 1981 until 1999 when he was dismissed by King Muhammad Ben al-Hassan VI. He was replaced by Colonel Hamido Laanigri. Before his appointment as minister of the interior, he had served as police commissioner, and later, in 1974, as secretary of state for the interior. Basri was considered the closest aide to the late King Hassan II. As minister of the interior, he conducted and oversaw a vast and intricate network of security forces. He acquired an immense authority, controlling not just the Interior Ministry but also communications and the kingdom's vast range of domestic affairs. From 1980 onward, most decisions made required Basri's approval. He arranged and supervised the performance of the country's elections and it was he who both advised Hassan II and implemented his will. Basri handled the portfolio of the disputed territories in Western Sahara that have been controlled by Morocco for the past 25 years. His position regarding this area may have been the reason for his dismissal, as demonstrations in this territory were brutally suppressed by forces under his direct command. However, the new king of Morocco, Muhammad Ben al-Hassan VI, declared publicly his desire to reign over a state of law, renouncing oppressive methods on behalf of the state, an approach that left Basri an undesired relic of the previous regime. *See also* MOROCCAN INTELLIGENCE.

BATEIKHI, SAMIH, AL-. Samih al-Bateikhi headed the Jordanian Mukhabarat (General Intelligence Department; GID) from 1996 to October 2000. In November 2003, he was sentenced by a special military court to four years in prison, reduced from eight, after he was convicted of corruption in a measure that was the first of its kind in Jordan. In addition, he received a fine and was ordered to repay the millions of dollars that he was accused of embezzling. The head of the GID at the time, Lieutenant General **Saad Kheir**, approved the sentence but ordered that the prison term be reduced from eight to four years. Saad Kheir himself was dismissed by King Abdullah II in November 2005. *See also* JORDANIAN INTELLIGENCE.

BATTLE OF BEERSHEBA. The battle of Beersheba, 1917, was the crucial battle of Great Britain's campaign of occupying Palestine, which was under Ottoman Empire rule. The success of this battle is due to the success of the intelligence and especially to Colonel **Richard Meinertzhagen** who headed the British military intelligence in Cairo.

After the British attempt to enter Palestine through coastal Gaza failed twice, Meinertzhagen (then a major) and Field Marshal Edmund Allenby spread rumors that another attack on the Turkish-German positions in Palestine would start from Gaza, while at the same time actually attacking from inland Beersheba. Part of this deception involved arranging for a satchel of documents to be "captured" by the Turks. Fake plans of the battle were dropped behind the Turkish lines in order to deceive them.

The British attack on Beersheba is a classic example of a deception tactics. The deception persuaded the Turkish command to reinforce their seaward flank at the expense of Beersheba. The Turks thought that they were safe in Beersheba and beyond the reach of any serious attack. By defying these expectations and reaching Beersheba in force, the Australian Light Horse Regiment gained both tactical and strategic surprise. *See also* BATTLE OF MEGIDDO II; BATTLES OF GAZA; BRITISH INTELLIGENCE IN EGYPT AND SUDAN.

BATTLE OF CAPE MATAPAN. The battle of Cape Matapan was a **World War II** naval battle fought by the British and the Australians against the Italians from 27–29 March 1941. A combined force of British Royal Navy and Royal Australian Navy ships under the command of the British Admiral Andrew Cunningham intercepted and sank or severely damaged ships of the Italian fleet off the Peloponnesian coast of Greece. As ships of the Royal Navy's Mediterranean Fleet were covering troop movements to Greece, an intelligence report was received regarding the sailing of the Italian battle fleet. Detection and interception of the Italian fleet was made possible by ULTRA (cryptanalysis of intercepted signals), but this was concealed from the enemy by a carefully directed reconnaissance plane. As a further deception, Admiral Cunningham is said to have made a surreptitious exit from a club in Egypt to avoid being seen going aboard ship. At the same time, there was a failure of intelligence on the Axis side. The Italians had been wrongly informed that the Mediterranean Fleet had only one operational battleship, when in fact there were three in addition to a lost British aircraft carrier that had been replaced.

BATTLE OF GALLIPOLI. Also known as the battle of Woodstock and the Dardanelles Campaign, this battle took place on the Gallipoli Peninsula in the Ottoman Empire during **World War I**. It lasted for nine months, from April 1915 until January 1916. The aim of the joint operation by British, French, Australian, and New Zealand forces was to knock Germany's ally, Turkey, out of the war and to eventually capture the Ottoman capital of Constantinople (now Istanbul). The attempt failed, with heavy casualties on both sides.

The Allies had struggled throughout the war to open an effective supply route to Russia. The German Empire and Austria–Hungary blocked Russia's land trade routes to Europe, while no easy sea route existed. The Black Sea's only entrance was through the Bosporus, which was controlled by the Ottoman Empire. When the Ottoman Empire joined the Central powers in October 1914, Russia could no longer be supplied from the Mediterranean Sea.

In November 1914, First Lord of the Admiralty Sir Winston Churchill proposed his first plan for a naval attack on the Dardanelles. Initially, the attack was to be made by the Royal Navy alone, with only token forces from the army being required for routine occupation tasks. A plan for an attack and invasion of the Gallipoli Peninsula was eventually approved by the British cabinet in January 1915.

On 19 February 1915, the first attack on the Dardanelles began when a strong Anglo–French task force, including the British battleship HMS *Queen Elizabeth*, bombarded Turkish artillery along the coast. A new attack was launched on 18 March 1915, targeted at the narrowest point of the Dardanelles where the straits were just a mile wide. A massive fleet containing 16 battleships tried to advance through the Dardanelles. However, nearly the entire fleet was damaged by sea mines that had been laid by the Turkish minelayer *Nusret*. The trawlers used by the British as minesweepers had retreated when the Turks opened fire on them. Although the mines were left behind, the fleet was sent in anyway. Three battleships were sunk and three others were badly damaged.

These losses prompted the Allies to cease any further attempts to force the straits by naval power alone. The defeat of the British fleet had also given the Turks a morale boost. The Turkish gunners had almost run out of ammunition before the British fleet retreated. If the

British had pushed forward with the naval attack, as Churchill suggested, then Gallipoli might not have been so great a defeat.

After the failure of the naval attacks, it was concluded that ground forces were necessary to eliminate Turkish mobile artillery. A first proposal to attack Turkey had already been suggested by French Minister of Justice Aristide Briand in November 1914, but it was not supported. A suggestion by British Naval Intelligence (Room 39) to bribe the Turks over to the Allied side was not taken up.

This would allow minesweepers to clear the waters for the larger vessels. On 24 April 1915, an amphibious force of British, French, Australian, and New Zealand troops began landing on the Turkish peninsula of Gallipoli. Despite the fact that only a small Turkish force awaited them on the cliffs overlooking the shore, the Gallipoli landing was a disaster. The defeat was caused by inadequate intelligence, insufficient attention to the terrain, and an underestimation of the enemy's strength and resilience in defense of their native soil. Nine months after landing, the Allies withdrew after incurring over 250,000 casualties, including over 46,000 fatalities. The result of the battle was a decisive Ottoman victory. The exact events and decisions made are controversial. However, it is clear that not enough use was made of intelligence regarding the landscape and topography of the peninsula and the enemy's positions and preparedness.

BATTLE OF GAZALA. The battle of Gazala was fought in North Africa around the port of Tobruk, Libya, from 26 May–21 June 1942 and culminated with the Allies losing Tobruk. The battle came after there had been a lull in the war in North Africa, with neither side able to deliver a knockout blow. The desert terrain made a cohesive strategy nearly impossible. However, German Field Marshal Erwin Rommel was anxious to continue his campaign in the region, and Prime Minister Winston Churchill wanted his military commanders there to adopt a more offensive approach. Although the loss of Tobruk was a huge blow to the morale of the Allies, the battle of Gazala has become known as Rommel's finest moment in battle. The tactics used at Gazala by Rommel were extremely similar to those involving a feint or fake in the north, followed by the real attack in the south. The Allied commanders had been informed by ULTRA about Rommel's intentions to attack and when, but not where and how. Rommel's plan achieved initial surprise and gained ground at first, but German intelligence had underestimated the strength of the Eighth Army. Rommel was practically encircled, but the Allies failed to counterattack. After regrouping and reestablishing his supply lines, Rommel took Tobruk on 21 June 1942 and pushed the Eighth Army further back toward Egypt, while exposing the inadequacy of its leadership. *See also* GERMAN INTELLIGENCE IN THE MIDDLE EAST; WORLD WAR II.

BATTLE OF MEGIDDO I. The battle of Megiddo I took place in 1479 BCE when Thutmose III moved against the king of Kadesh in Palestine, who had instigated other cities in the region to join him in revolt against Egypt, and who was undoubtedly backed by the military might of the Mitanni Empire. Mitanni had created a network of vassal city-states in this region during the early 15th century BCE.

An alliance of Canaanite cities was headed by the king of Kadesh on the Orontes and the king of Megiddo. In order to suppress them, Thutmose III marched his army in 10 days from his border fortress of Shiloh to Gaza, the main Egyptian stronghold in Canaan. After another 11 days they reached Yaham, where they held a war council.

The Canaanites concentrated their forces near Megiddo, to which there were three access routes: the northern and southern routes were longer than the central route through Aruna, but were less easily defensible. The generals had intelligence (as it turned out, wrong information) about the Aruna route being blocked by Canaanite forces and counseled the pharaoh to take the Tanakh route (nowadays this area is known as Yokneam). Thutmose III rejected the arguments of his generals, set out on the Aruna route and reached the Qinah River south of Megiddo without encountering any opposition.

The disposition of the Canaanite forces became clear. A contingent of infantry guarded the southern road from Tanakh, while the northern approaches of Megiddo were held by more infantry. The chariots were concentrated around Megiddo itself, waiting for the Egyptian forces to attack the infantry, who would quickly retreat as if they were fleeing. The pursuing Egyptians would break ranks and could be attacked by the hidden Canaanite charioteers.

The Egyptians rested during the night and dispersed their forces in three wings. The attacking Canaanites were routed and so hotly pursued that the defenders of Megiddo refused to open the gates and pulled their fleeing charioteers over the walls to safety. Instead of attacking the city, the Egyptians began to loot the abandoned camps, which gave the Canaanites time to organize their defense.

Thutmose led many more campaigns into Canaan, and eight years after the battle of Megiddo he took Kadesh on the Orontes. Following the conquest of Retenu, he built a big navy, which was instrumental in his extending Egyptian influence over much of the littoral Near East. His army could reach any coastal town in Syria by ship in four to five days, while by foot the journey would take more than a fortnight. Surprise became a major weapon in his arsenal. *See also* BATTLE OF MEGIDDO II.

BATTLE OF MEGIDDO II. This battle of Megiddo, Palestine, by British forces against the Ottoman Empire's forces started on 19 September and ended on 21 September 1918. This was a battle of movement because the land was not developed and there were no opportunities for the British army or the Ottoman army to carry out their maneuvers using motor cars, machine guns, and tanks. Aircraft had an important role in this battle for the successful British defense of the Suez Canal by providing reconnaissance of enemy formations and early warnings of attack. The role of the British Royal Flying Corps expanded in this theater and covered the breadth and depth of British efforts at the tactical, operational, and strategic levels. The Egyptian Expeditionary Force (EEF) of the British in Egypt prepared and conducted the battle against the Ottoman army across the plains surrounding Megiddo. It provided the EEF with intelligence of enemy positions, freedom to maneuver forces undetected, and the ability to attack more strongly the Turkish Army along the retreating route and thus to cause the annihilation of the Turkish units. The evolution of local air superiority in Palestine, properly coordinated with the ground offensive, was the decisive factor for victory in the battle of Megiddo. *See also* BATTLE OF BEERSHEBA; BATTLE OF MEGIDDO I; BATTLES OF GAZA. WORLD WAR I.

BATTLE OF OMDURMAN. Omdurman, in Arabic Umm Durmān, is the largest city in Sudan and Khartoum State, lying on the western banks of the Nile River, opposite the capital, Khartoum. It is known as the battle of Omdurman but actually the battle took place on 2 September 1898 in the nearby village of Kerreri.

During the British army's march up the Nile, British intelligence officer Colonel **Francis Reginald Wingate** obtained from the British Military Intelligence branch in London the maps of Sudan prepared by the leading intelligence officer, Lord Edward Gleichen. Based on this essential intelligence background and espionage obtained from Sudanese prisoners of war and refugees, it became possible for the British army to plan accurately their moves toward the Nile River. Secret agents were dispatched by Colonel Wingate, disguised as traders, warriors, and often as women. All of them obtained valuable information about the Sudanese forces. The intelligence contributed to the decisive battle, defeating the Sudanese Mahdist forces, and ensuring Great Britain's control over the Sudan.

BATTLE OF ROMANI. This battle took place during **World War I** on the Sinai Peninsula near the Egyptian town of Romani, which lies 23 miles east of the Suez Canal. The fort at Romani was a strategic location, as it controlled the northern approach to the Suez Canal. On the night of 3 August 1916, an Ottoman army attacked the British defenses at Romani, with the goal of controlling or destroying the Suez Canal in order to deny the use of the waterway to the Allies. After a night and day of fighting, the Ottoman assault was defeated. Thereafter, the Allies were on the offensive, pushing the Ottoman army back across the Sinai.

A previous Ottoman raid in early 1915 had succeeded in reaching the Suez Canal but was driven off by the British defenders. The commander of the Allied forces in Egypt, General Sir Archibald Murray, was confident that any future Ottoman attack would be made via the northern approach. Thus, he concentrated his defense at Romani, a position that was just out of artillery range of the canal.

On 18 July 1915, a large Ottoman force reached the area east of Romani undetected because they had marched at night all the way from Palestine. Over the next few weeks, the Turks consolidated their position and prepared for a large-scale assault on the British defenses. However, due to good intelligence, General Murray was anticipating that a Turkish attack was imminent. When the Turkish force—believed to be 8,000 strong—attacked, the battle of Romani ended in victory for the Allies.

BATTLE OF WOODSTOCK. *See* BATTLE OF GALLIPOLI.

BATTLES OF GAZA. When **World War I** broke out, Gaza was under the control of the Ottoman Empire, which was allied with the Central powers opposing Great Britain and France. The Turkish Army, which was made up of soldiers from all over the empire, launched an assault on Egypt in 1915. They were opposed by a British force comprised of imperial troops; under the command of Major General Sir John Maxwell, the attack was thwarted by using the Suez Canal as a barrier. When the Turks withdrew, Maxwell pushed his defensive line another 10 kilometers forward in order to keep ships in the canal out of artillery range of the enemy. The Turks then withdrew back to Gaza with a defensive line south to Beersheba, thus ending in a stalemate.

British forces acquired a new commander, General Sir Archibald Murray, whose mandate was still the defense of Egypt. He pushed forward into the desert, forming a base line from El Arish to Kossaima in the Sinai Peninsula and closer to the Turkish line. Because this strategy required the construction of a railway and water pipeline, it was March 1917 before Murray was ready to attack the Turks. Murray decided to attack Gaza itself by surrounding the town and taking it in one day. Unfortunately, early morning fog and other delays, such as tending to the cavalry horses, resulted in a failed attack and a Turkish victory in the first battle of Gaza.

The next month was spent by both sides feverishly building up their forces, with the British outnumbering the Turks in the end. The British now had a new commander, Lieutenant General Charles M. Dobell, and instructions from London to clear Palestine and take Jerusalem. However, the Turks were firmly dug in around Gaza, making encirclement difficult for an attack. On 17 April 1917, an Allied naval bombardment of the Turkish positions was launched, but with little effect. A full frontal attack was launched the next day, but this too did not breach the Turkish line. A third attack on 19 April 1917 also failed. The second battle of Gaza thus ended in another victory for the Turks due to bad planning and incompetence on the part of the British, as well as a resolute defense by the Turks. Once again, the two sides took some time to regain their strength.

Another new British commander, Field Marshal Edmund Allenby, arrived with definite orders to take Jerusalem by Christmas. His plan was simple. He decided to attack Beersheba and thus draw the Turks into the area and so weaken their troop numbers at Gaza. Allenby's intelligence officer, Colonel **Richard Meinertzhagen**, drew up a plan that hinted at a British attack on Gaza and, at great personal risk to himself, he arranged for it to fall into Turkish hands as a deception. The German commander, Friedrich Freiherr Kress von Kressenstein, was not completely taken in by this ploy, but shifted troops back from Beersheba to Gaza in order to counter a possible attack. On 30 October 1917, the British launched a surprise attack on Beersheba and a simultaneous attack on Gaza. Despite fierce Turkish resistance, Beersheba fell to the Australian Light Horse Regiment, and the main attack was then launched on Gaza. This third and final battle of Gaza ended with Allenby pushing the Turks back toward Syria. He entered Jerusalem on 4 December 1917, thus achieving his objective of taking Jerusalem by Christmas. *See also* BATTLE OF BEERSHEBA.

BEK, AZIZ (1883–?). Born in Rumalya, Turkey, educated in Istanbul, he started his career as a journalist and later fulfilled executive administrative roles in Gallipoli, Adirna, and Samasen. Recruited by the Ottoman security services in 1919, Bek began his active service in Turkey's internal affairs. Later he conducted surveillance on Arabic subjects suspected of anti-Turkish activities, such as young journalist Sharl Dubas; Shoufic al-Muid, who wanted an independent Lebanon; and Egyptian officer Aziz El-Matsri. Bek specialized in Arabic movements, of nationalistic and separatist character, in Lebanon and Egypt. He recruited Turkish loyalists to follow and keep under surveillance some of his principal subjects in Yemen and Libya.

On 1914 Bek arrived in Beirut, where he accepted the role of head of the Intelligence Department of the Fourth Army. He remained in this position until 1917. Bek's memoirs portray the pursuit of Christian missionaries in Lebanon, especially of the Maronite minority, and the apprehension of various Jewish underground networks in Palestine. Toward the end of 1917, he was appointed as head of the General Security Service of the Ottoman Empire. After the war he held several political positions; in 1927, he joined the political party of Mustafa Kamal Atatürk and was an active politician until his retirement. *See also INTELLIGENCE AND ESPIONAGE IN LEBANON, SYRIA, AND PALESTINE DURING THE WORLD WAR*; TURKISH INTELLIGENCE.

BELBACHIR, MUHAMMAD. Army General Muhammad Belbachir served as chief of the Moroccan military intelligence service until September 2006, when he was fired by King Muhammad VI because of his failure to prevent radical Islamists from infiltrating the military. Belbachir was replaced by the army's Colonel Muhammad Maaiche, who was assigned the task of rebuilding the military intelligence organization from the ground up after its being totally dismantled when the former chief was fired. *See also* MOROCCAN INTELLIGENCE.

BELL, GERTRUDE MARGARET LOWTHIAN (1868–1926). Gertrude Bell was a British writer, traveler, political analyst, administrator, and archeologist. She was born in England to a family of great affluence and was educated at Oxford, where she earned a degree in history in only two years. In May 1892, after leaving Oxford, Bell traveled to Persia, and over the next decade she made several more trips to the Middle East. At the outbreak of **World War I**, Bell's request for a Middle East post was initially denied.

In November 1915, however, Bell was recommended for war service to the newly established **Arab Bureau in Cairo**, headed by General **Gilbert Clayton**. At first she did not receive an official position, but in her first months there, she helped Lieutenant-Commander **George David Hogarth** organize and process data on the location and disposition of Arab tribes that could be encouraged to join the British against the Turks. On 3 March 1916, General Clayton sent Bell to Basra, which British forces had captured in November 1914, in order to advise Chief Political Officer Percy Cox regarding an area she had frequently visited. She drew maps to help the British army reach Baghdad safely. She became the only female political officer in the British forces and received the title of "liaison officer, correspondent to Cairo" for the Arab Bureau, where she had been assigned.

When British troops took Baghdad on 10 March 1917, Bell was summoned by Cox to Baghdad and presented with the title of oriental secretary. Bell, Cox, and **T. E. Lawrence** (Lawrence of Arabia) were among a select group of Orientalists convened by Winston Churchill to attend a 1921 conference in Cairo in order to find a way to reduce the expense of stationing troops in Great Britain's post–World War I mandates. Throughout the conference, Bell and Lawrence worked on promoting the establishment of the countries of Transjordan and Iraq and on persuading Winston Churchill to endorse kings **Abdullah** and Faisal, sons of the commander of the **Arab Revolt** against Turkey (1915–1916), Hussein bin-Ali, sharif and emir of Mecca. Bell and Lawrence are recognized as being almost wholly responsible for creating the Hashemite dynasty in Jordan. When the Ottoman Empire collapsed in late January 1919, Bell was assigned to conduct an analysis of the situation in Mesopotamia and the options for future leadership in Iraq. She drew up lines to create borders within Mesopotamia that later became the modern state of Iraq.

Faisal was crowned king of Iraq on 23 August 1921. As the first king of Iraq, Faisal sought advice from Bell on matters involving tribal geography and local business. Bell also supervised the selection of appointees for the cabinet and other leadership posts in the new government. Until her death in Baghdad, she served in the British High Commission advisory group in Iraq. Due to her influence with the new king, Bell earned the nickname "Al Khatun," the "Uncrowned Queen of Iraq."

King Faisal helped Bell to found the Baghdad Archeological Museum from her own modest artifact collection, which was initially located within the confines of the royal palace. She supervised excavations and examined finds and artifacts. Defying European opposition, she insisted that the excavated antiquities should remain in their country of origin, thereby ensuring that her museum would retain a collection of Iraq's antiquities. The museum was officially opened in June 1926. King Faisal also founded the British School of Archeology in Iraq to endow excavation projects from proceeds in Bell's will.

Bell briefly returned to Britain in 1925 and found herself facing family problems and ill health. Her family's fortune had begun to decline due to the onset of the economic depression in Europe. She returned to Iraq and soon developed pleurisy. When she recovered, she heard that her younger brother Hugo had died of typhoid. On 12 July

1926, Bell was discovered to have committed suicide with an overdose of sleeping pills. She had never married or had children. She was buried at the British cemetery in Baghdad, and her funeral was a major event attended by masses of people.

BEN-BARKA AFFAIR. Mehdi Ben-Barka, former tutor of King Hassan and ex-president of the Moroccan National Consultative Assembly, became an opponent of the Moroccan government after the mid-1950s, when he founded the Moroccan Socialist Party (USFP). He was involved in plots to topple the Moroccan monarchy and was twice sentenced to death by Moroccan courts in absentia. He lived in exile in Geneva, Switzerland, and King Hassan apparently decided to have the death sentence carried out wherever Ben-Barka lived. The king assigned the task to General **Muhammad Oufkir**, his interior minister, who was responsible for domestic security. General Oufkir, a close friend of his counterpart Meir Amit, director of the **Mossad**, approached Amit for assistance in this matter. Amit, concerned with the security of Jews worldwide, including Morocco, feared that his refusal to assist the Moroccan government might adversely affect the Jewish community there.

Amit and Oufkir met in France in the early fall of 1965 and reached an agreement whereby Mossad agents would not take part in Ben-Barka's slaying but would help to set the trap for him. On 29 October 1965, a Mossad agent persuaded Ben-Barka to leave Geneva for a meeting with a "movie producer" in Paris. Just outside a *brasserie* on the Seine's Left Bank, three French security officers, cooperating with the Moroccans, arrested Ben-Barka. On the evening of 30 October 1965, Ben-Barka was shot to death by Oufkir or one of his Moroccan agents. An investigation indicated that Ben-Barka's abductors acted with the complicity, if not the encouragement, of top officials of the French Service de documentation extérieure et de contre-espionnage (SDECE). *See also* ESPIONAGE MOVIES; MOROCCAN INTELLIGENCE.

BRITISH INTELLIGENCE IN EGYPT AND SUDAN. In the late 19th century, Egypt was an official province of the Ottoman Empire, but the empire was in a state of decline by then and unable to govern Egypt. In 1882, Egypt became a de facto British colony when Ahmed

Urabi led a revolt of Egyptian military officers and commoners against European and Ottoman domination of Egypt. A British expeditionary force was sent to crush the revolt, and although it was meant to be a temporary intervention, British troops stayed in Egypt. This marked the beginning of British occupation, which continued until 1922 when Egypt was granted its independence. Even then, however, British troops remained in the country and British influence continued to dominate Egypt's political life. The British were also involved in training and assisting the Egyptian Army following the creation of the kingdom of Egypt in 1922. True self-government did not occur until 1952 with the rise to power of Colonel Gamal Abdul Nasser.

The British army that was deployed in Egypt had to establish an intelligence network. They built an information-gathering system based on foreigners living in Egypt, especially journalists. They also recruited Arab informants to expand the scope of incoming information and to aid in interrogations of Egyptian and Arab subjects. This combination of sources proved to be effective. Following a decisive British victory, the preliminary intelligence network was dismantled but was later reorganized for use in the war conducted by the British army against the forces assembled in its province of Sudan (1883–1885). The Sudanese lived in tribal units and had never posed a serious threat to the administration until a nationwide revolt was launched against all foreign domination, whether Egyptian or British. The uprising was led by Muhammad Ahmed, who called himself "The Mahdi" (the Expected One).

These events led to the establishment of a permanent British intelligence branch in Egypt within the military framework. The commander of this intelligence unit was Major **Reginald Wingate**, who was appointed as director of British military intelligence in Egypt (1888–1898). During this period, the British reorganized and retrained the Egyptian Army according to traditional British military methods, making it far more suitable for an attempt to retake the Sudan. Under the command of General Horatio Kitchener, this campaign lasted for more than three years. Altogether, the British wars in Egypt and the Sudan lasted on and off for 17 years, during which British intelligence in the area grew from a small unit into an extensive department.

The governor of the Sudan was also accountable for the Sinai Peninsula, which at the time constituted a separate province and was not a part of Egypt. In 1896, a British intelligence officer, Major Wilfred Jenning-Bramly, conducted a thorough survey of the Bedouin tribes in the Sinai. The survey took him eight years to complete, but his diligent work was very productive to British intelligence. He was later able to use his personal connections to create an intelligence network of Bedouins in order to gather information on Turkish military movements in the Sinai, southern Palestine, and the area that is now the southern part of Jordan, watching for possible threats via the Suez Canal.

By the beginning of **World War I**, British intelligence consisted of 16 intelligence bodies assigned to four major fronts. One branch was responsible for Egypt, Palestine, and the Hijaz; one for Mesopotamia; one for Gallipoli; and one for Salonika and the Mediterranean basin. Each of these units was subdivided into departments according to function, and all expeditionary forces in the region contained intelligence units that were assigned to gather and evaluate field intelligence and produce assessments of the arena. They dealt with agents; interrogated prisoners of war and defectors; handled censorship, counterintelligence, and counterespionage; and produced propaganda and disinformation.

Due to its interest in creating a buffer zone between Europe and its sea routes to India, Great Britain became involved in the power struggles in the Middle East, particularly in Egypt after the construction and opening of the strategically vital Suez Canal in 1869. External debts forced Egypt to sell its share in the canal to Great Britain. By 1875, Great Britain owned about 40 percent of it. As the Suez Canal was a vital trade route between Great Britain and its colonies in Asia, control of the Asian side of it—namely Palestine—was deemed essential.

During World War I (in January–February 1915), a Turkish army crossed the Sinai to gain access to the canal. Although driven off, the threat of a similar attack forced Great Britain to keep troops assigned to that area. In 1916, Great Britain moved troops into the Sinai to protect both the canal and the railway. A series of battles ended the Turkish presence in the Sinai and opened the door to the invasion of Palestine. Great Britain's general command in the Egyptian–Palestinian front was reorganized under the command of Field Marshal Edmund Allenby, who launched an attack on the secondary defense line of the Turks and managed to sweep the remaining Turkish forces off the land. The Turks surrendered on 30 October 1918.

A 1936 treaty gave the United Kingdom the right to station troops on Egyptian soil in order to protect the Suez Canal, and the headquarters of the Royal Navy's Mediterranean Fleet was moved from Malta to Alexandria, Egypt. Although Egypt was technically neutral, Cairo soon became a major military base for the British forces leading up to **World War II**. In June 1939, Great Britain established the Middle East Intelligence Centre (MEIC) in Cairo for coordinating and supplying intelligence. In November 1940, the Combined Bureau Middle East (CBME) was created as a center for cryptanalytic activity. On 28 March 1941, **A Force** was officially established as a national brigade for the British Special Air Service. After World War II, the British remained in Egypt until 1955. *See also* BATTLE OF GALLIPOLI; BATTLE OF MEGIDDO II; BATTLE OF ROMANI; BATTLES OF GAZA; BRITISH INTELLIGENCE IN MESPOTAMIA; HOGARTH, DAVID GEORGE; LAVON AFFAIR.

BRITISH INTELLIGENCE IN MESOPOTAMIA. The surrender of Field Marshal Charles Townsend and his troops at Kut (also known as Kut-Al-Imara or Kut El Amara) in Mesopotamia (the region now known as modern Iraq, and parts of eastern Syria, southeastern Turkey, and southwest Iran) in April 1916 was considered to be the greatest humiliation of the British army during **World War I**. Great Britain had every reason to believe that the Turkish Army was no real match for theirs. Their experience in previous battles, as well as intelligence derived from foreign sources, indicated that the quality and motivation of the Turkish Army was low and that their military capabilities were quite poor. Reports attributed the Turkish Army's inadequate logistics to poor management and financial shortcomings.

Great Britain did not have a unified intelligence system in Turkey, as the Secret Service Bureau concentrated its main efforts against Germany and left intelligence in the Ottoman Empire to some local semiorganized networks of British sympathizers. Thus, the major source of intelligence on the Ottoman Empire came through the diplomatic services of the Foreign Office and was not necessarily militarily inclined.

There was concern in Great Britain about the possibility that Arab nations in the Persian Gulf would proclaim jihad and join the Axis forces. As a result, the British decided to send an expeditionary force to the Persian Gulf to secure their interests in the oil fields as well as to address the possible threat posed by Muslim **terrorism** in Bengal. The expeditionary force sent to the gulf was comprised of troops from the Indian Army, who had no knowledge of the terrain and almost no ability to communicate in Turkish.

Great Britain had no prior knowledge about possible changes in conditions, such as unexpected water shortages or sudden floods that could change the map of the battlefield overnight. Thus, the British expeditionary force was operating in a vast unknown territory and was completely disconnected from British forces in other arenas. Mesopotamia above Basra was mostly desert at the time, and land communication was very difficult. The main means of travel were the rivers, the Tigris and the Euphrates.

In the absence of sufficient aircraft reconnaissance, the British expeditionary force did not have accurate information on the deployment, size, or capability of the army they were about to face. It turned out that reports of the Turkish post in Basra had been exaggerated, and on November 1914, the British occupied Basra relatively easily, meeting with little resistance. After the arrival of the first airplanes, there was some improvement in field intelligence of the British forces.

By and large, the basic tactical and strategic intelligence used to assess the Turkish Army's strength and troop movement remained very much the same. Great Britain activated small units attached to headquarters for espionage missions. One of the subunits, later known as the Secret Service, was engaged in information gathering, mostly topographical data and estimates of mobility. However, this unit was very small and certainly inadequate to cover a country as large as Mesopotamia.

Thus, there was still no reliable source of information regarding the size, movements, intentions, or capabilities of the Turkish troops, and the British force in Mesopotamia had to rely on information received from other battle arenas and from prisoners of war—sources that are hardly sufficient for planning and troop allocation. Moreover, the Turkish moves could be unpredictable due to a lack of preplanning and a tendency to improvise according to circumstances. One source of information that proved useful was captured documents, including mail, though this did not occur often.

In retrospect, it can be said that the British found it exceptionally difficult to form a local espionage network. In Mesopotamia, the espionage network was activated under the assumption that the Arabs were anxious to free themselves from the Ottomans and would use the first opportunity to do so. However, the locals were reluctant to take the risk of engaging in active resistance or even spying for Great Britain, as Turkish retribution was severe. Those who were successfully recruited were poor and ill educated and did it only for the money. Much of the information they gathered was eventually dismissed as lies, exaggerations, and fabrications, even though verification was extremely difficult.

The British hope that the Arabs would rise against the Turks did not materialize. A general low assessment of the abilities and motivations of Turkish generals and the prevailing assumption that the Turkish troops were demoralized led an overconfident, poorly informed Townsend to his defeat in the battle on the banks of the Tigris at Kut. On the eve of this battle, the Turks managed to assemble several troops on the other side of the Tigris. Great Britain's intelligence failed to either notice or estimate accurately the movement of the troops. This lack of intelligence proved to be the downfall of Great Britain's expeditionary force, with the sudden unexpected arrival of one elite Turkish division turning the battle into a strategic disaster.

BRITISH INTELLIGENCE IN OMAN. In 1951 the sultanate of Muscat and Oman became independent and signed a treaty of friendship with Great Britain. Said bin-Taimour had been the sultan since 1932 when he was overthrown by his son, Qaboos bin-Said, in a bloodless coup in 1970, and the country was renamed the sultanate of Oman. Qaboos embarked on a more liberal and expansionist policy than his father. Since the mid-1950s, British intelligence has intervened in Oman, first in 1957 and then again in 1970.

In 1957, British intelligence assessed that Qaboos would be a better prospect as sultan than his reactionary father. As a result, Great

Britain inspired a coup to oust the sultan and replace him with his own son. In 1970 the British Special Air Service (SAS) was called in to support the sultan of Oman's armed forces in their fierce campaign against a communist armed insurrection. SAS was tasked not to obliterate the enemy but to persuade it to join the government's side and at the same time win the support of the civilians of the Jebel Dhofar (a hilly region of the area).

In Oman, SAS's small teams of elite soldiers took on a dedicated guerrilla army and destroyed it. SAS fought in complete secrecy, saving the Omani regime and preventing Soviet-backed guerrillas from seizing control of the Persian Gulf. *See also* LANDON, TIM.

BRITISH INTELLIGENCE IN THE PALESTINE CAMPAIGN OF 1914–1918. There was almost no institutionalized British intelligence agency functioning in the Middle East on a permanent basis until **World War I**. The war altered this situation completely, and the British set up a comprehensive intelligence apparatus in the Middle East. Field Marshal Edmund Allenby's victory in Palestine was attributable to the British intelligence that had provided him with every movement of the Ottoman Army. British deception operations in Palestine during World War I, and in particular the Haversack Ruse used in preparation for the third battle for Gaza, represent a modern revival of the use of deception in war. Allenby conceived of and planned his two major operations, Gaza and Megiddo, with deception as an integral part. His success against the Turkish–German armies in each of them was due, in large part, to his creative and thorough operational deception plans.

The advantages of strategic deception are its low cost, the element of surprise over the enemy, and the difficulty in countering such actions. However, sufficient intelligence feedback is necessary in order to assess whether the deceptive picture has fooled the enemy. Communications methods varied according to circumstances. Agents on short-term missions reported orally once they returned, while agents assigned to a target permanently or on a long-term basis were provided with codes or secret ink. Sending information in "innocent" letters was a widely used method, and telegrams were employed according to the urgency of the information and the agent's opportunities.

Although Great Britain used human intelligence, such as spies and prisoners of war, they did not rely too heavily on this source. In contrast, technical means, such as air reconnaissance and radio interceptions, were used intensively for their military campaign in Palestine and proved to be highly valuable in providing tactical intelligence. Early in 1916, a wireless intelligence unit was established and deployed at various sites in Egypt and Cyprus. Wireless intelligence became a key source of information on the Palestine front, and Great Britain became proficient in integrating the elements of interception, direction finding, and cryptanalysis into a unified system, as well as in utilizing the information more efficiently than their adversaries. As an alternative to sending intercepted messages to London for decrypting, which took up to four weeks, a civilian expert, Oliver Strachey, was sent to Egypt to organize a cryptanalytic group. His code-breaking staff was soon reading an average of 16 German and Turkish messages daily. Strachey went on to become one of the outstanding cryptanalysts of manual German codes and ciphers in **World War II**. *See also* BATTLE OF MEGIDDO II; BATTLES OF GAZA.

BRITISH INTELLIGENCE IN WESTERN DESERT BATTLES. During **World War II**, British intelligence played a key role in North Africa in the battle for supremacy in the Western Desert, though it was fraught with difficulties. Intelligence in the Mediterranean, and in particular ULTRA, the Allied codename for the Axis enigma ciphers, played a very significant part in helping the Allies devastate the Axis supply convoys. It was the Allied knowledge of the German Air Force (GAF) enigma ciphers that was of greatest use in North Africa. Since the GAF was involved in most operations in the Mediterranean and in the desert, its movements were an indication as to the whereabouts of enemy units and were thus useful in planning Allied air strategy. One of ULTRA's greatest contributions was in revealing that the Germans had induced the Italians into positive action against the British convoys, which resulted in the overwhelming British victory in the **battle of Cape Matapan** in March 1941. By keeping the Italian merchant fleet at port for the better part of the war, the British were able to take command of the Mediterranean, which ultimately led to victory in North Africa and made the Allied Operation Torch landings possible in November 1942.

The role of intelligence differed greatly between arenas and also between various aspects of warfare. For instance, intelligence played a much more significant role in the field of supplies than it did in land warfare in North Africa. ULTRA was only one intelligence source among many. Other sources ranged from reconnaissance (both ground and air), interrogation of prisoners of war, signals intelligence (SIGINT), and reports from contacts on the front line. ULTRA was never used as an infallible source but rather was corroborated by these other sources to gauge its reliability. Its significance as a whole to the North African Campaign was reduced considerably by numerous difficulties at every stage, from information gathering and analysis to distribution and application. Taken together, the bureaucratic, technical, and logistical limitations resulted in its potential not being exploited to the fullest.

ULTRA's role was severely limited in North Africa for several reasons. First, protection of the top-secret ULTRA source meant that the distribution of ULTRA intelligence findings was extremely slow and that by the time they reached the appropriate commanders, they were often outdated and therefore no longer relevant at best and dangerously misleading at worst. Therefore, when ULTRA decrypts were finally received by the commanders, they were not always trusted. Technological factors also slowed down the distribution of intelligence findings, as communications technology was not sufficiently developed to provide swift delivery over long distances with the required security.

Another limitation was that almost all of the intercepted SIGINT was low grade, occasionally revealing details of movements, equipment specifications, and supplies, but mostly containing trivial information. On rare occasions, high-grade SIGINT was intercepted and decrypted, but this never revealed the whole picture, warned of future attacks, or unveiled the enemy's strategy. Ciphers were regularly being changed and took valuable time to rebreak, with some never being broken. These operational problems added to the limitations faced by intelligence throughout the desert war. Of the thousands of decrypts that were analyzed, very few were found to be worthy of passing up to a higher authority, and of those, even fewer were actually acted upon.

Although ULTRA intelligence was consulted by commanders in planning stages or when an important decision was to be made, it did not generally constitute the basis of their decision. However, on occasion, intelligence was confused by the enemy's uncertainty, such as that preceding the **battle of Gazala** in North Africa in 1942. The Allies were completely misled into thinking that Field Marshal Erwin Rommel had lost the best part of his armor and was planning to deploy defensively, when in fact he had received new panzer tanks and was simply being indecisive about what strategy to take. He eventually decided on offensive action with superior armored forces. Thus, in May 1942, despite good general warning of the imminence of Rommel's attack, the British Eighth Army lost the battle of Gazala.

ULTRA still proved itself to be valuable on several occasions. Signal intercepts of information concerning the supply movements from Sicily and southern Italy to North Africa resulted in decisive strikes on Italian convoys by forces in Malta, Gibraltar, and Alexandria, forcing Rommel in August 1942 to strategically switch to the offensive when tactically he would not have done so otherwise. Thus, although intelligence in general, and ULTRA in particular, did not by itself enable the Allies to win the desert war, it did provide another important factor used to the Allies' advantage.

ULTRA achieved long-term successes in North Africa insofar as the consequences of its input were more long term than immediate. Although detailed ULTRA decrypts failed to stop the successful invasion of Crete, the Allied forces were able to pinpoint the precise plans of the invasion and helped to persuade the Axis powers to firstly postpone and then to cancel a similar invasion of Malta. ULTRA was also extremely useful to the Allies in planning future operations. The effectiveness with which intelligence was processed was significantly improved toward the end of the desert war, which led to its role being enhanced to some extent.

BRITISH–JORDANIAN INTELLIGENCE COOPERATION. In 1948 the intelligence cooperation between the British and the Jordanians began as soon as the British were asked by the Jordanians for assistance in establishing their military intelligence system. The general tendency of the British was to pass the Jordanians only material that could serve British interest. However, personal relations between British and Jordanian officers enabled additional information to pass unofficially. When the British evacuated Israel, they gave the Jordanians all the maps of the region they had in their possession. The

British provided the Jordanians with intelligence throughout the 1948–1949 Israeli War of Independence. It was especially evident toward the end of the hostilities when the British realized that the Israeli Army was about to conquer the Negev, which they perceived of strategic importance for the defense of the Suez Canal.

Several light airplanes were sent to photograph Israeli military activity in the Negev and to pass the information to the Jordanian and to Egyptian armies. The identity of these light aircrafts was revealed after some of them were shot down by Israeli air fighters.

British influence was also evident through the idea to create specific slogans for various units and by the decision to train snipers. Toward the end of the War of Independence, the high command of the Jordanian's **Arab Legion** dispatched its officers to Great Britain to be trained as intelligence officers.

BULL, GERALD (1928–1990). As a Canadian-born astrophysicist and metallurgist, Bull worked during the 1960s for the Canadian Defense Ministry as well as for the U.S. military. He was involved in a project to build a cannon powerful enough to launch satellites into space. From 1980 on, he lived in Brussels, where he offered his services as an artillery consultant to the military establishments of various countries, including Israel. Bull's offer was turned down by the Israelis. However, in the early 1980s, during the **Iran–Iraq War**, Bull was hired by Iraq to help with its project on the development of a megacannon capable of firing a huge projectile over a distance of 1,500 kilometers (930 miles). On 22 March 1990, Bull was shot dead from close range at the entrance to his home. The two assassins escaped without taking his briefcase or any of the documents and jewelry he was carrying. Various theories about who was responsible for the assassination were circulated in the international media, many of which asserted that the **Mossad** was behind it. Iraq and Iran were also identified as candidates, as was the Central Intelligence Agency. Bull's family members have their own theory, namely, that he was in touch with members of Israeli intelligence to whom he provided inside information about the Iraqi supergun project. According to another theory, the Mossad killed him for failing to provide complete information about the Iraqi program to extend the range of Scud missiles and to improve their accuracy. The circumstances of Bull's assassination are still shrouded in mystery and will probably remain so.

– C –

CAMILLA PLAN. This operation was conducted in December 1940 by the **A Force** and was designed to deceive the Italian forces in East Africa into thinking that Somaliland was being targeted in an up-coming attack. In so doing, they shifted the attention of the Axis units away from Libya, which was the real target. Under the command of Field Marshal **Archibald Percival Wavell**, A Force worked out the plan for the real attack as well as the cover. The plan entailed the launching of simultaneous attacks at the beginning of February 1941 on Eritrea from Sudan in the north and on Abyssinia and the south-ern part of Italian Somaliland from Kenya in the south. The northern attacking force, primarily the Fourth Indian Division, was withdrawn from the Western Desert in deep secrecy on the eve of the Sidi Bar-rani battle and sent southward via the Nile and the Red Sea.

Dudley Wrangel Clarke's task was to persuade Italian intelligence that any such moves which might be detected were in preparation for an amphibious attack on Italian-occupied territory from the east. The target was actually Italian-occupied British Somaliland, on which forces from Egypt and Kenya would converge in order to establish a base there for the reconquest of Abyssinia. According to the plan, Ital-ian forces would be concentrated in the eastern provinces of Abyssinia and not bothering to pay too much attention to the north and the south.

In order to ensure the success of this deception plan, Wavell put all his forces at the disposal of Clarke. Both naval and air raids were launched from Aden against targets in British Somaliland, and arrangements were made at Aden for the reception and dispatch of a large amphibious force. Maps and guides to British Somaliland were printed and issued to appropriate units. An elaborate radio deception plan was put into effect, while in Cairo rumors were circulated, leak-ages of information were arranged, and appropriate documents were allowed to go astray. All of these diversions contributed to the com-plete surprise when the attacks were launched, thus making the Camilla Plan a successful deception operation in the East African Campaign. *See also* WORLD WAR II.

CHARTER OF THE IRAQI NATIONAL INTELLIGENCE SER-VICE (INIS). The intelligence agencies of Saddam Hussein's regime in Iraq were routinely used to provide information to the Mukhabarat for the prevention and punishment of dissent. The new Iraqi National Intelligence Service was established in March 2004 by the transition government that was appointed after the ousting of Saddam Hussein. The Governing Council has published the complete charter of the Intelligence Service so that all Iraqis will know that the intelligence service has no further authorization to arrest people, report on domestic political issues, or involve itself in the political process as an abuse of power.

The INIS charter contains 12 chapters, including 44 articles that deal with intelligence activities relating to **terrorism**, domestic insurgency, espionage, narcotics production and trafficking, weapons of mass destruction, serious organized crime, and other issues pertaining to the national defense and the security of Iraq. The principles set forth in this charter are designed to achieve a balance between the work of the INIS and the protection of individual rights and liberties. The charter states that when the permanent constitution of Iraq is adopted, the activities of the **Iraqi intelligence** service will be conducted in accordance with that constitution.

CICERO AFFAIR. The Cicero affair, often called the most successful spy story of **World War II**, helped the Germans gain insight into British plans for forming an alliance with Turkey in order to win the war. Following Winston Churchill's strategy, the British ambassador to Turkey, Sir Hugh Knatchbull-Hugessen, tried to convince the Turks to enter the war in order to initiate a massive, coordinated offensive against Hitler's Eastern Front, but Turkey chose to remain neutral.

Between late 1943 and early spring 1944, the British embassy in Ankara was the source of a serious information leak due to a breach in security by the ambassador's assistant. The ambassador had the careless habit of bringing home top-secret documents from the embassy in Ankara for examination. His trusted assistant, Ilyas Bazna, a former convict, made duplicate keys and had free access to the house when Sir Hugh was not at home. The valet photographed a large number of important and secret documents that he then sold to a high-level German official. The Germans gave Bazna the cover name Cicero. Knatchbull-Hugessen made many attempts to clear his name after the episode but was ultimately unsuccessful.

CLARKE, DUDLEY WRANGEL (1899–1974). As a British army officer, Dudley Clarke was appointed to Field Marshal **Archibald Percival Wavell**'s staff in 1936. Clarke's main contribution to Wavell's staff began in January 1941 when he was asked to head a strategic deception unit that became known as **A Force** in North Africa. This unit developed the principles and methods of strategic deception that were later used during **World War II** in the Normandy landings in 1944. *See also* BRITISH INTELLIGENCE IN EGYPT AND SUDAN; CAMILLA PLAN.

CLAYTON, GILBERT (1875–1929). Gilbert Clayton served as a British officer and administrator in Egypt, Palestine, and Iraq. After serving under Lord Horatio Kitchener in the Sudan, Clayton filled the post of private secretary (1908–1913) to Sir **Francis Reginald Wingate**, the commander of Egypt's army and governor-general of the Sudan. He subsequently served as the Sudan agent in Cairo and director of intelligence of Egypt's army from 1913–1914, when he was promoted to the head of all intelligence services in Egypt, a post in which he remained until 1917. Clayton rose to the rank of brigadier general in 1916 and became chief political officer to Field Marshal Edmund Allenby of the Egyptian Expeditionary Force in 1917. He then served as adviser to the Ministry of the Interior in Egypt (1919–1922), replaced Wyndham Deedes as chief secretary in Palestine (April 1923–1925), and became the high commissioner and commander in chief in Iraq (1929).

In September 1914, Clayton wrote a secret memorandum to Lord Kitchener suggesting that Arabs could be of service to Great Britain during **World War I** and that an Arab leader friendly to Britain should be made caliph in place of the Ottoman sultan. Clayton and his fellow officers convinced Sir Mark Sykes that the Arabs in the Ottoman Empire might split from the Turks and join the Allies. Clayton argued against giving Syria to France and wanted Britain to take control of both Syria and Palestine. Although he believed that Britain should continue to govern the Arabs, he attempted to reconcile Britain's interests and Arab nationalist aspirations while serving as chief secretary in Palestine.

COMBINED BUREAU MIDDLE EAST (CBME). *See* BRITISH INTELLIGENCE IN EGYPT AND SUDAN.

COPELAND, MILES (1916–1991). Born in Birmingham, Alabama, Miles Copeland was a businessman, a musician, and a Central Intelligence Agency (CIA) officer who was closely involved in major foreign-policy operations from the 1950s to the 1980s, especially in the Middle East. After **World War II** and the establishment of the CIA, Copeland was tasked with organizing the agency's information-gathering unit in the Middle East. For this purpose Copeland was stationed in Damascus, Syria, as the CIA case officer with a cover title of "cultural attaché." While in Damascus, he was directly involved in the overthrow of the Syrian government, the first U.S. covert action of overthrowing of a foreign government. In Syria, while being exposed to Arabic music, Copeland learned Arabic, though he never spoke that language with the right accent.

In 1953, Copeland returned to private life at the consulting firm Booz Allen Hamilton, while remaining as a freelancer for the CIA. In this new job Copeland traveled to Cairo to offer Gamal Abdel Nasser advice on how to organize the Mukhabarat (**Egyptian intelligence**). Copeland soon became Nasser's closest Western advisor.

In 1955 Copeland returned to the CIA. During the **Suez crisis**, the U.S. decided to block France and Great Britain, which had invaded, and backed Egypt's independence and control of the Suez Canal. The purpose was to end the control of the region's oil resources and forestall the influence of the Soviet Union on regional governments by placing the United States on their side. Nevertheless, after the crisis Nasser moved closer to the Soviet Union and accepted massive military technology and engineering assistance for the Aswan Dam. Copeland, allied with Secretary of State John Foster Dulles and director of the CIA Allen Dulles (two brothers), reversed U.S diplomatic policy on Egypt at that time.

After King Faisal II (Iraq) was deposed by Colonel Abdul Karin Qassim in 1958, Copeland admittedly oversaw CIA contacts with the Iraqi regime and internal opponents, including Saddam Hussein and others in the Ba'ath party. His last job in the Middle East was in Beirut, Lebanon, where he was stationed with his family from 1957 until 1968.

– D –

DAHABI, MOHAMED AL-. Major General Mohamed Dahabi is one of Jordan's top antiterrorism officers and has served in the country's General Intelligence Department for more than 20 years. On 22 December 2005, he was assigned by King Abdullah II as director of the Mukhabarat (General Intelligence Department; GID). This appointment was made shortly after a deadly terrorist attack by **al Qaeda** took place in a hotel in Amman in November 2005.

Dahabi replaced Lieutenant General **Samih Asfoura**, who had been appointed to the position of director of the GID only six months earlier in July 2005. This was one of the country's three deadliest attacks ever, causing a major shake-up of political and security posts in the Arab kingdom. *See also* JORDANIAN INTELLIGENCE; JORDANIAN TERRORISM.

DAHHAM-MEJWEL, RAFI (1976–1999). Rafi Dahham-Mejwel was Saddam Hussein's second cousin and was also known as Rafi Dahham-Mejwel al-Tikriti, which means that he was born in the city of Tikrit. He was one of the well-known political figures in Iraq and was a member of the Iraqi Revolutionary Command Council and director of the Iraqi Intelligence Service. He was also the former Iraqi ambassador to Turkey, as well as former head of the Iraqi Secret Services. *See also* IRAQI DIRECTORATE OF GENERAL SECURITY; IRAQI INTELLIGENCE; IRAQI SPECIAL SECURITY ORGANIZATION.

DAHLAN, MUHAMMAD YUSUF (1961–). Muhammad Dahlan, also known as Abu Fadi, was one of the leaders of **Fatah** in the Gaza Strip and served as the head of its Preventive Security Service (PSS), one of the major security forces of the Palestinian National Authority (PNA). Dahlan later served as minister of state and security in the PNA under the 2003 government of Abu Mazen.

Born in the Khan Younis Refugee Camp in Gaza, Dahlan's political activity began as a teenager in Khan Younis, where he recruited friends into organized groups for civic projects, such as road sweeping. While studying business administration at the Islamic University of Gaza, he became a student leader and expanded his efforts into a network of charitable organizations, manned by children and teens. Members delivered food and medicine door to door in the community while at the same time preaching Palestinian nationalism. The group formally became the Fatah's "Young Guard" (Fatah Shabiba) in the Palestinian territories in 1981 and would be a driving force behind the first *intifada* (1987–1994). By the time he was 25, Dahlan had been arrested 11 times for his political organizing and all together spent five years in Israeli prisons.

After the first *intifada* broke out, Dahlan became one of the uprising's young leaders in Gaza, but he was swiftly arrested and deported by the Israelis to Jordan in 1988. He made his way to Tunis, where the Palestinian Liberation Organization (PLO) leadership was then based. From exile, he helped to organize the ongoing protests in the West Bank and Gaza, and he became a protégé of Yasser Arafat.

In 1993, he was involved in secret talks with Israel, which eventually culminated in the Oslo Accord of 1993. He returned to Gaza in July 1994, where Arafat rewarded him by giving him the position of security chief of the PSS and the Fatah movement in Gaza. The control of these two major organizations made Dahlan one of the strongest officials in the Palestinian National Authority. In this role, he enjoyed widespread popular support and continued to negotiate in several subsequent talks, such as the Camp David 2000 Summit.

As head of the newly formed PSS in the Gaza Strip, Dahlan was responsible for building a police force. With training assistance from the Central Intelligence Agency (CIA), he managed to amass a police force of more than 20,000 men under his control, creating a small empire in Gaza, which became informally known as "Dahlanistan." He maintained order, sometimes ruthlessly, and his PSS was accused by Palestinian and international human rights organizations of serious abuses, including torture. He also accumulated personal wealth from some of the PNA's monopolies in oil and cement and from the awarding of building contracts, and he purchased the largest house in Gaza for his family home.

Unlike other senior members of the Fatah "Old Guard," Dahlan was more insulated against public criticism from the Palestinian masses by virtue of the fact that he had served so many years in Israeli jails. Dahlan became highly popular among younger Fatah members, who identified with him more easily than with the rest of the senior Palestinian leadership. He was a vocal critic of the older generation of leaders who had returned from exile with Arafat in 1994, and he was considered as a leading contender to succeed Arafat.

As head of the PSS, Dahlan was responsible for restraining those Palestinian militants, specifically members of **Hamas** who rejected the Oslo process and hoped to sabotage a negotiated settlement through strategically timed attacks on Israeli targets. Dahlan is believed to have drawn up a plan for containing Hamas with senior Israel Defense Force (IDF) and Israeli Security Agency (ISA) officials in a meeting in Rome in January 1994. Until 2001, he met regularly with Israeli and American defense officials in order to coordinate security issues.

In 1995, following a series of Hamas suicide attacks on Israeli buses that were intended to push the Israeli electorate to the right and away from the Oslo-friendly Labour government of Shimon Peres, Dahlan cracked down hard on the Hamas infrastructure. On orders from Arafat, Dahlan disarmed and jailed about 2,000 known Hamas members and allegedly tortured some. His police also raided and closed Islamic charities, schools, and mosques. Dahlan and Arafat were able to crack down on Hamas at that time because in 1996 the PNA still generally enjoyed the support of the Palestinian public.

By 1997, however, Dahlan seemed to be distancing himself from his earlier crackdown on Hamas. He became a regular member, specializing in security issues, of the Palestinian team that negotiated Israeli redeployments, the return of Palestinians expelled since 1967, and prisoner releases during the Oslo process. He also participated in the Wye River (United States) negotiations in 1999 and was a member of the Palestinian negotiating team at Camp David (2000) and Taba (2001). Dahlan was generally regarded by the Israelis as a pragmatist with whom they could do business.

Dahlan's relations with the Israelis quickly cooled following the outbreak of the second *intifada* in October 2000 (also known as the al-Aqsa Intifada). As head of one of the main Palestinian security organizations, he negotiated with Israeli officials to try to arrange a cease-fire several times after the uprising erupted in September 2000. Dahlan maintained that he was unable to clamp down on militancy this time as he had done in 1995, since it was impossible for the PSS to curb the widespread anger at the peace process and Israel's response to the uprising. Dahlan reportedly tendered his resignation from the PSS on 5 November 2001, in opposition to the PNA's policy of arresting Popular Front for the Liberation of Palestine (PFLP) and Islamic Jihad members, but it was refused by Arafat.

In anticipation that pressure from the United States would force Arafat to unify the various PNA security forces into a single, manageable entity, Dahlan began to expand his power base beyond Gaza and into the West Bank. In the spring of 2002, he moved to bring low-level commanders in the West Bank Preventative Security Force under his control in order to undermine the influence of his West Bank counterpart, **Jibril Rajoub**. Dahlan and Rajoub had much in common: Both were considered pragmatic leaders who supported a negotiated solution to the Israeli–Palestinian conflict, who generally kept their security forces out of the *intifada*, and who favored the unification of PNA security forces under a single leader, trained by the CIA, and working in close coordination with the intelligence agencies of Egypt, Jordan, and Saudi Arabia.

Gaza's Gang of Five, initiated by Muhammad Dahlan, emerged as a significant force in the post-Arafat Palestinian leadership. It included Muhammad Dahlan; Nongovernmental Organization Affairs Minister Hassan Asfur, negotiator Saeb Urayqat, Muhammad Rashid, and Nabil Sha'th. They wanted a return to the Oslo format of direct negotiations with Israel; an end to the *intifada*, especially armed attacks; and a restructuring of the PNA's security into a single organization headed by Dahlan.

In late May 2002, reports surfaced in the Israeli press that the United States had approved Dahlan as head of a unified Palestinian security structure and preferred him as a potential successor to Arafat. In anticipation of his new appointment as the PNA's security chief and minister of the interior in President Arafat's imminent cabinet reshuffle, Dahlan resigned his post as head of the Gaza PSS on 5 June 2002. His gamble backfired, however, when Arafat declined to unify his security services and instead retained the vital position of interior minister for himself in the new government. Dahlan was offered a post as security advisor instead, but he did not accept this position.

Dahlan publicly expressed his support for political as well as security reform of the PNA by means of elections within Fatah. He intended to replace the elderly Central Committee members with the younger generation of Fatah members from whom he drew his support. Despite the broad support for Dahlan in the Gaza Strip, his attempt to launch an electoral challenge to Arafat came to an abrupt halt on 11 July 2002 when Arafat appointed Dahlan as his national security advisor, a promotion that in reality had no responsibilities and no effective control over the PNA security services. Dahlan resigned from the post after three months, blaming the PNA for a lack of leadership during the *intifada*.

After an intense struggle over the composition of the new cabinet, and under heavy pressure from the United States and Great Britain, Arafat agreed on 23 April 2003 that Abu Mazen would keep for himself the post of minister of the interior, but would bring Dahlan into the government as the Palestinian minister of state for security affairs. Within two weeks, Dahlan had been quietly authorized to restructure the PNA's Interior Ministry, effectively giving him control of the ministry and the PNA's security police, but without the official job title. Dahlan proposed negotiations with Hamas and smaller militant groups to bring about a cease-fire, which he achieved in July 2004. As for the PNA's security forces, Dahlan proposed taking up to 25,000 men from Fatah's Tanzim and the al-Aqsa Martyrs Brigades and turning them into a border police force deployed along the borders with Israel, Jordan, and the Golan Heights. In their place, the Palestinian cities would be policed by a newly created police force, made up of new recruits with no prior attachment to existing formations. Dahlan presented his intentions at the Aqaba Summit of 4 June 2003 and apparently won U.S. approval. However, Abu Mazen's government was unable to gain the necessary Israeli cooperation for Dahlan's proposals.

The cease-fire collapsed in its second month when Hamas and the Islamic Jihad withdrew following the Israel Defense Forces' assassination of a senior leader from each of their respective movements. Furthermore, Abu Mazen's government failed to win the release of any security prisoners from Israeli jails or the easing of restrictions on Palestinian mobility. Abu Mazen was replaced as prime minister by Ahmed Qureia (also known as Abu Ala). Dahlan was not included when Qureia announced his cabinet on 27 September 2003.

The decision to exclude Dahlan led to a wave of protests and chaos in the Gaza Strip. Thousands of demonstrators, some brandishing automatic rifles, marched in the streets, burning effigies and posters of "Old Guard" Fatah officials who opposed giving Dahlan a place in the new cabinet. The biggest protest took place in Khan Younis, Dahlan's birthplace. Dahlan launched a concerted campaign for long-overdue elections to Fatah governing institutions, which he hoped would bring "new blood" (that is, his supporters) into Fatah and reestablish control of its own militant groups. Dahlan campaigned on a reform and anticorruption ticket and tried to profile himself as an outspoken critic of Yasser Arafat, although many observers dispute his personal integrity.

Dahlan is believed to be behind the mass resignation in February 2004 of 300 low- and mid-level members of Fatah, who claimed that the lack of democracy and reforms was the reason for their protest. Dahlan was the driving force behind the weeklong unrest in Gaza following the appointment of Yasser Arafat's nephew **Moussa Arafat**, who was widely accused of corruption as head of the Gaza police force. It is also widely assumed that Dahlan was behind a series of leaks about PNA corruption designed to embarrass Arafat's close associates, including the allegations that $11.5 million had been channeled to the Paris bank account of Arafat's wife, Suha Tawhil, and that Ahmed Qureia's family cement business was making a huge profit from the construction of Israel's Separation Wall.

On 26 January 2006, Dahlan was narrowly elected to the Palestinian Legislative Council in the election of 2006 as a representative for Khan Younis. In January 2007, Dahlan took a tough stance against Hamas. In March 2007, despite objections from Hamas, Dahlan was appointed by Palestinian President Mahmoud Abbas to lead the newly reestablished Palestinian National Security Council, which is intended to oversee all security services in the Palestinian territories.

In July 2007, Dahlan resigned from his post as the Palestinian minister for civil affairs. The resignation was little more than a formality, since Mahmoud Abbas had issued a decree dissolving his National Security Council immediately after the Hamas takeover of Gaza in mid-June 2007. Dahlan has been blamed by many in Fatah for the rapid collapse of their forces in Gaza in the face of a Hamas offensive that lasted less than a week. During the fighting, Dahlan's house on the coast of Gaza, which many locals had seen as a sign of corruption by Fatah, was seized by Hamas militants and subsequently demolished. He and most of the other senior security commanders of the Fatah-dominated Palestinian National Authority security forces were not in Gaza during the fighting, leading to charges that their men had been abandoned in the field. *See also* PALESTINIAN NATIONAL AUTHORITY INTELLIGENCE; TENET PLAN.

DARDANELLES CAMPAIGN. *See* BATTLE OF GALLIPOLI.

DIRECTORATE FOR STATE SECURITY INVESTIGATIONS (GDSSI). *See* EGYPTIAN INTELLIGENCE.

DORI-NAJAFABADI, QORBAN-ALI. Hojatoleslam Qorban-Ali Dori-Najafabadi served as the third intelligence and security minister in Iran, succeeding Ayatollah **Ali Fallahian** in this position. Dori-Najafabadi is a legislator and did not have a background in intelligence or security affairs. However, he was welcomed as a relatively liberal and pragmatic cleric. Dori-Najafabadi has also served as a parliamentarian, member of the Assembly of Experts, head of the board of directors and secretary of the World Center for Islamic Science in Qum, as well as a member of the Council for the Discernment of Expediency, where he continues to serve. Dori-Najafabadi was forced to resign from the Intelligence and Security Ministry (MOIS) in 1999 over allegations that rogue elements within the ministry assassinated Iranian dissidents and intellectuals. *See also* IRANIAN INTELLIGENCE.

DORS, WARDA (?–1948). A Christian woman who was a friend of a British intelligence officer in Palestine. She worked in a coffee shop in Jerusalem that was patronized by several Israeli soldiers. Dors, who spoke Hebrew, English, and German fluently, presented herself as a Jewish girl, a new immigrant from Czechoslovakia, and encouraged the soldiers to speak freely. In the evenings, she used to pass reports of her findings to her British boyfriend. He, in turn, passed it to his contacts on the Jordanian side. Her spying role was eventually revealed. She was captured by members of the Irgun (the Jewish underground militia in Palestine) and was executed by the Irgun on 23 March 1948.

DOUBA, ALI (1935–). Born in the small village of Qurfais, Ali Douba served in the Syrian Air Force and became Syria's chief of military intelligence in the early 1970s. In 1994, Douba was promoted to lieutenant general and was feared for his rough treatment and physical abuse. Douba was an advisor to Syrian President Hafez al-Assad and enjoyed significant power until he was pushed aside by Bashir Assad, the son and heir apparent. Douba's retirement on 6 February 2000 was the result of Bashir asserting his authority at the highest levels of the Syrian government. Despite Douba's long history of friendship to the Assad family and over 25 years of distinguished service as chief of the military intelligence, Bashir al-Assad insisted that he leave his position. Although the 65-year-old general had just reached the official age of retirement, many other high-ranking Syrian military officers have retained their posts well beyond this limit. According to sources in Damascus, the main reason for Douba's disgraceful exit was that his alleged involvement in a number of financial scandals over the years clashed with Bashir's carefully cultivated reputation as a reformer. Douba had been linked to illegal activities since 1995, when his son, Muhammad, was arrested on charges of operating a car theft ring. In February 1999, his name surfaced in connection with the illegal trafficking of religious artifacts between Lebanon and Canada through a network under his protection since 1990. In the early 1990s, one of his sons was accused of kidnapping the son of Abu-Watfeh (the biggest Rolex dealer in Syria). Abu-Watfeh survived being thrown from a car on a highway at full speed. Since his retirement, Douba has been living in Paris, France. Douba was replaced by the deputy chief of military intelligence, General Hassan Khalil, who distinguished himself as a staunch supporter of Bashir's presidential ambitions. General Khalil played a high-profile role in negotiations with Israel in 1996 as a member of two committees related to borders and security. He has also directed Syrian relations with various Iraqi opposition groups headquartered in Damascus. *See also* GHAZALI, RUSTUM; KANAAN, GHAZI; LEBANESE INTELLIGENCE; SYRIAN INTELLIGENCE.

DRAISS, CHARKI (1955–). In September 2006, King Muhammad VI appointed Charki Draiss as the new chief of police in Morocco, officially known as the General Office of National Security (Direction

Générale de la Sûreté Nationale; DGSN). He replaced General **Hamidou Laanigri**, who assumed the position of general inspector of the Auxiliary Forces, with the task of supervising the southern and northern zones. Draiss is a political affairs specialist and former governor of Laayoune, western Sahara's main city (since June 2005), as well as *wali* (super-governor) of the southern region of Laayoune-Boujdour-Sakia Lhamra. According to official sources, the appointment of Draiss as the chief of police was part of a drive to name civilians to head key security services and sideline the influence of the military in security matters. *See also* MOROCCAN INTELLIGENCE.

DRUZE REVOLT. *See* GREAT SYRIAN REVOLT.

– E –

EARLY ISLAMIC INTELLIGENCE. The origin of Islam can be traced back to seventh-century Saudi Arabia. Islam is thus the youngest of the great world religions. The Prophet Muhammad introduced Islam in 610 CE after experiencing what he claimed to be an angelic visitation during which he dictated the Qur'an, the holy book of Islam. Muhammad was careful in protecting the new religion, keeping it a secret and underground religion for a period lasting three years, from 610 to 613 CE. This was the period during which the basis of intelligence in Islam was established.

As the Prophet Muhammad began his preaching during these first three years of secrecy, he was aware that he had to be extremely careful in order to ensure that the new religion would not become public. He had to choose the right people whom he could trust to expose to the ideas of the new religion. He chose his wife, his cousin, and a close confidant, who accepted the ideas and principles of the new religion and assisted him in preaching Islam while at the same time keeping it secret.

When the number of the new believers reached 30 people, the Prophet Muhammad changed his strategy. He set up his offices in a safe house, which became the first headquarters of the intelligence apparatus in Islam. As the number of believers in the new religion increased, the safe house could not accommodate all of them. Once again, the Prophet Muhammad adopted a new strategy by creating small cells in different locations. The meetings in the cells were held frequently but at different times, so that not all of the believers gathered simultaneously. The purposes of the meetings were to study the ideas and principles of the new religion, including the Qur'an, as well as to decide on the next strategic moves. This was the last stage of secrecy. From 613 CE onward, Muhammad moved into the next stage, during which he had to deal openly with those who opposed the new religion.

The main opposition came from the Quraysh tribe, who wanted to assassinate the Prophet Muhammad. In order to survive, Muhammad had to use deception and counterintelligence means against his opponents, and he undertook a new tactic to weaken the intelligence of the Quraysh. He encouraged the Muslims to emigrate from Mecca to what is known today as Ethiopia in 615 CE. The waves of the migration process (*Hijrah*) were carried out in a quick and secret manner. The intelligence apparatus of Muhammad became quite efficient, as evidenced by the number of believers, which grew from day to day. The migration process was successfully completed in 622 CE without the Quraysh knowing about it. It succeeded because of complete secrecy, effective counterintelligence, and an excellent level of organization. Another wave of migration took place from Mecca to Medina, both of which are presently in Saudi Arabia.

Thus, the first stages of creating a Muslim intelligence apparatus ended with gaining expertise in the tradecraft. From then on, the Muslims had to confront other challenges in the sphere of intelligence and security. In a sense, the first Islamic state was established in Medina, and great security challenges were faced in protecting it against the Quraysh tribe. An early Muslim victory in the battle of Badr in March 624 CE was the key to strengthening the political position of the Muslims in Medina by signaling to other tribes that a new power had emerged in Arabia. This victory was a turning point in Muhammad's struggle with the Quraysh and strengthened his authority as leader of the often-fractious community in Medina. Once Islam was established as a viable force in the Arabian Peninsula, local Arab tribes began to convert and ally themselves with the Muslims of Medina.

EGYPTIAN INTELLIGENCE. Egypt's intelligence apparatus was formed in 1955 under President Gamal Abdel Nasser, who assigned the task to **Zakareia Mohy El-Dien**. However, Egypt's main intelligence organization, the General Directorate for State Security Investigations (GDSSI; Mubahath al-Dawla) was established by **Salah Nasr**, who became its director in 1957 and served in this position for 10 years. Nasr succeeded in making the GDSSI a vital intelligence organ, but the name of the GDSSI director was a secret known only to high officials for several years.

Over the years, the GDSSI has scored many successes, such as planting Egyptian spies disguised as new immigrants in Israel. Several of them were active in Israel for years before they were detected and caught by the Israeli Security Agency (ISA). In 1970, in a covert operation known as Operation Al-Haffar, the GDSSI managed to trace an Israeli oil rig while being shipped from Canada to Sinai and detonated explosives along the way, crippling the rig. This operation was commanded by **Ameen Heweedy**.

The main strategic success of the GDSSI was in deceiving **Israeli intelligence** that the Egyptian Army was preparing its annual military maneuver, while in fact the GDSSI was concealing Egypt's plan to launch a massive military attack against Israel on 6 October 1973, starting the **Yom Kippur War**. The GDSSI prepared complicated logistic movement schedules for all Egyptian Army units in order to avoid mass troop movements at times when they could be spotted by satellites. The deception plan included planting false information and hidden messages in Egyptian President Anwar Sadat's speeches and interviews in the media. The Egyptian Army evacuated complete departments of Cairo hospitals a few days before the war started to be ready for receiving war casualties, while falsely claiming that those hospitals were infected with tetanus. Many details about the GDSSI deception plan are still classified.

The GDSSI is the main Egyptian intelligence organization that deals with matters of internal security. The entire Egyptian intelligence community is sometimes referred to as the State Security Investigations Sector (SSIS; Amn al-Dawla). Other Egyptian intelligence organizations are the Mukhabarat al-'Amma, which is under the president's responsibility, and the Mukhabarat al-Khabiya, which is the military intelligence division under the Egyptian Ministry of

Defense. In addition, the security apparatus operates special courts to hear cases related to national security threats that are tried under the criminal code, as well as other types of cases. These courts are referred to as either the National Security Courts or the Supreme State Security Courts (Mahkamat Amn al-Dawla al-'Ulya).

Since President Nasser's era in the 1950s, security forces have played a controversial political role in ensuring state control over dissent and opposition. Security forces have also held a strong position in other authoritarian Arab states, such as in Iraq, Syria, and Jordan, but in Egypt they are far more important than the police. In Egypt, the tactics of the security services have varied under different ministers of the interior. Their force was unleashed in the 1990s to vigorously combat the Islamist threat, and at times they have also demonstrated brutality in their attempts to assert control over nongovernmental organizations and to suppress the promotion of democratization. *See also* EGYPTIAN INTELLIGENCE SATELLITES; EGYPTIAN TERRORISM; NASSER'S ASSASSINATION ATTEMPTS; SADAT'S ASSASSINATION.

EGYPTIAN INTELLIGENCE SATELLITES. The Egyptian satellite company NileSat was established in 1996 for the purpose of operating satellites and their associated ground control station and other facilities. NileSat 101 has been in orbit since April 1998 and in service since June 1998; NileSat 102 has been in orbit since August 2000 and in service since September 2000.

In an effort to gather intelligence on Israel and other Middle Eastern countries from outer space, Egypt launched a new spy satellite from Kazakhstan. The Egyptian spy satellite, EgyptSat 1, was constructed in cooperation with the Yuzhnoye Company of the Ukraine and was launched in February 2007. The EgyptSat 1 is circling the Earth at an altitude of 668 kilometers. Its high-powered multispectrum telescopic camera can spot objects on the ground as small as four meters (13 feet) wide. With its ability to collect intelligence on Israel, the EgyptSat launching marks a significant change in the balance of space capabilities in the Middle East, thus giving it regional significance. In addition, another spy satellite, called DesertSat, is currently under construction in Italy. A launch date for this satellite has not been scheduled. *See also* EGYPTIAN INTELLIGENCE.

EGYPTIAN ISLAMIC JIHAD (EIJ). The Egyptian Islamic Jihad, an Egyptian Islamic extremist group, merged with Osama bin-Laden's **al Qaeda** organization in June 2001. Active since the 1970s, the EIJ's primary goals have traditionally been to overthrow the Egyptian government, replacing it with an Islamic state, and to attack United States and Israeli interests in Egypt and abroad. EIJ members who did not join al Qaeda retain the capability to conduct independent operations. In 1995, the EIJ joined forces with the Egyptian al-Agama's al-Islamiyya and **Sudanese intelligence**.

Today, EIJ probably has several hundred hard-core members, with most of its network being located outside Egypt in countries such as Yemen, Afghanistan, Pakistan, Lebanon, and Great Britain. Its activities have been centered outside Egypt for several years. The Egyptian government claims that Iran supports the Jihad, although it received most of its funding from al Qaeda after early 1998 through close ties that culminated in the eventual merger of the two groups. Some funding may come from various Islamic nongovernmental organizations, cover businesses, and criminal acts.

In February 2008, the Canadian Security Intelligence Service (CSIS) released information that in 1996 Mahmoud Jaballah had gone to Canada on a false Saudi passport and claimed refugee status. Jaballah was one of the chief leaders of the EIJ and was detained in February 2001 under charges from the federal government that he was a member of the Egyptian Islamic Jihad under Ayman al-Zawahiri and was alleged to have been the communications person for the 1998 bombings of U.S. embassies in Kenya and Tanzania that killed 213 people.

EGYPTIAN TERRORISM. Egypt has suffered from several waves of **terrorism** in its history in which Egyptian leaders were assassinated: in 1910, Prime Minister Boutros Ghali; in the second wave, two prime ministers, Ahmed Maher in 1944 and Mahmoud al-Nuqrashi in 1949; and in 1981, President Anwar al-Sadat. In the 1980s and 1990s, Egypt suffered from the scourge of terrorism, which claimed thousands of victims, as Islamic fundamentalists were determined to establish an Islamic Shari'a state. Egypt waged a bitter campaign of state violence, mass arrests, and financial crackdowns against **al-Gama'at al-Islamiyya** (Islamic Group) and the **Egyptian Islamic Jihad—**

Egypt's two largest Islamist terrorist groups—both of which are off-shoots of the much older Muslim Brotherhood and both of which have important ties to Osama bin-Laden's **al Qaeda** terrorist network. Indeed, many of al Qaeda's leaders are Egyptians, and many Egyptian militants have passed through al Qaeda training camps.

Terrorist organizations in Egypt had four main targets: public and administration figures and heads of the security establishment; foreign tourists, the Coptic minority, and Egyptian and other targets abroad. Striking against administration officials and heads of the security establishment became a very important goal for Islamic terrorist organizations since President Sadat's assassination by the Islamic Jihad in October 1981. As part of this campaign, fundamentalists assassinated the Speaker of Parliament, Rifat Mahgoub; police officers; and other senior security officials. Furthermore, President Mubarak barely escaped an assassination attempt in Addis Ababa in June 1995.

Beginning in mid-1992, the fundamentalists began targeting tourism in an effort to deal a blow to Egypt's tourism industry—the country's second-largest source of foreign currency, after fees from the Suez Canal. Two seasons of tourism were lost (1992 and 1993) due to terrorist activity, causing the economy direct damages of $3–5 billion. After the tourism industry recovered, it managed to thrive during 1995–1996 until the massacre in Luxor, which was the deadliest terrorist act in the history of Egypt. The wave of terrorism that broke out in Egypt in mid-1992 surprised the Egyptian government. The magnitude of the acts of terrorism was not anticipated and the Egyptian leadership did not have a suitable response. It lacked sufficient intelligence and a comprehensive strategy to fight back.

On 17 November 1997, Islamic fundamentalists armed with assault rifles attacked tourist groups in the courtyard of the famous Temple of Hatshepsut in Luxor. Sixty-eight people were killed in the massacre, with all but 10 of them foreign tourists. The terrorist attack, which was carried out by the largest Muslim terrorist organization in Egypt, the al-Gama'at al-Islamiyya, inflicted a severe blow to Egyptian tourism, caused significant damage to the national economy, scarred the image of the regime, and reversed the recent declining trend of terrorism. The attack occurred after Sheikh Omar Abdel Rahman, the spiritual leader of al-Gama'at al-Islamiyya, sent a *fatwa* (religious ruling) from the United States to his followers, permitting the murder of foreign tourists in Egypt. Altogether, 97 foreign tourists were killed in Egypt in six years of terrorism.

The third target of the terrorist organizations in Egypt was the Coptic minority, who symbolized the hated regime. Muslim fundamentalists view the Copts as outsiders, both religiously and ethnically, and are jealous of their economic success. Finally, the Muslim terrorist groups also carried out attacks abroad. In November 1995, a suicide bomber detonated a pickup truck loaded with explosives in the courtyard of the Egyptian embassy in Islamabad, the capital of Pakistan, and caused many fatalities. One month later, a car bomb exploded in the Pakistani city of Peshawar, killing at least 30 people. The Jihad organization, which claimed responsibility for the attack, asserted that the operation was carried out in reaction to the Pakistani government's decision to extradite wanted Islamists to Egypt.

The wave of terrorism that broke out in Egypt in mid-1992 surprised the regime both in its scope and its force. Egyptian leadership lacked sufficient intelligence and a comprehensive strategy to fight back. Under these circumstances, the regime reacted to the terrorist attacks by applying force, imposing curfews, conducting house-to-house searches, and carrying out mass arrests in order to capture wanted fundamentalists and to uncover weapon supplies. Following the mass arrests, Egypt's prisons were quickly filled beyond capacity, to the point where it was no longer possible to separate the fundamentalist prisoners from the common criminals. Often the fundamentalists controlled the inmates, forcing them to join their organizations and in effect turning the prisons into schools of terrorism.

Finding itself cornered, the regime tried to reach an agreement with the fundamentalists through dialogue and negotiation. This experiment was conducted by Minister of Interior Abdel Halim Moussa in early 1993. The leadership of al-Gama'at al-Islamiyya set conditions for an agreement, according to which most of the fundamentalist prisoners would be released in exchange for a *hudna*, or cease-fire agreement. In the absence of trust between the parties, the negotiations ultimately failed. The interior minister paid for the failure with his job, and the regime never again returned to the negotiating table with the fundamentalists. In 1997, the leaders of al-Gama'at al-Islamiyya approached the government at least three times with offers of a cease-fire, but in light of the previous experience in trying to reach an agreement with the fundamentalists in 1993, the regime rejected the proposals outright.

In the second half of 1993, the Egyptian government adopted a different strategy for combating terrorism. The program focused on recruiting agents from within the fundamentalist organizations, establishing a computerized information database on the fundamentalists and their activities, implementing direct strikes against leaders of terrorist organizations, and reaching intelligence and operational cooperation agreements with Arab and Western countries. Egyptian internal security forces and intelligence agencies implemented this comprehensive approach successfully to combat terrorism. Many agents were recruited from among the terrorist groups and supplied important information to the security forces. The information enabled more focused strikes on terrorist cells and arrests of their leaders and members. Enlisted soldiers with suitable qualifications were drafted to internal security units and special antiterrorist units were established. Extremist groups were barred from using mosques as a forum for disseminating their ideas. The computerized database supplied the security forces with a constant flow of up-to-date information. Communication networks between terrorist organizations and their cells were dismantled, and their financing channels were blocked and frozen. The smuggling of arms from Sudan to terrorist cells in Egypt has also been successfully prevented. The fundamentalists have been pushed out of the Cairo area, where they used to draw young followers from the city's slums. The terrorist organizations do not enjoy significant public support, except in the south of the country. Indeed, since the end of 1994, there has been a decline in the fear of violence and terrorism among the public, especially in Cairo and the north. The number of terrorist incidents has dropped, and the presence of security forces in the large cities has diminished.

However, despite the Egyptian government's success in reducing terrorist attacks inside Egypt, there are still occasional attacks perpetrated against tourists. These terrorist attacks have virtually decimated Egypt's tourism industry, one of its most important sources of income. On 7 October 2004, three explosions shook popular resorts on Egypt's Sinai Peninsula, where many Israelis were vacationing. At least 30 people were killed and 114 wounded, and witnesses gave unconfirmed reports that all three explosions were caused by car bombs. The first blast shook the Hilton Hotel in the Taba resort, only yards from the Israeli border.

EIGHTH CORPS. The Turkish Eighth Corps was the most important military unit within the Ottoman Fourth Army during **World War I** in the Levant theater. It was the military body responsible for espionage and spy hunting. The commander of the Eighth Corps was Akhmed Dormash Bek, and his senior deputies were Rashdi Bek and Abdel Rahman Elnatzuli. *See also* TURKISH INTELLIGENCE.

EL-ALAMEIN, SECOND BATTLE OF. *See* OPERATION BERTRAM.

EMANI, SAEED (1959–1999). Also known as Saeed Eslami and Mojtaba Ghavami, Saeed Emani served as the deputy minister of intelligence under **Ali Fallahian**. After spending several years in the United States pursuing his studies in mechanical engineering, Emani returned to Iran after the revolution and became involved in intelligence gathering. In 1984, when the Majlis (Parliament) approved the establishment of the Ministry of Intelligence, he officially applied for a job. After initially being rejected, he later joined the ministry and became its deputy during the tenure of Ali Fallahian. He also served as an intelligence officer who was charged with the self-organized assassinations of dissidents. In 1999, after being charged with orchestrating the Chained Murders (a series of murders and disappearances of Iranians who had been critical of the Islamic Republic system), he reportedly committed suicide in prison by consuming a strong chemical while bathing. *See also* IRANIAN INTELLIGENCE.

EPPLER, JOHANNES. Johannes Eppler was a German of Egyptian descent who was recruited by the Abwehr, the German military intelligence service, in **World War II** to infiltrate Egypt, from where he was to send radio messages direct to Field Marshal Erwin Rommel's headquarters with information about British troop and naval movements. Count **László Almásy** helped him to carry out the infiltration in a hazardous drive across the desert from Tobruk. However, the wireless operator in Rommel's headquarters, who was meant to receive Eppler's transmissions, was captured and never replaced. Thus,

Eppler's messages were never received, and Eppler was arrested in July 1942. During his interrogation, it was revealed that his code-name was Moritz.

ESPIONAGE MOVIES. Espionage stories taking place in the Middle East have attracted many movie producers. The best known movies are *Raid on Entebbe*, *I Saw Ben-Barka Getting Killed*, *OSS 117: Cairo, Nest of Spies*, and *Penetration*.

Raid on Entebbe is a 1977 TV movie directed by Irvin Kershner about the freeing of the Israeli hostages at Entebbe Airport, Uganda, on 4 July 1976, and is considered to be fairly accurate. The rescue operation also attracted many movie producers, and other versions were the TV movie *Victory at Entebbe* (1976) and *Entebbe: Operation Thunderbolt* (1977), directed and produced by Menahem Golan.

I Saw Ben-Barka Getting Killed (J'ai vu tuer Ben-Barka) was directed by Serge Le Péron in 2004 as a docudrama. This French movie is about the **Ben-Barka affair**, France's great political scandal of 1965–1966 about the disappearance of Mehdi Ben-Barka from Paris. Ben-Barka was a Moroccan opposition leader in exile and an international left-wing Third World activist. Ben-Barka's corpse has never been found.

Ben-Barka was lured to Paris "for making a movie" about decolonization with the great French director Georges Franju (Jean-Pierre Léaud) and the writer Marguerite Duras (Josiane Balasko). The project had been organized by Georges Figon (Charles Berling), a Dostoyevskian petty criminal and littérateur, who himself had been recruited by local gangsters brought into the game through the French secret services, working with Moroccan authorities in conjunction with the Central Intelligence Agency (CIA). In his movie, Jean-Pierre Léaud succeeded in describing the historical context of the postcolonialism of Morocco, its independence, and the postcolonial internal power struggles between different political entities in the Morocco, but it was also a moral story of Morocco.

OSS 117: Cairo, Nest of Spies, known by the French title *OSS 117: Le Caire nid d'espions* is a 2006 movie that is a continuation of the OSS 117 series of spy movies from the 1950s and 1960s, which were in turn based on a series of novels by Jean Bruce. This is a French movie directed by Michel Hazanavicius. It is a parody of the spy movie genre. The movie follows the exploits of a French secret agent, OSS 117, in Cairo in 1955. Jean Dujardin stars as secret agent Hubert Bonisseur de la Bath, also known as OSS 117. The main plot starts with the disappearances of an OSS agent, Jack Jefferson, and a Russian cargo ship in Cairo. Agent OSS 117 is sent to investigate the events, since he and Jefferson share a history, shown in a short opening sequence and in flashbacks throughout the movie. OSS 117 stumbles into a web of international intrigue that involves the French, separate factions of Egyptians, Russians, a goofy Belgian spy, and even Neo-Nazis. Throughout the movie, the main character has two main romantic interests. The first is Egyptian Princess al-Tarouk, who cannot resist the charms of OSS 117. The second is the former assistant of Jack Jefferson, Larmina El-Akmar Betouche, who at first shows no interest in the main character but warms up to him in the end.

The most recent movie about espionage in the Middle East is *Penetration* (titled in the United States as *Body of Lies*), released in 2008. *Penetration* is a spy thriller directed by Ridley Scott, scripted by William Monahan, and based on David Ignatius's novel *Penetration*. According to the movie, Leonardo DiCaprio is an idealistic CIA agent stationed in Jordan and tasked with infiltrating a terrorist cell. During his stay in Jordan he comes up with a plan to sow seeds of suspicion among the members of the terrorist cell. Russell Crowe plays DiCaprio's CIA boss. The plan puts DiCaprio's life in jeopardy. In order to complete his plan, he teams with the head of Jordan's intelligence agency, which leads to personal and cultural clashes between the two men. *See also* LAWRENCE, THOMAS EDWARD; OPERATION ENTEBBE.

– F –

FADL, MOHSEN. Mohsen Fadl was an Egyptian member of the Pyramid Organization of German spies in Cairo, who was recruited in October 1941 in Paris, at a café on the Bois de Boulogne, by Hungarian aristocrat Count **László Almásy**. Fadl was arrested after being identified by Sobhi Hanna, an Egyptian lawyer arrested for espionage in 1942. The British Security Intelligence Middle East (SIME) in Egypt interrogated Fadl, who was convicted of espionage and sentenced to jail. *See also* BRITISH INTELLIGENCE IN EGYPT AND SUDAN.

FAISAL ISLAMIC BANK OF EGYPT (FIBE). The Faisal Islamic Bank of Egypt was founded in 1976 as part of the banking empire built by Saudi Prince Muhammad al-Faisal. Several of the founders, including Sheikh Abdel Rahman, were leading members of the Muslim Brotherhood. The growth of Islamic banking directly funded the political growth of the Islamist movement and allowed the Saudis to pressure the poorer Islamic nations, like Egypt, to shift their policies to the right. The FIBE was also closely associated with the infamous **Bank of Credit and Commerce International** (BCCI), which was deeply involved in the illegal arms and narcotics trades, as well as with the funding of terrorist organizations, until it collapsed in 1991. Investigators also found that the BCCI held $589 million in "unrecorded deposits," $245 million of which were placed with the FIBE. In 2001, the U.S. Office of Terrorism and Financial Intelligence (TFI) revealed that the FIBE with connection to the BCCI was involved in financing **terrorism**.

FALLAHIAN, ALI (1949–). Born in Najafabad, Iran, into a religious family, Ali Fallahian became a conservative Islamic mullah after studying theology in a Qum seminary. Fallahian was an ardent follower of the Ayatollah Khomeini and spent time in the shah's jails for spreading antigovernment propaganda. His political rise began after the 1979 revolution, when he was appointed as a revolutionary court judge. He quickly won a reputation as a hanging judge because of his inclination for handing down death sentences. He was appointed to the leadership of the Revolutionary Committee in 1982 and, in coordination with Iran's Islamic Revolution Guards Corps (IRGC), he participated in the dismantling of the Mujahedin Khalq Organization.

Fallahian began working at the Intelligence and Security Ministry (MOIS) in 1984 as a deputy minister, moved on to become prosecutor in the Special Court for the Clergy in 1986, and was made head of the Armed Forces Inspectorate in 1988. He served as the second minister of intelligence and security from 1989 until 1997 in Hashemi Rafsanjani's government and then as a member of the Assembly of Experts. Fallahian is believed to have played a key role in organizing covert operations abroad and to be responsible for at least two dozen assassinations of foreign-based opposition figures during his tenure in the ministry. In an August 1992 interview on Iranian television, Fallahian openly boasted of his organization's success in stalking Tehran's opponents.

In 1996, a German court issued an international arrest warrant for Ali Fallahian for his part in the Mykonos Restaurant terror incident in Berlin, in which three of Iran's exiled Kurdish leaders were gunned down, allegedly by mixed Iranian–Lebanese agents. Fallahian was also the most prominent member of a group of five Iranians and Lebanese for whom international arrest warrants were issued in March 2007 as the principal conspirators in the bombing of the Jewish community building in Buenos Aires in July 1994, which killed 85 people. Ali Fallahian was also charged by a Swiss court with masterminding the assassination of Kazem Rajavi, a renowned human rights advocate, near Geneva in broad daylight on 24 April 1990. *See also* IRANIAN INTELLIGENCE.

FATAH, AL-. This Palestinian group was founded in exile in 1957 by Yasser Arafat, who remained its leader until his death in 2004. Over the years, al-Fatah has become one of the leading Palestinian groups. In the 1960s and 1970s, al-Fatah offered training to a wide range of European, Middle Eastern, Asian, and African terrorist and insurgent groups and carried out numerous acts of international **terrorism** in Western Europe and the Middle East. Al-Fatah became increasingly important in the 1960s, gaining full control over the Palestinian Liberation Organization (PLO) in 1969, which it had joined in 1967. During this period, the PLO started to carry out guerrilla actions inside Israel. It has since been linked to terrorist attacks against Israeli and foreign civilians in Israel and the occupied territories.

From late 2004 until 12 November 2006, al-Fatah was led by Farouk Kaddoumi, the remaining living cofounder of al-Fatah. Kaddoumi was subsequently replaced by the Palestinian president, Mahmoud Abbas. Al-Fatah was committed to full independence for Palestinians, focusing on direct military confrontation with Israel in order to win back "lost land." Al-Fatah remains the most powerful group of the PLO, controlling the power of the Palestinian National Authority until the elections in 2006, when **Hamas** won and formed its government.

The politics of al-Fatah have changed drastically from the military line of the 1950s and 1960s into the pragmatic politics of a democratic Palestine, even if this approach is more constrained than that for which many Western observers and Palestinians would have hoped. Al-Fatah has had close, long-standing political and financial ties to Saudi Arabia, Kuwait, and other Persian Gulf States, although these relations were disrupted by the **Gulf War** of 1990–1991. It has also established links to Jordan and received weapons, explosives, and training from the former Soviet Union and the former communist regimes of Eastern European states. China and North Korea have reportedly provided weapons as well. Since the Palestinian National Authority was formed in 1994, al-Fatah has operated a vast intelligence network cooperating with the U.S. Central Intelligence Agency. Al-Fatah controlled spying operations carried out in Arab and Muslim countries for the benefit of the United States and other foreign governments. In several instances, Fatah's intelligence operatives cooperated with the Israeli Security Agency (ISA) to target Islamist leaders for assassination. The CIA supplied al-Fatah's intelligence with sophisticated intelligence-gathering equipment, including eavesdropping technology. The CIA even utilized al-Fatah's agents for covert intelligence operations in other Middle Eastern countries. One of the key figures cooperating with the CIA on behalf of al-Fatah was **Muhammad Dahlan**. After 2004, when Hamas won the election in Gaza Strip, the connection between al-Fatah and the CIA almost ceased.

FATAH AL-ISLAM. Fatah al-Islam emerged in November 2006 when it split from Fatah al-Intifada (Fatah Uprising), a Syrian-backed Palestinian group based in Lebanon. Operating under the auspices of **Syrian intelligence**, Fatah al-Islam's goals are to destabilize Lebanon's political and territorial situation, to reform the Palestinian refugee community in Lebanon according to Islamic Shari'a law, to oppose Israel, and to expel the United States from the Islamic world. Fatah al-Islam is led by Shakir al-Abssi, a well-known Palestinian militant who was sentenced to death in absentia in Jordan for killing a U.S. diplomat, Laurence Foley, in Amman in 2002. It is unclear whether Fatah al-Islam is linked to **al Qaeda**.

The group is believed to have between 150 and 200 armed members, all in the Nahr al-Bared refugee camp north of Tripoli. Fatah al-Islam has accused the Lebanese government of trying to pave the way for an offensive against Palestinian refugee camps in Lebanon. The camps are widely seen as a breeding ground for radical Islam, but Beirut continues to adhere to a 1969 United Nations agreement allowing the camps to remain autonomous, provided they disarm their militias.

On 20 May 2007, Lebanon's worst internal violence since the end of its civil war in 1990 left at least 41 dead. The fighting between Fatah al-Islam and Lebanese troops began when Lebanese security forces investigating a bank robbery raided an apartment north of Tripoli, Lebanon. In response, members of Fatah al-Islam seized control of army posts at the entrance of the Nahr al-Bared refugee camp, which Lebanese Army tanks then proceeded to shell. The camp's electricity, phone lines, and water were cut off. On-and-off fighting continued for weeks, leaving scores dead or wounded. Fatah al-Islam is regarded as a tool of Syrian intelligence.

FORUZANDEH, MUHAMMAD (1953–). Muhammad Foruzandeh is the current head of the Oppressed and Disabled Foundation, which funds the Iranian Islamic Revolution Guards Corps (IRGC) activities through overseas enterprises that serve as fronts for IRGC operations. After the Islamic revolution, he served as governor-general of Khuzestan Province. In 1986, Foruzandeh served as chief of staff for the IRGC, and in 1993 he was appointed defense minister by President Ali-Akbar Hashemi-Rafsanjani. *See also* IRANIAN INTELLIGENCE.

FRENCH INTELLIGENCE IN THE MIDDLE EAST. The influence of France in North Africa began with the 1881 Bardo Treaty, which established its protectorate in Tunisia. Since then French influence in North Africa expanded to Morocco, Algeria, and to a certain extent even Egypt. During the era of colonialism in the Maghreb, France regarded political and military intelligence as an effective tool for promoting its interests in the region. France used its intelligence agencies especially during times of political and ethnic resistance to its colonial rule, particularly in Algeria. In Morocco, France formed the Mission Scientifique au Maroc (Scientific Mission to Morocco) in 1904, which was tasked with intervening politically whenever it was necessary. The Scientific Mission was active until France's protectorate rule was established in 1912.

After **World War II**, when French colonialism in the Maghreb ended, France played the role of Africa's sentinel. French interference in the Maghreb was mainly through its military bases or through the intelligence activities and disguised behind its multinational corporations.

In the Middle East, French influence started with its League of Nations mandate on Syria in 1920. This aroused the anger of various ethnic groups, which led to the 1925 **Great Syrian Revolt**. During World War II, soldiers of Free France were still fighting alongside the British against the Nazis in Europe. The two colonial powers were engaged in a clandestine struggle in the Middle East. During the summer of 1944, French intelligence succeeded in recruiting a Syrian agent who had access to top-secret correspondence between Syrian President Shukri al-Quwatli and Foreign Minister Jamil Mardam to Middle Eastern statesmen and leaders of Great Britain, the Soviet Union, and the United States. The agent—for a small fortune, of course—smuggled the secret correspondence from Damascus to the French intelligence headquarters in Beirut, sealed as diplomatic mail. He provided his French handlers with about a hundred classified letters every week. In Beirut a French intelligence officer translated the contents of the letters into French. When it was necessary, the translator used to add several comments and interpretations. Free France under the command of General Charles de Gaulle found great interest in the contents of the correspondence. Therefore, a special airplane was dispatched to pick up the documents from Beirut and deliver them to de Gaulle's headquarters in London.

By the middle of the 1950s, France obtained from its secret agent in Syria the classified draft of the British–Syrian agreement, according to which Great Britain and the United States intended to forge an anti-Soviet regional alliance with the participation of Iraq, Syria, and Turkey; this plan was later known as the Baghdad Pact. It is unknown if France brought this information to the attention of the Kremlin.

In the aftermath of World War II, France was still involved in the Middle East as France secretly armed Israel in the 1950s and the early 1960s. France assisted Israel in the construction of the nuclear reactor in Dimona. In 1956, France joined Britain as a principal actor in the Middle East in the ill-conceived Suez expedition of 1956. Since the 1980s, a substantial number of Middle Eastern and North African citizens have immigrated to France. On 3 October 1980, in front of the Jewish synagogue on Rue Copernic, a motorcycle bomb exploded, killing four peopled and wounding 11. Since this was the sixth case of anti-Jewish violence in Paris, the immediate assumption was that it was an anti-Semitic act done by a Neo-Nazi movement in France. In fact, this was just the beginning of a long campaign of foreign terrorists trying to influence France's Middle East policy. On 14 December 1980, Ahmed Ressam, an Algerian by origin and holding a Canadian passport, was arrested on the United States–Canada border with a trunk fully loaded with explosives. The French antiterrorism investigation later revealed that Ressam was connected to the group that carried out the wave of terrorist actions against the Jewish community in France in the 1980s.

By the beginning of the 1980s, France's policies in the Middle East were conflicting with the interests of Iran, Lebanon, and Syria, the main terror-sponsoring states of the Middle East. The most devastating act of terror occurred in 1983 when a suicide bomber killed 58 French troops in the French contingent of the Multinational Force in Lebanon. Since then, France's intelligence activity regarding the Middle East has targeted mainly **terrorism**. Two French intelligence agencies became involved in analyzing this terror: Direction générale de la sécurité extérieure (DGSE; External Documentation and Counterespionage Service) and the Direction de la surveillance du territoire (DST; Directorate of Territorial Surveillance). But at the time of the troop bombing, the DST was not really capable of dealing with the threat of terror.

Under President Nicolas Sarkozy, who was elected in May 2007, France has a vision of renewing its influence in the Middle East. This would require it to target its intelligence agencies on the Middle East. *See also* ISRAELI NUCLEAR WEAPONS PROGRAM; OPERATION MUSKETEER.

– G –

GAMA'AT AL-ISLAMIYYA, AL-. Al-Gama'at al-Islamiyya is also known as Jama'a Islamia, which in Arabic means the Islamic Group. Al-Gama'at al-Islamiyya, Egypt's largest militant group, has been active since the late 1970s and appears to be loosely organized. It also has an external wing with supporters in several countries worldwide.

In November 1992, **Egyptian intelligence** repeatedly warned U.S. intelligence that Sheikh Abdel Rahman's principal mosques in the United States, the al-Salaam and al-Farouq mosques in Brooklyn, were "hotbeds of terrorist activity," and that Abdel Rahman was plotting a new round of terrorist attacks in Egypt. On 12 November 1992, members of the al-Gama'at al-Islamiyya militant group led by Abdel Rahman machine-gunned a busload of Western tourists in Egypt, injuring five Germans. Between 6 and 11 February 1993, agents of the Federal Bureau of Investigation (FBI) visited Cairo to discuss Egyptian concerns about al-Gama'at al-Islamiyya. The Egyptian representatives to the discussion even warned about the activities of certain terrorist cells of al-Gama'at al-Islamiyya connected to Abdel Rahman in the United States. However, the warning was not concrete. There was not even a hint of what was supposed to happen in the World Trade Center (WTC), New York, later that year. By the summer of 1993, the Central Intelligence Agency realized that Osama bin-Laden had been paying for training al-Gama'at al-Islamiyya's members in Sudan, where he lived.

The group also claimed responsibility for the June 1995 attempt to assassinate Egyptian President Hosni Mubarak in Addis Ababa, Ethiopia. Al-Gama'at al-Islamiyya has never specifically attacked an American citizen or facility but has threatened American interests.

Senior members signed Osama bin-Laden's *fatwa* in February 1998 calling for attacks against the United States. The group subsequently issued a cease-fire in March 1999, but its spiritual leader, Sheikh Omar Abdel Rahman, was sentenced to life imprisonment in January 1996 for his involvement in the 1993 WTC bombing. Al-Gama'at al-Islamiyya has not conducted an attack inside Egypt since August 1998. Prior to the cease-fire, al-Gama'at al-Islamiyya conducted armed attacks against Egyptian security and other government officials, Coptic Christians, and Egyptian opponents of Islamic extremism. From 1993 until the cease-fire, al-Gama'at al-Islamiyya launched attacks on tourists in Egypt, most notably the November 1997 attack at Luxor that killed 58 foreign tourists.

At its peak, al-Gama'at al-Islamiyya probably commanded several thousand hard-core members and a like number of sympathizers. The 1999 cease-fire and security crackdowns following the 1997 Luxor attack and, more recently, security efforts following 11 September 2001, have probably resulted in a substantial decrease in the group's numbers. Unofficially, the group has split into two factions: one that supports the cease-fire, led by Mustafa Hamza, and one led by Rifa'i Taha Moussa that is calling for a return to armed operations. In early 2001, Moussa published a book in which he attempted to justify terrorist attacks that would cause mass casualties; he disappeared several months later, and reports as to his current whereabouts are conflicting.

Al-Gama'at al-Islamiyya operates primarily in the al-Minya, Asyut, Qina, and Sohaj governorates of southern Egypt. The group also appears to have support in Cairo, Alexandria, and other urban locations, particularly among unemployed graduates and students, and has a worldwide presence in Great Britain, Afghanistan, Yemen, and various locations in Europe. The Egyptian government believes that Iran, bin-Laden, and Afghan militant groups support al-Gama'at al-Islamiyya, which may also obtain some funding through various Islamic nongovernmental organizations. *See also* EGYPTIAN TERRORISM.

GENERAL DELEGATION OF DOCUMENTATION AND SECURITY (DGDS)/DELÉGATION GÉNÉRALE DE DOCUMENTATION ET SÛRETÉ. *See* ALGERIAN INTELLIGENCE.

GEOMILITECH (GMT). GeoMiliTech (GMT) Consultants Corporation was established in 1983 as a dummy company by U.S. intelligence in cooperation with Israeli military industries. Its aim was to assist Iran in the war against Iraq (1980–1988) through weapons sales. A number of far right-wing, high-ranking American and Israeli military officials became involved in the company, which operated from corporate offices in both Washington and Tel-Aviv. Barbara F. Studley, a conservative talk show host, served as the company's president, and Ron S. Harel, a veteran of the Israeli Air Force, served as its executive vice president. Vice presidents were Bruce E. Herbert, a U.S. Navy captain, and Joel Arnon, a former assistant director general in the Israeli Ministry of Foreign Relations.

The founding of GMT marked the beginning of arms sales from the United States to Iran through Israel and North Korea. The illicit traffic in arms sales was facilitated by Israeli companies used as intermediaries. Many of these sales were approved by the Central Intelligence Agency and the Ronald Reagan administration. Israel's political motive in selling arms to the Iranian Islamic regime was to ensure that the **Iran–Iraq War** was as long and destructive as possible. Beyond profit making, the motive of the U.S. officials involved was less clear but most probably was to gain leverage for requesting the release of the U.S. citizens captured by the Lebanese Shi'ites in Lebanon and held there as hostages. However, several academic scholars maintain that these U.S. arms sales preceded the hostage incidents in Lebanon, which were later claimed by U.S. officials as the motive for arms sales to Iran. *See also* IRANGATE AFFAIR.

GERMAN INTELLIGENCE IN PALESTINE. In August 1933, the Jewish Agency signed an agreement with German officials to allow tens of thousands of German Jews to migrate to Palestine and transfer their capital. For this purpose, the Jewish Agency formed a company under the name Haavara (Hebrew for "transfer"). When **World War II** broke out in August 1939, the activities of Haavara aroused suspicion within British intelligence in Palestine, which placed the directors of Haavara under arrest and conducted interrogations for their contacts with the Germans. Through their contacts with Haavara, German intelligence made the first step in penetrating Palestine.

Initial reports about Nazi agents penetrating Palestine disguised as immigrants from Germany were attributed by the British to the Arab hatred toward Jews, rather than to direct German involvement. However, the Jewish community in Palestine placed a larger importance on the activities of the Nazi agents and their followers. Informers provided information to the Arab Department of the Jewish Agency and the Haganah (the underground militia of the Jewish community in Palestine) about the activities of German agents and propagandists operating undercover as journalists in order to infiltrate the Arab media, spread anti-British propaganda, and finance antigovernmental Arab newspapers.

Agents of the Haganah conducted surveillance about the activities of German citizens in Palestine and even bugged their telephone conversations, which revealed their involvement in political subversion, spying, fund-raising, and the transfer of money and weapons from Germany to the Arabs in Palestine. The German activities were concentrated mainly in youth organizations, consulates, and Shneller, a German orphanage in Jerusalem that served as a center for hiding Arabs wanted by the law.

The interest of the British intelligence in the activities of the Germans in Palestine and the Middle East increased with time as international tensions worsened. By 1939, the British were receiving news about an increase in illegal activities by the Nazis in Palestine. In one instance, Jewish intelligence agents faked for the British a copy of the check that two Germans from Haifa gave to an Arab agent to spread propaganda. They also reported Germans and Italians who were trying to get photographs of the damage caused to Arabs by British army activity so that they could distribute them to newspapers abroad.

One of the main information sources of the Haganah on German activity in Palestine was a Jewish man named Fable Pollocks. In 1937, Pollocks was sent by the Haganah to meet with German representatives about the transfer of Jewish property from Germany to Palestine. The Gestapo attempted to recruit Pollocks as a double agent, for which he appeared to offer his cooperation in return for giving preference to the migration of German Jews to Palestine over other countries. Pollocks also requested that the Germans release a number of Jews from concentration camps in exchange for money from Jewish sources in Palestine and the United States. Pollocks claimed that he agreed to serve as a double agent only with the Haganah's knowledge in order to distribute disinformation to the Germans. *See also* GERMAN INTELLIGENCE IN THE MIDDLE EAST; JEWISH AGENCY IN PALESTINE; ITALIAN INTELLIGENCE IN PALESTINE.

GERMAN INTELLIGENCE IN THE MIDDLE EAST. Germany joined the struggle for influence in the Middle East only in the last decade of the 19th century. Since the beginning of **World War I**, several prominent emissaries of German intelligence were simultaneously working in the Middle East. The most outstanding was Karl Wassmus, who had influence on a number of Iranian tribes. Wassmus managed to set up an impressive human intelligence cell that covered Persia, the gulf region, and the eastern area of Afghanistan.

After 1936, Germany increased its espionage activities in the Middle East. Many German agents came to the region, and every one of them had a cover story. The agents had paid attention to the anti-British moods of the Arab population and to the establishment of ties with leaders of national minorities, in particular, the Kurds. Fritz Grobba of the German Foreign Ministry and Franz Mayer of German intelligence achieved special success in organizing Germany's covert activities in the Middle East. Grobba used his cover of a diplomatic position as Germany's ambassador to Iraq and Saudi Arabia (1936–1941). Grobba was assisted by Franz Mayer of German intelligence. Grobba also used the diplomatic cover of secretary in the German embassy in Ankara, Turkey. In the spring of 1941, Grobba and Mayer played one of the key roles in organizing a pro-German mutiny in Baghdad. In turn, Mayer, who had a good command of the Russian and Farsi languages, headed the German Secret Service network in Persia from the fall of 1940 until late summer 1943. Mayer managed to organize from scratch the Iranian Army and to recruit many politicians, including those from the shah's inner circle. To neutralize German intelligence, in August 1941, the Soviet Union and Great Britain dispatched their troops to Iran. In addition to Iraq and Iran, German secret services had an appreciable influence in Turkey, Syria, Palestine, Egypt, and other North African countries.

After **World War II** ended, leaning on old ties among the Arab nationalists, many former army and Secret Service officers of the Third Reich found refuge in the Middle East. According to figures published in the Western press, their number in the Middle Eastern countries reached 8,000 persons by the mid-1950s. Many of them had played a decisive role in the formation of army special units and departments of intelligence and counterintelligence in Arab countries.

In 1946, the former chief of Foreign Armies East (Fremde Heere Ost) in Germany's Wehrmacht, Reinhard Gehlen, enjoyed American support and, with the assistance of his former comrades-in-arms, set up a Secret Service unit that was subsequently transformed into West German subordinates located in Arab countries, an extensive agent network in the Middle East.

Gehlen succeeded especially in tracing the activities of the Soviet Union in the Middle East. For this reason, Gehlen became especially attractive for the United States and its Western allies, who sought to cooperate with the Bundesnachrichtendienst (BND; Federal Intelligence Service). In the late 1950s, Gehlen initiated cooperation with **Israeli intelligence**. After the establishment of diplomatic relations between West Germany and Israel in spring 1965, the intelligence cooperation between the two countries extended further. The cooperation between West Germany's BND and the Israeli **Mossad** continued after Gehlen's retirement in 1968.

Since the beginning of the 1990s, German intelligence has played a key role in negotiations to release prisoners of war and hostages. In December 1991, Bernd Schmidbauer was appointed the new coordinator of German intelligence at the chancellor's bureau. After tough negotiations with Lebanese Shi'ites, Schmidbauer declared the release of the German captives in Lebanon. Schmidbauer got acquainted with prominent figures in the Israeli establishment, with leaders of **Hizballah**, and also with ministers of intelligence and security of the Islamic Republic of Iran. As a consequence, on 17 June 1992, two German citizens who were being held as hostages in Lebanon by the Hizballah, Heinrich Strubig and Thomas Kemptner, returned home. This was only the beginning of Germany's active participation in the release of war prisoners, convicts, and hostages in the Middle East. Until the end of the 1990s, owing to the efforts of Schmidbauer and his assistants, Berlin (the key Western partner of Iran) became the main mediator in secret contacts between Hizballah and Israel.

Between 1991 and 2004, almost all of the deals of releasing prisoners and hostages were arranged by German mediators. No other state ever managed to establish such an effective secret contact between Hizballah and Israel. After the Lebanon War II broke out in July 2006, Israel and Hizballah addressed Berlin with the request to arrange the next exchange of captives. The director of German intelligence served as the main negotiator with Hizballah, Iran, and **Syrian intelligence**. *See also* GERMAN INTELLIGENCE IN PALESTINE; HIJAZ OPERATION.

GHAZALI, RUSTUM. In 2002, Rustum Ghazali was appointed by Syrian President Bashir al-Assad as the commander of **Syrian intelligence** in Lebanon. He replaced Colonel **Ghazi Kanaan**. Rustum Ghazali, as was common to Syrian intelligence officers, became involved in the local drug trade. After the assassination of former Lebanese prime minister Rafik al-Hariri in early 2005, Syria was forced by the international community to withdraw its army from Lebanon. Syrian indeed withdrew its 15,000 men from Lebanon, and Ghazali relocated to Syria. However, some feel that Syria still interferes in Lebanese politics through parts of its intelligence apparatus left behind in the country; Syria denies the charges. *See also* LEBANESE INTELLIGENCE.

GLUBB PASHA (1897–1986). Lieutenant General Sir John Bagot Glubb, better known as Glubb Pasha, was a British officer who led and trained Transjordan's **Arab Legion** as its commanding general from 1939 to 1956. His career in the Middle East started in 1920, after serving in the Royal Engineers for five years. He was transferred to Iraq, which was then governed by Great Britain under a League of Nations mandate. In 1922, Glubb was appointed as an intelligence officer. In 1930, he became an officer of the Arab Legion, where he subsequently served in different high positions. The next year he formed the Desert Patrol, a force consisting exclusively of Bedouins, which successfully curbed the Bedouin practice of raiding neighboring tribes in the southern part of the country. In 1939, Glubb succeeded Frederick G. Peake as the commander of the Arab Legion and went on to transform it into the best trained force in the Arab world.

During **World War II**, he led attacks on Arab leaders in Iraq, as well as the Vichy regime in Lebanon and Syria. Glubb remained in charge of the defense of the West Bank following the armistice between Israel and the Hashemite kingdom of Jordan in March 1949. He served as the commander of the Arab Legion until March 1956, when he was dismissed by King Hussein, who wanted to distance himself from the British and disprove the contention of Arab nationalists that Glubb was the actual ruler of Jordan. Differences between Glubb and Hussein had been apparent since 1952, especially over defense arrangements, the promotion of Arab officers, and the funding of the Arab Legion. Despite his decommission, however, he remained a close friend of the king. He spent the rest of his life writing books and articles, mostly on his experiences in the Middle East.

GORBANIFAR, MANUCHER. An Iranian exile, Gorbanifar served in the shah's security forces and later acted as a businessman trading in carpets. He was reported to have deep connections in the ayatollah's regime of postrevolution Iran, serving as a middleman in the secret affair between Iran and the West that later came to be known as the Iran–Contra or Irangate affair. This affair was a triple-sided weapons deal conducted between the United States, Israel, and Iran that involved selling antitank Lau missiles and later antiaircraft Hawk missiles to Iran from Israel, with an upgrading of the Israeli weapons along the way, in return for Iranian intervention in the release of the U.S. hostages kidnapped by terror organizations around the world (the first being the Reverend Benjamin Weir, who was kidnapped in Beirut in 1984). In the other direction, the Israelis would secretly convey weapons to the Nicaraguan underground Contras (Contrarevolucionarios) to support their fight against the pro-Soviet Sandinista government, thereby obviating the need to inform the U.S. Congress about the matter.

GREAT ARAB REVOLT. The Great Arab Revolt, also known as the Arab Revolt in Palestine, lasted from 1936 until 1939 and consisted of a strike and acts of sabotage against British forces, as well as the assassination of British officials and Jewish civilians. The Great Arab Revolt is sometimes referred to by the Arabs as the Great Uprising and is known in Hebrew as Meoraot or Praot (riots). It is not to be confused with the **Arab Revolt** led by **Thomas Edwards Lawrence** and Sharif Hussein in the Arab Peninsula during **World War I**. The revolt was triggered by Arab dissatisfaction with the relatively large number of Jewish immigrants arriving in the early 1930s and worsening economic conditions due to the world depression and other factors. This revolt signaled the real beginning of active involvement of the Arabs in the Palestinian cause.

In 1935, the followers of Sheikh Izz ad-Din al-Qassam, who was killed in a shootout with the British, initiated a general strike in Jaffa and Nablus and then launched attacks on Jewish and British installations. During the first days of the strike, 85 Jews were killed by

Arabs. As the months wore on, sporadic attacks by villagers gave way to armed bands. The Arabs attacked British police, officials, and soldiers as well as Jews, and caused extensive property damage to oil pipelines and railways.

The Arab Higher Committee (AHC) officially condemned such violence while behind the scenes it provided incitement and possibly financing as well. The armed bands and the AHC were probably funded by Fascist Italy and perhaps by Nazi Germany. The Sherut Yedioth (SHAI; Information Service), which was the intelligence arm of the Haganah (the Jewish underground militia in Palestine), found evidence of German funding, which was later confirmed by captured documents.

Early in the rebellion, **Ord Charles Wingate** was stationed in Palestine as a captain in the British intelligence service. Wingate organized special night squads staffed by British soldiers and the Haganah, which were probably the first effective counterguerilla forces in modern times. The British hired some 3,000–6,000 Jewish policemen, and the Haganah grew to a force of 6,000 to 12,000 volunteers during the period of the revolt.

On 26 September 1937, Lewis Andrews, the British district commissioner for the Galilee, was assassinated in Nazareth by Arab gunmen. The British finally began to show some resolution to end the violence, and an entire division was brought in from Egypt. They adopted harsher methods, dynamiting houses in Jaffa and Nablus as a punitive measure and a means to control dense neighborhoods. The armed bands were eventually surrounded and forced to leave Palestine but were not arrested. The British also built a network of security roads, including a security fence along the northern border to prevent the infiltration of terrorists.

In an attempt to put an end to revolt, the Peel Commission's members arrived in Palestine on 11 November 1937 headed by William Wellesley Peel. After hearing both Palestinian Arab and Jewish arguments, the Peel Commission (formerly known as the British Royal Commission of Inquiry) concluded that the two sides were irreconcilable and recommended the partition of Palestine. The Jewish executive group accepted the proposal, but the AHC rejected the partition offer. The AHC rejection of the partition plan led to the resumption of the revolt.

The official Jewish response was one of restraint. However, this policy of restraint and cooperation with the British was frustrating for the general Jewish population, which was under attack. It provided a natural political target for the revisionist faction (Irgun), which insisted on armed action and had never wanted to cooperate with the British in the first place. The Irgun, which was another underground militia of the Jewish community in Palestine, began a bombing campaign against Arab civilians despite the official condemnation of such acts by the Zionist movement. The first such attack killed two Arabs in a bus depot in Jerusalem, followed by a number of fatal attacks throughout the country. In April 1938, the Irgun ambushed an Arab bus. The ambush resulted in no deaths, but the British caught the three perpetrators and hanged Shlomo Ben Yosef, the only Jew to be hanged in the uprising. Finally, in 1939, the Great Arab Revolt calmed down. *See also* ISRAELI INTELLIGENCE.

GREAT SYRIAN REVOLT. The Great Syrian Revolt of 1925 is also known as the Druze Revolt. However, many other tribes besides the Druze took part in the revolt. In 1918, the League of Nations carved the new country of Syria out of the defeated Ottoman Empire and placed it under French mandate following **World War I**. Several states that had been part of the Ottoman Empire were forcefully united as Greater Syria. Many of these states remained as displeased with the French mandate as they had been under the Ottoman Empire, and their dissatisfaction was reflected in anti-French revolts.

Although France occupied the country against the wishes of most of its inhabitants, the French intelligence assessment was that the situation was calm and stable. In 1925, the political and military situation in Syria was already deteriorating. For more than five years, the supporters of a plan for a "Pan-Arabic Kingdom" had been openly stirring up anti-French feeling among the Druze. The death of Emir Selim, the pro-French governor of the Djedel Druze, was the spark that set off open revolt among the tribes. The arrest and detainment of several Druze leaders in July 1925 resulted in a violent revolt led by Sultan al-Atrash.

On 25 July 1925, some 7,000 Druze warriors threatened Soueida and defeated the French troops led by Captain Normand. Reinforcements were sent but were again attacked in turn on 2–3 August 1925, killing nearly 600 and wounding 300 in the process. Another request for reinforcements was met by a squadron headed for an operational area some 45 miles south of Damascus on 2 September 1925. On 11 September, they received orders to take up a defensive position at Messifre after intelligence reports that 3,000 rebels were moving on Messifre. On 16 September, a patrol was attacked by 800 Druze rebels but managed to break away with one dead and four wounded.

On 17 September 1925, the attack was launched. Waves of warriors on foot and horseback attacked the Legionnaires, who fought all night. The Druze managed to reach the foot of the walls, killing all the guards. It was only on the second night, after bombardment by three French aircraft, that the Druze rebels finally withdrew. The battle cost them about 500 dead and the same number of wounded. Of the French forces, 47 were killed and 83 wounded at Messifre.

On 5 November, a French Legion cavalry unit set up quarters in the old citadel of Rachaya, a half-ruined fort dominating a large village of about 3,000 inhabitants. Reconnaissance indicated that an equal number of rebels to that of the village population were converging on the fort. Patrols were increased, and the position was put in a state of defense. On 18 November, two sections were attacked while on patrol, leaving them with two dead, three wounded, and three missing.

This was followed on 20 November by heavy fire from the surrounding hilltops and then the next day by a major Druze attack on the village. In the face of resistance by the Legionnaires, who were already running short of ammunition, the Druze retreated, but only to gather reinforcements and return the next day. A rush by the Druze overwhelmed the defenders of the gate, and the Legionnaires fell back, at a cost of about 100 wounded. The position was looking desperate when French aircraft suddenly appeared and bombed the Druze amassed around the walls. On the morning of 24 November, the siege was lifted and the Druze pulled back into the mountains, with some 400 dead and 34 wounded. Thus, although the Druze initially defeated the French in August and September, the turning point in the revolt was when the fighting reached Damascus and the French bombed the city.

French intelligence had initially regarded the violence as inconsequential, concluding that there was no need to alarm Damascus about a prospective outbreak of armed revolt. Those intelligence assessments proved to be wrong, and Druze discontent continued to expand. Actually, there were several anti-French revolts during the mandate period in Syria. Theoretically, there was nothing to hinder a successful revolt except failure by the French intelligence services. That they did not act was a reflection of the political instability of the government in France itself. The lack of continuity in military and political policies made the French in Syria hesitant about initiating any drastic moves and further fueled the revolts.

However, the revolts were poorly planned and coordinated for the most part and suffered from a lack of resources. Few were little more than the actions of a disorganized mob, and all of the revolts failed. The Druze Revolt in southern Syria was the only one with better coordination, and the French had to fight much harder to defeat the attack. Indeed, it was the largest and longest-lasting insurgency against colonial rule in the interwar Middle East. The fact that the rebels were divided helped the French put an end to the revolt. Had the planners of the revolts been able to unify their forces and had there been even more French intelligence failures, the outcome might have been different. By mid-1927, the revolts were essentially over. But despite the failure of the Great Syrian Revolt to liberate Syria from French occupation, it provided a model of popular nationalism and resistance that is still followed in the Middle East today. *See also* FRENCH INTELLIGENCE IN THE MIDDLE EAST.

GULF WAR (2003). *See* OPERATION IRAQI FREEDOM; U.S. PROPAGANDA IN IRAQ.

– H –

HAFEZ, MUSTAFA. In the 1950s, Colonel Mustafa Hafez was the commander of **Egyptian intelligence** in Gaza. That was the time when Egypt customarily sent cells of marauding Arabs (*fedayeen*) from the Gaza Strip into Israel for the purpose of terrorizing Israeli society by murdering Israelis. Hafez was in charge of those operations.

In June 1956 the director of the Israeli Military Intelligence, Major General Yehoshafat Harkabi, and Colonel Haim Levakov proposed a plan to assassinate Hafez, which succeeded. Hafez was killed on 12 June 1956 by an explosive device hidden in a book handed to him by an Egyptian double agent. The agent, who did not know what he was carrying, was blinded in the blast. Another book bomb was sent the next day via the East Jerusalem post office to Colonel Salah Mustafa, the Egyptian military attaché in Amman, who had dispatched infiltrators via the West Bank to Israel. He opened the package and was killed by the blast.

In the 1960s, mail bombs became a central assassination tool of **Israeli intelligence**, especially as part of the Damocles operation against former Nazi German scientists who were developing a missile program for Egypt.

HAMAS. In Arabic, Hamas is an acronym for Harakat Al-Muqawama Al-Islamia, which means Islamic Resistance Movement; *hamas* is also a word meaning "zeal." Formed in late 1987 as an outgrowth of the Palestinian branch of the Muslim Brotherhood, this radical Islamic fundamentalist organization became active in the early stages of the *intifada*, operating primarily in the Gaza Strip but also in Judea and Samaria. Various Hamas elements have used both political and violent means, including **terrorism**, to pursue the goal of establishing an Islamic Palestinian state in place of Israel. Loosely structured, some elements work clandestinely while others work openly through mosques and social service institutions to recruit members, raise money, organize activities, and distribute propaganda. In the January 2006 election, Hamas won a majority of seats in the Palestinian legislature.

Hamas activists, especially those in the Izz al-Din al-Qassam brigades, have conducted many attacks—including large-scale suicide bombings—against Israeli civilian and military targets. In the early 1990s, they also targeted suspected Palestinian collaborators and **Fatah** rivals. Hamas increased its operational activity in 2002 and 2003, claiming numerous attacks against Israeli interests. The group has not targeted American interests, although some U.S. citizens have been killed in Hamas operations; instead, it continues to confine its attacks to Israelis inside Israel and the occupied territories.

Hamas probably has tens of thousands of supporters and sympathizers and likely receives some funding from Iran, but it primarily relies on donations from Palestinian expatriates around the world and private benefactors in moderate Arab states. Some fund-raising and propaganda activity takes place in Western Europe and North America. In December 2005 the Israel Security Agency (ISA) exposed Hamas terrorist infrastructures in the regions of Hebron and Ramallah that perpetrated severe terrorist attacks prior to and during the lull in the fighting (including a suicide bombing attack in Beersheba). The uncovering of the infrastructures prevented numerous additional terrorist attacks planned to be perpetrated during the lull.

The Central Intelligence Agency of the United States and the British MI6 gathered information about Hamas; accordingly, after Hamas achieved control of the Gaza Strip in 2006, its leaders seized intelligence files that included the personal files of its leaders and their involvement in terrorism. The files detailed al-Fatah contacts with Iran, **Hizballah**, Hamas, Islamic Jihad, and **al Qaeda**.

With the support of Iranian intelligence and **Syrian intelligence** directorates, Hamas blocked al-Fatah in its attempt to renew its support bases in Palestinian society. Hamas's intelligence windfall prevented Fatah from significantly resisting Hamas's consolidation of control over the Gaza Strip and the expansion of Hamas's rule to Judea and Samaria.

HANAM, AISHA (1895–?). Born in Istanbul, Aisha Hanam was the daughter of Rifat Bek, who was a member of the **Turkish intelligence** community. Bek was executed by the members of "Unity and Progress," who accused him of involvement in the counterrevolution of 1909. On the eve of **World War I**, Aisha Hanam was recruited by British intelligence while living in Cairo, where she worked as a companion to a local dignitary. She established complex spying and sabotage networks comprised of local Arabs and conducted comprehensive espionage activities in Lebanon, Israel, Syria, and Jordan.

HARIRI'S ASSASSINATION. Rafik al-Hariri served as Lebanon's prime minister from 1992 to 1998 and again from 2000 until his resignation on 20 October 2004. He was a self-made billionaire and business tycoon who played a leading role in the reconstruction of Beirut. He headed five cabinets during his tenure. Hariri was assassinated by explosives on 14 February 2005 as his motorcade was driving through downtown Beirut. The International Independent Investigating Commission, which was convened under the supervision of the United Nations, suggested in its October 2005 report that both **Syrian intelligence** agents and Lebanese were involved in the assassination plot. However, the Syrian government has categorically denied having any prior knowledge of the bombing.

HARMER, YOLANDE (?–1959). Born in Egypt to a Turkish–Jewish mother, her maiden name was Yolande Gabai and her Hebrew name Yolande Har-Mor. She is thought of as the Israeli Mata Hari. Harmer was a widow with one son from her third husband, a wealthy South African businessman. She was recruited in Egypt to the Political Department of the Jewish Agency during a visit to that country by the head of the department, Moshe Sharett, in 1945. Posing as a journalist, Harmer made many important contacts within high Egyptian echelons, including senior editors of the leading Cairo newspaper *al-Ahram*. Harmer also made exceptional contacts with foreign diplomats in Egypt. Following meetings of the Arab League in Cairo in December 1947 and February 1948, she reported to the Political Department in Tel-Aviv on the resolutions adopted, mailing them via Europe. From her sources, she found out the plans of the Egyptian and other Arab armies following the approaching termination of the British mandate in Palestine. From a British officer stationed in Egypt, she obtained information about relations between Great Britain and the kingdom of Jordan. Much of the material Harmer obtained was of high strategic value. She also set up an espionage network in Egypt, although it collapsed upon the Arab invasion of Israel on 15 May 1948.

In June 1948, Harmer was arrested in Egypt. In prison she fell ill, and by some means she received help to be released. In August 1948, she left Egypt for Paris, where she kept in touch with her Egyptian contacts. After October 1948, Harmer became the key figure of the Paris branch of the Israeli Foreign Ministry's Middle East Department. In the 1950s, she worked for Israel in Madrid.

HASAN, BARZAN IBRAHIM, AL- (1951–2007). Barzan Ibrahim al-Hasan was Saddam Hussein's stepbrother and was also known as Barzan Ibrahim al-Tikriti, which means that he was born in the city of Tikrit. Al-Hasan was appointed as one of the heads of the Directorate (M4) of the Iraqi Mukhabarat, the Iraqi Intelligence Service (IIS), in the 1970s. During his career in **Iraqi intelligence**, al-Hasan also performed jobs for the Iraqi secret police and played a key role in the Iraqi regime's execution of opponents at home and assassinations abroad. He was also known for his ruthlessness and brutality in purging the Iraqi military of anyone seen as disloyal. In 1989, al-Hasan became Iraq's representative to the United Nations Human Rights Committee in Geneva, Switzerland, for almost a decade. Under the cover of this diplomatic position, he carried out many clandestine operations.

When the 2003 **Operation Iraqi Freedom** began, al-Hasan became one of the top targets for U.S. forces. In April 2003, warplanes dropped six satellite-guided bombs on a building in the city of Ramadi, west of Baghdad, where he was thought to be hiding. By late summer 2003, al-Hasan was captured alive with a large entourage of bodyguards by U.S. Army Special Forces in Baghdad. He was turned over to Iraq's interim government on 30 June 2004, and his trial started on 19 October 2005. On 5 November 2006, al-Hasan was sentenced to death by hanging, and on 5 January 2007, the death sentence was executed. *See also* IRAQI DIRECTORATE OF GENERAL MILITARY INTELLIGENCE; IRAQI DIRECTORATE OF GENERAL SECURITY; IRAQI SPECIAL SECURITY ORGANIZATION.

HASSAN, ALI (1941–). Ali Hassan Abd al-Majid al-Tikriti was born in the city of Tikrit and was Saddam Hussein's first cousin. He served as the head of **Iraq's Directorate of General Security** (DGS), also known as the Internal State Security or the Secret Police (al-Amn al-Amm), from 1980–1987 and was then appointed by Saddam Hussein as minister of defense. Ali Hassan was one of the key figures in the Iraqi campaigns against rebel forces (Kurds, Shi'ites, and other religious dissidents). He undertook repressive measures, including deportations of the population and mass killings. He also ordered the use of chemical weapons against the Iraqi Kurds, earning him the nickname "Chemical Ali." Ali Hassan was captured during the 2003 **Operation Iraqi Freedom** by U.S. forces and charged with war crimes. In June 2007, he was convicted and was sentenced to death for crimes committed in the al-Anfal campaign of the 1980s. An appeals court upheld the death sentence in September 2007. On 28 February 2008, his death sentence was approved by the Iraqi government, but there is no clear-cut information that Ali Hassan was in fact executed. *See also* IRAQI DIRECTORATE OF GENERAL MILITARY INTELLIGENCE; IRAQI INTELLIGENCE; IRAQI SPECIAL SECURITY ORGANIZATION.

HEWEEDY, AMEEN (1921–). Ameen Heweedy was appointed in the 1970s as director of the Egyptian State Security Investigations (GDSSI; Mubahath al-Dawla). In that year, Heweedy managed to detect an Israeli oil rig being shipped from Canada to Sinai. In a covert action, clandestine GDSSI agents and frogmen succeeded in tracing the oil rig and detonated explosives that crippled it. *See also* EGYPTIAN INTELLIGENCE.

HIJAZ OPERATION. The Egyptian Expeditionary Force (EEF) in Cairo coordinated the entire signals intelligence (SIGINT) operation throughout the Middle East during **World War II**, initially only interception but later on cryptanalysis as well. Several Special Wireless Sections (SWS) were established throughout the region, covering German and Ottoman wireless transmissions in Turkey, Syria, Palestine (including Transjordan), and the Hijaz.

The first Ottoman wireless station in the Hijaz was set up in Medina in June 1915 at the initiative of the Germans, who were interested in utilizing it for communicating with their troops in East Africa. There is no evidence, however, that it was actually operated regularly before the outbreak of the **Arab Revolt**. By late 1916, most of German and Ottoman codes and ciphers in the Middle East were successfully broken and regularly read. Decrypted German messages in northern Palestine and Syria disclosed the imminent arrival of troop reinforcements, armaments, munitions, and supplies. In the Transjordan and Hijaz regions in particular, almost no military movement went unnoticed.

Radio communication between stations in the Hijaz and Transjordan and the main headquarters in Damascus became one of the most important sources for information on the Arab Revolt and on the intentions and capabilities of the Ottoman forces there. After late 1916, the Fourth Army headquarters in Damascus operated a special wire transmission network with the stations in the Hijaz and Transjordan, conducted in the Turkish language and entirely by Turkish wireless operators. Other networks that connected Damascus to stations in Syria and Palestine were operated in German.

The contribution of the Hijaz-derived SIGINT to the war effort is evident from the fact that the vulnerability of cables to sabotage in the Hijaz after the outbreak of the Arab Revolt in June 1916 forced dependence on the wireless stations for contact with the north. At the same time in Palestine and Syria, however, the Ottomans were able to rely on a landline system during the entire period of the war, with wireless communication used mostly as a backup. In the Hijaz, there were two separate telegraphy circuits running alongside the railway: a line for civilian and military purposes, and a "traffic line" for the internal use of the 89 railroad stations. Arab raiding parties damaged telegraph lines as hundreds of telegraph poles were pulled down and long sections of wire were cut. With the spread of the Arab Revolt to the Ma'an area in June 1917, damage caused to the line reached a level that seriously hampered Ottoman efforts to repair it. At least 30 more raids involving damage to the telegraph system were reported during July–October.

T. E. Lawrence boasted that it was he who instigated cutting the lines, with the aim of forcing the Ottomans to use wireless transmissions. The British read their messages in order to keep the military movements of the Turks public. It is unclear if they actually initiated this activity or merely benefited by it, but clearly this form of sabotage was one of the main causes of the extensive use made by the Ottomans of wireless in that region.

After October 1916, wireless intelligence developed into the most important means of information gathering on the Ottoman Army in the Hijaz and Transjordan. Owing to wireless stations established within a year in Medina, Hadia, Mada'in, Tabuk, Ma'an, and Dar'a, British intelligence was privy to every detail of the defense of the Hijaz, including operational plans and deliberations over such difficult decisions as whether to allocate the few unassigned forces in the region to reinforce the Hijaz or Palestine. The intercepted messages detailed all troop movement schedules and updates when delays occurred, in addition to a complete picture of the enemy's military structure and organization, order of battle, deployment, fitness, casualties and losses, level of food and ammunition stocks, division of responsibility, and morale of all the units in the area. This information also served to verify and correct reports received from Arab sources, whose credibility with the British was low, thereby contributing toward a more balanced evaluation of the revolt.

The massive collection of SIGINT from the Hijaz expanded even further during 1918, when the Ottomans increased the number of wireless stations there to at least eight high-frequency static and mobile stations, all controlled by a central station in Damascus. Hence, information on enemy intent was obtained regularly and practically in full, with only occasional and partial interception in Palestine. Information derived from radio interception was routinely distributed to parties that interacted with the Arab forces, such as the Arab Bureau. A considerable portion of the summaries on the enemy situation that were prepared by Lawrence for the *Arab Bulletin* was, in fact, based on this source. Circumstantial evidence of the direct contribution of radio intelligence to operations in Arabia leads to the conclusion that actions were taken by British officers in the Hijaz on the basis of technical information gleaned from intercepted messages of Ottoman wireless operators.

Monitoring the Hijaz and Transjordan communications also provided a source for intelligence regarding Ottoman intentions and capabilities in Palestine through messages sent to both sectors detailing the transfer of units from one sector to another as reinforcement. Telegrams transmitted to Palestine addressees were routed via relatively secure wire-line circuits, but the same messages were simultaneously sent by wireless to the Hijaz and picked up by intelligence. *See also* ARAB BUREAU IN CAIRO.

HILMI, ABBAS. In 1964, Captain Hilmi, a pilot in the Egyptian Air Force (EAF) dissatisfied with the Nasser regime, defected to Israel flying his Soviet-made Yak trainer aircraft. Israel was more interested in obtaining a Soviet-built MiG fighter, but Abbas Hilmi was still given a very warm reception. He provided **Israeli intelligence** with important information about the EAF. His main use, however, was for propaganda purposes. In widely broadcast interviews, he condemned the Egyptian intervention in Yemen and revealed that Nasser used poison gas against the Yemeni royalists. He was offered a well-paid job in Israel, but it was difficult for him to get used to the Jewish state and its customs.

Hilmi rejected an offer of political asylum in Israel, where he could remain in relative safety, and instead insisted on moving to South America. The **Mossad** arranged a new identity for him, gave him a generous sum of money to build his new life, and taught him the basics of remaining safe under his new assumed identity. However, Hilmi committed a series of fatal errors in Buenos Aires, including mailing a postcard from Argentina to his mother in Egypt. The way to tracing him was soon open. He later met a young Arab woman at a nightclub who invited him to her apartment in Buenos Aires. It was an Egyptian trap. Egyptian secret agents lay in wait for him at the apartment; they took him and smuggled him aboard an Egyptian cargo vessel bound for Cairo. Hilmi was convicted of treason in an Egyptian court and executed. *See also* STEALING THE MIG-21.

HINDAWI AFFAIR. In April 1986, the Syrians attempted to blow up an El Al airplane departing from London's Heathrow Airport with a bag of explosives taken onboard by an unwitting courier, but the plot was foiled. The courier had been dispatched by Nizar Hindawi, a Jordanian of Palestinian origin who was directly controlled by the Air Force Security Directorate headed by Syrian Major General **Muhammad al-Khouli**. Hindawi was convicted by a court in Great Britain, and for a short period thereafter Britain severed its relations with Syria; the United States also withdrew its ambassador from Damascus.

The Syrian attempt to blow up the El Al aircraft occurred after the **Mossad** and Israeli Military Intelligence had obtained information that the chief Palestinian terrorists—George Habash, Nayef Hawatmah, Ahmed Gibril, and **Abu Nidal**—were flying back from Tripoli, Libya, to Damascus, Syria. This information was not correct, however. Four Israeli F-16 jets forced the Gulfstream airplane to land in a military airport in the north of Israel. The passengers were taken out of the airplane with their hands up. **Israeli intelligence** found that not one of the wanted men was among the passengers, although some Syrian officials close to President Hafez Assad were.

HINDI, AMIN FAWZI, AL- (1940–). Born in Gaza, Amin Fawzi al-Hindi served as the senior security officer in **Fatah** in the 1970s. Al-Hindi coordinated relations between the Palestinian Liberation Organization (PLO) and the U.S. Central Intelligence Agency (CIA) through the 1980s. After the establishment of the Palestinian National Authority (PNA) in 1994, he became chief of the PNA's General Intelligence Service (GIS; Mudiriyat al-Amn al-Amma) with the rank of general. Al-Hindi served as a member of the Palestinian Higher Committee of Negotiations. On 16 July 2004, he decided to resign because of the state of chaos in the PNA and the lack of reforms, but his resignation was postponed. In April 2005, the chair of the PNA, Mahmoud Abbas, accepted his resignation, and Amin al-Hindi was replaced by **Tareq Abu Rajab** as chief of the GIS.

HIZB UL-MUJAHIDIN (HM). Hizb ul-Mujahidin, the largest Kashmiri militant group, was founded in 1989 and officially supports the liberation of Jammu and Kashmir and its accession to Pakistan, although some cadres are pro-independence. HM most likely has several hundred members in Indian-controlled Kashmir and Pakistan.

As the militant wing of Pakistan's largest Islamic political party, the Jamaat-i-Islami, HM is currently focused on Indian security forces and politicians in Jammu and Kashmir and has conducted operations jointly with other Kashmiri militants. It reportedly operated in Afghanistan through the mid-1990s and trained alongside the Afghan Hizb-i-Islami Gulbuddin (HIG) in Afghanistan until the Taliban takeover. The group, led by Syed Salahuddin, is made up primarily of ethnic Kashmiris. The group is getting direct support from **Pakistani intelligence** and most probably from Bangladeshi intelligence.

HM has conducted a number of operations against Indian military targets in Kashmir. The group also occasionally strikes at civilian targets in Kashmir, but it has not engaged in terrorist acts elsewhere.

HIZBALLAH. This Lebanon-based radical Shi'ite group takes its ideological inspiration from the Iranian Revolution and the teachings of the late Ayatollah Khomeini. Hizballah was formed in 1982 in response to the Israeli invasion of Lebanon and is dedicated to eliminating Israel from the region. The Majlis al-Shura (Consultative

Council) is the group's highest governing body and is led by Secretary General Hassan Nasrallah. Hizballah's television station, al-Manar, uses inflammatory images and reporting in an effort to encourage the *intifada* and promote Palestinian suicide operations.

Hizballah is closely allied with and often directed by Iran but has the capability and will to act alone. The group has actively participated in Lebanon's political system since 1992, though it formally advocates the ultimate establishment of Islamic rule in Lebanon. It has also been a strong ally for Syria, helping the country advance its political objectives in the region. In 2003, Hizballah established a presence in Iraq, but its activities there have been limited thus far.

Hizballah operates mainly in the southern suburbs of Beirut, the Bekaa Valley, and southern Lebanon. The group has also established cells in Europe, Africa, South America, North America, and Asia. It receives financial aid, training, weapons, and explosives, as well as political, diplomatic, and organizational assistance, from Iran. It also receives diplomatic, political, and logistical support from Syria and financial support from sympathetic business interests and individuals worldwide, largely through the Lebanese diaspora.

Following their slogan "Death to America," the group was responsible for the kidnapping and detention of Americans and other Westerners in Lebanon during the 1980s. Hizballah is known or suspected to have been involved in numerous anti-American and anti-Israeli terrorist attacks, including the suicide truck bombings of the U.S. embassy and Marine barracks in Beirut in 1983 and the U.S. embassy annex in Beirut in September 1984. Three members of Hizballah—**Imad Mugniyah**, Hasan Izz-al-Din, and Ali Atwa—are on the Federal Bureau of Investigation's list of the 22 most-wanted terrorists for the 1985 hijacking of TWA Flight 847 during which a U.S. Navy diver was murdered.

Hizballah attacked the Israeli embassy in Argentina in 1992 and the Israeli cultural center in Buenos Aires in 1994. In fall 2000, Hizballah operatives captured three Israeli soldiers in the Shab'a Farms and kidnapped an Israeli noncombatant who may have been lured to Lebanon under false pretenses. On 12 July 2006, Hizballah carried out the most serious terrorist attack against Israeli forces and communities along the Israeli–Lebanese border since the Israel Defense Forces (IDF) withdrew from Lebanon in May 2000. During the attack, two Israeli soldiers were abducted, eight soldiers and one civilian woman were killed, and approximately 54 soldiers and civilians were wounded.

On the same day, the Israeli government convened an emergency meeting and stated that it viewed the Lebanese government as solely responsible for the Hizballah attack. In response to the attack, the IDF shelled Lebanese infrastructures and Hizballah targets in both north and south Lebanon. Hizballah responded by firing Katyusha rockets at Israeli population centers in the northern part of the country. These attacks are part of the Lebanon War II (2006); Lebanon War I started in June 1982.

In September 2006, Hizballah's special security apparatus had been broken up by two spy network of Lebanese agents that the Israeli **Mossad** had planted inside Hizballah before and during Lebanon War II. One network operated out of Beirut, and the second network operated out of south Lebanon. The two networks planted bugs and surveillance equipment at Hizballah command posts before and during the war. They also sprinkled special phosphorus powder outside buildings housing Hizballah's war command and rocket launchers as markers for air strikes. The result was that the Israeli Air Force (IAF) was able to dispatch its warplanes and helicopters to hit these locations with great accuracy.

Prior to Lebanon War II, the Beirut network penetrated the inner circles of Hizballah's upper echelon and was reporting on their activities and movements to their Israeli handlers. Hizballah's headquarters were located in Beirut's Shi'ite district of Dahya, the Hizballah stronghold. Short anonymous phone calls would give agents the meeting locations for picking up orders and spy equipment and dead drops for relaying their information.

The second network was composed of two subnetworks operating out of the village of Itrun opposite Kibbutz Yaron and Bint Jubeil farther west. It was run by veterans of the South Lebanese Army and commanded by Mahmoud al-Jemayel. This network was tasked to "paint" targets for the IAF and artillery. Envelopes with their orders and espionage devices were left at a preassigned spot along the security fence on the Lebanese–Israeli border. Halil Mantsur, an Itrin resident, was in charge of communications through the security fence; Muhammad Bassem, a Shi'ite from Bint Jubeil, ran field operations.

The network activated operatives recruited from south Lebanese villages and a number of Palestinians from the camps around Tyre and Sidon. They were paid US $500 per month for spying on Hizballah. A local taxi driver drove the operatives to their assignments and returned them to their homes.

The Beirut network was the more sophisticated. In addition to tactical intelligence gathering, its work spread outside Lebanon. The commander of this network was Faisal Mukleid, a young Shi'ite from the village of Jarjuara. In addition, he was captain of a fleet of small freighters that carried smuggled drugs and stolen goods between Mediterranean ports on the Italian and Egyptian coasts. The job of being a captain was used by him as a good cover story.

In 2000, Mukleid was picked up by the Italian Navy in a customs raid. In a cell awaiting trial, he was contacted by the Mossad. In no time, he was sprung and flown to Israel where he spent several months learning how to use eavesdropping and surveillance equipment.

The Lebanese Shi'ite sea captain's first mission in Lebanon was to recruit relatives and fellow Shi'ites and get them planted inside the Hizballah leadership. Toward the end of the year, he and his wife joined up as members of Hizballah. Their "devotion and zeal" was such that they were soon promoted to high ranks in the organization. Together with the agents they recruited, they quickly reached positions on the personal staffs of top political and military leaders, whom they accompanied more than once on trips to Tehran.

Exposing the Israeli spy network in their midst has made Hizballah's leaders extremely jumpy and suspicious. The networks succeeded in revealing Hizballah's command structures in south Lebanon and were heavily penetrated by agents working for the **Israeli intelligence** community. On 29 August 2006, Hizballah security officers arrested two non-Lebanese Arabs wandering around the ruined Dahya district, taking photos and drawing maps. Several forged passports were found in their possession. These agents were detained by Hizballah.

HOGARTH, DAVID GEORGE (1862–1927). As a British archeologist and scholar, David Hogarth traveled to excavations in Cyprus, Crete, Egypt, and Syria between 1887 and 1907. He was the keeper of the Ashmolean Museum in Oxford from 1909 until his death in

1927. When **World War I** broke out, Hogarth served as lieutenant commander in the Royal Navy and a key figure in British intelligence in the Middle East. He joined the Geographical Section of the Naval Intelligence Division and was later assigned to head the Arab Bureau, the special unit established to deal with the Arab Middle East. In that capacity, Hogarth worked under **Gilbert Clayton**, who was made head of all British civilian and military intelligence in Egypt. Hogarth and several others associated with the **Arab Bureau in Cairo** believed that the Arabs could not govern themselves and ought to be ruled by Europeans. *See also* BRITISH INTELLIGENCE IN EGYPT AND SUDAN.

HORESH, JOSHUA (1920–?). Born in Baghdad to Jewish parents, Horesh left Iraq in 1938 as Nazi influence spread across the country. His unique background allowed him to work with **British intelligence in Egypt** during **World War II**, where he served with distinction until jailed in Cairo. Horesh was sentenced to deportation from Egypt to Beirut, but he succeeded in escaping to Palestine and joined the British forces. This time, he secretly served the Palestinian Jewish underground, providing information on British policies toward the Jews. After the establishment of the state of Israel, Horesh served as an intelligence officer in the 1948–1949 War of Independence and successfully broke Egypt's military codes. Horesh joined the newly established **Mossad** intelligence organization and worked for it primarily in Turkey and Austria under an assumed Arab identity. *See also* IRANIAN INTELLIGENCE.

HOUSSEINIAN, RUHOLLAH (1955–). Ruhollah Hosseinian was appointed as the deputy minister of intelligence in Iran after **Saeed Emani** committed suicide in 1999. In April 2007, he was appointed by President Mahmoud Ahmadinejad as the security advisor to the president and is a member of the Council for Spreading Mahmoud Ahmadinejad's Thoughts.

HUEIJI, IBRAHIM. General Ibrahim Hueiji served as the head of Syrian Air Force Intelligence in the late 1990s and the beginning of the 2000s. General Hueiji is an Alawite from the Haddadin tribe. He was elected to the Ba'ath Party's Central Committee on 17 June 2000.

HUSSEIN, KAMIL (?–1996). General Kamil Hussein Hasan al-Majid was a first cousin and son-in-law of Iraqi President Saddam Hussein. He commanded **Iraq's Special Security Organization** (SSO; al-Amn al-Khas) from 1983 until 1989. By 1987, he had also become the overseer of the Military Industrial Commission (MIC), the Republican Guard (including the Special Republican Guard), Saddam's Special Presidential Guard, and the Ministry of Oil. Kamil Hussein had the power to fire anyone or have them placed under suspicion. In 1991, he was briefly appointed to and eventually fired as the Iraqi minister of defense. After that he was appointed by Saddam Hussein to be the minister of the Military Industrial Commission.

In August 1995, Kamil Hussein defected to Jordan. However, he believed Saddam Hussein's promise for safety upon returning to Iraq. On 23 February 1996, Kamil Hussein returned to Iraq and was assassinated by **Qusay Saddam Hussein**. In January 1997, Nawfal Mahjoom al-Tikriti was appointed as head of the SSO. *See also* IRAQI DIRECTORATE OF GENERAL MILITARY INTELLIGENCE; IRAQI DIRECTORATE OF GENERAL SECURITY; IRAQI INTELLIGENCE.

HUSSEIN, QUSAY SADDAM (1966–2003). Qusay Saddam Hussein, the son of Iraqi President Saddam Hussein, was appointed by his father as the commander of **Iraq's Special Security Organization** (SSO) in late 1991. By that time, and especially after the 1991 **Operation Desert Storm**, the SSO had lost much of its influence. Because Qusay was considered young and inexperienced, many of the responsibilities were not passed on to him. Qusay served as a civilian commander of the SSO without any military rank. He was assisted by **Kamil Hussein**, a former experienced commander of the SSO, who provided assistance particularly in the fields of collecting information and covert action. In that way, the SSO succeeded in deceiving the United Nations Special Commission's inspectors, while Qusay was engaged in commanding the Republican Guard and the Special Republican Guard. As the son of Saddam Hussein, Qusay had almost absolute power in the Iraqi regime. Officially, Qusay ended his position of commander of the SSO after he was elected as one of two deputies in charge of the military branch of the Ba'ath Party on 19 May 2001. *See also* TAWFIQ, WALID HAMID.

– I –

INTELLIGENCE AND ESPIONAGE IN LEBANON, SYRIA, AND PALESTINE DURING THE WORLD WAR. This is the translation from Arabic of the title of General **Aziz Bek**'s book. The book was published as the memoirs of Aziz Bek, who commanded the intelligence services of the Fourth Ottoman Army that ruled the Levant during **World War I**. The book reviews the espionage and sabotage actions of Jews, Arabs, and British in the Levant countries during **World War II**. The book presents the view of a **Turkish intelligence** person who perceived these actions as insidious treacheries endangering the security of his country, the Ottoman Empire.

The book was published in the Lebanese press as a serial in 1932, and a year later it was published under the title *Syria and Lebanon during the World War: Intelligence and Espionage in the Ottoman Empire.* This book covers the period from 1909 to 1917 and is written from a personal angle. The writer described events in which he played a central role and focused on the struggle with various underground movements and espionage networks.

In 1936, Bek published a second book, *Intelligence and Espionage in Syria, Lebanon, and Palestine during the World War.* This book takes into account the responses and remarks generated by the first book and keeps sequential chronological order. The first part of the book tells about the pursuit of Jewish–Israeli networks, and the second part deals with the pursuit of British–Arabic spy networks.

IRAN–IRAQ WAR. The Iran–Iraq War of 1980–1988 was multifaceted and was launched as a result of religious (Sunni versus Shi'ite) and ethnic (Arab versus Persian) differences, border disputes, and political conflicts. The outbreak of hostilities in 1980 was, in part, just another phase of a centuries-old conflict, aggravated by modern border disputes. Another contributing factor to the war was the personal animosity between Saddam Hussein and the Ayatollah Khomeini, who was bitter over his expulsion from Iraq in October 1978 after being in exile there for 14 years. Now that Khomeini was able to freely communicate with opposition forces, he quickly became the focus as an alternative to the shah, giving fundamentalist religious forces an enormous boost. On 1 February 1979, Khomeini set up an opposition government, and on 31 March, Iran became an Islamic Republic.

This turn of events disturbed Hussein, who, as a Sunni Arab, was deeply suspicious of the loyalties of the Shi'ite Muslim population in Iraq, many of whom were of Iranian ethnic origin. Persecution of Shi'ites in Iraq soon followed. The Iraqis perceived Iran's new revolutionary leadership and Islamic militant agenda as threatening not only their delicate Sunni–Shi'ite balance but also their pan-Arabism as well. Above all, Saddam Hussein's decision to invade Iran was based on his ambition to strengthen Iraq's rising power in the Arab world and to replace Iran as the dominant Persian Gulf state.

The Iran–Iraq War followed months of rising tension between the fundamentalist Islamic Republic of Iran and secular nationalist Iraq. Baghdad became more confident as it watched the once invincible Imperial Iranian Army disintegrate and as a new rebellion caused the Khomeini government severe troubles in the Kurdish region. As the Ba'athists planned their military campaign, they had every reason to be confident. Iran's armed forces, including the Pasdaran (Revolutionary Guard) troops, who were led by religious mullahs with little or no military experience, had to contend with Saddam Hussein's army of 190,000 men, 2,200 tanks, and 450 aircraft. Not only did the Iranians lack cohesive leadership, but the Iranian armed forces, according to **Iraqi intelligence** estimates, also lacked spare parts for their American-made equipment. Since the shah's overthrow, only a handful of tank units had been operative, and the rest of the armored equipment had been poorly maintained. Baghdad, on the other hand, possessed fully equipped and trained forces, and morale was running high.

The principal events that touched off the rapid deterioration in Iraqi–Iranian relations occurred during the spring of 1980. Iraq's main Shi'ite Islamic opposition group, the Iranian-supported al-Dawa, was a major factor precipitating the war. In April 2000, stirred by Iran's Islamic Revolution, al-Dawa attempted to assassinate Iraqi Foreign Minister Tariq Aziz. Shortly after that failed attack, al-Dawa was suspected of attempting to assassinate another Iraqi leader, Minister of Culture and Information Latif Nayyif Jasim. In response, the Iraqis immediately rounded up members and supporters of al-Dawa and deported thousands of Shi'ites of Iranian origin. In the summer of 1980, Saddam Hussein ordered the execution of presumed al-Dawa leader Ayatollah Sayyid Muhammad Baqr al Sadr and his sister.

In September 1980, border skirmishes erupted in the central sector of Iran with an exchange of artillery fire by both sides. On 17 September 1980, Saddam Hussein annulled a border agreement with Iran and claimed the whole Shatt el-Arab waterway that connects Iraq with the Persian Gulf. Five days later, Iraq invaded Iran, beginning what would become a long and costly war. Six Iraqi army divisions simultaneously entered Iran on three fronts in an initially successful surprise attack, where they drove as far as eight kilometers inland and occupied 1,000 square kilometers of Iranian territory.

For Iraqi planners, the only uncertainty had been the fighting ability of the Iranian Air Force, which was equipped with some of the most sophisticated American-made aircraft. On 22 September 1980, Iraq launched a massive preemptive air strike on Iranian air bases with the aim of destroying the Iranian Air Force on the ground. Iraqi forces succeeded in destroying runways and fuel and ammunition depots, but much of Iran's aircraft inventory was left intact because Iranian jets were protected in specially strengthened hangars.

Although the United States was officially neutral and claimed that it was not supplying arms to either side, it began shifting policy in favor of Iraq, having decided that an Iranian victory would not serve its interests. Thus, the United States began supporting Iraq by providing it with intelligence and military support (in secret and contrary to its official neutrality). In February 1982, the State Department removed Iraq from its list of states supporting international **terrorism**. In addition to the massive financial support already provided by the Persian Gulf States to Iraq for the war effort, assistance through loan programs was now being offered by the United States as well. In addition, U.S. authorities applied pressure to the Export-Import Bank to give Iraq financing and to enhance its credit standing so as to enable it to obtain loans from other international financial institutions.

During the Iran–Iraq War, Washington used intensively its intelligence apparatus. First the Ronald Reagan administration planned a covert action and provided Iraq with critical battle-planning assistance at a time when the U.S intelligence community was alert to the warning that Iraqi commanders would employ chemical weapons in waging the decisive battles of the Iran–Iraq War. The covert program was carried out at a time when President Reagan's top aides, including Secretary of State George P. Shultz, Defense Secretary Frank C. Carlucci, and the National Security Adviser General Colin L. Powell were publicly condemning Iraq for its use of poison gas, especially after Iraq attacked Kurds in Halabja in March 1988.

Reagan's administration decided it was imperative that Iran be thwarted so it could not overrun the important oil-producing states in the Persian Gulf. The United States provided intelligence assistance to Iraq in the form of satellite photography to help the Iraqis understand how Iranian forces were deployed against them. The information that the U.S. intelligence community provided to Iraq was the general order of battle, albeit not operational intelligence.

Though senior officials of the Reagan administration publicly condemned Iraq's employment of mustard gas, sarin, VX, and other poisonous agents, the U.S. intelligence community never withdrew its support for the highly classified program in which more than 60 officers of the Defense Intelligence Agency (DIA) were secretly providing detailed information on Iranian deployments, tactical planning for battles, plans for air strikes, and bomb-damage assessments for Iraq.

In early 1988, the Iraqi Army, assisted by U.S. planning, retook the Fao Peninsula in an attack that reopened Iraq's access to the Persian Gulf. Defense intelligence officer Lieutenant Colonel Rick Francona was sent to tour the battlefield with Iraqi officers. Francona reported to Washington that Iraq had used chemical weapons.

During the Iran–Iraq War, the main concern of the CIA and the DIA was that Iran might spread the Islamic revolution to Kuwait and Saudi Arabia. Therefore, these two agencies decided to support Iraq by providing intelligence information. The CIA provided Iraq with satellite photographs of the war front. During the 1988 February battle in the Fao Peninsula, the CIA assisted Iraq by blinding Iranian radar for three days. *See also* IRANGATE AFFAIR; IRANIAN INTELLIGENCE; OPERATION EAGER GLACIER; OPERATION EARNEST WILL; OPERATION PRAYING MANTIS; U.S. INTELLIGENCE IN IRAN.

IRANIAN BIOLOGICAL WEAPONS PROGRAM. Iran ratified the Biological Weapons Convention on 23 August 1973. However, it has advanced biologic and genetic engineering research programs supporting an industry that produces world-class vaccines for both domestic use and exportation. The dual-use nature of these facilities means that Iran, like any country with advanced biological research programs, could easily produce biological warfare agents. According to a 2005 report published by the U.S. State Department, Iran began work on offensive biological weapons during the Iran–Iraq War. Iranian activities indicate a maturing offensive program with a rapidly evolving capability that might soon include the ability to deliver these weapons by various means. Iran is known to possess cultures of many biological agents for legitimate scientific purposes that have been weaponized by other nations in the past or could theoretically be weaponized. And though it is not alleged that Iran has attempted to weaponize them, Iran possesses sufficient biological facilities to potentially do so.

In June 2004, the U.S. intelligence community stated in a 721-page report to the U.S. Congress that Iran maintains an offensive biological warfare (BW) program. Iran continued to seek dual-use biotechnical materials, equipment, and expertise. While such materials had legitimate uses, Iran's BW program could be benefiting from them. *See also* IRANIAN CHEMICAL WEAPONS PROGRAM; IRANIAN NUCLEAR WEAPONS PROGRAM.

IRANIAN CHEMICAL WEAPONS PROGRAM. Iran was a victim of chemical warfare (CW) on the battlefield that caused suffering to hundreds of thousands of both civilians and military personnel in chemical attacks during the 1980–1988 **Iran–Iraq War**. As a result, Iran has promulgated a very public stance against the use of chemical weapons, making numerous vitriolic comments against Iraq's use of such weapons in international forums. Iran did not resort to using chemical weapons in retaliation for Iraqi chemical weapons attacks during the Iran–Iraq War, though it would have been legally entitled to do so under the then-existing international treaties on the use of chemical weapons, which only prohibited the *first* use of such weapons. Following its experiences during the Iran–Iraq War, Iran signed the Chemical Weapons Convention on 13 January 1993 and ratified it on 3 November 1997.

However, according to a 2001 Central Intelligence Agency report, Iran has manufactured and stockpiled chemical weapons—including those that cause blistering, bleeding, and choking. These are most probably nerve agents, and bombs and artillery shells are used to deliver them. During the first half of 2001, Iran continued to seek production technology, training, expertise, equipment, and chemicals from Russian and Chinese entities that could be used to help Iran reach its goal of having indigenous nerve-agent production capabilities.

As a signatory of the Chemical Weapons Convention, Iran is banned from delivering chemical weapons, delivery systems, or having production facilities. Iran has not made any declaration of a weapons stockpile under the treaty.

In June 2004, the U.S. intelligence community reported in its unclassified Report to Congress on the Acquisition of Technology Relating to Weapons of Mass Destruction and Advanced Conventional Munitions that Iran continued to seek production technology, training, and expertise that could further its efforts to achieve an indigenous capability to produce nerve agents. *See also* IRANIAN BIOLOGICAL WEAPONS PROGRAM; IRANIAN NUCLEAR WEAPONS PROGRAM.

IRANIAN INTELLIGENCE. The Iranian intelligence agency during the shah's regime was called Sazeman-i Ettelaat va Amniyat-i Keshvar (SAVAK; Organization for Intelligence and National Security). It was founded in 1957 with the assistance of the Central Intelligence Agency (CIA) and the Israeli **Mossad. Ya'acov Nimrodi**, the Israeli military attaché to Tehran who was also the Mossad representative in Iran, was in charge of forming SAVAK, and by so doing, became the shah's confidant. The mission of the new organization was to monitor opponents of the shah's regime and to undertake the repression of dissident movements. SAVAK used intimidation, exile, incarceration, and torture, and sometimes also assassination. The organization was first headed by General **Taimour Bakhtiar**. The second director was General **Hassan Pakravan**, who was one of the people executed by the Revolutionary Guard after the demise of the shah's regime. The third director, General **Nematollah Nassiri**, a close associate of the shah, was appointed in 1965 and reorganized the organization to enable it to cope with the rising Islamic and communist militancy and the general political unrest.

SAVAK had virtually unlimited powers of arrest and detention, and had its own detention centers, such as the notorious Evin Prison. It is universally accepted that SAVAK subjected detainees to physical torture on a regular basis. The tasks of the organization extended beyond domestic security and included surveillance of Iranians (especially students on government stipends) abroad, especially in the United States, France, and Great Britain.

SAVAK was also involved in internal power struggles. Its first director, Taimour Bakhtiar, was assassinated by the organization in 1970, and the telephones of its U.S. director, Mansur Rafizadeh, and of General Nassiri were bugged. A personal confidant of the shah, Hussein Fardust, previously of SAVAK, was appointed head of the Imperial Inspectorate, also known as the Special Intelligence Bureau, which worked independently from the SAVAK and monitored top government officials, including SAVAK directors. SAVAK was also responsible for the planning and execution of the events of Black Friday (1978), although it is believed that Palestinian Liberation Organization operatives were also involved; there is no certainty either way. CIA monitored SAVAK and also provided it with intelligence on possible targets for elimination, especially communists, many of whom were detained or mysteriously vanished. It is believed that the last director of SAVAK was on the CIA payroll.

As late as 1978, accurate information concerning SAVAK was still restricted. Pamphlets issued by the revolutionary regime indicated that SAVAK was not just a security agency but rather a full-scale intelligence agency with more than 15,000 full-time personnel and thousands of part-time informants. The organization was monitored directly by the office of the prime minister, and its director was deputy to the prime minister for national security. Although officially it was a civilian agency, SAVAK was in fact an extension of the military, as many of its officers served simultaneously in various forces of the army.

As an organization that was initially founded to round up members of the outlawed Tudeh, SAVAK's activities expanded to include gathering intelligence and neutralizing all the regime's opponents. It developed an elaborate system monitoring practically everything and everyone, by methods such as censorship to monitor journalists, literary figures, and academics throughout the country; it was also given the power to deal with those "failing to behave." All institutions and public movements such as universities, labor unions, peasant organizations, and the like were spied on by paid informants working for the SAVAK surveillance network. The agency had active offices abroad that specialized in monitoring Iranian students who might be considered a threat to the Pahlavi rule.

Over the years, SAVAK became completely independent from the regular legal system and was given the authority to arrest and detain suspects indefinitely. SAVAK operated its own prisons such as Komite and Evin in Tehran and additional facilities throughout the country. Its activities were not monitored by the authorities. Thus, after the Islamic Revolution of 1979, the organization and its top officials were targeted for reprisals, while its headquarters was trashed, and its leadership tried and executed by *komiteh* representatives. Of the 248 military personnel executed by the state after the revolution, 61 were SAVAK officers.

In May 1979, Ayatollah Rouhollah Khomeini created the Islamic Revolutionary Guard Corps (IRGC), which was charged with protecting the revolution and its achievements. The IRGC is known in Farsi as Pasdaran. It is separate and distinct from the "regular" military, and the rivalry between the two military branches has been ever present since the founding of the Islamic Republic. Soon after the IRGC was created, it had 120,000 troops. In 1982, the IRGC dispatched troops to Lebanon in support of the Shi'ite guerrillas in their struggles against Israel. Since then, the IRGC has become active in supporting Islamic revolutionary movements in other parts of the Muslim world. The IRGC is one of the most powerful supporters of Palestinian militant groups in the West Bank, including the Palestinian Islamic Jihad and **Hamas** movements. As a result of the weapons embargo that the United States imposed after the 1979 embassy takeover in Tehran by Khomeini supporters, the IRGC built its own weapons infrastructure, procuring arms from China, North Korea, and the Soviet Union. The IRGC has overall responsibility for the country's nuclear program. It has set up several civilian companies to work on the program whose activities are being deliberately concealed from the United Nations nuclear inspection teams.

Another intelligence agency created by the Khomeini regime was the Ministry of Intelligence and Security (MOIS). It is one of the most enigmatic entities operating in the Islamic Republic and reliable information about its structure and reach is hard to come by. The supreme leader of the Islamic Revolution (Ali Khamenei) controls all of Iran's matters of defense, security, and foreign policy, and a special law dictates that the head of the MOIS must be a cleric, which deepens the supreme leader's influence.

According to the MOIS foundation law, which was passed by the Iranian Parliament in 1983, the ministry is charged with the "gathering, procurement, analysis, and classification of necessary information inside and outside the country." It is responsible for disclosing conspiracies that sabotage the integrity of the Islamic Republic. The MOIS is known in Farsi as VEVAK (Vezarat-e Ettela'at va Amniat-e Keshvar) and later it became known as SAVAMA (Sazman-e Ettela'at va Amniat-e Melli-e Iran). *See also* IRANIAN TERRORISM; ROOSEVELT, KERMIT.

IRANIAN NUCLEAR WEAPONS PROGRAM. Iran has had a nuclear weapons program for close to 50 years, beginning with a research reactor purchased from the United States in 1959. The shah's plan to build 23 nuclear power reactors by the 1990s was regarded as grandiose but not necessarily viewed as a "back door" to a nuclear weapons program, possibly because Iran did not then seek the technologies to enrich or reprocess its own fuel.

There were a few suspicions of a nuclear weapons program, but these abated in the decade between the 1979 Iranian Revolution and the end of the **Iran–Iraq War**, both of which brought a halt to nuclear activities. Iran's current plans—to construct seven nuclear power plants with 1,000 megawatts (MW) each by 2025—are still ambitious, particularly for a state with considerable oil and gas reserves. Iran argues, as it did in the 1970s, that rising domestic energy consumption should be met by nuclear power, leaving oil and gas sales to generate foreign currency. Few observers believe that such an ambitious program is necessary or economic for Iran, and many question Iran's motives in developing enrichment uranium before even a single power reactor is in operation.

Iran has asserted repeatedly that its nuclear program is strictly peaceful, stating in May 2003 that it considers the acquiring, development, and use of nuclear weapons as inhumane, immoral, illegal, and against the country's basic principles. Iran essentially asserted that such weapons have no place in its defense doctrine.

Iranian government spokesman Gholam Hussein Elham said in July 2006 that the Islamic Republic will never produce weapons of mass destruction. At the same time, Supreme Leader Ali Khamenei said in November 2004 that Iran would not give up its enrichment at any price, and former President Khatami stated in March 2005 that ending Iran's uranium enrichment program would be completely unacceptable.

Uranium enrichment can be used for both peaceful (nuclear fuel) and military (nuclear weapons) uses. However, two decades of clandestine activities have raised questions about Iran's intentions, and many have called for Iran to rebuild world confidence by refraining from enrichment and reprocessing—perhaps indefinitely. Nonetheless, the further Iran proceeds down the path of enrichment, the more difficult it will become to stop, if only for financial reasons.

In 2002, the National Council of Resistance (NCR) of Iran helped expose Iran's undeclared nuclear activities by providing information about nuclear sites at Natanz (uranium enrichment) and Arak (heavy-water production). Three years of intensive inspections by the International Atomic Energy Agency (IAEA) revealed significant, undeclared Iranian efforts in uranium enrichment (including centrifuge, atomic vapor laser, and molecular laser isotope separation techniques) and separation of plutonium, as well as undeclared, imported material. Iranian officials have delayed inspections, changed explanations for discrepancies, cleaned up facilities, and in one case, Lavizan-Shian, razed a site.

Iran tried to cover up many of its activities. Among other activities, Iran admitted in 2003 that it had conducted bench-scale uranium-conversion experiments in the 1990s, required to be reported to IAEA, and later, admitted that it had used some safeguarded material for those experiments that had been declared lost in other processes, which was clearly a safeguards violation.

Since 2003, the IAEA inspections have revealed two decades' worth of undeclared nuclear activities in Iran, including uranium enrichment and plutonium separation efforts. Inspections revealed two enrichment plants at Natanz—a pilot-scale facility planned to have 1,000 centrifuges, and a commercial-scale plant under construction, planned to have 50,000 centrifuges. The pilot-scale plant (PFEP) started up in June 2003, only to shut down after Iran suspended enrichment activities in December 2003. Since February 2006, when Iran resumed enrichment-related activities, Iran has tested small cascades of 10, 20, and then 164 machines with uranium hexafluoride gas (UF_6), all under IAEA safeguards.

Iran agreed in 2003 to suspend sensitive activities in negotiations with Germany, France, and the United Kingdom (known as the EU-3), which broke down in August 2005. On 24 September 2005, the IAEA Board of Governors found Iran to be in noncompliance with its Nonproliferation Treaty (NPT) safeguards agreement and reported Iran's case to the United Nations Security Council (UNSC) in February 2006. The UNSC called upon Iran to resuspend enrichment and reprocessing, reconsider construction of its heavy-water reactor, ratify and implement the 2003 Additional Protocol, and implement transparency measures. However, Iran has continued its enrichment activities, failing to meet deadline after deadline. In November 2005, Iran finally admitted that the Pakistani A. Q. Khan network supplied it with information on nuclear weapons casting and machining parts.

Unresolved questions about the process of the Iranian nuclear weapons program development are the sources of highly enriched uranium (HEU) particles at sites in Iran. Iranian officials asserted that HEU particles found at the Natanz pilot plant in 2003 were contaminants from foreign centrifuge assemblies, a first clue pointing to the Khan network. Iran admitted to enriching uranium to just 1.2 percent, while the particles sampled ranged from 36 percent to 70 percent U-235. In October 2003, Iranian officials admitted they tested centrifuges at the Kalaye Electric Company using UF_6 between 1998 and 2002. The IAEA report of 2006 revealed that components also came from another country besides Pakistan.

The second unresolved issue is how far Iran has pursued more sophisticated centrifuge and laser enrichment technology. The third unresolved issue is the question of the heavy-water program, which raises the question of Iran's intentions. Iran first told the IAEA that it planned to export heavy water, then suggested that the heavy water would be used as a coolant and moderator for the planned IR-40 reactor for research and development, radioisotope production, and training. However, Iran's design information for the facility, which omitted necessary hot-cell equipment for producing radioisotopes, conflicted with reported Iranian efforts to import hot-cell equipment.

Construction of the IR-40 reactor has continued, despite the IAEA board's continued calls for a halt, although Iranian officials predict that the reactor will not be operational until 2011. The heavy-water production plant reportedly has been operational since 2004. In fact, in August 2006, Iranian officials announced they would double its production.

The 2005 U.S. National Intelligence Estimate (NIE) assessment was that Tehran probably does not yet have a nuclear weapon and probably has not yet produced or acquired the fissile material. Thus, it appears it would be at least 10 years before Iran has a bomb.

On 6 June 2006, Russia, China, and the United States offered Iran a new negotiating proposal that included incentives such as affirming Iran's inalienable right to peaceful nuclear energy, assistance in building state-of-the-art light-water reactors for Iran, fuel supply guarantees, dismissing UNSC consideration of Iran's NPT noncompliance, membership in the World Trade Organization (WTO), and ending certain U.S.-imposed embargos that would enable Iran to purchase agriculture appliances and Boeing aircraft parts. In return, Iran would suspend enrichment- and reprocessing-related activities, resume implementation of the Additional Protocol, and fully cooperate with the IAEA. Iran's moratorium could be reviewed once several conditions had been met, including resolving all issues and restoring international confidence in the peaceful nature of Iran's nuclear program. The proposal also outlined several measures targeted at Iran's nuclear program should the country not agree to cooperate, including a ban on nuclear-related exports, a freeze of assets, travel and visa bans, suspension of technical cooperation with the IAEA, a ban on investment in related entities, and an end to Iranians studying abroad in nuclear- and missile-related areas. Broader measures could include an arms embargo, no support for WTO membership, and a general freeze on assets of Iranian financial institutions.

Since June 2006, the UNSC has demanded Iranian compliance and transparency, and Iran has failed to respond. The P5 (the five permanent members of the United Nations Security Council) discussed sanctions through the fall, and the UNSC ultimately adopted UNSC Resolution 1737 on 23 December 2006, which required states to prevent the supply, sale, or transfer of equipment and technology that could contribute to enrichment-, reprocessing-, and heavy-water-related activities to or missile delivery systems in Iran, as well as to freeze the funds of persons and entities involved in the nuclear and ballistic missile programs. Iran was given a deadline of 60 days to comply with the resolution and it expired on 21 February 2007. Thus, Iran did not comply with the UNSC Resolution 1737, and as a result, the UNSC resumed the discussion on imposing further sanctions on Iran.

It is unknown if Iran received the same nuclear weapon design that A. Q. Khan gave Libya. If not, then the most difficult technical stage would be the production of the fissile material. In January 2007, U.S. director of national intelligence John Negroponte delivered the U.S. Intelligence Assessment to Congress, which stated that Iran was determined to have been developing nuclear weapons. This assessment was based mainly on Iran's continuous efforts to pursue uranium enrichment.

On 3 December 2007, the U.S. National Intelligence Estimate published its analyses according to which, since 2003, Iran has probably been seeking to acquire nuclear weapons. One of Iran's interests in acquiring nuclear weapons lies in its goal of becoming the dominant state in the Middle East. By gaining a nuclear capability, Iran would also have more leverage when dealing with rival countries such as the United States, Israel and, previously, Iraq. Nuclear weapons would help solidify regime survival in Tehran and prevent outside states, such as Israel, from responding effectively to Iranian encroachment in the region. On 8 December 2007, Iran sent a formal protest to the Swiss embassy in Tehran, maintaining that the United States was "spying" on Iran's nuclear activities.

The British and **Israeli intelligence** arrived at differing conclusions. A senior British official delivered a withering assessment of U.S. intelligence-gathering abilities in the Middle East and revealed that British spies shared the concerns of Israeli defense chiefs that Iran was still pursuing nuclear weapons.

Major General Ali Jafari, the commander of the IRGC, declared on 4 August 2008 that Iran had test-fired a new naval weapon that could destroy any vessel within a range of 300 kilometers. However, Western intelligence sources were skeptical about the IRGC commander's boast of a sophisticated sea missile as "propaganda fantasy" and unfounded. By mid-August 2008, Western intelligence services assessed that the deliveries of the sea launcher were due in early September, which would have seriously impeded a possible Israeli Air Force strike against Iran's nuclear facilities. *See also* IRANIAN BIOLOGICAL WEAPONS PROGRAM; IRANIAN CHEMICAL WEAPONS PROGRAM; IRANIAN INTELLIGENCE.

IRANIAN TERRORISM. During the regime of Shah Muhammad Reza Pahlavi, Iran was not considered to be a sponsor of **terrorism**. However, during the shah's regime, human rights in Iran were not honored and opposition groups were brutally punished. Since the 1979 revolution, led by the Ayatollah Khomeini, toppled the American-backed regime of the shah, the country has been governed by Shi'ite Muslim clerics committed to a stern interpretation of Islamic law. Iran still has a price on the head of the Indian-born British novelist Salman Rushdie for what Iranian leaders call blasphemous writings about Islam in his 1989 novel, *The Satanic Verses.*

Iran today has two main leaders: Mahmoud Ahmadinejad, who is the popularly elected president, and Ayatollah Ali Khamenei, who is the supreme leader. Ahmadinejad is a conservative, anti-American, anti-Western nationalist. Since the 1979 Islamic Revolution, Iran has been involved in various terrorist activities. In November 1979, Iranian student revolutionaries widely thought to be linked to the Khomeini government occupied the American Embassy in Tehran. Iran held 52 Americans hostage for 444 days. The U.S. State Department first listed Iran as a terrorist sponsor in January 1984, and it has borne that designation every year since, despite Iran's denials of involvement. The State Department currently views Iran as the leading state sponsor of terrorism. The Islamic Revolution Guards Corps (IRGC) and the Ministry of Intelligence and Security (MOIS) are considered by U.S. intelligence as the main Iranian institutions that are involved in and support terrorist activities.

Iran mostly backs Islamist groups, including the Lebanese Shi'ite militants of **Hizballah**, which Iran helped found in the 1980s, and such Palestinian terrorist groups as **Hamas** and Palestinian Islamic Jihad. A few months after Hamas won the Palestinian National Authority (PNA) elections in January 2006, Iran pledged $50 million to the near-bankrupt PNA. The United States, among other nations, has cut off aid to the PNA because of Hamas terrorist ties. Iran has given support to the Kurdistan Workers'

Party, a Kurdish separatist movement in Turkey, and to other militant groups in the Persian Gulf region, Africa, and Central Asia. Some reports also suggest that Iran's interference in Iraq has included funding, safe transit, and arms to insurgent leaders like Muqtada al-Sadr and his forces.

U.S. officials claim that Iran supported the group behind the 1996 truck bombing of Khobar Towers, a U.S. military residence in Saudi Arabia, that killed 19 American servicemen. Observers maintain that Iran had prior knowledge of Hizballah attacks, such as the 1988 kidnapping and murder of Colonel William Higgins, a U.S. marine involved in a United Nations observer mission in Lebanon, and the 1992 and 1994 bombings of Jewish cultural institutions in Argentina. Iran was also reportedly involved in a Hizballah-linked January 2002 attempt to smuggle a boatload of arms to the PNA.

Iran is suspected of encouraging Hizballah's July 2006 attack on Israel in order to deflect international attention from its nuclear weapons program. With help from Russia, Iran is building a nuclear power plant, but U.S. officials claim that Iran is more interested in developing a nuclear weapon than in producing nuclear energy. In April 2006, President Ahmadinejad announced that Iran had successfully enriched uranium. Experts say that Iran could have enough highly enriched uranium (HEU) to produce a bomb in 3–10 years. The international community has called on Iran to stop its nuclear program.

The MOIS uses barracks and military bases belonging to the IRGC and belonging to the Iranian Army or the conventional army for training non-Iranian agents. The MOIS has turned IRGC barracks into secret training bases for terrorists. The military barracks that have been used for training terrorists are the Lavizan Training Camp in the Lavizan District, Tehran, which is also being used as an army center for intelligence and counterintelligence courses. The instructors are from the Iranian Army. The MOIS also uses this camp for training its cadres and terrorists. Other sites are the Abyek Training Center, which is used by MOIS for training and carrying out paramilitary exercises for terror activities. The Abyek Training Center is based in a camp that looks like a normal city with shopping centers and residential houses.

The Mostafa Khomeini Training center also looks like a normal city but is being used by the MOIS for training terrorists. The candidates learn the tradecraft of security, espionage, and the latest methods of torture in this barracks. The Ali Abad Barracks is located 40 kilometers from Qum on the Tehran–Qum Highway. The MOIS has a dedicated quarter in this barracks for training terrorists. The candidates are getting experience in firing on a giant 320 mm mortar in this area. Intelligence agent candidates are trained in Abyek Training Center in firing Katyusha rockets toward civilian targets. Korreit Camp is located 40 kilometers from the Ahwaz on Ahwaz–Mahshahr Highway very close to the IRGC Habibollahi barracks, which is controlled by the IRGC. The commander of Korreit Camp is Seyed Abbas Mousavi, an experienced intelligence instructor who has trained many MOIS agents. Fateh Ghanni Barracks is located on Tehran–Qum highway and is being used as a training place for foreign agents. Graduates of this barracks took part in the following terror activities: the assassination of Tooran Dourson, a Turkish journalist, in August 1990; the kidnapping and murder of a Mujahedeen-e Khalq (MEK) member called Ali Akbar Ghorbani in 1993; and the assassination of Ughoor Momjoo, a Turkish journalist, by putting a bomb in his car in June 1993.

The Ghayoor Asli Barracks is located 30 kilometers from Ahwaz–Khoramshahr Highway and is used for training foreign agents. The Quds Force and the Intelligence Ministry use this center simultaneously. This barracks also has a branch in Khoramshahr.

Other terrorist training centers are Navab Safawi's school for teaching theoretical training of agents, and the Hezballah Barracks in Varamin, which have been used in the past for training terrorists to infiltrate Iraq for terrorist activities. The Amir Al-Mo'amenin barracks in Ban Roushan is located 35 kilometers away from Ilam. This place belongs to the IRGC in Ilam. The Kawthar training barracks is located on the Dezful–Shushtar Highway; it is one of the regime's terrorist training centers. An IRGC commander, Hassan Darvish, teaches the terrorists.

The MOIS selects candidates through the Islamic Culture and Communications Organization or the Cultural Advisor. Then, through a number of tours that are organized by the regime's intelligence officers, those candidates with the right qualifications are introduced to the MOIS or to Quds Force, which provide the candidate with clerical training as well as military and intelligence training. The following curriculum is typical of the first stage of military and intelligence training: espionage and intelligence training; the tradecraft of infiltration into various sensitive locations and key buildings such as factories, airports, computer centers, and control rooms in arms factories; infiltration into meetings, gatherings, and various organizations; handling all types of sound equipment and recording people's voices; map reading, location, and identification skills; ordinary and infrared photography; communications techniques and instruments, control and management of communications; handling, installing, and controlling bugging devices; and persuasion and observation.

During the second stage, the candidates learn the tradecraft of explosives materials, buildings and bridges, handling of plastic explosives for making booby traps for the purpose of assassination, and handling of plastic explosives as bombs for installing in suitable places for the purpose of demolition or assassination. After graduating from the first two levels, the candidates learn techniques for assassination. *See also* IRANIAN INTELLIGENCE; IRANIAN NUCLEAR WEAPONS PROGRAM; IRANIAN TERRORISM IN ARGENTINA.

IRANIAN TERRORISM IN ARGENTINA. On 18 July 1994, a terrorist car bomb attack was perpetrated on the Jewish community's Argentine Israelite Mutual Association (AMIA) building in Buenos Aires, Argentina, killing 200 people and injuring 250 others. The AMIA building was totally destroyed and heavy damage was caused to the surroundings. A similar plan had been used in the 17 March 1992 attack on the Israeli embassy in Buenos Aires in which 30 people were killed and over 200 injured. The Argentinean Intelligence Service charged Iran's Intelligence Ministry with implementing the attacks via **Hizballah**.

The decision to mount another terrorist attack in Argentina was influenced by the success of the 1992 attack on the Israeli embassy in Buenos Aires and by the deteriorating relations between Argentina and Iran, particularly in terms of their strategic cooperation agreements. Beyond Iran's desire to hit Israeli and Jewish interests wherever and whenever possible, Iran may also have blamed Israel and the Jews in Argentina for these adverse developments in bilateral relations.

In August 1993, Iran's Supreme National Security Council made the decision to launch the attack on the AMIA building. Present at the meeting were spiritual leader Ayatollah Khamenei, President Hashemi Rafsanjani, Foreign Minister Ali Akbar Velayati, head of Intelligence and Security Affairs Mohamed Hijazi, and Intelligence Minister **Ali Fallahian**. The responsibility for planning the attack was placed on Fallahian, who determined that Hizballah's attack apparatus abroad, headed by **Imad Mugniyah**, would perpetrate the attack in the same way as it had on the Israeli embassy in Buenos Aires.

Hizballah's preferred method is to use local collaborator networks to set up dormant terrorist cells that can be called upon to assist in attacks like the ones in Argentina. Similar networks of Hizballah's Lebanese expatriates abroad have been exposed elsewhere in the world, including in Southeast Asia and the Middle East. Its extensive network of collaborators in Argentina was carefully built and nurtured by the Iranian embassy in Buenos Aires as early as the 1980s, using propaganda to increase support for the Islamic revolution in Muslim communities.

This goal was furthered by the Foreign Ministry in Iran, which supplied diplomatic cover for a branch of Iran's Ministry of Intelligence and Security (MOIS) in Argentina. Iran's Revolutionary Guard Corps (IRGC) also worked together with the Intelligence Ministry to build terrorist infrastructures and plan attacks abroad in accordance with the regime's interests. In the case of the AMIA building terrorist attack, the IRGC provided extensive support for Hizballah with training as well as financial and logistical assistance.

In retrospect, it was possible to detect several signs indicating changes in the routine of those involved during the days prior to the attack in mid-July. For example, the **Iranian intelligence** station chief in Buenos Aires left Argentina suddenly 10 days before the attack, and the Iranian ambassador in Argentina was also absent from his post at the time. Moreover, in the days before the attack, many telephone calls were recorded between Iranian and Hizballah collaborators in Argentina, Lebanon, and Iran, and there was a sharp increase in Iranian diplomatic couriers visiting Argentina. It can be assumed that they were transferring explosives or making other preparations for the attack and that their role as diplomatic couriers was a cover for their true activity as Iranian intelligence agents.

MOIS's Buenos Aires representative, Mohsen Rabani, was particularly instrumental in planning the attack, as was the Lebanese community in the Argentina–Brazil–Paraguay border triangle. For example, in late 1993, Rabani made several inquiries about purchasing a Renault commercial vehicle, which was used later to mount the attack. Rabani also traveled to Iran several times before returning there permanently in March 1994 prior to the attack.

Several days before the attack, the suicide bomber, Ibrahim Hussein Berro, entered Argentina through the border triangle. He belonged to Hizballah in Lebanon and was accompanied by a Hizballah collaborator in the area. Apparently, the car bomb was prepared somewhere in Buenos Aires. It is known that the car was parked in a public lot not far from the AMIA building some three days before the attack. On 18 July 1994, a few hours before the attack, Berro called his family in Lebanon to tell them that "he was going to be united with his brother," who had been killed in a car bomb against Israel Defense Forces in Lebanon in August 1989. Later that day, Berro drove the Renault loaded with hundreds of kilograms of explosives into the entrance of the AMIA building and detonated it.

Hizballah denied responsibility for the terrorist attack in Buenos Aires, and it only announced the death of its perpetrator after a great delay and under fabricated circumstances. Several months later, on 9 September 1994, it was announced on Hizballah's radio station Nur in Lebanon that Ibrahim Hussein Berro had been killed in action in south Lebanon, ostensibly unconnected with the attack on the AMIA building. It is in this way that Hizballah attempts to portray the organization as operating only in Lebanon, thereby avoiding identification as a terrorist organization and certainly not one that operates internationally. *See also* IRANIAN TERRORISM.

IRANGATE AFFAIR. Israel, along with the United States, was unprepared for repercussions after the fall of the shah of Iran at the end of 1979. The Israeli leaders assumed that consistent geopolitical interests would eventually triumph over religious ideology and produce an accommodation between Israel and Iran. The onset of the **Iran–Iraq War** in 1980 gave Israeli leaders a special incentive to keep their door open to the Islamic rulers in Iran. The director-general of Israel's Foreign Ministry, David Kimche, recommended selling arms to relatively moderate Iranians in positions of power, such as Ali Akbar Hashemi Rafsanjani. Israeli Defense Minister Ariel Sharon supported the idea. He believed that Israel's vital interest was a continuation of the war in the Persian Gulf, with an eventual Iranian victory. The Irangate arms deal was held strictly as covert action by former officials of the intelligence communities of the countries involved.

The head of the Jaffee Center for Strategic Studies at that time, Aharon Yariv, a retired major general and former director of Military Intelligence (DMI), stated at a scholarly conference at Tel-Aviv University in late 1986 that it would be to Israel's advantage if the Iran–Iraq War ended in a stalemate, but it would be even better if it continued; when that war ended, Iraq might open an "eastern front" against Israel. Uri Lubrani, Israel's chief representative in Iran under the shah, also justified the continued sale of Israeli arms to Iran since it might lead to the disappearance of Khomeinism. Strengthening the relatively moderate Iranian faction was thought potentially to be capable of toppling Khomeinism. Israeli leaders in talks with their American counterparts occasionally raised the notion of restoring the shah's regime; such an event might afford Israel and the United States influence in Iran once more.

Israel had its own considerations for deciding to continue selling arms to Iran: it was simply good for business. One out of 10 Israeli workers was then employed in arms-related industries; military items constituted more than a quarter of Israel's industrial exports. Israeli pro-Iranian policy was guided by the profit motive rather than strategic considerations. It resulted from the situation of severe unemployment that hit the Israeli arms industry in 1979 after the Iranian market shriveled.

The first renewed Israeli arms sales to Iran in 1980 included spare parts for U.S.-made F-4 Phantom jets; a later deal that year included parts for U.S.-made tanks. Israel informed Washington only after the fact, when deliveries were well underway. Israeli policymakers feared that a request for U.S. approval in advance would be turned down out of hand.

In November 1979 in the early days of the Iranian Revolution, Iranian radicals had seized the U.S. embassy in Tehran and taken 66 American diplomats hostage. The administration of President Jimmy

Carter was in fact outraged that its embargo had been blatantly violated when it learned of Israel's secret supply of American spare parts to the Iranians during the hostage crisis. Until the diplomats were released in January 1981, U.S. Secretary of State Edmund Muskie demanded that Israel cease its shipments. Israeli Prime Minister Menahem Begin promised to comply with U.S. demands, but in fact Israel continued to sell arms to Iran without U.S. approval. Israeli officials maintained they were simply selling domestic Israeli-produced arms, not embargoed U.S. weapons.

On 24 July 1981, **Ya'acov Nimrodi**, an Israeli businessman engaged in arms sales, signed a deal with Iran's Ministry of National Defense to sell Iran arms worth $135,842,000, including Lance missiles, Copperhead shells, and Hawk missiles. A sale of such a magnitude must have had Israeli government acquiescence. Nimrodi, a comrade in arms of Ariel Sharon during Israel's 1948–1949 War of Independence and a close personal friend, won his approval for the deal.

The new U.S. administration of Ronald Reagan entered office in 1981. Toward the end of that year, Kimche approached U.S. Secretary of State Alexander Haig and National Security Adviser Robert McFarlane to discuss proposed Israeli shipments of U.S.-made spare parts worth $10–15 million to the relatively moderate faction in Iran. Haig did not give his approval.

In November 1981, Sharon visited Washington and asked his U.S. counterpart Caspar Weinberger for approval to sell arms to Iran. Weinberger referred him to Haig, who unequivocally opposed any violation of the embargo. In May 1982, a clandestine gathering took place between Al Schwimmer, a Jewish American billionaire who had founded the Israeli aircraft industry, Nimrodi, Kimche, and Sharon and his wife Lily, together with Sudanese president Gaafar Numeiri, at a Kenyan safari resort owned by Saudi business tycoon Adnan Khashoggi. At the meeting, Israel won Numeiri's agreement to allow Ethiopian Jews safe passage through Sudan when they migrated to the Jewish state. In return, Numeiri required that Israel would later get him out of the country if his regime was toppled. Sharon and Kimche went further and proposed to Numeiri that Sudan become a gigantic arms cache for weapons produced or captured by Israel. Saudi Arabia would finance the project, aimed largely at selling weapons to exiled Iranian generals of the ousted monarchical regime for a major coup attempt.

The **Mossad** foiled the plan behind Sharon's back by persuading the late shah's son, then in Morocco, to veto it.

Under U.S. pressure, Israel halted arms sales for a while, but private Israeli citizens, particularly Nimrodi, continued making plans to resume trade with Iran. In 1985, Nimrodi succeeded in obtaining approval for his plans from Israel's national unity government, headed by Shimon Peres. Nimrodi and his partner Schwimmer, a close friend of Peres, were authorized to provide Iran with LAU antitank missiles and Hawk antiaircraft missiles from Israel's warehouses. These deals were part of what was later known as "Irangate" (echoing the Watergate scandal of the Nixon administration in the early 1970s).

In the mid-1980s, Schwimmer played a key role in persuading the U.S. administration itself to sell arms to Iran. Through a secret agreement between the United States and the Israeli Defense Ministry in 1985, the arms to Iran passed through Nimrodi. The United States replenished the supplies Israel transferred to Iran. One aspect of the deal was that Iran was to exert pressure on its protégé, the **Hizballah** organization in Lebanon, to release U.S. and Western hostages kidnapped after 1982. The Reagan administration was fully aware of these attempts at freeing the hostages by means of unsanctioned arms sales to Iran.

News of Irangate first began to appear in the press toward the end of 1986. The scandal also became known as the Iran–Contra affair. It revealed how deeply the United States was involved in arms sales to Iran, breaching its own laws that prohibited the sale of U.S. weapons for resale to a third country listed as a "terrorist nation"—which occurred precisely at a time when Washington was publicly calling for a worldwide ban on sending arms to Iran. The money Iran paid for the arms was used by senior officials in the Reagan administration to buy arms for the Contra rebels in Nicaragua. This went against the Boland Amendment of 8 December 1982, which specifically prohibited military assistance to the Contras. One of the administration officials involved was Colonel Oliver North, military aide to the U.S. National Security Council, who reported in the White House to National Security Adviser Robert McFarlane and later to his successor, John Poindexter. The entire scheme was conducted without Congress's knowledge, again contravening a law requiring sales above $14 million to be reported to Congress.

IRAQI COUP. In the 1920s, Great Britain occupied Mesopotamia, which had been taken from the Ottoman Empire and had created Iraq. An Arabian prince, driven into exile by the al-Saud family, was made king, to ensure that Iraq remained pro-British. But when **World War II** began in 1939, Arab nationalists became pro-German. The anti-Semitism of the Nazis appealed to Arabs. When the German Afrika Korps advanced across North Africa toward Egypt, pro-German Iraqi Army officers staged a coup in Iraq in early April 1941. The new Iraqi government did not declare war on Great Britain, it just wanted to be on the right side when the Germans won the war. The new Iraqi government was assisted and funded by Nazi Germany's intelligence.

Great Britain's intelligence was aware of the developments in Iraq, and Great Britain still had a few hundred troops in Iraq. By treaty, it had the right to move troops through Iraq and to maintain two airbases (one outside Baghdad and the other near Basra in the south, mainly for training). Without saying anything to the Iraqis, the British began moving the 10th Indian Infantry Division from India to Basra. The first brigade of the division arrived in Basra on 18 April 1941. On 27 April 1941, the Iraqis violated the treaty by demanding that the British land no more troops until the brigade already in Basra had left Iraq. The British announced to the Iraqi government that they would ignore that request. The violation of the treaty was regarded by Great Britain as *casus belli* for war. The British took over Basra, thus protecting their airbase outside the city. They also flew 400 troops to the Habbaniya airbase outside Baghdad, as they knew that the Iraqis were already moving troops to seize the base. The British had a battalion of Assyrian (Iraqi Christians) militia, plus a company of Kurds and Arabs, protecting Habbaniya and sent additional troops to show the Assyrians that they would be supported. The airbase had about 90 aircraft, but nearly all were biplane trainers because the base was used mainly for training pilots. But the pilots were of good quality, particularly the instructors. The Iraqi Air Force was also equipped mainly with 60 aircraft, mostly biplanes from three different countries, but the Iraqi pilots were not very competent. A British intelligence officer spread rumors directly to the Iraqi Army that 100 British tanks were going to move toward Baghdad. Actually this was a deception.

The Iraqi Army consisted of four infantry divisions, one mechanized brigade (a battalion with 16 light tanks and 14 armored cars, plus two battalions of infantry in trucks). Many of the officers and noncommissioned officers had served in the Turkish army. These troops were not qualified for battle. On 30 April 1941, the Iraqi Army moved 50 batteries of artillery and 9,000 troops to Habbaniya. Most of the troops were just militiamen.

The Iraqis occupied the high ground about a thousand yards from Habbaniya, and warned the British army that they would use their artillery if any British aircraft took off. At dawn on 2 May 1941, the British aircraft took off anyway and attacked the Iraqi troops. Over the next five days, British aircraft launched 584 sorties, dropped 45 tons of bombs, and fired over 100,000 rounds of machine-gun ammunition. The Iraqi artillery did some damage to the British forces, but the Iraqi infantry and militias began to flee on 6 May 1941. The rest of the 10th Indian Division landed at Basra on 6 May 1941 and started to move toward Baghdad. On 7 May 1941, the Iraqi troops were fleeing from British warplanes. The British army succeeding in organizing a mobile brigade and a battalion-sized force from Palestine, and it was dispatched quickly to Baghdad. Together with the same troops from the **Arab Legion**, the British forces invaded Baghdad on 9 May 1941.

The Iraqi Army realized the extent of the trouble, looked for stronger allies, and asked Nazi Germany's intelligence for further assistance. German and Italian bombers began bombing missions out of Mosul but suffered from a lack of aviation fuel. On 23 May 1941, the British force crossed the Euphrates River and moved toward Baghdad. Iraqi resistance was ineffective and on 30 May 1941 the Iraqi rebels surrendered.

IRAQI DIRECTORATE OF GENERAL MILITARY INTELLI-GENCE (DGMI). The Iraqi Directorate of General Military Intelligence (al-Istikhbarat al-Askariyya) was one of the oldest **Iraqi intelligence** agencies, dating back to the 1921 British mandate on Iraq. With its staff of 6,000 people, the DGMI's main functions were ensuring the loyalty of the army's officer corps and gathering military intelligence from abroad. However, the DGMI was also involved in foreign operations, including assassinations.

In contrast to other Iraqi intelligence agencies, the commanders of the DGMI were not immediate relatives of Saddam Hussein. In order to ensure that none of the commanders of the DGMI would become powerful enough to challenge the president, Saddam Hussein used a tactic of constantly shifting the commanders. After the 2003 **Operation Iraqi Freedom**, the DGMI, like all of Saddam Hussein's intelligence agencies, was dismantled by U.S. forces. *See also* IRAQI DIRECTORATE OF GENERAL SECURITY; IRAQI SPECIAL SECURITY ORGANIZATION.

IRAQI DIRECTORATE OF GENERAL SECURITY (DGS). Iraq's Directorate of General Security, also known as the Internal State Security or the Secret Police (al-Amn al-Amm), was the oldest security agency in the country, established in 1921 when Great Britain's mandate imposed the Hashemite monarchy on Iraq. The DGS was responsible for domestic counterintelligence operations and had representatives in all of the other **Iraqi intelligence** agencies. The headquarters of DGS was located in Baghdad, from which it guided the work of the DGS branches throughout the country.

During Saddam Hussein's presidency, the DGS had a staff of 8,000 people. Saddam Hussein used to appoint his relatives to key positions in the DGS. During the 1980s **Iran–Iraq War**, Saddam Hussein appointed **Ali Hassan** al-Majid commander of the DGS. Ali Hassan became the architect of the Iraqi regime's anti-Kurdish campaign and ordered the use of chemical weapons against the Kurds.

In 1991, Saddam Hussein established a paramilitary unit under the command of the DGS, known as Quwat al-Tawari, to reinforce law and order. This unit monitored the daily lives of the population and had a pervasive local presence, with officers present in every Iraqi neighborhood, every office, every school, every hotel, and every coffee shop in order to enforce the law. In many cases, agents of Quwat al-Tawari would disguise themselves as members of an opposition group and approach Iraqi officials, offering to recruit them for some opposition or espionage purpose and then arresting them if they did not report the incident. The DGS also used to watch for foreigners who might be breaking Iraqi law or seeking to stir up antiregime feelings among native Iraqis.

After the 1991 **Operation Desert Storm**, Quwat al-Tawari was involved in hiding Iraqi ballistic missile components. Quwat al-Tawari also operated the notorious Abu Ghuraib prison outside of Baghdad, where many of Iraq's political prisoners were detained. After the 2003 **Operation Iraqi Freedom**, the DGS—like all of Saddam Hussein's intelligence agencies—was dismantled by U.S. forces. *See also* IRAQI DIRECTORATE OF GENERAL MILITARY INTELLIGENCE; IRAQI SPECIAL SECURITY ORGANIZATION.

IRAQI INTELLIGENCE. After the Ba'athist coup of 1968, Saddam Hussein, then vice president of Iraq, began to exercise indirect control of Iraq's politics. He established the vast network of Iraq's security apparatus and created or expanded the various existing intelligence agencies. The largest and most renowned intelligence agencies during Saddam Hussein's regime were the Iraqi Intelligence Service (IIS; Mukhabarat); the **Iraqi Directorate of General Military Intelligence** (DGMI; al-Istikhbarat al-Askariyya); the **Iraqi Directorate of General Security** (DGS; al-Amn al-Amm); and the **Iraqi Special Security Organization** (SSO; al-Amn al-Khas). Iraq's Directorate of General Security, also known as Internal State Security or the Secret Police (al-Amn al-Amm), was established first and was the oldest security agency in the country, dating back to 1921 when Great Britain's mandate imposed the Hashemite monarchy on Iraq.

The Iraqi Intelligence Service was used for collecting intelligence on foreign countries and domestic Iraqi affairs. In addition, in the late 1990s, the IIS was responsible for deception activities aimed at foiling the inspectors of the United Nations Special Commission (UNSCOM) who were searching for unconventional weapons arsenals in Iraq. The IIS consisted of over 20 compartmentalized directorates, seven of which were engaged in surveillance of the UNSCOM inspectors and concealing the Iraqi weapons of mass destruction (WMD) programs. The directorates exchanged information whenever members of one directorate discovered intelligence related to the other directorate's responsibilities.

- The Directorate of Military Industries, known also as al-Munzhumah, provided security for all Military Industrial Commission (MIC) and Iraqi Atomic Energy Commission (IAEC) sites.

- The Directorate of National Monitoring was assisted by the Directorate of Military Industries with purging MIC facilities of documents to be concealed from United Nations inspectors. In August 1998, Saddam ended cooperation with UNSCOM inspections, and soon after he ordered the creation of a committee to purge all MIC records of sensitive documentation related to past prohibited programs. This directorate also handled security within MIC facilities, as well as the security staff at gates of industrial complexes, weapons manufacturing plants, and chemical production plants.
- The Directorate of Internal Security monitored the loyalty of all IIS employees and was responsible for the physical security of the MIC and IIS headquarters.
- The Directorate of Protective Services was responsible for external security to protect IIS facilities and also provided convoy security for shipments of WMDs during transport from one location to another.
- The Directorate of Foreign Intelligence was the primary directorate for foreign intelligence collection and foreign operations. Also known as the Secret Service Directorate, it was focused primarily on collecting political, military, and economic information about foreign countries. It also targeted Iraqi opposition groups operating outside Iraq.
- The Directorate of Counterintelligence conducted domestic monitoring and counterintelligence activities within Iraq and was engaged in collecting information about domestic businesses, such as restaurants, hotels, travel services, and souvenir shops.
- The Directorate of Clandestine Operations was responsible for technical monitoring, such as surveillance photography, electronic eavesdropping, and counterintelligence functions at Iraqi embassies abroad and for UN officials in Iraq.
- The Directorate of Signals Intelligence (SIGINT) monitored, collected, and analyzed external signals and voice communications and intercepted foreign military communications. It also monitored internal Iraqi communications to ensure communications security, including surveillance of foreign embassies, UN headquarters, and UNSCOM inspectors.

- The Directorate of Science and Technology developed chemical and biological weapons, producing toxins, poisons, and lethal devices for assassination operations.
- The Directorate of Special Logistics was involved in the analysis of chemical and biological substances; X-ray and bomb detection devices used in Iraqi embassies; document authentication, and diplomatic mail security.
- The Directorate of Explosives was responsible for detecting and disabling explosive devices in the mail or in vehicles. It also produced new designs or methods for concealing explosive materials to be used in assassination operations, including books, briefcases, belts, vests, thermoses, car seats, floor mats, and facial tissue boxes.
- The Directorate of Special Operations was responsible for training and conducting special operations activities. It trained operatives from Egypt, Lebanon, Iraq, the Palestinian National Authority, Sudan, Syria, and Yemen in counterterrorism, explosives, marksmanship, and foreign operations at its training facilities. This directorate was composed of both foreign and domestic sections and performed government-sanctioned assassinations inside or outside Iraq, largely by activating suicide bombers.

In the sphere of military intelligence, the Directorate of General Military Intelligence (DGMI) was Iraq's main organ. The DGMI collected intelligence on the military capabilities of the neighboring countries of Iraq, as well as on Kurdish forces. The directors of the DGMI reported directly to the presidential secretary, despite the subordination of the DGMI to the Iraqi Ministry of Defense. In addition to functioning as a conventional military intelligence unit, the DGMI served as an internal police force within and assigned its intelligence officers to each military unit, down to the battalion level.

The third Iraqi intelligence organ was the Directorate of General Security (DGS), which was charged with the task of collecting intelligence on various opposition groups, such as the Kurds, in Iraq. The SSO was created from within the DGS in 1984 during the **Iran–Iraq War**. It emerged as the most powerful agency in the Iraqi security apparatus during Saddam Hussein's presidency and was the only unit responsible for providing bodyguards to the country's leaders. Saddam Hussein selected only the most loyal agents to serve in this newly established agency.

After the 2003 **Operation Iraqi Freedom**, U.S. forces dismantled Saddam Hussein's military and security services, including all of the existing Iraqi intelligence agencies. The newly established Iraqi government proposed the creation of an independent intelligence agency, which they considered to be essential for collecting and analyzing intelligence. Initially, the United States suspected that an independent Iraqi intelligence organization would reduce U.S. influence and enhance the indirect control of a Shi'ite-dominated government, bringing it closer to Iran.

However, the United States finally decided to allow the establishment of a new Iraqi intelligence organization. In 2004, Paul Bremer, former administrator of the U.S-led occupation of Iraq, announced the formation of the Iraqi National Intelligence Service, which was funded from secret funds totaling $3 billion over three years. The agency was aimed at carrying out covert Central Intelligence Agency operations within Iraq, as well as Afghanistan to a lesser extent.

In April 2004, the **charter of the Iraqi National Intelligence Service** (INIS) was promulgated. According to the charter, the INIS is the intelligence agency of the new Iraqi government established on the authority of the Coalition Provisional Authority (CPA). The purpose of the new intelligence agency is to address threats to the national security of Iraq, **terrorism** and insurgency, proliferation of weapons of mass destruction, narcotics production and trafficking, and serious organized crime, espionage, and other acts threatening to Iraqi democracy.

IRAQI NUCLEAR WEAPONS PROGRAM. Iraq's modest civilian nuclear program dates all the way back to the Atoms for Peace program in 1956, when the United States led the international community in establishing nuclear research programs in nations around the world. In 1962, construction began on Iraq's first research reactor. In 1968, Iraq signed the nuclear Nonproliferation Treaty (NPT), with other non-nuclear nations, providing them with access to nuclear technology in exchange for agreeing not to acquire nuclear weapons and to allow inspections. But in late 1971, a secret plan was initiated to breach the treaty and set up clandestine operations. At that time, the program was run by the Iraq Atomic Energy Commission (IAEC), a small department within the Iraqi Ministry of Higher Education. Moyesser al-Mallah, the newly appointed secretary of the IAEC, and Husham Sharif approached Khidir Hamza, who was the chairman of the Physics Department of the Nuclear Research Center (located at the IAEC facilities at al-Tuwaitha, 17 kilometers south of Baghdad) and requested that Hamza develop a plan for acquiring nuclear weapons, one that used an ambitious and carefully designed civilian nuclear program to obtain the technologies, skills, and infrastructure required to successfully create a nuclear weapons arsenal. They promised that this plan would secure greatly increased funding from Saddam Hussein for Iraq's nuclear program, which thus far had been small and poorly funded by international aid programs. Saddam Hussein was then vice chairman of the Iraqi Revolutionary Command Council (RCC).

Khidhir Hamza became the founder of the nuclear weapons program and assumed the position as head of nuclear bomb development. The core of Hamza's plan for designing and testing a nuclear explosive was to acquire a foreign reactor to use for producing plutonium. However, the reactor was supposed to be under the biannual safeguards of the International Atomic Energy Agency (IAEA). Iraq's nuclear program demonstrates how easily it could be used for producing nuclear weapons.

Hamza's plan was reviewed by a group affiliated with the RCC, and in 1972, it was approved by Saddam Hussein. In September 1973, Hamza and the minister of higher education, Hisham al-Shawi, went to Vienna to lobby for Iraq to gain a seat on the IAEA board of governors. Al-Shawi was given the seat.

In order to further penetrate the IAEA's operations, a special intelligence office was created at the Iraqi embassy in Vienna. The position of "scientific attaché" was created and filled by Suroor Mahmoud Mirza, a brother of Saddam's senior bodyguard. The inside knowledge of IAEA operations acquired through these sources allowed Iraq's activities to go undetected by the IAEA. Al-Shawi was even successful in getting an Iraqi nuclear physicist, Abdul-Wahid al-Saji, appointed as an IAEA inspector. Hussein soon tightened his control over the program even further. Moyesser al-Mallah and

Husham Sharif, both of them U.S. educated, were dismissed by Saddam Hussein from the IAEC. Saddam Hussein transferred the IAEC to the RCC and appointed himself as its chair, an appointment that was never disclosed to the IAEA.

By late 1974, about 200 Iraqis were on the staff of the IAEC. In April 1975, reputed nuclear physicist Jafar Dhia Jafar returned to Baghdad after several years working at European nuclear physics laboratories. Jafar quickly took a leading role in the Iraqi nuclear weapons program and initiated Iraq's first uranium enrichment project. By 1979, Jafar had become vice chairman of the IAEC, and the internationally known radiochemist Hussein al-Shahristani headed the plutonium separation program.

In 1974, Iraq sought a large reactor suitable for substantial plutonium production. It approached Canada and France and requested to obtain a nuclear power reactor. Iraq opted for a large materials test reactor (MTR) from France, which was a type of high-power experimental reactor fueled by highly enriched—that is, weapons-grade—uranium. It was one of the largest of its type in the world. Hamza traveled to France and negotiated for the MTR. Since the reactor was a derivative of the French Osiris reactor and the French were selling it to Iraq, they dubbed this export model the "Osiraq" reactor. Although this was the name under which it was commonly known, the Iraqis called the reactor the "Tammuz-1," named after the month of the Islamic calendar when the Ba'ath came to power in 1968. Along with Tammuz-1, Iraq also contracted for a second lower power reactor called Tammuz-2.

The Iraqis had several objectives in obtaining Tammuz-1 (Osiraq). The principal one was to produce enough plutonium for one or more bombs, but even if not, to obtain a complete suite of modern reactor technology for study and to provide experience in high-flux reactor operation and in plutonium production, refining, and manufacturing. For his part, Saddam Hussein was not secretive about his intentions. Just before flying to France to close the Osiraq deal in September 1975, he gave an interview to a leading Arabic-language news magazine from Beirut in which he declared that his country was engaged in the first Arab attempt at nuclear arms.

The agreement for purchasing the reactors was finally concluded in 1976. France began to have second thoughts about the wisdom of providing such an efficient irradiation facility and tried to amend the contract to provide a model using a lower enrichment fuel. Significantly, Iraq had never expressed interest in the type of light-water power reactors with limited proliferation potential and was clearly seeking only power reactors with high-proliferation capabilities. Iraq had actually requested an underground facility but had been turned down by the French. The infrastructure was built during 1976 and 1979, and in 1979 construction of the reactor itself commenced.

In 1979, Iraq contracted with the Italian company SNIA-Techint for a plutonium separation and handling facility, and a uranium refining and fuel-manufacturing plant. These facilities were not subject to IAEA safeguards. Iraq also obtained large shipments of uranium from Portugal, Brazil, and Nigeria that were not safeguarded.

During the 1970s, the IAEC nuclear weapons program spent some $750 million, $300 million of it for the French reactor, and $200 million on the fuel plant and plutonium separation facility. It built up a staff of 500 engineers and technicians. In addition, a program in uranium enrichment using laser isotope separation (LIS) was started in the late 1970s and was conducted in complete isolation and secrecy from the IAEC. LIS was a new area of technology that at that time had yet to be demonstrated successfully even by the United States. Not surprisingly, Iraq produced no apparent results. The LIS program was initiated under Humam al-Ghafour, who replaced Saddam Hussein as the chairman of the IAEC in the late 1970s and remained the chief executive of the Iraqi nuclear program into the mid-1990s.

In June 1979, Saddam Hussein moved to consolidate the power that he had been accumulating over the years. The increasingly unwell Bakr was forced to resign all his positions, and Saddam Hussein took over as president of the republic, secretary general of the Ba'ath Party, chairman of the RCC, and commander in chief of the armed forces. The political environment in and surrounding Iraq deteriorated through 1979 and 1980, as events were leading up to the outbreak of the **Iran–Iraq War** in 1980.

The real proliferation potential of Osiraq was long the subject of considerable controversy. Osiraq was placed under IAEA inspection, which, it was widely argued at the time, would make significant cheating all but impossible. Thus, the conventional wisdom of the arms control community was that this reactor was not a proliferation threat. Yet Iraq had no peaceful need or purpose for this reactor, something that was evident to any serious observer even at the time. It already had one experimental reactor and was acquiring a second with Tammuz-2. It was training an enormous cadre of nuclear technicians (400 were sent abroad for training), yet had no experimental program. The massive construction of buildings at al-Tuwaitha without any declared purpose and off limits to outsiders indicated activities unconnected with legitimate research. Unlike the energy-poor nation of India, oil-rich Iraq did not have the argument that it needed to develop indigenous nuclear power for domestic needs.

Although the IAEA was unaware of Iraq's intentions, it is more than likely that these indications about Iraq's true plans and intentions were fully grasped by **Israeli intelligence**. Israel had plenty of reason to be suspicious of the capabilities that Iraq was acquiring and had specific knowledge of Iraq's plans. Israel's first attempt to disrupt those plans occurred at 3 A.M. on 6 April 1979. The two reactor cores lay in storage at a French firm near Toulon awaiting shipment to Iraq. A **Mossad** operation known as **Operation Sphinx** smuggled in seven operatives, who placed five explosive charges on the cores and detonated them, damaging both cores and setting back Iraq's program by at least half a year. The most severely damaged cores were repaired, but X-rays revealed hairline fractures throughout the core of Osiraq that could not be fixed without completely rebuilding it, a process that would take two years. Rather than incur additional delay, Iraq decided to accept the core as it was.

This led to Israel's second attack on Osiraq. The Mossad kept a team operating in France in order to continue its assault on the Iraqi project after the bombing at Toulon. But after the sabotage of the reactor core, Israel's next target was Yahya al-Meshad, who was a respected Egyptian nuclear engineer hired by Iraq to make up for the serious problems in staffing the nuclear program The Mossad made an attempt to recruit al-Meshad in order to obtain information on the program. However, al-Meshad declined to reveal any information and to cooperate with foreign agents.

At 6:35 P.M. local time on 7 June 1981, **Operation Opera** (known also as Operation Babylon) was put into action. In the Israeli attack on Tammuz-1, eight Israeli F-16 Falcons dropped 13 bombs in a matter of 80 seconds, blowing a hole in the concrete dome and completely demolishing the reactor core and the building down to its foundation. The attack was carried out before the reactor was completely operational, so no radiation was released. Israel emphasized that it planned the attack in order to minimize casualties by attacking the reactor before it began operation and became radioactive.

This was the longest-range attack in Israeli Air Force history, carried out at 1,100 kilometers, the extreme limit of combat range of the F-16 fighter bombers. At the time of the attack, it was widely reported that laser-guided bombs had been used, given the precision of the bombing. One bomb blew a hole in the reactor containment vessel, the other bombs hit directly through the hole, and only one bomb fell elsewhere. In fact, laser-guided bombs were not used, and the attack was simply carried out by precision visual bombing. It has even been suggested that the bomb that missed the reactor was not dropped in error. It hit a 30-meter tunnel connecting the reactor with a large laboratory that was also an important target. A van was found parked next to the tunnel with a guidance transmitter inside, and a French technician, who had been recruited by Mossad, was reportedly asked to deposit a briefcase containing a homing device inside the building.

The attack was carried out at sunset, and this timing provided several advantages. Emerging from the setting sun minimized the opportunity for Iraqi air defenses at the site to detect them visually. In addition, the target was easy to spot, with the near-horizontal sunlight illuminating the light-colored dome for the approaching F-16s. The main reason given by the Israelis for the timing of the attack was that if any aircraft had been lost, search-and-rescue missions could have been conducted under cover of darkness.

A critical factor in planning the timing of the attack was Israeli intelligence about the behavior of the reactor's operators and when they were expected to be absent. The workers in the reactor had the habit of taking dinner and leaving their post at 6 P.M., shutting off the missile radar. The Israeli attack was timed such that the aircraft came into range of the radar several minutes after it had been shut off. The French scientists and the technicians working in the plant most probably had advance knowledge of the attack and on 7 June at 5 P.M. they vacated the premises.

After the Osiraq reactor was destroyed, Iraq initially attempted to replace it, but by 1985 had realized that it could not buy a replacement. The reason that Iraq eventually dropped this effort is not entirely clear. Saudi Arabia offered to finance a replacement, and partial financing was actually obtained. French President François Mitterrand declared an in-principle agreement to rebuild Osiraq after consultations with Iraqi Deputy Prime Minister Tariq Aziz in August 1981. However, France wanted to tighten its controls on the project, including the addition of a reactor core surveillance system. Concerns about international awareness of reactor programs may be part of the reason that none of the available options were openly pursued, including the possibility of building its own reactors using natural uranium technology to capitalize on its established plutonium-based weapons infrastructure.

Following the 1991 **Gulf War**, however, inspectors uncovered a startling range of nuclear activities, leading to the assumption that Iraq was within a year or two of producing enough highly enriched uranium for nuclear weapons. These discoveries came as a shock to the international nonproliferation apparatus, revealing major weaknesses in inspection routines, export controls, and intelligence gathering and sharing. In contrast, Iraqi efforts to obtain plutonium had been unsuccessful, and it appears that Iraq was unable to resurrect its plutonium program after the Israeli bombing of the unfinished plutonium-production reactor at Osiraq in 1981.

In the 1990s, as part of UN Security Council Resolution 715, Iraq was subjected to the most intrusive weapons-inspection system ever implemented. Despite long searches, the inspectors did not uncover any evidence that a hidden reactor, plutonium separation plant, or associated nuclear waste site existed anywhere in Iraq. Indeed, after the U.S. invasion of Iraq in March 2003, the Central Intelligence Agency (CIA) reported that Saddam Hussein did not possess stockpiles of illicit weapons at the time of the invasion and that Iraq's nuclear program had ended after the 1991 Gulf War. *See also* OPERATION ROCKINGHAM.

IRAQI SPECIAL SECURITY ORGANIZATION (SSO). Established in 1984, Iraq's Special Security Organization (al-Amn al-Khas) was the most powerful Iraqi security agency during Saddam Hussein's presidency. The SSO was highly secretive and operated on a functional, rather than a geographical, basis. With its staff of 2,000 officers, the SSO was subdivided into two main organs. The Security Bureau was charged with providing personal security, including bodyguards, for high-ranking government officials and presidential facilities. The Political Bureau was responsible for collecting and analyzing intelligence on all Iraqi dissidents, as well as implementing actions against "enemies of the state," such as arrests, interrogations, and executions.

The SSO carried out numerous clandestine operations, particularly in suppressing domestic opposition to the regime. It used its own military brigade to preempt several coup attempts, such as the one in January 1990 by members of the Jubur tribe. The SSO also played an active role in crushing the March 1991 Shi'ite rebellion in the south of Iraq. In August 1996, together with the **Iraqi Intelligence** Service (IIS), agents of the SSO infiltrated the Kurdish enclave in the north of Iraq and captured operatives of the Iraqi opposition. The SSO was also allegedly involved in various assassination attempts abroad.

The SSO played a key role in secretly buying dual-use material for the Iraqi weapons of mass destruction (WMDs) program. During the 1991 **Operation Desert Storm**, the SSO was charged with concealing WMDs and hiding documents related to WMDs from United Nations Special Commission inspectors. After the 2003 **Operation Iraqi Freedom**, the SSO—like all of Saddam Hussein's intelligence agencies—was dismantled by U.S. forces. *See also* IRAQI DIRECTORATE OF GENERAL MILITARY INTELLIGENCE; IRAQI DIRECTORATE OF GENERAL SECURITY.

IRAQI TERRORISM. Iraq has been accused by the U.S. State Department and the Central Intelligence Agency (CIA) of both sponsoring terrorist activities and supporting terrorist organizations. In the area of supporting terrorist organizations, Iraq has supported the Palestinian Liberation Organization (PLO) as the political representative for the Palestinian people. In the early 1970s, Iraq hosted the headquarters of the **Abu Nidal Organization** (ANO), one of the most active Palestinian terrorist organizations. Although later, in the 1980s, the ANO headquarters moved to Syria and then to Libya, in 1990 it was relocated to Iraq. The ANO was responsible for attacks that killed some 300 people. Its leader, Abu Nidal, was found dead in Baghdad in August 2002.

Iraq has provided safe haven, training, and financial support to specific terrorists wanted by other countries in violation of international law. Among them were Palestinian Liberation Front (PLF) leader Abu Abbas, who was responsible for the 1985 hijacking of the *Achille Lauro* cruise ship in the Mediterranean; two Saudis who hijacked a Saudi Arabian Airlines flight to Baghdad in 2000; and Abdel Rahman Yasin, who is on the Federal Bureau of Investigation's (FBI) most wanted terrorists list for his alleged role in the 1993 World Trade Center bombing.

Iraq has also provided financial support for Palestinian terror groups, including **Hamas**, Islamic Jihad, the PLF, and the Arab Liberation Front. It has channeled money to the families of Palestinian suicide bombers, increasing the amount of such payments from $10,000 to $25,000 in April 2002. It has helped the Iranian dissident leftist group **Mujahedeen-e Khalq** (MEK), which fought to overthrow the shah of Iran; the Kurdistan Workers' Party (PKK), a separatist organization fighting the Turkish government; and several far-left Islamist Palestinian splinter groups that oppose peace with Israel. Prior to the 2003 invasion, the CIA cited Iraq's increased support for such organizations as reason to believe that Baghdad's links to **terrorism** could continue to increase. Experts say that by promoting Israeli–Palestinian violence, Saddam may have hoped to make it harder for the United States to win Arab support for a campaign against Iraq. However, there is no evidence that Iraq cooperated, hosted, or dealt with **al Qaeda**. Although the Iraqi government never expressed sympathy for the United States after the attacks, it did deny any involvement. In late 2001, Czech intelligence officials reported that the 9/11 ringleader, Muhammad Atta, had met with an **Iraqi intelligence** agent in Prague in April 2001, but many American and Czech officials have since disavowed the report and there is no evidence to substantiate such a claim.

The U.S. list of state sponsors of international terrorism has been compiled by the State Department since 29 December 1979. Iraq was initially included on the list, and inclusion leads to the imposition of strict sanctions. The State Department's reason for including Iraq was that it provided bases to the MEK, the PKK, the PLF, and the ANO. Iraq was removed from the list in 1982 to make it eligible for American military technology while it was fighting Iran in the **Iran–Iraq**

War (1980–1988). It was later put back on the list in 1990 following its invasion of Kuwait and has since been removed following the 2003 invasion. Following the invasion, U.S. sanctions against Iraq were suspended on 7 May 2003, and President George W. Bush announced the removal of Iraq from the list on 25 September 2004. *See also* IRAQI NUCLEAR WEAPONS PROGRAM; U.S. PROPAGANDA IN IRAQ.

ISMAIL, ALI AHMAD (1917–1974). Ali Ahmad Ismail served with the Allies in the Western Desert during **World War II** and fought as a brigade commander in the first Arab–Israeli War (1948–1949). He later trained in Britain, fought the Franco–British–Israeli forces during the **Suez crisis** of 1956, undertook further training in the Soviet Union, and was a divisional commander in the **Six Days' War** of June 1967. In March 1969, Ismail was dismissed by President Gamal Abdel Nasser. President Anwar al-Sadat, who succeeded Nasser, appointed him chief of intelligence in September 1970. In October 1972, Ismail accompanied Prime Minister Aziz Sidqi on a visit to Moscow and on his return stifled a coup against the president. That same month, he replaced the anti-Soviet General Muhammad Sadeq as minister of defense and was promoted to full general. During the 1973 **Yom Kippur War**, Ismail served as the commander in chief of Egypt's army and planned the crossing of the Suez Canal. In November 1973, Ali Ahmad Ismail was promoted to the rank of field marshal in the Egyptian Army. *See also* EGYPTIAN INTELLIGENCE.

ISRAELI INTELLIGENCE. Until 1939, no single body existed to coordinate Jewish intelligence actions. Rather, four different organizations were operating throughout the country; although no regular or formal connection existed between these bodies, important pieces of information were channeled to the Jewish Agency's Political Department in Jerusalem. To some extent, the commanders of the Haganah, the Jewish militia, in the various districts and settlement blocs found this arrangement to be advantageous. The next stage in the development of an intelligence system came in 1939, with the publication of the British white paper on Palestine, which intensified the confrontation between Jewish settlements and their British rulers over the future status of Palestine.

Upon the outbreak of **World War II**, the first attempt to unify the four intelligence organizations was made by the Haganah. The prime mover in this effort was Shaul Avigur, who, together with Moshe Sharett and the national Haganah command, was instrumental in creating the official Information Service, known by its Hebrew acronym SHAI. It was divided into departments, and the essential function of counterespionage was integrated into its ranks. The SHAI's departmental system remained in effect with hardly any changes until the body was disbanded soon after the state of Israel was established in May 1948.

Despite the fact that most of its members were lacking in formal intelligence experience, it appears that the SHAI was well organized and was able to penetrate most areas necessary for obtaining intelligence. The SHAI had the benefit of a considerable number of Arabic-speaking Jews, most of whom had been born in Arab countries and could pass as Arabs. Some were sent back to their countries of birth as Israeli agents, and some infiltrated Palestinian Arab villages and towns inside the borders of the British mandate, all for purposes of collecting information.

The SHAI did engage in some successful operations, such as the "Night of the Bridges." By obtaining the plans of the bridges between Palestine and its neighbors, Haganah forces blew up those bridges on 17 June 1946. However, in the end, the SHAI lacked the central direction and systematic thinking essential for an intelligence organization, as all of its departments were more politically than militarily oriented. SHAI was ill prepared for its real mission during the crucial years of 1947 and early 1948 in the struggle for the creation of the independent state of Israel, when most SHAI resources, in terms of manpower, money, and effort, were devoted to the Internal Department for collecting information on dissident Jews.

After the United Nations voted for the partition of Palestine on 29 November 1947, the SHAI, like the intelligence units of the other underground militias, lost many of its contacts with Palestinians and other Arabs. From 29 November 1947 to 14 May 1948, the period marking Israeli statehood, the SHAI performed rather poorly. It managed to learn the planned routes of the Arab invasions of the fledgling Jewish state only a week before they were launched. Many in the Jewish leadership did not believe that the British would really leave or that the regular Arab armies would attack, but they were mistaken on both counts. Arab informers could no longer be contacted once the fighting broke out, due to communication difficulties as well as to unwillingness on the part of many to continue working against their own people. The SHAI failed to evaluate the military strength of the Arab states on the eve of Israel's War of Independence in May 1948. The young state knew very little about enemy plans, and Israeli army forces were surprised by the numbers and strength of the Arab armies. A heavy price was paid for this assessment error.

The SHAI was formally disbanded on 30 June 1948, a month and a half after the declaration of Israeli statehood. Despite its ineffectiveness in many spheres, the SHAI's apparatus and personnel provided the infrastructure on which the new state's military intelligence and security services were founded. Thus, Israel's intelligence community was built on the foundations laid by the SHAI during the few years of its existence.

Besides the SHAI, other underground militias also performed intelligence tasks. The Palmah had the Arab Platoon, which was composed of Arabic-speaking and Arab-looking Jews who conducted work similar to that of the SHAI's Arab Department. There was also Rekhesh (Acquisitions), a secret organization with a mission to secretly obtain weaponry by whatever means available. Finally, the **Mossad** Le'Aliyah Beth organized and brought illegal immigrants to Palestine in violation of the British white paper of 1939. After the Information Service was disbanded on 30 June 1948, three Israeli intelligence organizations were formed: Military Intelligence (MI), the Israeli Security Agency (ISA), and the Political Department in the Foreign Ministry. MI was established as a department in the General Staff of the Israel Defense Forces (IDF) and was known by its Hebrew name, Mahleket Modi'in. In December 1953, it was renamed the Directorate of Military Intelligence, known in Hebrew as Agaf Modi'in (Aman).

MI serves as the professional authority for the Israeli Air Force's Air Intelligence Squadron, the Israeli Navy's Naval Intelligence Squadron, and intelligence units at the headquarters of the various field corps and in the regional commands. MI collects information on the Arab armies and is responsible for state-level intelligence evaluation for war and peace, for providing a warning of war and of hostile and terrorist acts, and for indicating the rise of opportunities for political agreements. When it was established, MI was also engaged in counterespionage; however, this function has since been transferred to the ISA.

MI is structured as two main units: the Collection Department and the Research Division. The Collection Department is responsible for signals intelligence (SIGINT) and for imagery intelligence (IMINT). SIGINT collects intelligence information by plugging into the telephone systems of Arab countries to eavesdrop and record landline conversations. The Collection Department also operates human intelligence (HUMINT) by sending agents and informers over Israel's borders. The Collection Department is responsible for gathering information from open sources (OSINT) by scanning the print and electronic media, including the Internet, for unwittingly exposed military matter.

The Research Division is the largest part of the MI, with 3,000–7,000 officers and other ranks. This division receives and analyzes information assembled by the entire Israeli intelligence community, including the MI itself, the ISA, and the Mossad (the most well-known Israeli intelligence agency). It publishes the *Daily Information Digest* and other periodical assessments, of which the best known is the *Annual National Intelligence Evaluation*. The Research Division is organized into subunits, divided according to geographical and functional targets.

MI is also responsible for assigning military attachés to Israeli embassies overseas. A special task is press censorship and information security (previously known as field security) to prevent the leakage of secret matters. There is a unit for liaison with foreign intelligence communities and another engaged in computer hardware and software to assist in intelligence collection. Following the disbanding in April 1951 of the Foreign Ministry's Political Department, its intelligence missions in Arab countries were transferred to a new unit in MI responsible for dispatching spies, collecting intelligence, and sabotage in Arab countries. In 1963, that unit was dismantled and moved to the Mossad. Another unit was charged with conducting propaganda in Arab countries.

The Sheruth Bitahon Klali literally means General Security Service, but the organization's official English name is Israeli Security

Agency. The ISA is also known as the Security Service, Sheruth Bita-hon, or Shin Bet, which are the Hebrew initials. It was established with the declaration of Israeli independence in the Israel Defense Forces. At that time, all its personnel were IDF officers and soldiers. In 1950, responsibility for ISA activity was moved from the IDF to the Israeli Defense Ministry, and soon after it was moved again, this time to the office of the prime minister.

Upon establishment, the ISA was divided into units, which later became sections. The first section was concerned with preventing subversion by members of the Israeli extreme right. In practice, this referred to political espionage, which entailed the collection of information about the adversaries of the then-ruling party, Mapai. The importance of that section declined with the rising perception of Israel as a democratic state, and political espionage was terminated. The ISA was then transformed from an organization close to the ruling party to a state body without political affiliation.

Other sections of the ISA were charged with counterespionage (espionage obstruction), in particular the section for Arab affairs. Besides monitoring and tracing the political mood of the Arabs in Israel, this section was also responsible for the obstruction of espionage by Arab states and for the prevention of hostile sabotage activity. Since the **Six Days' War**, the major missions of this section have been the fight against subversive action in the occupied territories and the struggle against Palestinian terrorist organizations.

Another ISA unit was concerned with new immigrants, specifically with obtaining information on the Soviet Union and the communist bloc by means of questioning new immigrants from Eastern Europe in order to detect any spies who might attempt to enter Israel in the guise of a new immigrant. The information obtained in this way was important to the state of Israel, as it greatly assisted in establishing intelligence relations with the United States. The information was passed on to intelligence agencies in the United States, which at that time was locked in the Cold War with the Soviet Union. Other sections were responsible for the security of installations of the defense system, including technical services for eavesdropping equipment, microcameras, recording devices, invisible ink, and so forth.

Today the ISA is responsible for security against any party who seeks to undermine Israel by terrorist activity or violent revolution. It is also charged with providing the IDF with intelligence for counterespionage and for supporting counterterrorist operations in the West Bank and the Gaza Strip. After the 1967 Six Days' War, the ISA was assigned to monitor terrorist activity in the occupied territories. This has become the organization's most important role, but it was ill prepared for this mission and its challenges. Its workforce until then had consisted of 600 agents. After a few years, however, it adjusted to the new missions, and its agents became known as "intelligence fighters."

After the 1993 Oslo Accords, the ISA was obliged to undergo another adjustment to collecting intelligence in areas over which the IDF no longer held control under the Oslo agreement. During the Palestinian uprising known as the al-Aqsa Intifada, which erupted in the fall of 2000 after the collapse of the Camp David summit, the ISA reacted speedily to the Arab violence. Since then, it has become a prominent player in Israel's war against the Palestinian **terrorism** that has plagued Israeli cities. The ISA produces intelligence enabling the IDF to stop some of the suicide bombers before they reach their destinations through preventive arrests and the deployment of roadblocks.

In addition, the ISA cooperates with the Israeli Air Force (IAF) to pinpoint and kill terrorist masterminds and leaders by precise air strikes, known as "targeted killings." The targets are field commanders and senior leaders of Palestinian militant factions that Israel considers to be terrorist organizations, mainly those of **Hamas** but also of the Palestinian Islamic Jihad, al-Aqsa Martyrs' Brigades, and al-**Fatah**, as well as the Iranian–Lebanese group **Hizballah**. The ISA task is to provide intelligence on when and where the target will be vulnerable to the strike without endangering civilians.

The ISA has succeeded in uncovering dozens of terrorist groups within Israel's Arab population. In terms of quality and quantity of intelligence gathering, the ISA is considered to be one of the best intelligence services in the world. It relies mainly on human intelligence (HUMINT) from the local population for collecting information about planned terror attacks or about the location of terror leaders. The organization has enjoyed overwhelming success with informants in its targeted killings. As a result, the Palestinian groups, mainly al-Aqsa Martyrs' Brigades, have started lynching suspected collaborators or killing them on the street without trial.

The ISA also obtains information by interrogating suspects. Until the 1980s, the ISA used controversial methods, including beatings, to extract information. However, after complaints of excessive use of violence in interrogations of Palestinian prisoners, the Landau Commission published a directive in 1987 setting criteria for lawful interrogation methods. Only moderate physical pressure was to be permitted, and then only in the case of an imminent terrorist attack. In 1999, the Israeli Supreme Court assessed the ISA interrogation methods and ruled that physical pressure was to be banned altogether. Accordingly, the ISA now bases its interrogations solely on psychological pressure, in which it has become highly effective. However, complaints about physical pressure continue. In 2002, the Knesset passed the Israeli Security Agency Law regulating ISA activity. According to the law, the prime minister carries ministerial responsibility for this activity, but the law's provisions concerning interrogation methods have not been made public.

The Director of Security for the Defense Establishment (DSDE) is the head of a certain unit in the Israeli Defense Ministry known by its Hebrew acronym MALMAB; however, the full title of this unit is not known exactly because of its extreme secrecy. The exact date that MALMAB was established is also unknown, though according to certain documents released by the Defense Ministry, MALMAB was created in the 1960s as part of the Bureau of Scientific Liaison (LAKAM).

MALMAB is apparently responsible for physical security of the Defense Ministry and its research facilities, including the nuclear reactor at Dimona. MALMAB is also charged with preventing leaks from the Israeli security institutions, including the Mossad and the Israeli Security Agency. MALMAB, together with Security Support (SIBAT) in the Ministry of Defense, closely supervises Israeli arms manufacturers with the aim of reducing any potential damage caused by too widely disseminating Israeli weapons technology around the world. Yet, for all its enormous power, MALMAB is not an autonomous intelligence organization, in contrast to the Mossad or the ISA, and in fact does not engage in any information collecting.

Another Israeli intelligence agency is Nativ. Formerly called Bilu, this intelligence organization was established in March 1951 after the dismantling of the Mossad Le'Aliyah Beth, which was active in illegal immigration to Palestine during the period of the British mandate. Nativ was responsible for the connection with Jews in the Soviet Union and Eastern Europe and for immigration to Israel from those countries. Over the years, Nativ became an inseparable part of the Israeli intelligence community, establishing research and intelligence-gathering units and carrying out clandestine operations, such as sending agents under diplomatic cover to Israeli consulates in countries behind the iron curtain. Nativ also ran secret operations to establish contact with Jews and to provide them with informational materials about Israel, prayer books, Hebrew dictionaries, and the like. To this end, it recruited Jews who were citizens of countries other than Israel and members of youth movements abroad. As a cover for its operations, Nativ operatives were planted on vessels of the Israeli merchant fleet that visited Soviet harbors, especially Odessa.

In 1961, Nativ expanded its operations and set up a unit called Bar, which received funding from organizations in the United States controlled by the Central Intelligence Agency (CIA), among others. The unit was charged with spearheading a movement among Jewish organizations and leaders throughout the world to apply pressure on the Soviet Union to allow Jews to immigrate to Israel. The Kremlin considered Nativ a hostile espionage organization that was inciting the Jewish population to emigrate, and every effort was made to repress it, including placing Nativ operatives under surveillance by the KGB. The expansion of its operations enabled Nativ to set up stations at Israeli embassies in Western Europe, Latin America, and the United States. The benefit to the United States from supporting Nativ was access to intelligence about the Soviet Union and other communist bloc countries, which the Israelis obtained from questioning new immigrants in order to detect any spies who might attempt to enter Israel in the guise of new immigrants. In fact, Nativ, with its interviewing of new immigrants, was the main instrument of the intelligence community in its efforts to gather information about the Soviet Union and its satellites.

The organization was behind the worldwide propaganda and information campaign whose slogan was "Let my people go." For about 30 years, Nativ secretly organized the emigration of Jews from Romania through an agreement with the regime of dictator Nicolae Ceausescu. Ceausescu and other senior officials in his regime received bribes in return for this agreement, which over time amounted to tens of millions of dollars deposited in secret bank accounts in Austria and Switzerland.

Nativ's clandestine operations to bring immigrants from the Soviet Union and Eastern Europe largely terminated with the end of the Cold War and the collapse of the Soviet Union. After the renewal of diplomatic relations between Israel and the Eastern Bloc countries at the end of the 1980s, and still more with the disintegration of the Soviet Union, Jews were increasingly able to emigrate freely from those countries. Occasionally, the old methods of using clandestine operations still had to be employed. In September 1992, Nativ organized two airlift operations to take Jews out of Georgia and out of Tajikistan, which were under attack by members of extremist Muslim rebel groups.

Still, the overall change raised questions about the need for a clandestine organization like Nativ. At its peak, Nativ had about 500 employees operating from its Tel-Aviv headquarters and from branch offices in Israeli embassies in the former Soviet Union countries as well as in Israeli consulates in the West. Clearly, the current situation no longer calls for such a large-scale operation. In July 2000, the Israeli government decided on a substantial reduction in Nativ's annual budget, dismantled Nativ's unit for research and intelligence, and transferred part of its functions to other governmental bodies. *See also* BULL, GERALD; ISRAELI INTELLIGENCE SATELLITES; ISRAELI NUCLEAR WEAPONS PROGRAM; JEWISH AGENCY IN PALESTINE; NILI; TENET PLAN.

ISRAELI INTELLIGENCE SATELLITES. In 1979, Israel and Egypt signed a peace treaty according to which Israel agreed to return all control over Sinai Peninsula to Egypt sovereignty, albeit as a demilitarized zone. Verifying that the Sinai Peninsula remains a demilitarized zone without violating Egypt's sovereignty required the development of spy satellites. The 1991 **Operation Desert Storm** and the threats of developing weapons of mass destruction by Iraq, Iran, and Libya required the development of spy satellites as well.

The first Israeli spy satellite, Ofeq-1 (Horizon, in Hebrew), was launched in 1988. The purpose of this launch was just to test the ability of launching a satellite into space. In 1990, Ofeq-2 was launched.

In 1995, Ofeq-3 was launched. The attempted launch of Ofeq-4 in 1998 failed. This failure prompted the Israeli defense establishment to launch the commercial observation satellite Eros-A. It was launched in 2002 and it is still in orbit. In 2002, Ofeq-5, an optical surveillance satellite, was launched. It has a resolution of 1 meter and it is still in orbit.

On 6 September 2004, Ofeq-6 was launched. During the third stage of the Shavit rocket launching, just a couple of minutes after initiation, the launch failed; the satellite did not achieve orbit and crashed into the Mediterranean Sea. Ofeq-6 had been expected to be used for monitoring Israel's neighbors in the Middle East and was intended to replace Ofeq-5. In April 2006, Israel launched another commercial observation satellite, the Eros-B. Although the Eros series are commercial satellites, they were used for obtaining intelligence especially about the Arab world. On 10 June 2007, Ofeq-7 was successfully launched under a cloak of secrecy. It has the ability to eavesdrop on Iran and Syria.

On 23 January 2008, the TECSAR satellite was launched successfully. The TECSAR launch was postponed a number of times, largely due to weather conditions. The TECSAR satellite was manufactured by Israel Aerospace Industries (IAI) as a commercial satellite, but it can boost **Israeli intelligence**-gathering capabilities, especially about Iran. TECSAR has an enhanced footage technology that allows it to transmit clearer images regardless of the time of day and under adverse weather conditions, including dense clouds, and is considered Israel's most advanced satellite in orbit to date. TECSAR uses radar to identify targets, and it differs from the Ofeq series, which rely on cameras.

Israel also has the Amos series satellites. Amos-1 was launched on 16 May 1996 from the European Space Center in French Guiana. Amos-2 was launched on 28 December 2003 from Baikonur, Kazakhstan. The technology of the Amos series satellite is based on experience from Ofeq reconnaissance. Although the Amos satellites are defined as communication satellites, they are used also for espionage purposes. On 28 April 2008, Amos-3 was launched and it is supposed to replace Amos-1 and to remain in space for 18 years. Amos-4 is expected to be launched in mid-2010. *See also* IRAQI NUCLEAR WEAPONS PROGRAM.

ISRAELI NUCLEAR WEAPONS PROGRAM. In 1948, soon after its establishment as a state, Israel began to examine the nuclear option. In 1949, Science Corps C, a special unit of Israel Defense Force's Science Corps, began a two-year geological survey of the Negev Desert to discover uranium reserves. Although no significant sources were found, recoverable amounts were located in phosphate deposits.

Israeli and French research institutes worked closely together. Before **World War II**, France had been a leader in nuclear physics research but subsequently lagged far behind the United States, the Soviet Union, and Great Britain. Israel and France were at a similar level of expertise, so nuclear technology in both countries developed in close alignment in the early 1950s. For example, Israeli scientists were involved in the construction of the (military) G-1 plutonium production reactor and the UP-1 reprocessing plant at Marcoule. In the 1950s and early 1960s, France was Israel's major arms supplier, and as instability spread in the French North African colonies, Israel provided valuable intelligence obtained from those countries.

The Israeli Atomic Energy Commission was established in 1952. By then Science Corps C had succeeded in perfecting the process to extract uranium found in the Negev. It was also able to produce heavy water for a research reactor. Israel decided on the use of heavy water for cooling and of natural uranium as fuel. Normal light water would require enriched uranium, and that was too difficult to obtain. Heavy-water reactors with natural uranium fuel could produce plutonium extremely efficiently.

On 3 October 1957, France and Israel concluded an agreement for the construction of a 24-megawatt research reactor at Dimona in the Negev Desert. France also undertook building a chemical reprocessing plant, although this understanding was not committed to writing. French and Israeli operatives started building the complex in secret. French customs officials were told that certain components, such as the reactor tank, were being shipped to a desalinization plant in Latin America. Moreover, the French Air Force secretly flew as many as four tons of heavy water to Israel, after the French purchased it from Norway on condition that it would not be transferred to a third country,

In 1960 the construction work encountered problems when France urged Israel to submit Dimona to international inspections. France feared a scandal when it became clear that it had aided Israel, especially with respect to the reprocessing plant. Israel worked out a compromise: France would supply the uranium and components that were promised and would not insist on international inspections. For its part, Israel assured France that it had no intention of making nuclear weapons.

The reactor's existence could not be kept secret from the world. In 1958, U-2 reconnaissance spy planes took pictures of the facility under construction, but the United States did not identify it at that time as a nuclear reactor. It was variously explained as a textile plant, an agricultural station, or a metallurgical research facility. Eventually, however, it was impossible to deny that the facility was anything other than a reactor because of its characteristic dome shape. In December 1960, Israeli Prime Minister David Ben Gurion stated that Dimona was a nuclear research center for "peaceful purposes."

Dimona became critical in 1964. French officials were surprised to discover that the cooling circuits were designed to support three times the original power level (24 MW). Without additional cooling, power was indeed scaled up to 70 MW years later.

Besides the reactor and the underground reprocessing plant at Dimona, there was a uranium processing facility, a waste treatment plant, a fuel-fabrication facility, a laboratory, and a depleted uranium bullets factory. It would also contain a facility for uranium enrichment tests.

Presently it is feared that the aged reactor, functioning for more than 40 years, is in a poor state. Former workers have revealed to the media that safety procedures are alarmingly inadequate, and that longtime workers become contaminated after exposure to high levels of radiation.

Israel has always encountered problems acquiring uranium for the reactor because it has not signed the Nonproliferation Treaty (NPT). However, it was able to develop some capability of extracting uranium from phosphate ores at Dimona; it also used "gray market" channels to fuel the reactor. In 1965 up to 100 kilograms of highly enriched uranium were lost from the American Nuclear Materials and Equipment Corporation (NUMEC) in Apollo, Pennsylvania. The existence of certain nuclear material deals between the NUMEC chairman and Israel led to the belief that the uranium had gone to Israel. Other reports suggested that much of the missing uranium was recovered from floors and ventilation ducts when the facility was eventually decommissioned. Furthermore, in 1968 a 200-ton load of uranium (yellow cake) was stolen (or just misdelivered) from the German vessel *Scheersberg A*.

Cooperation between Israel and South Africa on nuclear technology seems to have started around 1967. It lasted through the 1970s and 1980s, during which time South Africa was a principal uranium supplier for Dimona. Israel might have played a part in a nuclear weapons test in the Indian Ocean on 22 September 1979; it was and is generally believed to have been a joint South African–Israeli test.

Israel has long had close relations with the United States. In 1955, before the contract for Dimona had been signed, the United States agreed to sell a 5 MW swimming-pool research reactor to an Israeli facility at Nahal Soreq, south of Tel-Aviv. But the United States required Israel to accept safeguards because it would be supplying highly enriched uranium fuel for the reactor. With the 1960 official announcement that Israel had a reactor for "peaceful purposes," relations between the United States and Israel cooled over the issue. Publicly Washington accepted Israel's declaration of peaceful purposes, but privately it exerted pressure. As a result, Israel finally agreed to admit U.S. inspection teams once a year. These inspections took place between 1962 and 1969 but were in fact a sham. The inspectors saw only above-ground parts of the facility, with simulated control rooms; access to the underground rooms was hidden from them, and it was there, on many levels, that the plutonium reprocessing actually took place. The U.S. inspectors could report no obvious scientific research or that a civilian nuclear power program was evident to justify such a large reactor, but they found no hard evidence of "weapons-related activities" such as the existence of the plutonium reprocessing plant.

In 1968, however, based on information from Edward Teller, father of the U.S. hydrogen bomb, the Central Intelligence Agency (CIA) concluded that Israel had started producing nuclear weapons. Teller had heard this, he said, from Israeli friends in the scientific and defense establishment. He counseled the CIA to make a final assessment without waiting for an Israeli nuclear test, which would never be conducted. In 1981 the U.S. embargoed further shipments of highly enriched uranium fuel to the Nahal Soreq reactor.

After the opening of the Dimona reactor in 1964, it started producing plutonium. During the 1967 **Six Days' War** the first two developed bombs may have been armed. It was also reported that, fearing defeat in the 1973 **Yom Kippur War**, the Israeli Army readied 13 bombs of 20 kilotons each for use. Missiles and aircraft were armed with the bombs for an attack on Egyptian and Syrian targets. During the 1991 **Operation Desert Storm**, Israel went on full-scale nuclear alert when seven Iraqi Scud missiles were fired at Israeli cities. Only three missiles hit Tel-Aviv and Haifa, with only minor damage. But the Israeli government warned Iraq of a counterstrike if the Iraqis used chemical warheads; this clearly meant that Israel intended to launch a nuclear strike if gas attacks occurred.

In 1986, former Dimona worker Mordechai Vanunu revealed details of the Dimona plant to the London *Sunday Times*. His descriptions and the photographs he took during his employment supported the conclusion that Israel had a stockpile of 100 to 200 nuclear warheads. Following his revelations, Vanunu fell into a trap by the **Mossad** and was kidnapped. In a closed door trial, he was sentenced to an 18-year prison term (to be spent in isolation).

In the late 1990s, however, U.S. intelligence organizations gave a different figure, estimating that Israel possessed between 75 and 130 nuclear warheads, which, they believed, could be used in Jericho missiles and as bombs in aircraft. Israel has never conducted a weapons test of its own, apart from the (believed) joint test with South Africa in 1979. However, a subcritical test (with no real nuclear explosion) may have been carried out in November 1966 at Al-Naqab in the Negev Desert.

Israel conducted several acts of sabotage against Iraq out of concern about that country's nuclear weapons development. In April 1979, the Mossad was believed responsible for two explosions at a construction yard in Seine-sur-Mer in France. Two research reactor cores destined for Iraq were badly damaged. In June 1980, Yahya al-Meshad was assassinated in Paris, where he was negotiating a contract for Iraq to take over Iran's share of the French Eurodif enrichment plant. Even earlier, in 1978, unknown attackers had tried to kill him when he was a technical liaison officer with France for the export of the Osiris research reactor.

Israel's most famous act of sabotage is the bombing of the Tammuz-1 research reactor at the Tuwaitha Nuclear Research Center near Baghdad. On 7 June 1980, Israeli aircraft bombed and destroyed the

70 MW reactor completely. According to Israel, Iraq was about to start producing plutonium in the reactor for the manufacture of a nuclear weapon.

Recently, concerns have been expressed that Israel considered bombing Iranian nuclear facilities, where Iran is continuing its construction with the help of Russia. *See also* IRANIAN NUCLEAR WEAPONS PROGRAM; IRAQI NUCLEAR WEAPONS PROGRAM; OPERATION SPHINX.

ITALIAN INTELLIGENCE IN PALESTINE. Under the fascist regime of Benito Mussolini, the Italian government used propaganda and subversive activities in the Middle East from 1935 until 1940, when Italy entered **World War I**. On the one hand, this fascist propaganda was part of Mussolini's foreign policy and his attempts to build an Italian empire with further territorial expansion in Africa. On the other, Rome was courting the Arab nationalist movements in Egypt and Palestine, which were seeking the support of external forces capable of providing political, financial, and military backing needed to revolt against foreign rulers, such as the British and the French.

The relations between Great Britain and Italy were tense against the background of Italy's invasion of Ethiopia. Italy initiated its activities in Palestine under the British mandate in order to ensure Arab support on their side. **British intelligence in Palestine** was aware of the fact that Italy was active in funding the **Great Arab Revolt** of 1936 in Palestine. Italian diplomats, journalists, and businessmen in Palestine, Egypt, Syria, and Lebanon were under constant surveillance, and in particular their contacts with Arabs were watched carefully.

Informers in Arab countries reported to the Jewish Agency in Jerusalem about the activities of Italian agents in Arab countries. Nahum Vilansky, an agent of the Jewish Agency in Cairo obtained information about the Italian activities in Egypt against the British and the Jewish community in Palestine. Information was obtained about the Italian bank Banco di Roma in Beirut, which served as a channel for transferring money from Italy to the Arab leaders in Palestine. The Jewish Agency also received information about a French pilot who serviced Italy and was smuggling money from Egypt to Palestine on a regular basis.

The surveillance of the contacts between the Italians and the Arabs in Palestine extended as far as Geneva. It became known to British intelligence and to the Jewish Agency that Italian delegates went to Switzerland in 1936 in order to meet Jamal al-Husayni, president of the Palestine Arab Party and delegate to the League of Nations discussions on the future of Palestine. After Grand Mufti Haj Muhammad Amin al-Husseini fled to Lebanon in 1937, the British were informed that the Italians planned to take the mufti to Rome. Most of the information about the relations between Mufti Amin al-Husseini and Italian agents was provided by Eliezer Rothstein, who was a double agent.

It was also suspected that diplomatic channels were being used to smuggle money and weapons into Palestine via the Italian consulate in Jerusalem. Other information was obtained about the methods the Italians used to transfer money from their propaganda bureaus and from the diplomatic representative in Cairo by couriers to Palestine. The information aroused suspicion that the Italians were using the diplomatic mail for smuggling purposes. The names of the couriers and of the end receivers became known to the Jewish Agency agents. It was also known that anti-Jewish and British propaganda material was being smuggled into Palestine.

In 1938, British intelligence in Palestine began to worry about Italian and German involvement in the events in Palestine and in the neighboring Arab countries in the case of a outbreak of all-out war and a coordinated Arab resistance to the British mandate in Palestine. At that point, the British increased their surveillance on the Arabs in Palestine and on the Nazi German and Italian activities in Palestine. As a result of these efforts on the part of the British, the center of the Italian activities in the Middle East moved from Palestine to Baghdad, Iraq. Information about the involvement of the Axis—Italy and Germany—in planning another **Arab Revolt** in Palestine increased toward the summer of 1938, and the contacts between Italian agents in Palestine and Syria became more frequent. The Italian involvement in Palestine and in the Middle East continued during World War II and ended completely with the surrender of the Axis by the end of the war. *See also* GERMAN INTELLIGENCE IN PALESTINE; JEWISH INTELLIGENCE IN PALESTINE.

– J –

JABALI, GHAZI AL-. Ghazi al-Jabali was the Gaza Strip chief of the Preventive Security Service, appointed by the Palestinian National Authority in 1994. In February 2004, a gunfight erupted between his police officers and forces loyal to **Muhammad Dahlan**. In March 2004, his offices were targeted by gunfire. In April 2004, a bomb was detonated, destroying the front of his house. In July 2004, al-Jabali was kidnapped at gunpoint following an ambush of his convoy and the wounding of two bodyguards. He was released several hours later. Following his kidnapping, Yasser Arafat dismissed al-Jabali from his post. He was also a member of the Central Committee of the Palestinian Liberation Organization. In 1998, Israel demanded his transfer to Israeli custody, accusing him of coordinating Palestinian attacks on Israel. *See also* PALESTINIAN NATIONAL AUTHORITY INTELLIGENCE.

JALIL, TAHIR (1950–). General Tahir Jalil al-Habbush was born in Tikrit. In 1997, Jalil was appointed by Saddam Hussein to replace **Taha Abbas** as the commander of **Iraq's Directorate of General Security** (DGS). He served in this position until 1999, when he was replaced by **Rafi Tilfah**. Jalil was then appointed director of the **Iraqi Intelligence** Service (IIS). After the 2003 **Operation Iraqi Freedom**, Jalil was listed as wanted by U.S. forces in Iraq. Rumors spread that Jalil had succeeded in escaping to France on a counterfeit passport. The French authorities announced that if they were able to trace him, his passport would be cancelled and he would be arrested. It remains unclear whether Jalil entered France or found asylum in Syria. *See also* IRAQI DIRECTORATE OF GENERAL MILITARY INTELLIGENCE; IRAQI SPECIAL SECURITY ORGANIZATION.

JEWISH AGENCY IN EGYPT. During the 1936 **Great Arab Revolt** in Palestine, many Middle Eastern countries, including Syria, Lebanon, and Iraq, were involved in supporting the Palestinians in Palestine. In Egypt, this effort was led by the Muslim Brotherhood, which was founded in 1928 by Hassan al-Banna. At the beginning of the revolt, there was no attempt made by the **Jewish Agency in**

Palestine to collect any information about the involvement of the Muslim Brotherhood. The Political Department of the Jewish Agency was satisfied with the intelligence work being supplied by its agent in Egypt, Nahum Wilensky, and took action in Palestine based on that information. Wilensky was a journalist who was assigned by the Jewish Agency to cover the events unfolding in Egypt.

After Mufti Haj Amin al-Husseini's escape from Palestine to Lebanon in the fall of 1937, the number of Palestinian and Syrian exiles in Egypt increased. Two Palestinian exiles, Abed al-Hadi and Munaif al-Husseini, were directing the main activities of the Palestinian struggle in Egypt, including a campaign to disseminate propaganda and collect funds for the cause. The Political Department in Jerusalem authorized Wilensky to enlarge his activities by recruiting local human sources in Egypt. Wilensky became intensively engaged in conducting surveillance on the movements and activities of the Palestinian and Syrian exiles in Egypt. He obtained his information from open sources as well as from secret agents in Egypt.

Wilensky reported directly to the Political Department of the Jewish Agency in Jerusalem about the information he had gathered on the current events in Egyptian domestic politics. Wilensky closely followed the contacts between the Palestinian exiles in Egypt and the mufti in Lebanon. He even managed to obtain their mail correspondence, which became a valuable source for assessing the mufti's behavior. The Political Department of the Jewish Agency tried, through Wilensky, to examine the chances for direct negotiation with the Arabs. Wilensky also used disinformation published in local newspapers as a means of psychological warfare aimed at diverting the public in Egypt from the problems in Palestine. This disinformation was quoted by the Syrians and the Lebanese in their local newspapers. *See also* JEWISH AGENCY IN SYRIA.

JEWISH INTELLIGENCE IN PALESTINE. From the time the modern Jewish community in Palestine became an entity, following the first and second waves of immigration (from 1870 until the outbreak of **World War I** in 1914), every Jewish settlement faced the necessity of protecting itself. At the time, protection was necessary mainly against local Arab thieves, both individuals and organized gangs. In Palestine under Ottoman rule, young men who lived in the settlements around Zikhron Ya'akov formed an organization called the Gideonites. During the war, this organization served as the basis for the establishment of **NILI**, the Jewish underground espionage network. However, their intelligence work was amateurish and conducted randomly rather than systematically. Furthermore, no attempts were made to assess the reliability of the information or the sources, and it was therefore difficult to provide any concrete early warnings about Arab political unrest in the streets.

As a result of this failure, the Jewish Agency decided to establish the Information Service (Sherut Yediot; SHAI) in the Haganah, the underground militia of the Jewish community, in Palestine with forces operating in Jewish neighborhoods and settlements. When the **Great Arab Revolt** in Palestine broke out in 1936, these local Jewish intelligence organs became the information-collecting branches of the SHAI.

In the 1940s, the SHAI was reorganized into three separate departments: the Political Department, the Internal Department, and the Arab Department. The Political Department was charged with conducting surveillance on the British mandate authorities in Palestine, while the Internal Department conducted internal surveillance. The Arab Department was mainly tasked with conducting surveillance on the Arab mood in the street, and an attempt was also made to gather and assess intelligence on the Arab infrastructure by training intelligence field experts. As a result of the reorganization, the counterespionage unit of the SHAI and the Arab Department of the Jewish Agency were united, though the SHAI was still under the command of the Haganah.

Despite the confrontation between the Jewish community and the British mandate authorities in Palestine, some cooperation continued in order to conduct intelligence gathering on the Axis countries in Europe and their activities in Palestine and the Middle East. For these reasons, the Jewish Agency dispatched agents to Arab countries and to Europe. Eliyahu Eilat (Epstein) and Eliyahu Sasson were dispatched to Iraq in the beginning of 1937 to assess how deeply the Nazi German propaganda had penetrated into Iraq.

In Transjordan, the Jewish Agency had contacts with Emir as-Sayyid Abdullah (who became King **Abdullah I** in 1946). Abdullah actually supported partition so that the allocated areas of the British mandate for Palestine could be annexed to Transjordan. Abdullah went so far as to have secret meetings with the Jewish Agency (future Israeli prime minister Golda Meir was among the delegates to these meetings), which resulted in a mutually agreed-upon partition plan that even had approval from British authorities.

After **World War II** ended, the SHAI became aware of resumed Arab organizing against the Jewish community, with the smuggling of munitions into Palestine from other Arab countries. However, the SHAI regarded the effort as a local Arab initiative and rejected the likelihood that the Arabs in Palestine would get substantial assistance from the **Arab League** due to its own internal conflicts. This assessment was most probably the result of the lack of information and the lack of experienced intelligence experts in the Jewish community in Palestine.

By the end of 1947, David Ben Gurion came to the conclusion that the intelligence apparatus had to be reorganized in order to focus more on the Arab countries and not just on the Arabs in Palestine. For this purpose, he appointed Reuven Shiloah as his intelligence adviser. Following the declaration of independence of the state of Israel (15 May 1948), the Israel Defense Forces (IDF) established an intelligence department. The advantage of the newly established intelligence department was in the military experience of its staff. The SHAI was dismantled and its activities were divided between the IDF and the Ministry of Foreign Affairs. *See also* ISRAELI INTELLIGENCE.

JEWISH AGENCY IN SYRIA. During the 1936 **Great Arab Revolt** in Palestine in April 1936, many Middle Eastern countries, including Syria, Lebanon, and Iraq, became involved in supporting the Palestinians in Palestine. Based on information gathered in Syria by agents of the Jewish Agency in Damascus, the analysts of the agency's Political Department assessed that there was a linkage between the Palestinian uprising and the uprising in Syria against the French mandate. These agents obtained information about Syrians who were planning to burn the main Jewish synagogue in Damascus and to attack Jewish villages along the border between Syria and Palestine.

The Political Department of the Jewish Agency became actively involved in surveillance of the Mufti Haj Amin al-Husseini after he escaped in the fall of 1937 from Palestine to Lebanon. The agency enlarged its network of agents recruited in Lebanon and Syria to follow the movements of al-Husseini and to thwart the plans of the Palestinian revolt in Palestine. Jewish Agency headquarters in Jerusalem received regular reports from its agents in Syria about current events, including information about the active support and collection of funds for the Palestinian struggle. Nasib al-Bakri was one of the leaders from Damascus who was recruited and paid for gathering information about the activity of the leadership of the Syrian revolt and passing it to the Jewish Agency.

At the same time, the Jewish Agency agent in Cairo, Nahum Wilensky, was holding conversations with Syrian exiles in Cairo about the possibility of negotiations between Jews and Arabs in Palestine. Following these preliminary discussions, Eliyahu Epstein was dispatched by the Jewish Agency to Damascus, where he met Farhi al-Baradi and other Syrian officials in order to establish direct contacts between the Jewish Agency and the Maronite community in Lebanon. *See also* JEWISH AGENCY IN EGYPT.

JORDANIAN INTELLIGENCE. The Jordanian intelligence organization, called the General Intelligence Directorate (GID; Dairat al Mukhabarat), was established in 1964 as the agency responsible for the collection and analysis of intelligence information and for internal security measures to protect the interests of the Jordanian government. Additional duties include fighting corruption, arms and drug smuggling, and counterfeit operations. Its intelligence reports are submitted to key decision makers in the government, and the GID helps other government agencies maintain awareness of security and strategic issues. The GID is regarded today as one of the United States' most effective allied counterterrorism agencies in the Middle East.

American–Jordanian military and intelligence relations have flourished regardless of the temporary strain caused by the reluctance of the late King Hussein of Jordan to participate in the first **Gulf War**. King Abdullah II, who served previously as commander of Jordan's Special Operations force, has actively forged military and intelligence ties with the United States. During the 1990s, as the Iraqi population and commerce in Jordan expanded, the cooperation of Jordanian intelligence with the Central Intelligence Agency (CIA) grew closer, and many of the Iraqi refugees, businessmen, and defectors who settled in Jordan were recruited. Amman became a regional center for anti-Saddam operations. After 11 September 2001, the United States increased funding and technological support to the GID, and the close relations enabled the United States to build permanent signals intelligence (SIGINT) monitoring stations in Jordan. On 19 September 2001, Jordan was officially designated as a combat zone for U.S. military and intelligence personnel and became the "secret" base for U.S. operations in western Iraq to oust Saddam Hussein.

As the GID has the authority to track both internal and external security threats, it plays a leading role in monitoring opponents of King Abdullah II's regime. With its wide reach and access to Islamic organizations, the GID has a long record of successful penetration into extremist groups. In the 1970s, the GID played a leading role in the crackdown on Palestinian radical organizations that threatened to topple the monarchy. In the 1980s, the CIA and the GID collaborated in a campaign aimed at subverting and crippling the organization led by Abu Nidal, which was then considered to be one of the most dangerous terrorist organizations worldwide. The GID also aggressively hunted Abu Musab al-Zarqawi, the Jordanian-born head of **al Qaeda** in Iraq, and arrested several al-Zarqawi associates suspected as perpetrators of the truck bomb attacks on the U.S. embassy and government targets in Amman. The agency has powers of detention and it operates a network of detention centers. There have been reports in intelligence circulation indicating the possibility that Jordanian secret services and intelligence personnel perform "dirty jobs" for the benefit of the Americans, including interrogations, torture, and targeted killings. *See also* ABDULLAH I; ABU NIDAL ORGANIZATION; ASFOURA, SAMIH; JORDANIAN TERRORISM; ZAHABI, MOHAMED AL-.

JORDANIAN TERRORISM. In 1923, Great Britain recognized Jordan's independence, subject to the mandate. In 1946, grateful for Jordan's loyalty in **World War II**, Britain abolished the mandate. That part of Palestine occupied by Jordanian troops was formally incorporated by action of the Jordanian Parliament in 1950. From its early days, Jordan was plagued by **terrorism** and pressure to change its political stands, which are characterized by moderation and rationality in a region torn by extremism and instability. In addition to the Jordanian citizens, institutions, embassies, and diplomats abroad who have been the target of terrorism, Jordan lost its founder King Abdullah bin al-Hussein in 1951, as well as two of its prime ministers (Haza'a al-Majali and Wasfi al-Tal) to terrorism.

From the beginning of King Hussein's reign in 1952, he had to steer a careful course between his powerful neighbor to the west, Israel, and the rising Arab nationalism that frequently posed a direct threat to his throne. Jordan was swept into the 1967 Arab–Israeli War and lost East Jerusalem and all of its territory west of the Jordan River, the West Bank. Embittered Palestinian guerrilla forces virtually took over sections of Jordan in the aftermath of defeat, and open warfare broke out between the Palestinians and government forces in 1970. By mid-1971, Hussein, ignoring protests from other Arab states, had crushed Palestinian strength in Jordan and shifted the problem to Lebanon, where many of the guerrillas had fled.

On 26 October 1994, King Hussein and Israeli Prime Minister Yitzhak Rabin signed a peace agreement, though a clause in it calling the king the "custodian" of Islamic holy shrines in Jerusalem angered the Palestinian Liberation Organization. In the wake of the agreement, relations improved between Jordan and the United States, as well as with the moderate Arab states, including Saudi Arabia. In January 1999, King Hussein unexpectedly deposed his brother, Prince Hassan, who had been heir apparent for 34 years, and named his eldest son as the new crown prince. A month later, King Hussein died of cancer, and Abdullah, 37, a popular military leader with little political experience, became king.

A terrorist plot targeting four sites in Jordan was planned by members of the terrorist group **al Qaeda** to occur on or near 1 January 2000. The 2000 millennium attack sites were chosen to target tourists from the United States and Israel: a fully booked Radisson hotel in Amman; the border between Jordan and Israel; Mount Nebo, a Christian holy site; and a site on the Jordan River where John the Baptist is said to have baptized Jesus. However, the terrorist plot was foiled by Jordanian authorities.

On 30 November 1999, **Jordanian intelligence** intercepted a call between Abu Zubaydah, the leader of the plot, and Khadr Abu Hoshar, a Palestinian militant. In the conversation, Zubaydah stated that the time for training was over. Sensing that an attack was imminent, Jordanian police arrested Hoshar and 15 others on 12 December 1999. The most active participant was a Boston taxi driver named Raed Hijazi. The authorities put 28 suspects on trial, and 22 of them were quickly found guilty. Six of them, including Hijazi, were sentenced to death. Zubaydah was sentenced to death in absentia. Loa'i Muhammad Haj Bakr al-Saqa and Abu Musab al-Zarqawi, who later became the leader of al Qaeda in Iraq, were sentenced in absentia in 2002 for their part in the plot, which included using poison gas during the bombing.

On 9 November 2005, a series of coordinated suicide bombings blasted three hotels in Amman, killing 60 people and wounding 115 others—almost all of whom were Jordanians. The three hotels are often frequented by Western military contractors and diplomats. Al Qaeda in Iraq claimed responsibility for the attacks, contending that Jordan had been targeted because of its friendly relations with the United States. The explosions took place at the Grand Hyatt Hotel, the Radisson SAS Hotel, and the Days Inn. The bomb at the Radisson SAS Hotel exploded in the Philadelphia Ballroom, where a wedding hosting almost 300 guests was taking place. In addition to killing a total of 38 people, the explosion destroyed the ballroom and caused damage to other parts of the hotel. The bomb that exploded in the lobby bar of the Grand Hyatt Hotel was equally devastating.

A number of Iraqis were among the more than 100 suspects who were arrested in the days following the attacks. On 12 November 2005, Deputy Prime Minister Marwan Muasher reported that the attacks had been carried out by the Jordanian-born al-Zarqawi's group. According to Jordanian officials, the attackers had entered the country from Iraq three days before the attacks, and police claimed to have found maps that were used in planning the attack.

Although Jordanian police initially stated that there were only three attackers, King Abdullah shortly thereafter announced the arrest of a woman believed to be a fourth would-be suicide bomber, whose explosive belt had failed to detonate at the Radisson. The three dead suicide bombers were identified as Ali Hussein Ali al-Shamari (Radisson SAS); Rawad Jassem Muhammad Abed (Grand Hyatt); and Safaa Muhammad Ali (Days Inn). The woman in custody was identified as Sajida Mubarak Atrous al-Rishawi. She was married to al-Shamari and was the sister of a close aide of al-Zarqawi.

JOSHUA'S SPIES. Joshua was one of the two surviving spies who had participated in the spy operation conducted under Moses. Under the leadership of Joshua, things proceeded in a different manner. He chose two young men, whose names are not recorded, and instructed them to survey the city of Jericho. The spies went to Jericho and visited a harlot named Rahab, who hid the spies and kept them from being captured by the local authorities, despite their knowledge of the spies' presence. She told the two spies that the people had been expecting an Israelite invasion for some time and that they were frightened of the Israelites, even though the city was well fortified and the army was well trained. The escape of the Israelites from the Egyptians, their successful crossing of the Red Sea, the subsequent destruction of the pharaoh and his armies, and their exploits during the 40 years of wandering in the desert were well known to the people and had convinced them of the Israelites' superiority. Rahab likewise was convinced that the city would fall and made an agreement with the spies that she would help them leave the city and not reveal the plan if in return they would spare her and her family during the attack. The spies agreed, and with Rahab's help, they successfully escaped capture and eventually made their way back to their own people.

The spies reported to Joshua everything that had happened, especially the information given to them by the harlot regarding the people's fear of an impending attack by the Israelites. Using this information, Joshua made plans for the invasion and reported his plan to the 12 tribes. The plan was approved, the invasion proceeded, and the attack, capture, and subsequent destruction of the city of Jericho were successful. As promised, Rahab and her family were spared by Joshua during the battle of Jericho. *See also* MOSES' SPIES.

– K –

KAKA, AHMAD HASSAN. Ahmad Hassan Kaka al-Ubaydi was an official of the Ba'ath party and an officer of the **Iraqi Intelligence** Service (IIS) under Saddam Hussein's regime. After the 2003 **Oper-**

ation Iraqi Freedom, the Central Criminal Court of the new Iraqi regime issued an arrest warrant for Kaka on 9 January 2005. *See also* IRAQI DIRECTORATE OF GENERAL MILITARY INTELLIGENCE; IRAQI DIRECTORATE OF GENERAL SECURITY; IRAQI SPECIAL SECURITY ORGANIZATION.

KANAAN, GHAZI (1942–2005). Born in Bhamra near Kerdaha, Syria, to a prominent Alawite family, Major General Ghazi Kanaan was the powerful commander of **Syrian intelligence** in Lebanon from the mid-1970s until 2002. Ghazi Kanaan is also known to his associates as Abu Yo'roub, after the name of his eldest son. All high-ranking Lebanese officials reported directly to Kanaan, and he had the final word on all major political and security decisions made by the Lebanese government.

Kanaan joined the Syrian military early in his career. During his army career, he commanded a Syrian Army unit facing Israeli forces in the Golan Heights during the 1970s. Kanaan rapidly advanced through the army officer corps. He attained the rank of colonel and served as head of Syrian intelligence in Homs until 1982, when he was appointed to replace Colonel Muhammad Ghanem as commander of Syrian intelligence (Mukhabarat) in Lebanon.

During the Lebanese Civil War of the 1970s, Syria's intelligence in Lebanon united under Kanaan's command. He decided to locate the Syrian intelligence headquarter in Lebanon in Anjar, an Armenian village in the Bekaa Valley. Ghazi Kanaan established more Syrian intelligence bases and detention camps in west Beirut.

Ghazi Kanaan gradually tightened Syria's grip over the Lebanese government during the 1980s by cultivating alliances with members of Lebanon's militia elite. In 1983, Kanaan ordered his militia allies to destroy the 17 May agreement between Lebanon and Israel that was brokered by U.S. Secretary of State George P. Shultz. In 1984, Kanaan masterminded the 6 February mutiny in west Beirut that led to the breakdown of the Lebanese central government and the withdrawal of multinational peacekeeping forces, including U.S. marines, from Lebanon. By the late 1980s, Syrian influence pervaded throughout the country as militia leaders of all sectarian persuasions came under Kanaan's influence. All those who expressed a rejection of Syrian influence were either executed or imprisoned.

Kanaan's most significant achievement during the 1980s was to trace Lebanese Christians who belonged to the Lebanese Forces (LF) militia and influence them to defect to the Syrian side. Among them were Elie Hobeika, who was one of the commanders who ordered his men to carry out the 1982 massacre of Palestinians in Sabra and Shatila. Kanaan also succeeded in influencing LF Commander Samir Geagea to collaborate with Damascus in October 1990, when Syrian forces invaded east Beirut and ousted the constitutional government of Lebanon headed by Interim Prime Minister Michel Aoun.

After Aoun was ousted, Syrian control of Lebanese politics became complete and Ghazi Kanaan became the key decision-making figure. The election of the new president in Lebanon was strictly subject to his official approval. In October 1995, just weeks before the expiration of Lebanese President Elias Hrawi's term in office, Kanaan attended a party hosted by former prime minister Umar Karami and ordered numerous members of the Lebanese Parliament to amend Article 49 of the Lebanese Constitution and extend Hrawi's tenure for three more years. Soon after, members of the Lebanese Parliament obediently convened and extended Hrawi's term in office.

Ghazi Kanaan's power extended far beyond his political capacity. Due to the extensive network of Syrian intelligence officers and local operatives under his command, little of importance happened in Lebanon without his knowledge. The commander of Lebanon's Sureté Générale (General Security Directorate), Major General Jamil Sayyed, reported directly to Kanaan, often bypassing the civilian leadership of the Lebanese regime. Kanaan, who had the power to order the arrest and indefinite detention of anyone in Lebanon, was the most feared man in the country. Kanaan used his influence for personal gain as well. His involvement in narcotics production and trafficking in the Bekaa Valley, counterfeiting, and other illegal activities made him a very wealthy man. With the shadow of Syrian power lurking behind him, few in Lebanon were willing to stand their ground in disputes with Kanaan.

Kanaan's success in subduing Lebanon earned him tremendous accolades in Damascus. Ghazi Kanaan replaced **Ali Douba** as the head of Syria's entire intelligence apparatus. Kanaan's early support of Bashir Assad considerably strengthened his influence within the regime. Ghazi Kanaan also had good relations with several U.S. officials, particularly in the intelligence community. He even visited Washington, D.C., on at least one occasion, in February 1992.

In 2002, Ghazi Kanaan was summoned back to Damascus and was offered the position of minister of interior. Kanaan was succeeded in Lebanon by **Rustum Ghazali** in 2004. He then served as Syrian minister of interior until 12 October 2005 when he was killed in his office by a gunshot. According to one rumor, Kanaan was killed because he objected to Assad's decision to extend the term of the pro-Syrian Lebanese President Émile Laoud, siding with the then Lebanese prime minister, Rafik al-Hariri, with whom he is reported to have had a good relationship. *See also* LEBANESE INTELLIGENCE.

KARINE-A. On January 2002, elements of the Palestinian National Authority's (PNA) **Fatah** movement attempted to smuggle 50 tons of weaponry and ammunitions worth $15 million into the Gaza Strip, including Katyusha rockets, mortars, sniper rifles, antitank missiles and mines, and general ammunition. The ship was purchased in 2001 by Ali Muhammad Abbas, an Iraqi citizen, under the name *Rim-K* and renamed *Karine-A* and registered under a Tonga flag. It was brought by Captain Omar Akawi, a former Fatah member, to the island of Kish, close to the Iranian coast, and loaded with the weapons purchased by a member of Yasser Arafat's staff, Adel Moghrabi Salameh. The cargo of the vessel included civilian freight that concealed the weapons. When the Palestinian plan was revealed by **Israeli intelligence**, the Israeli Air Force and Navy carried out a combined operation on 3 January 2002 to capture *Karine-A* in the Red Sea about 300 miles off the shore of Israel. The operation was successfully completed without firing a single shot, and the ship was brought to Israel. Based on the captain's interrogation and intelligence information, Israel blamed the PNA for the incident.

KHEIR, SAAD (1951–). Holding a bachelor's degree in political science from the University of Jordan, Lieutenant General Saad Kheir joined the Mukhabarat (General Intelligence Department; GID) as an intelligence cadet and made his way up the ranks over nearly three decades. Kheir became second-in-command of the GID in 1996 and was appointed to the position of director on 9 November 2000. In

2001, King Abdullah II of Jordan bestowed upon him the title of "maali," which is equivalent to the rank of minister, with all inherent privileges. He was appointed director of the State Security Council in May 2001 and then adviser to King Abdullah on security affairs in March 2002. Saad Kheir was dismissed by King Abdullah in November 2005. *See also* JORDANIAN INTELLIGENCE.

KHOULI, MUHAMMAD AL-. Major General Muhammad al-Khouli was the trusted advisor to President Hafez Assad and occupied an adjacent office to Assad in the presidential palace. Al-Khouli commanded the Syrian Air Force Intelligence for nearly 30 years, until the **Hindawi affair**, the attempted bombing of an Israeli airliner at London's Heathrow Airport in April 1986. The subsequent investigation revealed that the primary suspect, Nizar Hindawi, who had tricked an unsuspecting woman into carrying explosives onto the aircraft, was operating in coordination with al-Khouli and his aide, Lieutenant Colonel **Haitham Sayid**, in Air Force Intelligence. The two officials had promised the Jordanian national Hindawi UK £250,000 in exchange for placing a bag of explosives on an El Al flight to Tel-Aviv and had taken part in the planning, financing, training, and recruiting for the operation. As a result of this incident, the British government severed diplomatic relations with Syria. *See also* SYRIAN INTELLIGENCE.

KILOWATT GROUP. International cooperation between intelligence services is by default bilateral, but close coordination in and around Europe is achieved informally through the so-called Bern Club, formed in 1971. "Kilowatt" is the codename of the International Counterterrorist Intelligence Network. This group was formed in 1977 at the instigation of Israel, largely in response to the 1972 Munich massacre of Israeli athletes at the Olympic Games. The purpose of the Kilowatt Group was to ensure the free flow of intelligence about terrorist groups and political extremists through a secure telex clearinghouse network.

The members of the Kilowatt Group are the European Union countries, Canada, Norway, Switzerland, the United States (represented by the Central Intelligence Agency [CIA] and the Federal Bureau of Investigation [FBI]), South Africa, and Israel (represented by the

Mossad and Israeli Security Agency [ISA]). The group is dominated by Israel because of its strong position in information exchange on Arab-based terrorist groups in Europe and the Middle East. Since 1977, the Kilowatt Group may have changed its name, and probably its codename, to another that is not yet known publicly.

It is believed that the Mossad's links with the German Intelligence Services (BND) undoubtedly hold the most comprehensive registry of information on international **terrorism** and political extremism, using high-speed, hyperencrypted communications known as "C37A" from a signals intelligence (SIGINT) site near Tel-Aviv and "6XM8" from a similar site at Monschau, near Hoefen, on the Belgian border. Unit 8200, with its huge SIGINT facilities just outside Herzliya near Tel-Aviv, and the ISA feed their information straight to the Situation Information Center of the Kilowatt Group. It is believed that the Mossad supplies the CIA with information on terrorism and extremists, especially those of the Middle East.

In 1991, it emerged that Israeli Mossad agents were operating illegally on Norwegian territory, posing as Norwegian police, with the consent and support of Norwegian security. The disguised Israelis interrogated Palestinians seeking asylum in Norway. The Israeli–Norwegian operation was run within the framework of the Kilowatt Group.

KUSSA, MOUSSA. Head of the Libyan External Security Organization (ESO), Moussa Kussa is known in Libya as a ruthless killer who has no problem using extreme force. He is responsible for the murder and mutilation of dissidents in the country and in exile. He is the man who orchestrated the bombing of Pan Am Flight 103 that crashed over Scotland. He also enables the use of the Libyan Islamic Call Society as a factor in various subversive efforts in West Africa and other parts of the continent. *See also* LIBYAN INTELLIGENCE.

KUWAITI INTERNAL SECURITY. Before the **Gulf War** in 1991, Kuwait maintained a small military force consisting of army, navy, and air force units. The majority of equipment for the military was supplied by Great Britain. Aside from the few units that were transferred to Saudi Arabia, all of this equipment was either destroyed or taken by the Iraqis. Much of the property returned by Iraq after the

Gulf War was damaged beyond repair. Moreover, Iraq retained a substantial amount of captured Kuwaiti military equipment in violation of United Nations resolutions. Since the end of the war in February 1991, Kuwait, with the help of the United States and other allies, has made significant progress in increasing the size and modernity of its armed forces. The government also continues to improve its defense arrangements with other Arab states, as well as United Nations Security Council members.

A separately organized National Guard maintains internal security. The police constitute a single national force under the purview of civilian authorities of the Ministry of Interior. Kuwait's internal security and police services are considered to be well trained and organized. These services receive growing support from Saudi Arabia, Bahrain, and the United Arab Emirates as part of a broad effort among the Persian Gulf States to improve cooperation in reporting on the activities of various radical groups and religious factions as well as labor problems.

KZAR, NADHIM. Nadhim Kzar, an Iraqi Shi'ite, was the first commander of **Iraq's Directorate of General Security** (DGS). He was appointed to this position in 1969 by Saddam Hussein, then vice president of Iraq, after DGS had deteriorated under 10 years (1958–1968) of army rule. Kzar was known for his sadism, and under his command the DGS tortured and killed thousands. Much of this violence was directed against the Iraqi Communist Party and the Iraqi Kurds. He even attempted twice to assassinate the Kurdish leader Mustafa Barazani. His goal was to promote the Shi'ites and to put an end to the Sunni regime. In 1973, Kzar initiated an unsuccessful coup attempt against Iraqi President Ahmed Hassan al-Bakr. Bakr was supposed to be assassinated when his plane landed in Baghdad, but his flight was delayed and Kzar was forced to change the plan. Kzar planned to escape to Iran, but he was captured and found guilty on 7 July 1973 by the Iraqi Revolutionary Command Council and executed. *See also* IRAQI DIRECTORATE OF GENERAL MILITARY INTELLIGENCE; IRAQI INTELLIGENCE; IRAQI SPECIAL SECURITY ORGANIZATION.

– L –

LAANIGRI, HAMIDOU (1943–). General Hamidou Laanigri was appointed in September 2006 as general inspector of Morocco's Auxiliary Forces, with the task of supervising the southern and northern zones in Morocco. Laanigri, who previously served as chief of the Direction Générale de la Sûreté Nationale (DGSN; General Office of National Security) became the second top general to lose his position as chief of the DGSN. Prior to his appointment to the position of DGSN police chief, Laanigri had served as the head of the domestic intelligence service, Direction de la Surveillance du Territoire (DST; Territory Security Directorate) until shortly after the 2003 suicide bombings in Casablanca killed 45 people. *See also* MOROCCAN INTELLIGENCE.

LAHOUD, GABY (1931–). After graduating from the military school al-Madrasa al-Harabia in 1952, Gaby Lahoud enrolled in a military education program in France in 1954. In 1959, he joined the **Lebanese intelligence** agencies and played an important role during the presidency of Fuad Chehab (1958–1964). In 1964, Lahoud was appointed as head of the intelligence agency under President Charles Helou (1964–1970).

Lahoud and the organization he headed were accused of persecuting the Palestinian *fedayeen*. He did not support their attacks on Israel in the 1960s, as he saw that the damage inflicted by the Israelis on the Lebanese in retaliation for each Palestinian action was much larger than the damage caused by the Lebanese side. He also perceived the Palestinian activity from Lebanon against Israeli targets as a violation of the armistice agreements signed between Lebanon and Israel in 1949.

Lahoud's position ended with the presidential election of Suleiman Kabalan Beik Frangieh to the presidency in 1970. Lahoud had supported Elias Sarkis in the 1970 elections as the candidate who could revitalize Lebanon, which had been deteriorating since the mid-1960s. Lahoud was dismissed from his position and removed from the army. He left for Spain and returned to Lebanon at the end of Sarkis's presidency (1976–1982). President Amine Gemayel appointed Lahoud as a major general in the Lebanese Army, but after a while he went back to Spain, where he lives at present. *See also* LEBANESE INTELLIGENCE.

LANDON, TIM (1942–2007). Born in Vancouver to a British army officer and a Canadian mother, he was educated at Eastbourne College and the British Royal Military Academy Sandhurst. Brigadier Tim Landon was a remarkable British intelligence officer and even a mysterious figure. His particular theater was Oman, where he organized a peaceful coup d'état, and is said to have amassed a fortune of more than £200 million.

The foundation of Landon's success was his friendship with Sultan Qaboos bin-Said. The two men had been classmates at Sandhurst and went on to serve in different regiments of the British army. Landon's introduction to Oman came in the late 1960s, when he was appointed a junior intelligence officer in Dhofar, serving under the command of Brigadier Malcolm Dennison. At the time Oman was ruled by Qaboos's father, Sultan Said bin-Taimour, and was involved in a struggle against communist insurgents. Landon secretly helped Qaboos overthrow his father in 1970.

As the new sultan's military adviser and confidant, Landon was in a position to help broker arms deals to reequip the newly pro-Western gulf state. Landon demonstrated his ability to facilitate development contracts for British companies. However, his great achievement was to assist a young and inexperienced ruler in the application of good governance and in the creation of a modern state. *See also* BRITISH INTELLIGENCE IN OMAN.

LAVON AFFAIR. The Lavon affair is known also as "the Bad Business" and by its codename, Operation Susannah. In 1951, the Israeli Military Intelligence (MI) established a network of agents inside Egypt with the capability of attacking civil and military installations. In 1954, as pressure mounted for the British and French to turn over the Suez Canal to the Egyptians, director of Military Intelligence Binyamin Gible ordered the network under its Israeli commander, Avri El-Ad, to launch a series of attacks designed to discredit the Egyptian government. The Israeli MI included the United States Information Service (USIS) libraries in Cairo and Alexandria as targets for the attack. A failed attack in Alexandria led to the rolling up of the network. Soon after, it aroused a big scandal and the question quickly became "Who authorized the attacks on U.S. and British installations in Egypt?" Minister of Defense Pinchas Lavon denied that he authorized the attacks. However, he was forced to resign. *See also* IS-RAELI INTELLIGENCE.

LAWRENCE, THOMAS EDWARD (1888–1935). T. E. Lawrence studied archeology and graduated with honors from Oxford in 1910. Then he served as an assistant at a British Museum excavation in Mesopotamia, where he met **Gertrude Bell**. When **World War I** broke out in 1914, Lawrence spent a brief period in the Geographical Section of the General Staff in London, and soon was stationed in the Military Intelligence Department in Cairo. In Cairo, Lawrence served as an intelligence officer and succeeded in gathering and analyzing intelligence on the Turkish Empire and its troops and producing maps illustrating the Turkish forces. Lawrence collected intelligence from various sources about the Ottoman Army, such as telegrams from Sofia, Belgrade, Petrograd, Athens, Basra, and Tiflis. He also wrote a book based on the collected intelligence, *Handbook of the Turkish Army*. The handbook was designed for extensive circulation and Lawrence, together with his comrades in the British Intelligence Department in Cairo, used to update the handbook frequently as new information was obtained. From January 1915 to February 1916, Lawrence published eight editions of this handbook.

In June 1916, Sharif Hussein bin-Ali of Mecca initiated a revolt of the Arabs living in the Hijaz against Turkish rule. At first, the revolt went well; however, with time the momentum waned when the Arabs failed to capture Medina. **British intelligence in Egypt and Sudan** came to worry about the possibility that the revolt would not achieve its aim of getting rid of Ottoman Empire rule in Arabia. Lawrence was then still an intelligence officer in the British Intelligence Department in Cairo, but he decided take a leave from this job and go to Arabia to encourage the rebels to continue their struggle against the Ottoman Empire.

On 13 October 1916, Lawrence and the oriental secretary to the British civilian administration in Cairo, Ronald Storrs, left Cairo to visit the Hijaz. Lawrence and Storrs arrived in Jeddah on 16 October 1916 and had a meeting with Emir Abdullah, Hussein's second son.

Three days later, Lawrence met Emir Ali, Sharif Hussein's oldest son, and his youngest son, Emir Zeid. On 23 October 1916, Lawrence met Faisal bin-Abd al-Aziz bin-Saud (the founder of Saudi Arabia).

Lawrence's major contribution to the revolt was convincing the Arab leaders (Faisal and Abdullah bin al-Hussein) to coordinate their actions in support of British strategy. He persuaded the Arabs not to drive the Ottomans out of Medina; instead, he recommended that the Arabs attack the Hijaz railways on many occasions. This tactical move tied up more Ottoman troops, who were forced to protect the railway and repair the constant damage. From Hijaz, Lawrence reported to Cairo how things were progressing.

In November 1916, Lawrence returned to Egypt and was officially transferred to the **Arab Bureau in Cairo** and wrote reports about what was necessary for the success of the **Arab Revolt**. This included regular supplies, weapons, ammunition, and most of all, money. In his reports, Lawrence identified Faisal as the most suitable person to lead the revolt. In December 1916, Lawrence was sent back to the Hijaz to rejoin Faisal as his personal liaison officer. He remained with him until October 1918 and together they guided the Arab army north to Damascus.

Lawrence's major contribution to the revolt was convincing Faisal and Abdullah to coordinate their actions in support of the British strategy. Finally the Arab Revolt succeeded. Lawrence became popularly known as Lawrence of Arabia. *See also* HIJAZ OPERATION.

LEBANESE INTELLIGENCE. The official name of the Lebanese intelligence is the General Security Directorate (GSD; Sureté Générale). The agency was established in 1921, and in 1945 it was placed under the authority of the Ministry of the Interior, with headquarters in Beirut. The GSD is assigned by the government to gather and analyze political, economic, and social information; to monitor the preparation and implementation of security measures; to combat threats and acts of sabotage that might jeopardize the security of the state; and to perform judicial investigations. The GSD is also engaged in organizing and monitoring services related to foreigners visiting the country, including everything from arrival to departure. It prepares documentation regarding deportation, implements travel bans and restrictions for entry to the country, issues Lebanese passports and permanent and temporary residence permits, monitors all documentation issued to Palestinian refugees living in Lebanon, and supervises all procedures related to naturalization. The GSD is also responsible for media censorship of audiovisual broadcasting and publication of written materials, including the press. *See also* LAHOUD, GABY.

LIBYAN BALLISTIC MISSILES PROGRAM. The bulk of Libya's ballistic missile inventory consisted of aging FROG and Scud-B missiles imported from the Soviet Union. Western intelligence reports indicated that potential delivery vehicles included short-range antiship cruise missiles, air-launched tactical missiles, fighter aircraft, bombers, artillery, helicopters, and rockets. It does not appear that Libya had an active program underway to develop a missile delivery system for nuclear warheads.

Throughout the late 1980s and early 1990s, Libya made several apparently unsuccessful attempts to purchase more sophisticated missiles, such as the Surface-to-Surface (SS)-12, SS-23, and SS-21 from the Soviet Union, the DF-3A, M-9, and M-11 from China, and extended-range Scuds or No-Dong missiles from North Korea. Libyan attempts to modify its older Scuds in order to extend their range also proved to be unsuccessful. The Central Intelligence Agency (CIA) in 1993 noted that, although Libyan leaders had expressed a desire for ballistic missiles capable of reaching North America, an actual commitment to such an expensive and technically and politically risky development program was doubtful. For over 15 years, Libya did attempt to develop an indigenous missile, al-Fatah, with an intended range of 950–1,000 kilometers. This would have allowed it to target Sardinia, Sicily, southern Italy (including Rome), and U.S. forces in the Mediterranean. If these missiles were based near Tobruk, they would be able to hit Israel, Greece, western Turkey, and almost all of Egypt. However, Libya only succeeded in producing liquid-fueled rockets with a range of about 200 kilometers, and al-Fatah never moved beyond the testing stage.

On 12 September 1981, U.S. space and intelligence analysts and the West German company Organisation, Revisions und Treuhand AG (OTRAG) were building installations at Sebha, Libya, as part of Libya's overall effort to develop an indigenous production capability in missile parts and related technology. On 5 June 1982, British intelligence claimed that Libya delivered Marte antiship air-to-surface missiles to Argentina, and another British report maintained that the missiles were the Israeli-made Gabriel sea-skimming ones. Libya's missile development was hampered by the imposition of United Nations sanctions between 1992 and 1999 that restricted the flow of ballistic missile technology. Central Intelligence Agency (CIA) director John Deutch listed Libya as one of the recipients of North Korean Scud missiles (possibly the Scud-B or -C).

According to the assessment of the U.S. Defense Intelligence Agency (DIA), Libya's missile program has only succeeded in producing missiles with ranges of about 200 kilometers. Libya hoped that al-Fatah missile would reach ranges of up to 950 kilometers. Libya has also sought to acquire the North Korean No-Dong series missiles. In November 1996, the CIA stated that Serbian scientists were also assisting Libya in the production of ballistic missiles. In January 2001, the DIA assessed that Libya had some success in circumventing sanctions and obtaining ballistic-missile-related components and technology from companies abroad, most notably China, India, and the former Yugoslavia. In the 1990s, Libya also maintained cooperation with Iran in developing missile technology and components. The CIA reported in August 2000 that Libya was continuing its efforts to obtain ballistic-missile-related equipment, materials, technology, and expertise from foreign sources. An example was the 1999 attempt to ship liquid-fuel rocket engine components as "auto parts" from a firm in Taiwan to Libya, intercepted in Great Britain.

Libya's only possibly operational ballistic missile system was the 300-kilometer-range Scud-B, acquired from the former Soviet Union. Its inventory was quite large, estimated at 80 launchers and between 240 and 800 missiles. In 1986, Libya actually fired two Scuds at a U.S. Coast Guard facility on the Italian island of Lampedusa. According to a 1996 report, they were sufficient to provide a tactical strike against Libya's regional neighbors, including Egypt, Chad, Niger, and Algeria, as well as offshore islands in the Mediterranean, but they could not threaten the mainland of southern Europe. However, according to a U.S. Pentagon report in January 2001, these were aging missiles and their operational status was questionable due to poor maintenance. Eventually, Libya agreed to cease its programs on weapons of mass destruction on 19 December 2003.

In September 2004, the United States announced that its verification of the dismantling of Libya's nuclear, biological, and chemical (NBC) weapons program, including the Missile Technology Control Regime (MTCR), was essentially complete. *See also* LIBYAN BIOLOGICAL WEAPONS PROGRAM; LIBYAN CHEMICAL WEAPONS PROGRAM.

LIBYAN BIOLOGICAL WEAPONS PROGRAM. When Libya signed the 1925 Biological and Toxin Weapons Convention (BTWC) in December 1971, it declared that it would only be bound to the protocol as long as other signatory countries did not pose a threat to Libya's sovereignty by failing to comply with the protocol. On 19 January 1982, Libya signed the BTWC without reservations and ratified it. However, there were a number of allegations in Western intelligence reports that Libya had pursued offensive biological warfare capabilities and had produced limited quantities of proscribed biological agents in violation of its international commitments. Libya's possible possession of biological weapons agents was considered to be a significant threat because dissemination by terrorists of an agent such as anthrax would be capable of inflicting massive civilian casualties.

In the mid-1990s, it was believed by the U.S. Central Intelligence Agency (CIA) that Libya had a biological weapons program in the early research and development stage. Its arsenal reportedly included an unconfirmed number of microbial and toxic agents, though it did not succeed in developing effective delivery systems. Despite little knowledge about the locations of the facilities manufacturing biological weapons agents, Libya's Rabta facility, primarily a chemical weapons plant, was believed to also contain biological weapons research facilities. Like Rabta, the Tarhunah chemical weapons plant was also thought to be possibly manufacturing biological agents, though these suspicions were based on previous research and development programs and there was no solid evidence of production capacity.

After the Cold War ended, the CIA's analysts described the biological weapons programs of two great powers, Russia and China, as being in the process of change, and identified Iran, Iraq, North Korea, and Libya as rogue nations seeking to acquire weapons of mass destruction.

In early 1995, U.S. intelligence sources claimed that Libyan ruler Muammar Qaddafi attempted to recruit South African scientists to Tripoli to assist in Libya's development of biological weapons. These scientists had secretly developed biological weapons that were allegedly used to assassinate opponents of South Africa's apartheid regime. Despite such foreign assistance, it would have taken several years for Libya to be capable of producing effective biological weapons and missile warheads suitable for use at the proper altitude without killing the microbes.

Libya's international relations, especially with the United States, were further damaged by allegations that Libya was seeking to acquire biological weapons technology from Cuba in May 2002. There were also reports in June 2003 that Libya was employing approximately 400 Iraqi scientists in its biological and chemical weapons programs. Further, a November 2003 CIA report concluded that there was evidence suggesting that Libya also sought dual-use capabilities, which could be used to develop and produce biological weapons.

On 19 December 2003, after considerable pressures from the United States and others, Libya announced that it would dismantle its programs for weapons of mass destruction (WMDs) and that it would adhere to its commitments under the BTWC. Following the announcement, American and British inspectors were allowed to enter Libya to monitor and verify the destruction of WMDs, including biological weapons, in order to prove the country's commitment to complying with international agreements. Although no evidence of an advanced biological weapons program was found, the inspectors did corroborate that Libya had a limited research and development program for biological weapons. However, Libya was not found to have the technological base to manufacture biological agents and thus was unable to move beyond the research and development phase in any case. Libya's renunciation of WMD and acceptance of international inspections prompted the administration of George W. Bush to lift the trade sanctions imposed in 1992 and to allow the resumption of trade and investment between Libya and the United States. *See also* LIBYAN BALLISTIC MISSILES PROGRAM; LIBYAN CHEMICAL WEAPONS PROGRAM.

LIBYAN CHEMICAL WEAPONS PROGRAM. In 1985, the U.S. intelligence community took the first satellite pictures of what was going on in the Libyan desert. The pictures revealed secret and mysterious huge construction projects in the desert, with dead dogs around the newly constructed plant, most probably not having died from starvation. Then came more pictures showing oversized ventilation equipment in the plant near the town of Rabta.

The assessment of the U.S. intelligence analysts was that the dogs were dying of chemical contamination by some kind of chemical weapon synthesized at the Rabta factory. After the *New York Times* published the story based on Central Intelligence Agency findings, Libya maintained that the new plant near Rabta produced medicine. Libya did not allow any foreigner to visit what was the largest chemical factory in the Third World. The information obtained from the pictures was cross-checked with information obtained from European suppliers, and it became clear that the newly constructed factory in the Libyan desert was in fact a chemical weapons manufacturing site.

In a regional conflict in 1987, the Libyan military proved that it possessed chemical weapons by attempting to use them against troops in neighboring Chad. Libya was reportedly producing mustard and nerve agents, as well as actively training and supporting insurgencies and terrorists worldwide in its efforts to counter Western influence. After Libya's chemical weapons capabilities were limited by United Nations sanctions in effect from 1992 to 1999, the country had to work to reestablish its chemical weapons program. Although it was pursuing an indigenous production capability, it was still highly dependent on foreign suppliers.

On 20 December 2003, Libya agreed to give up its research programs for biological and chemical weapons and to allow unconditional inspection and verification by U.S. and British inspectors. The official reason given by Colonel Muammar Qaddafi was that his country was ready to play its role in building a world free from all forms of **terrorism**. The favored speculation about the real reason is that he was fearful of "regime change," as had been imposed in Iraq against Saddam Hussein by the West. Libya declared that it had 3,563 empty chemical weapons air bombs, 23.62 tons of sulfur mustard, and more than 3,000 tons of chemical weapons precursors. Libya stated that it had never transferred chemical weapons and declared that it had an inactivated chemical weapons production facility at Rabta and two chemical weapons storage facilities. *See also* LIBYAN BIOLOGICAL WEAPONS PROGRAM.

LIBYAN INTELLIGENCE. Libya has three separate intelligence agencies. One is the Military Intelligence Force (Istikhbarat Askaria), whose major task is to gather all intelligence information on domestic and foreign matters. The Guide's Intelligence Bureau (GIB; Maktab Maaloumat al-Kaed), whose headquarters is in the center of Tripoli at the Bab al-Aziza barracks, is an internal security force affiliated with the police; its area of responsibility is domestic political espionage, flushing out dissidents of all kinds. The Jamahiriya Security Organization (JSO; Haiat amn al Jamahiriya), also called the External Security Organization (ESO) and Libyan Intelligence Service (LIS), is divided into two branches: Internal Security and Foreign Security. It contains sub-branches, such as a Foreign Liaison Office, responsible for most overseas intelligence operations and a subdirectorate that maintains direct contacts with international terrorist groups. The JSO was Libya's principal intelligence agency in the country's support of terrorist organizations, providing state sponsorship to certain terrorist actions.

In addition, the Security Battalions (Kataeb-al-Amn), also known as the Green Brigades, are responsible for the regime's security in the major cities. The Security Battalions are fully equipped with modern military and police equipment. A new agency called the Revolutionary Guard (Al Haras Assauri) was established in the 1980s and became an influential organization in the wake of a coup attempt of May 1985. The Revolutionary Guards, supported by a paramilitary organization called the Revolutionary Committees, arrested thousands of people suspected of possible connection with the coup. It is relatively small organization, with an estimated manpower of 1,000 to 2,000, equipped with light tanks, armored cars, personnel carriers, multiple rocket launchers, and SA-8 antiaircraft missiles. After the

1988 bombing of Pan Am Flight 103 over Lockerbie, Scotland, the Revolutionary Guard—like other armed forces, including the Libyan Army—was deprived of access to new weaponry due to the international embargo.

The Anti-Imperialism Center (AIC; Al-Mathaba) was the Libyan center for anti-imperialist propaganda and funding of Third World guerilla groups. The AIC was established in 1982 to support revolutionary groups throughout the world. It sponsored a number of anti-Western conferences in Tripoli. It is believed that in 2004 the AIC was tasked with identification and recruitment of radicals for ideological indoctrination and military training in Libya, during which some individuals were selected for advanced training, including preparation of explosive devices. The AIC ran its independent operations by using the offices of its agents in Libyan embassies worldwide. These special offices also handled the payments and channeled funds to terrorist, insurgent, and subversive groups in various parts of the world.

From 1992 on, the AIC was headed by **Moussa Kussa**, a personal confidant of Muammar Qaddafi who also served as Libya's deputy foreign minister. On 1995, Moussa Kussa was appointed head of the Libyan External Security Organization (ESO), as well as director of al-Mathaba.

The Secretariat of the Interior administers intelligence services responsible for the preservation of national security, and protection of government buildings and officials.

Libya employs a variety of other special police forces, such as the People's Security Force and the National Police. These agencies combine intelligence and law enforcement duties. However, elite elements of these special branches units also operate as secret police forces, arresting and detaining any suspects of antigovernment activity. *See also* MEGRAHI, ABDELBASET ALI MOHAMED, AL-; TERRORISM.

– M –

MASKELYNE, JASPER (1902–1972). Jasper Maskelyne was a British star magician. His sleight-of-hand techniques came in useful during **World War II** in the campaign to defeat Field Marshal Erwin Rommel's German Army in North Africa. Maskelyne was assigned to **A Force**, where he was able to apply his skills to the task of concealing British forces from German aerial reconnaissance. He assembled a group, known informally as the Magic Gang, whose 14 members were professionals in analytical chemistry, electrical engineering, and stage set construction. The Magic Gang rapidly became the nucleus of a small industry devoted to trickery and military deception.

Maskelyne's team members were skilled and imaginative, qualities that they brought to bear in various techniques of deception. Using their professional knowledge of cheap and lightweight construction techniques, the group produced dummy tanks made of plywood and painted canvas and even devised a means of faking tank tracks after the dummies had been moved into position. They also used similar techniques to disguise real tanks as supply trucks by placing removable plywood structures over them.

In 1941, Maskelyne was involved in an elaborate operation to divert German bombers from the port of Alexandria by setting up a fake harbor in a nearby bay. This operation involved constructing dummy buildings, a dummy lighthouse, and even dummy antiaircraft batteries with explosive special effects. Maskelyne also made it difficult for German bombers to locate the Suez Canal by fitting searchlights with a revolving cone of mirrors that produced a wheel of spinning light beams nine miles across.

After the war, Maskelyne resumed his stage career but found that jobs as a stage magician were becoming scarce. He did not receive any decoration or honor in recognition of the part he had played in the war effort, and official accounts of the war in North Africa made little or no mention of him. Embittered at the lack of official recognition, as well as widowed and estranged from his children, Maskelyne immigrated to Kenya to start a new life running a driving school.

MEGRAHI, ABDELBASET ALI MOHAMED, AL- (1952–). A former director of the Libyan Center for Strategic Studies and the head of security for Libyan Airlines, allegedly an intelligence officer. Al-Megrahi was convicted by a Scottish court as being responsible for bombing Pan Am Flight 103 from London to New York on 21 December 1988. The blast from the aircraft killed 270 people, including Scottish residents of the town of Lockerbie over which the plane exploded. On 12 November 1991, following the investigation and police report, arrest warrants were issued against al-Megrahi as well as another Libyan national, al-Amin Khalifa Fhimah.

Al-Megrahi's extradition was facilitated in 1999 when Libya started conducting talks with the United Nations on the removal of sanctions. Subsequently, Libya agreed to provide compensation to the victims' families in return for the lifting of sanctions and removal from the list of terror-sponsoring countries by the United States. Since it is commonly believed that the terrorists were acting in concert with Libyan authorities, it is considered the first case of a terror-sponsoring country that somehow acknowledged its actions and agreed to make amends. On 31 January 2001, a panel of Scottish judges returned a guilty verdict of murder against Abdelbaset Ali Mohamed al-Megrahi. *See also* LIBYAN INTELLIGENCE; TERRORISM.

MEINERTZHAGEN, RICHARD (1878–1967). Colonel Richard Henry Meinertzhagen was a British intelligence officer who was stationed in various places in India, Africa, and Palestine. He led many battles during **World War I** and was most well known for leading secret British missions against the Turks in Palestine. During the Sinai and Palestine Campaign, Meinertzhagen let false British battle plans fall into the hands of the Ottoman military, thereby contributing significantly to the surprise British attack that led to the capture of Beersheba and all of Gaza.

In May 1917, Meinertzhagen arrived in Cairo to join Field Marshal Edmund Allenby's Intelligence Section. It was in this context that he became acquainted with the realities of the Jewish settlement of Palestine and with the support the Jews gave to the Allies during World War I. Following Allenby's capture of Jerusalem in December 1917, Meinertzhagen was assigned to the War Office in London, and he subsequently became a member of the British delegation to the Paris Peace Conference, with responsibility for the Middle East. This work brought him into close contact with Zionist leaders, such as Chaim Weizmann, and with Arab leaders such as Faisal, the brother of King **Abdullah I** of Jordan. This was followed by a nine-month assignment as Allenby's chief political officer, beginning in September 1919 and spanning the period of the 1920 Arab riots against the Jews.

Meinertzhagen attained the rank of colonel but was dismissed from the service for insubordination in 1926; his crucial support for Palestinian Jews against the overt anti-Semitism of the British administration cost him his job. In the 1920s–1930s, he was an admirer of fascism but hated the Nazis for their racist policies. He was also a great admirer of Zionism and for decades promoted the founding of Israel. His retirement was interrupted during **Word War II** when, at the age of 61, he was recalled to the War Office and worked in intelligence planning. During that period, Meinertzhagen also joined the Home Guard and participated in the Dunkirk evacuation. *See also* BATTLE OF BEERSHEBA; BATTLES OF GAZA; BRITISH INTELLIGENCE IN THE PALESTINE CAMPAIGN OF 1914–1918.

MIDDLE EAST INTELLIGENCE CENTRE (MEIC). *See* BRITISH INTELLIGENCE IN EGYPT AND SUDAN.

MOHSENI-EJEI, HOJATOLESLAM GHOLAM-HUSSEIN (1956–). Hojatoleslam Gholam-Hussein Mohseni-Ejei had a long background with the Iranian Ministry of Intelligence and Security (MOIS), dating to its creation in the mid-1980s. He served with the MOIS until 1990, then served with the Tehran Prosecutor's Office, then returned to the MOIS as the judiciary's representative until the mid-1990s. Mohseni-Ejei served with the Special Court for the Clergy from 1995 until 2003, first as a prosecutor and then as its head.

Mohseni-Ejei is associated with Hojatoleslam **Muhammad Muhammadi-Reyshahri**, the first chief of the MOIS, and their careers have paralleled one another. Muhammadi-Reyshahri served as chief judge of the Iranian Military Revolutionary Tribunal in the immediate postrevolutionary period, headed the MOIS from 1984 until 1989, and later served as prosecutor of the Special Court for the Clergy. In 2005 Mohseni-Ejei was appointed by Iranian President Mahmud Ahmadinejad as chief of the MOIS, succeeding Hojatoleslam **Ali Yunesi**. *See also* IRANIAN INTELLIGENCE.

MOHTASHAMI-PUR, ALI-AKBAR HOJATOLESLAM. Hojatoleslam Ali-Akbar Mohtashami-Pur served as the Iranian ambassador to Damascus from 1981 until 1985, interior minister from 1985 to 1989, and a parliamentarian from 1989 to 1993 and again from 2000 to 2004. Mohtashami-Pur was deeply involved in the creation of **Hizballah** and makes no effort to hide his close association with it. He was also tied to the 1983 bombing of the U.S. Marine Corps barracks in Beirut. Mohtashami-Pur was secretary-general of the International Conference to Support the Palestinian Uprising (*intifada*), which was held in Tehran in April 2001 and June 2002 and was attended by representatives from Hizballah, **Hamas**, Palestinian Islamic Jihad, and the Peoples' Front for the Liberation of Palestine. *See also* IRANIAN INTELLIGENCE.

MOHY EL-DIEN, ZAKAREIA (1918–?). Zakareia Mohy El-Dien was a member of the Egyptian Revolutionary Command Council from 1952 until 1956. He served with the Egyptian Army in Sudan and in 1948 became the chief of staff of the first brigade, which was later besieged at Falouga. After infiltrating enemy lines from Rafah to Falouga and returning to the besieged brigade, he was rewarded for his bravery with the Mehmet Ali Golden Award. From 1953 until 1958, Mohy El-Dien served as Egypt's minister of the interior. In 1955, President Gamal Abdel Nasser assigned him the task of establishing the first intelligence apparatus to be responsible for Egyptian national security. He served as central minister of the interior for Egypt and Syria from 1958 until 1961, during the period of the United Arab Republic, and as finance minister from 1961 until 1962. He was then appointed as vice president of Egypt and served in this position until 1968. After Nasser's resignation, Mohy El-Dien declined Nasser's offer to take over the position of president and instead retired from public life in 1968.

MOROCCAN INTELLIGENCE. Morocco is situated in a strategic location on the African side of the Straits of Gibraltar, making the country the gateway between Africa and Europe. It gained independence in 1956 and has engaged ever since in efforts to expand its borders, especially by annexing the western Sahara, which Morocco calls it Southern Province.

Morocco maintains military commando and intelligence units to protect its national interests within its own territory and also disputed areas such as the western Sahara. The main government intelligence agency is the Directorate of Territorial Surveillance (DST; Direction de la Surveillance du Territoire). The DST conducts most of Morocco's intelligence operations, both foreign and domestic, including joint operations with allied foreign intelligence services. The DST is known to serve a double purpose: it is an intelligence agency and a secret police force. As such, it conducts inner political espionage. Its largest organizational department is the counterintelligence unit.

Since independence, Morocco has endured waves of political unrest. However, political reforms undertaken recently have brought Morocco stability during the past decade, making the country and the government more able to cope with the recent rise of extremist Islamic groups in North Africa. Morocco has openly fought **terrorism** ever since bombers struck the city of Casablanca in May 2003. In response, Parliament approved the Ministry of Interior's wide-ranging Antiterrorism Law that enabled the arrests of 4,000 suspected extremists. On 11 November 2003, the Moroccan police arrested 17 men suspected of being affiliated with **al Qaeda**, two of whom had previously been imprisoned at Guantanamo Bay.

After the events of 11 September 2001, the Moroccan intelligence community cooperated with U.S. and British efforts to contain the spread of the al Qaeda terrorist network. Surveillance operations carried out by the DST have led to the arrest of several suspects and the seizure of money and weapons earmarked for terrorist cells in Europe and North Africa. Despite this cooperation with international antiterrorism efforts and ongoing government reforms, Morocco's intelligence and security services remain on the "black list" of several human rights organizations that have accused various branches of DST of torture of political dissidents. The DST, known also as General Directorate for Territorial Surveillance (DGST), wages an uncompromising war against terrorism. The fact that these efforts are conducted with disregard to human rights does not help the government's image of modern regime. *See also* OUFKIR, MUHAMMAD.

MOSES' SPIES. Moses conducted the earliest spying operations recorded in the Bible. He chose 12 prominent individuals, one from each of the 12 tribes, to be his spies and instructed them to go to the Promised Land of Canaan and find out what they could about the lay of the land. He instructed his spies to return with samples of fruit in order to provide proof that indeed it was a "land flowing with milk and honey." These spies spent 40 days in the Promised Land, returning as instructed with information and delivering the requested samples of fruit. They reported their findings publicly to Moses and the 12 tribes regarding the cities and the population, and declared that the countryside was indeed "flowing with milk and honey." Ten of the spies, however, reported that the people were so physically large and well organized that if an invasion were attempted, the Israelites would be destroyed.

Moses was distraught at the loss of confidence by the Israelites, especially after they had been safely delivered out of Egypt and had successfully crossed the Red Sea. Their attitude brought them dangerously close to losing their status as God's chosen people, but Moses argued successfully on their behalf. They were nevertheless severely punished for their failure. They were told that they would be required to remain in the wilderness one year for every day the spies spent in the Promised Land—that is, 40 years for the 40 days spent spying. They were furthermore told that everyone over the age of 20 would be denied entry into the Promised Land, and that the only exceptions would be the two spies who had maintained their faith. Even Moses was told he would not enter the Promised Land. *See also* JOSHUA'S SPIES.

MOSSAD. Officially the Israel Secret Intelligence Service (Mossad Le'Modi'in Ule'Tafkidim Meyuhadim), the Mossad was established in Israel on 13 December 1949 as the Institution for Coordination, at the recommendation of Reuven Shiloah, adviser to Prime Minister David Ben Gurion. Shiloah wanted a central body to coordinate and improve cooperation among the existing security services: Military Intelligence (MI), the Israeli Security Agency (ISA), and the Political Department, which was the intelligence unit of the Foreign Ministry. Shiloah proposed establishing the Mossad as a central institution for organizing and coordinating the intelligence and security services. The Mossad began life under the wing of the Foreign Ministry. For all practical purposes, it was the Political Department, although in fact not all of the Political Department was transferred to the Mossad. However, it soon underwent a reorganization process.

On 8 February 1951, Ben Gurion, after consulting with Foreign Minister Moshe Sharett and Mossad director Shiloah, decided to reorganize the Mossad. The Political Department was to be dismantled and its intelligence collecting and operational activities in foreign countries were to be assigned to the Mossad. In March 1951, it was made a part of the prime minister's office, reporting directly to the prime minister. The immediate result was that senior operations officers of the Political Department collectively submitted their resignations in what became known as the Spies' Revolt. The revolt did not last long, and the day it broke, 1 April 1951, is considered the Mossad's official birth date. That day, the operations branch of the Political Department was replaced in the Mossad by the Foreign Intelligence Authority (Rashut Le'Modi'in Be'Hul), also known by its codenames Rashut (Authority) or Rashut Green (Green Authority). The authority was headed by Haim Ya'ari. Operational activities and operating spies in Arab countries were assigned to MI.

Over the years, the Mossad was given several more tasks previously fulfilled by Israel's other intelligence agencies, such as handling Israeli spies abroad. This mission was assigned to the Mossad in 1963; until then it had been accomplished by Unit 131 of MI. In 1963, the Mossad was given the Hebrew name Mossad Le'Modi'in Ule'Tafkidim Meyuhadim (Institute for Intelligence and Special Operations).

The Mossad is a civilian organization. Its employees do not have military ranks, although most of them have served in the Israel Defense Forces (IDF) and many even served in MI. Its current staff is estimated at 1,200 to 2,000 employees. The Mossad is organized into several main units, with headquarters in Tel-Aviv. Tsomet is the largest branch, with responsibility for collecting intelligence information, mainly by its case officers who activate spies and operatives in target countries. Nevioth (formerly known as Queshet) collects intelligence for the Mossad via break-ins, street surveillance, listening devices, and other covert methods. The special operations division, known as Metsada (formerly known as Caesarea), conducts sabotage and paramilitary projects. A top-secret classified subdepartment known as Kidon (Bayonet) conducts assassinations, as approved by Committee X, which is chaired by the prime minister. The Intelligence Branch is responsible for LAP, the putative abbreviation for

Literature and Publications, though it is actually the Hebrew acronym for Lohama Psikhologit—meaning psychological warfare, for which it is indeed responsible, along with propaganda and deception operations. The Intelligence Branch is also responsible for collecting information on prisoners of war and those missing in action, nonconventional weapons, and hostile sabotage activities. The political action and liaison department, known as Tevel, conducts political activities and liaison work with friendly foreign intelligence services and with nations with which Israel does not have normal diplomatic relations. Tsafririm is a unique department distinguished by its concern for the security of the Jewish people around the globe. This department, among other things, directed Operation Moses (Mivtsa Moshe) and Operation Solomon (Mivtsa Shlomo) with the goal of bringing Ethiopian Jews to Israel. In the 1950s and 1960s, Tsafririm was engaged in setting up defense groups in Jewish communities outside of Israel, mainly in the Maghreb, known by the name Misgeret (Framework).

All of the above units come under the aegis of the deputy director of the Mossad for activating the force. The administrator for construction of the force is responsible for the following units: Training Branch, Personnel and Finances, Technology and Spy Gadgets, Research, and the Chief Security Officer.

The Mossad is one of the leading intelligence agencies in the world in the field of high-tech electronics. It has developed a powerful computer database, known as PROMIS, that can store and retrieve enormous quantities of information. This technology is even sold by the Mossad to intelligence communities of foreign countries. Since its establishment, the Mossad's best-known successful operations have been obtaining of Nikita Khrushchev's speech in 1956; Adolf Eichmann's capture in 1960; Operation Wrath of God after the 1972 Munich massacre; the kidnapping of Mordechai Vanunu in 1986; providing the intelligence background for the Osiraq nuclear reactor bombing by Israel in 1981 (**Operation Opera**); assisting in the immigration of Ethiopian Jews to Israel; and furnishing intelligence for IDF operations thousands of miles away from Israel, such as Operation Yehonathan in 1976 and **Abu Jihad's assassination** in Tunisia in 1988.

The Mossad's best-known mishaps have been the Lillehammer affair, which was the killing in 1973 of Ahmed Bouchiki, an innocent

Moroccan waiter mistakenly identified as the leader of the Black September terrorist organization, Ali Hassan Salameh; the Khaled Mash'al fiasco, which was the failed assassination of Sheikh Khaled Mash'al, a leader of the Palestinian militant group **Hamas**, by poison injection in 1997 on Jordanian soil when Mossad agents used forged Canadian passports, which angered the Canadian government no less than the Jordanians; the use of forged British passports, discovered in 1981 in a grocery bag in a London telephone booth, which sparked a diplomatic row between Great Britain and Israel over the Mossad's involvement in an attempt to infiltrate China; and an attempt in July 2004 by Uriel Kelman and Eli Cara (formerly head of Nevioth) to fraudulently obtain New Zealand passports.

From time to time, the Mossad undergoes a reorganization. Efraim Halevy, as director of the Mossad, wanted to pattern it on the U.S. Central Intelligence Agency (CIA), with a few big divisions. He envisioned three such wings: a collection wing, a research wing, and an operations wing. All the departments described above would have been incorporated in one way or another into these three large wings. Halevy actually succeeded in establishing the first two wings. To date, the operations wing has not been created—not even by Halevy's successor, who devotes special attention to operations. The current director, Meir Dagan, created the Forum of Unit Directors, which includes the deputy director of the Mossad for activating the force and the administrator for construction of the force.

The Mossad director, together with the directors of MI and of the Israeli Security Agency (and of Nativ in its early stages) constitute the Committee of Directors of the Intelligence Services (Va'adat Rashei Hasherutim, or VARASH).

Since its establishment, the Mossad has had 10 directors: Reuven Shiloah (1951–1952), Isser Harel (1952–1963), Meir Amit (1963–1968), Zvi Zamir (1968–1974), Yitzhak Hofi (1974–1982); Nahum Admoni (1982–1990), Shabtai Shavit (1990–1996), Danny Yatom (1996–1998); Efraim Halevy (1998–2003), and Meir Dagan, who assumed the office in 2003 and is still serving. *See also* IS-RAELI INTELLIGENCE.

MUGNIYAH, IMAD FAYES (1962–2008). Born in Tayr Dibba, a poor village in southern Lebanon, Mugniyah joined Yasser Arafat's

Security Force-17 in 1976. He was known by his nickname, "the Fox," and later joined forces with the Lebanese **Hizballah** and rose to become a senior operations officer for the organization. Mugniyah, also sometimes described as the Hizballah's senior intelligence officer, is considered responsible by Western and **Israeli intelligence** agencies for most of the organization's worldwide terror activities and was implicated in many terrorist attacks carried out in the 1980s and 1990s, primarily with American and Israeli targets. Among those attacks were the 1992 bombing of the Israeli embassy in Buenos Aires and the April 1983 bombing of the U.S. embassy in Beirut, which killed 63 people, including 17 Americans. He was later blamed for the October 1983 simultaneous truck bombings against the French paratrooper barracks that killed 58 French soldiers and the U.S. Marine Corps barracks that killed 241 marines. Almost a year later, in September 1984, he attacked the U.S. embassy annex building. The United States indicted him for the June 1985 hijacking of TWA Flight 847, which resulted in the death of U.S. Navy diver Robert Stethem.

Mugniyah was also linked to numerous kidnappings of Westerners in Beirut throughout the 1980s, most notably that of Terry Anderson. Some of those individuals were later killed, including U.S. Army Colonel William Francis Buckley. The remainder were released at various times; the last one, Terry Anderson, was released in 1991. In 1985, his group also kidnapped four Soviet Embassy officials, one of whom, Arkady Katkov, was killed.

Mugniyah is considered to have ties with several Palestinian elements and to have helped with the attempt to smuggle 50 tons of weaponry into the Palestinian National Authority on board the ship *Karine-A* in 2002. He is also suspected to have ties with other worldwide terror organizations, such as **al Qaeda**, leading some to believe that he might be linked to several terror acts carried out in Saudi Arabia, including the Khobar towers bombing (1996) and the attack on the USS *Cole* destroyer (2000). He is known to have ties with Iran, which is funding and controlling the Hizballah, and is considered to be one of the links between the Iranian leadership and the Hizballah. Although his exact status following the second Lebanon War is unknown, it is speculated that his role in the Hizballah leadership and his ties with Iran have been expanded.

Mugniyah had the blood of many hundreds of Americans and Israelis—not to mention Frenchmen, Germans, and Britons—on his hands. For this reason, he became a top target for Israeli and U.S. intelligence. On 12 February 2008, Imad Mugniyah was killed by a car bomb blast in the Kfar Suseh neighborhood of Damascus, Syria. Israel denied being behind the killing. U.S. director of National Intelligence Mike McConnell suggested that internal Hizballah factions or Syria may be to blame for the killing. Mugniyah's widow has suggested Syria was involved in his assassination. Iran has condemned the killing. Regardless of who killed Imad Mugniyah, there was considerable relief in Tel-Aviv and Langley, Virginia, (the Central Intelligence Agency's headquarters) following his death. The day after Imad Mugniyah was killed, Prime Minister Ehud Olmert announced publicly that he decided to extend Meir Dagan's term as director of the **Mossad**. This would make Dagan one of the longest-serving Mossad directors. According to some sources, the extension came in the wake of the killing of Imad Mugniyah. *See also* TERRORISM.

MUHAMMADI-REYSHAHRI, HOJATOLESLAM MUHAMMAD. Hojatoleslam Muhammad Muhammadi-Reyshahri served as chief judge of the Military Revolutionary Tribunal in the immediate post-Islamic revolution period in Iran. Muhammadi-Reyshahri headed the Iranian Ministry of Intelligence and Security (MOIS) from 1984 until 1989 and later served as prosecutor of the Special Court for the Clergy. In 1991, he replaced Ahmad Khomeini as leader of the Iranian delegation to the Hajj pilgrimage. Muhammadi-Reyshahri founded the Society for the Defense of Values of the Islamic Revolution in 1996 and stood as its candidate in the 1997 presidential election. In April 1997, he was appointed to the Council for the Discernment of Expediency by Supreme Leader Ayatollah Seyyed Ali Khamenei, and later became a member of the Assembly of Experts. Muhammadi-Reyshahri also heads the Shah Abdolazim shrine foundation. *See also* IRANIAN INTELLIGENCE.

MUJAHEDEEN-E KHALQ (MEK). The Mujahedeen-e Khalq was formed in the 1960s based on an ideology of Marxism mixed with Islamism. MEK's history is filled with anti-Western attacks as well as terrorist attacks on the interests of the clerical regime in Iran and abroad. Expelled from Iran after the Islamic Revolution in 1979, MEK's primary support came from the former Iraqi regime of Saddam Hussein after the late 1980s. MEK currently advocates the overthrow of the Iranian regime and its replacement with the group's own leadership.

MEK's worldwide campaign against the Iranian government stresses propaganda, although it occasionally uses **terrorism**. During the 1970s, MEK killed U.S. military personnel and American civilians working on defense projects in Tehran and supported the 1979 takeover of the American embassy in Tehran. In 1981, MEK detonated bombs in the head office of the Islamic Republic party and the premier's office, killing some 70 high-ranking Iranian officials, including Chief Justice Ayatollah Muhammad Beheshti, President Muhammad-Ali Rajaei, and Premier Muhammad-Javad Bahonar. Near the end of the **Iran–Iraq War** (1980–1988), Baghdad armed MEK with military equipment and sent it into action against Iranian forces. In 1991, it assisted the Iraqi government in suppressing the Shi'a and Kurdish uprisings in southern Iraq and the Kurdish uprisings in the north. In April 1992, MEK conducted near-simultaneous attacks on Iranian embassies and installations in 13 countries, demonstrating the group's ability to mount large-scale operations overseas. In April 1999, the group targeted key military officers and assassinated the deputy chief of the Armed Forces General Staff. A year later, in April 2000, MEK attempted to assassinate the commander of Nasr Headquarters—Tehran's interagency board responsible for coordinating policies on Iraq. The normal pace of anti-Iranian operations increased during Operation Great Bahman in February 2000, when the group launched a dozen attacks against Iran, such as a mortar attack against the leadership complex housing the offices of the supreme leader and president in Tehran. In 2000 and 2001, MEK was regularly involved in mortar attacks and hit-and-run raids on Iranian military and law enforcement units as well as government buildings near the Iran–Iraq border, although MEK terrorism in Iran declined throughout the remainder of 2001.

MEK provided the U.S. intelligence community with false and misleading information about Iran's nuclear capabilities. In 2002, MEK provided critical information about Iran's nuclear-enrichment complex at Natanz and a heavy-water production facility at Arak.

MEK has most probably some real sources inside Iran. However, in light of the misinformation surrounding the claims of Iraq's weapons programs, U.S. policymakers have become doubly cautious about its claims and pursuit of aggressive deterrence operations against Iran.

Coalition aircraft bombed MEK bases during **Operation Iraqi Freedom**, forcing MEK forces to surrender in May 2003. The future of the MEK forces remains undetermined. MEK's approximately 3,800 members remain confined to Camp Ashraf, the group's main compound near Baghdad, where they remain under coalition control. As a condition of the cease-fire agreement, the group relinquished its weapons, including tanks, armored vehicles, and heavy artillery.

In the 1980s, Iranian security forces forced MEK's leaders to flee to France. Upon resettling in Iraq in 1987, almost all of its armed units were stationed in fortified bases near the border with Iran. Although the bulk of the group has been limited to Camp Ashraf since Operation Iraqi Freedom, an overseas support structure remains, with associates and supporters scattered throughout Europe and North America. Prior to Operation Iraqi Freedom, MEK received all of its military assistance—and most of its financial support—from the former Iraqi regime. MEK has also used front organizations to solicit contributions from expatriate Iranian communities.

MUKHLIF AL-DULAYMI, KHALAF MUHAMMAD. Khalaf Muhammad Mukhlif al-Dulaymi, also known as Abu Marwan, was the former director of the Directorate of Commercial Projects in the Iraqi Intelligence Service (IIS). Al-Dulaymi was in charge of numerous Iraqi front companies that moved funds abroad for Saddam Hussein. After the 2003 **Operation Iraqi Freedom**, Abu Marwan fled Iraq with millions of U.S. dollars. According to Western intelligence sources, he provided funds and organized the smuggling of weapons into Iraq for the insurgency against the U.S. forces. He was listed as wanted by the new Iraqi government. *See also* IRAQI DIRECTORATE OF GENERAL MILITARY INTELLIGENCE; IRAQI DIRECTORATE OF GENERAL SECURITY; IRAQI INTELLIGENCE; IRAQI SPECIAL SECURITY ORGANIZATION.

– N –

NAIF, ABDUL RAZZAZ AL- (1933–1978). Abdul Razzaz al-Naif served as chief of **Iraq's Directorate of General Military Intelligence** (DGMI) from the end of the 1950s and into the 1960s. Al-Naif provided Saddam Hussein with secret assistance in the form of military intelligence during the crucial days when Saddam Hussein needed to base his regime in Iraq. *See also* IRAQI DIRECTORATE OF GENERAL SECURITY; IRAQI INTELLIGENCE; IRAQI SPECIAL SECURITY ORGANIZATION.

NAJI, NUHAD. Nuhad Naji al-Adhari al-Dulaymi was the former director of the Iraqi Intelligence Service (IIS). After the 2003 **Operation Iraqi Freedom**, Naji became the leader of Baghdad's Former Regime Elements (FRE) cell. The Central Criminal Court of the new Iraqi regime issued an arrest warrant for Nuhad Naji on 9 January 1995. *See also* IRAQI DIRECTORATE OF GENERAL MILITARY INTELLIGENCE; IRAQI DIRECTORATE OF GENERAL SECURITY; IRAQI INTELLIGENCE; IRAQI SPECIAL SECURITY ORGANIZATION.

NASR, SALAH AL-NOGOMY (1920–1982). In 1957, Salah Nasr was assigned to the position of director of the Egyptian State Security Investigations (GDSSI; Mubahath al-Dawla) by President Gamal Abdel Nasser. Nasr served in this position until 1967 and succeeded in establishing the GDSSI as a major **Egyptian intelligence** agency with separate divisions. In order to finance the intelligence apparatus, Nasr established a dummy import-export company, which flourished and was eventually separated from the GDSSI under independent management. The GDSSI came to own many companies in Egypt, especially in the fields of tourism, aviation, and construction.

NASR, YOUSEF (1943–). Born in Palestine, Yousef Nasr is the Palestinian National Authority's interior minister. He was formerly the chief of the public security apparatus in the Gaza Strip and West Bank and now serves as the commander of the National Security Force in his new position. He is responsible for overseeing the police force, which has up to 45,000 members (three times the number permitted by the 1993 Oslo Peace Declaration of Principles and subsequent agreements), many of whom carry automatic weapons and use armored cars as though they were a militia or an army.

NASSER'S ASSASSINATION ATTEMPTS. Several attempts were made to assassinate Egyptian president Gamal Abdel Nasser. The first attempt to assassinate Nasser was on 26 October 1954 when he was speaking to a large crowd in Alexandria. Eight gun shots rang out. Nasser heard the bullets whizzing past his ears. Happily for him, the gunman, Mahmoud Abd al-Latif, a member of the Muslim Brotherhood, was a bad shot even at close range.

In 1965, the Islamic religious militia was able to recruit a member of the Presidential Security Unit, Ismail al-Fayoumi, a sharpshooter, to await Nasser's arrival at Cairo International Airport as he returned from his trip to Moscow and then assassinate him. The discovery of the sniper through informants and the eventual apprehension of al-Fayoumi took place only 30 minutes before Nasser's plane landed, thus foiling this assassination attempt. A second attempt in 1965 involved detonating a truck as Nasser's presidential railcar passed by on its way from Cairo to Alexandria. Upon discovering the bomb, it was determined that the detonation device was radio controlled. In a third attempt, two hit squads were strategically placed along the route of Nasser's motorcade in Alexandria as he traveled from Mamoora to Ras-El-Tin Palace.

After the 1967 **Six Days' War**, yet another elaborate plot to kill Nasser was discovered when he visited the city of Suez. This attempt involved Egyptian investigators using primitive bugging devices against the perpetrators instead of immediately staging arrests. Although the devices malfunctioned, they revealed an elaborate trail in which Egyptians were recruited in Saudi Arabia during their Hajj pilgrimage to Mecca. *See also* EGYPTIAN INTELLIGENCE; SADAT'S ASSASSINATION.

NASSIRI, NEMATOLLAH (1911–1979). General Nematollah Nassiri was the third director of Sazeman-e Ettelaat va Amniyat-e Keshvar (SAVAK) during the rule of Muhammad Reza Pahlavi. Nassiri was a personal friend of the shah. In 1953, Nassiri personally delivered to Prime Minister Muhammad Mossadeq the warrant for his arrest. On 21 January 1965, Nassiri was appointed director of the SAVAK, succeeding **Hassan Pakravan**, but was imprisoned in 1978. When the shah left Iran on 16 January 1979, Nassiri remained in prison until the fall of Shahpour Bakhtiar's government on 11 February 1979. He was executed two days later by firing squad. *See also* IRANIAN INTELLIGENCE; OPERATION TPAJAX.

NILI. The Hebrew acronym for the biblical phrase *netzah yisrael lo yeshaker* ("the Everlasting of Israel will not lie"; 1 Sam. 15:29) was the name given to a Jewish espionage network established in Israel during the last years of the Ottoman Empire in **World War I**. NILI was formed in 1915 by Sarah Aaronsohn, her brother Aharon Aaronsohn, and Avshalom Feinberg. Other key members were Yosef Lishansky and Naaman Belkind. The founders believed that by spying for the British they could bring about a British victory over the Turks, who then ruled Palestine, and thereby gain a Jewish state. The main mission of NILI was to assist the British forces under Field Marshal Edmund Allenby to conquer Palestine, thus helping to realize Zionist aspirations.

For almost two years Aharon Aaronson, a botanist by training, entreated the British to accept information from him on the movements of the Turkish army in Palestine and on the conditions of the terrain. When approval was received, the entire burden of activating the NILI underground fell to Aharon's sister Sarah, whose other siblings, apart from Aharon himself—namely, Alexander, Shmuel, and Rivka—were then abroad.

Once every two weeks, Sarah Aaronsohn would hold parties at the botanical experimental station that were as "licentious as those conducted in the palaces of Rome," as **Aziz Bek**, the head of **Turkish intelligence**, described them in his diary. Among the guests at the parties were officers of the Turkish coast guard. When they got drunk, they gave away information, which was conveyed to a British ship lying offshore.

The group was able to operate only eight months before being detected. The members of the NILI spy network were careless in every aspect of subterfuge and secrecy, and they endangered the entire village of Zichron Yaakov, where they lived and out of which they operated. The group was exposed because they used carrier pigeons to send messages. Using these birds requires expert skills that the NILI people lacked, so it is not surprising that not one of the pigeons dispatched by the NILI members reached its destination. All but two were lost; one of the two surviving birds alighted in the pigeon coop of Ahmad Bey, the Turkish governor in Caesarea, precisely when he was feeding his own pigeons. He caught it and discovered attached to its foot a note that Sarah had written in code.

In October 1917, at the close of the Jewish festival of Tabernacles, the Turks surrounded Zichron Yaakov and arrested Sarah, her father Fischel Aaronsohn, her brother Zvi, and several more members of NILI. They were taken to the command post in the center of the village, where their captors tortured them to extract the hiding place of Lishansky and other members of the network. Sarah Aaronsohn bravely withstood the torture even when they hung her by her hands, whipped the soles of her feet, placed scorching eggs in her armpits and between her thighs, and pulled out her fingernails. The torments continued for three days, and the screams were heard all through the village. About to be sent to Damascus to be hanged, Sarah received permission to go home to change her clothes. Making use of the opportunity, she shot herself there. After her death, NILI's activities ceased. With the death of Aharon Aaronsohn in an air accident in May 1919, the group finally broke up. Officially the leadership of the Jewish community in Palestine dissociated itself from NILI's activities. *See also* ISRAELI INTELLIGENCE.

NIMRODI, YA'ACOV (1926–). Born in Iraq to a poor family with 10 children, Nimrodi was brought up from childhood in Jerusalem. At age 15 he joined the Shahar, the Arab Platoon of the Palmah underground militia. After Israel's War of Independence, Nimrodi became an intelligence officer in Military Intelligence (MI) as an agent runner. In 1955, Nimrodi assumed the position of Israeli military attaché in Tehran with the rank of colonel. In fact, he was an agent of MI and of the **Mossad** charged with developing relations with Iran as part of Israel's **Periphery Doctrine**.

No Israeli representative in Iran during the shah's regime was more significant or influential than Nimrodi. He reportedly helped organize and encourage the rebellion of Kurdish tribesmen against Iraq, the shah's main political and military rival in the region. Nimrodi was actually the "chief government agent for Israel's burgeoning arms industry." He was known as an all-purpose "fixer" and was on intimate terms with the shah and his generals. He would even boast to his friends that he was in "partnership" with the shah. Among other coups, Nimrodi sold the Iranian Army on the Israeli-made Uzi submachine gun. As the Mossad agent who could properly boast of having "built" the Iranian National Organization for Intelligence and Security (SAVAK) into an efficient but brutal intelligence service, he was no less intimate with the keepers of the shah's secrets.

Nimrodi ended his term in Iran in 1969 and returned to Israel. There he lobbied for the job of military governor of the West Bank, occupied by Israel in the 1967 **Six Days' War**. Upon being turned down, he resigned from the army.

As a private citizen, Nimrodi became a merchant selling arms and other Israeli products to Iran. All the sales to Iran that he had previously arranged during his "low-salary" military career were now handled by Nimrodi as a private businessman. In the Six Days' War, massive quantities of Soviet weapons were captured by the Israel Defense Forces (IDF) from the Arab armies, and Israel decided to transfer these weapons to the Kurds of Iraq. Nimrodi served as the main channel for this transaction. He, like other wealthy businessmen, invested millions in the shah's Iran, and as a result accumulated an enormous fortune. This profit making came to an end with the Iranian Islamic Revolution in 1979. However, Nimrodi had banked wisely in Europe and was not hurt. He moved to London, where he maintained his contacts with exiled Iranians.

In the first half of the 1980s, Nimrodi, still a private businessman, resumed his engagement in arms sales. As partners he had David (Dave) Kimche, former deputy director of the **Mossad** and then director-general of the Israeli Foreign Ministry, with a lasting penchant for clandestine activity; Al Schwimmer, a Jewish American billionaire who had founded the Israeli aircraft industry and was a close friend of Shimon Peres; and the Saudi tycoon Adnan Khashoggi. These men became key figures in an arms deal with revolutionary Iran known later as the **Irangate affair**. Nimrodi is now in retirement but still has many varied investments in Israel. *See also* IRANIAN INTELLIGENCE; ISRAELI INTELLIGENCE.

– O –

ÖCALAN'S CAPTURE. Abdullah Öcalan was born in 1948 in Ömerli, a village in southeast Turkey. After completing his degree in political science at Ankara University, he entered the civil service. Öcalan believed that the Turkish state was denying the Kurdish people the right to live according to their own cultural identity. He became an active member of the Democratic Cultural Association of the East, a group promoting the rights of the Kurdish people. In 1974, Öcalan founded the Kurdistan Workers' Party (PKK), which was formally named as such in 1978. The group, composed primarily of Turkish Kurds, began to launch attacks in 1984 against the governments in Turkey, Iraq, Iran, and Syria, with the goal of creating an independent Kurdish state. Approximately 30,000 people have died as a result of conflict between the PKK and the Turkish state, which therefore considers Öcalan a terrorist.

Syria harbored Öcalan until 1998, when the Turkish government openly threatened to stop Syria from supporting the PKK. As a result, the Syrian government forced Öcalan to move out of the country rather than handing him over to the Turkish authorities. Öcalan went to Russia first, and from there he moved to various countries, including Italy, Greece, and Kenya.

In late November 1998, Turkish Prime Minister Bluent Ecevit appealed to Israeli Prime Minister Benjamin Netanyahu to help capture Öcalan. Netanyahu agreed, as Israel considered a close working relationship with Turkey to be an important strategic point. The **Mossad**'s plan to trace Öcalan for Turkey was given the codename "Watchful." Six Mossad agents were dispatched to Rome and set up surveillance on Öcalan's apartment close to the Vatican. When Öcalan managed to leave Italy before being apprehended, the Mossad team began a search for him in other Mediterranean countries. The Mossad learned that on 2 February 1999 Öcalan had attempted to enter the Netherlands but was turned away by the Dutch authorities. Sources in the Schiphol Airport security informed the Mossad that Öcalan had boarded a flight to Nairobi. Kenya was considered easy terrain for the Mossad, since relations between the two intelligence communities were already well developed.

Soon Öcalan was traced near the Greek embassy compound in Nairobi, and the Mossad team reported daily on every move around the compound. The order was simply to continue to watch until the instruction was given to capture Öcalan. By intercepting phone calls from the Greek embassy, the Mossad learned that Öcalan had been turned down for political asylum in South Africa and other African countries and that he was starting to ponder the idea of moving to the mountains of northern Iraq. A member of the Mossad team with a Kurdish appearance approached one of the Kurdish bodyguards from the embassy to express concern for Öcalan's life and to suggest that Öcalan consider a move to Iraq, where he would be safer.

Öcalan took the bait. On 15 February 1999, a Falcon 900 executive jet landed at Nairobi's Wilson airport. The pilot told the airport authorities that he had come to pick up a group of businessman. In fact, Öcalan was by some means placed aboard the jet. According to some versions, Öcalan was drugged by the Mossad agents. Some versions even maintain that capturing Öcalan was a joint venture by the Central Intelligence Agency and the Mossad. Although no one has publicly admitted that the Mossad was involved in the Öcalan affair, the case reveals how the Mossad sometimes works as a contractor for other governments, as in the **Ben-Barka affair**.

Öcalan was flown to Turkey for trial and since his capture has been held in solitary confinement on the Imrali Island in the Turkish Sea of Marmara. In August 1999, he declared a "peace initiative," ordering members to refrain from violence and ending the 15-year rebellion. However, in February 2004, the group's hardline militant wing, the People's Defense Force (HPG), took control of the group and soon afterward renounced the PKK's self-imposed cease-fire of the previous five years. Although Öcalan was initially sentenced to death, his sentence was commuted to life imprisonment when the death penalty was conditionally abolished in Turkey in August 2002. *See also* PERIPHERY DOCTRINE; TURKISH INTELLIGENCE.

OCTOBER WAR DECEPTION. *See* YOM KIPPUR WAR DECEPTION.

OMANI INTERNAL SECURITY. Oman has not been the target of terrorist acts and has not been exposed to a significant internal threat since the defeat of the Dhofari insurgents in 1975. Home guard (*firqat*) units, which were trained for counterinsurgency operations by troops of the British army's Special Air Services, have remained as paramilitary tribal police and defense forces for the mountain people in the areas infiltrated by the Dhofari insurgents during the rebellion. However, tribal dissension is considered unlikely to recur because most tribal chiefs and leading families share the benefits of rising oil income.

Still, it is possible that, due to the lack of a designated successor for Sultan Qaboos bin-Said, an internal power struggle could ensue over the selection of a new ruler. The sultanate faces few problems from the narcotics trade and considers the level of general crime to be remarkably low. The foreign labor force is large, estimated at 58 percent of the working population, and most foreign workers are Indians and Pakistanis who are not politically active.

The security services are described as large and efficient, but not overly intrusive. The Royal Oman Police (ROP), commanded by the inspector-general of police and customs, is under the supervision of the Ministry of Interior. The principal crime-fighting unit is the Directorate General of Criminal Investigation. An oil installation division has responsibility for security of the oil industry, including the patrolling of pipelines, oil rigs, and oil terminals. The mounted division patrols border areas on horseback and camel and also provides security control at airports and border points. The coast guard contingent is equipped with AT-105 APCs and inshore patrol craft.

Great importance is attached to ensuring that the armed forces are up to date and at a high standard of combat capability. The Royal Army of Oman (RAO) is trained in the latest techniques in the military sciences, with up-to-date weaponry and equipment and a solid support system. The modernization and development of the Sultan's Armed Forces (SAF) reflects the strategic and military vision of Sultan Qaboos bin-Said, who is the supreme commander of the armed forces and of the Royal Oman Police.

A rarely used security court system handles internal security cases. The government can search private residences and monitor telephones and private correspondence without warrant but generally confines such actions to investigations of potential security threats and individuals suspected of criminal activity. Torture, mistreatment, and cruel punishment are not systematically practiced or condoned by Omani authorities. The traditional punishments authorized by Islamic law, such as amputation and stoning, are not imposed. *See also* BRITISH INTELLIGENCE IN OMAN.

OPERATION ALPHA. This was a joint Anglo–American project aimed at forging an Arab–Israeli peace agreement at the beginning of the 1950s. The plan called for Israel to cede parts of the Negev Desert to Egypt and Jordan in exchange for peace negotiations between Israel and each of these two countries. In the view of the United States and Great Britain, this exchange would enable Egypt and Jordan to gain territorial continuity.

The British MI6 became the architect of this covert operation and secretly suggested it to each of the three countries involved. Israel considered the idea of ceding parts of the Negev as an unacceptable demand and rejected the plan, worsening its already strained relations with the United Kingdom. The failure of **Operation Alpha** paved the way for another covert peace-promoting initiative between Israel and Egypt, albeit this time planned by the United States by the Central Intelligence Agency. *See also* OPERATION GAMMA.

OPERATION BERTRAM. This was the codename for the second battle of El Alamein, which lasted from 23 October to 3 November 1942. Following the first battle of El Alamein (1–27 July 1942), which stalled the Axis advance, this battle marked a significant turning point in the Western Desert Campaign of **World War II**.

The German forces under the legendary Field Marshal Erwin Rommel knew that a British counterattack was coming, so the trick was to mislead them as to where and when it would take place. The Magic Gang, headed by **Jasper Maskelyne**, used its techniques of trickery to build a dummy pipeline, the construction of which would lead the Axis to believe that the attack was planned for a much later date and much farther south. To enhance the illusion, dummy tanks consisting of plywood frames placed over jeeps were constructed and deployed in the south. In a reverse deception ploy, the tanks destined for battle in the north were camouflaged as supply trucks by placing removable plywood structures over them.

The Axis troops were dug in along two lines and had laid about half a million mines in what was called the Devil's Garden. The attack was actually to take place near the coast at the northern end of the German line. In readiness, 1,000 tanks were disguised as trucks at the north of the line, while 30 miles south 2,000 fake tanks were assembled, complete with explosive special effects. To further throw the enemy off track, a fake railway line was built and there were even fake radio broadcasts and sound effects to mimic the noise of construction. In addition, a fake water pipeline was built to supply the simulated armies, and its progress could easily be tracked from the air by German planes. The trick was to convince the Germans that it would not be ready before November 1942 and that no attack could be launched until that time.

The actual attack began on the night of 23 October 1942, catching the German forces unprepared. After 10 days of bloody fighting, the British forced the Germans into retreat, with almost two thirds of the more than 30,000 casualties sustained by the German side. The role played by the element of surprise in weakening the enemy's defenses was later acknowledged by Sir Winston Churchill, who paid tribute in the House of Commons to the deception operation that had contributed to the victory. After the success in El Alamein, there was no further need for deception tactics in the North African venue and the Magic Gang disbanded. Indeed, the Allied victory at El Alamein marked the end of German expansionism, including their hopes of occupying Egypt, controlling access to the Suez Canal, and taking over Middle Eastern oil fields.

OPERATION COMPASS. This was the first major **World War II** Allied military operation in the Western Desert Campaign. After the Italian declaration of war on France and Britain on 10 June 1940, the Italian forces in Libya and the Commonwealth forces in Egypt began a series of cross-border raids. Benito Mussolini urged the Libyan governor-general, Marshal Italo Balbo, to launch a large-scale offensive against the British in Egypt. Mussolini's immediate aim was to capture the Suez Canal, ultimately wanting to link up his forces in Libya with those in Italian East Africa. But, for many reasons, Balbo was reluctant. After Balbo's accidental death on 28 June 1940, Mussolini was just as adamant in urging his replacement, General Rodolfo Graziani, to attack. Like Balbo, however, Graziani too was reluctant.

Operation Compass resulted in British Commonwealth forces pushing across a great stretch of Libya and capturing over 100,000 Italian soldiers, with very few casualties of their own. It was the first occasion in which Australian troops saw action in World War II. Operation Compass was originally envisaged as a spoiling attack, combined with a reconnaissance in force to disrupt the Italian forces that had advanced into Egypt in September 1940.

On 8 December 1940, British army and Indian army units, under the command of Major General Richard O'Connor, attacked the Italian positions in the rear. O'Connor proceeded to launch what amounted to a British blitzkrieg. In less than two months, the British forces swept 500 miles along the coast of North Africa. The Seventh Armored Division raced across the desert to cut off the retreating Italians, and O'Connor's men destroyed nine Italian divisions and took 130,000 prisoners. In March 1941, German forces under the command of Field Marshal Erwin Rommel and the Afrika Korps landed at Tripoli, Tunisia.

As a counterespionage measure, many of the troops involved in Operation Compass were not informed that the operation was not an exercise until they were very nearly engaged in combat. The intelligence and the counterespionage measure involved mainly **A Force** under the command of Field Marshal **Archibald Percival Wavell**. *See also* BRITISH INTELLIGENCE IN WESTERN DESERT BATTLES.

OPERATION CREDIBLE SPORT. *See* OPERATION EAGLE CLAW.

OPERATION DESERT STORM. On the morning of 2 August 1990, the Iraqi Republican Guard invaded and seized control of Kuwait. In reaction to the invasion, the United States launched Operation Desert Shield in order to deter an invasion of Saudi Arabia, Kuwait's oil-rich neighbor. On 7 August 1990, the deployment of U.S. forces began. On 20 August 1990, President George H. W. Bush signed National Security Directive (NSD) 45, "U.S. Policy in Response to the Iraqi Invasion of Kuwait," which outlined U.S. interests in the region and the principles that would guide U.S. policy during the crisis. The directive called for the "immediate, complete, and unconditional withdrawal of all Iraqi forces from Kuwait" and the "restoration of Kuwait's legitimate government to replace the puppet regime installed by Iraq." It also articulated "a commitment to the security and stability of the Persian Gulf." This NSD was the first of two key presidential directives that guided U.S. policy and actions in response to Saddam Hussein's invasion of Kuwait.

The U.S. intelligence involvement in the Iraqi invasion of Kuwait can be divided into the preparation for the U.S.-led coalition attack against Iraq, the collection and analysis of information during the war as support for the military operation, and the search for weapons of mass destruction in Iraq.

In regard to preparation, the U.S. intelligence community invested six months of planning, deployment, training, and intelligence gathering prior to beginning Operation Desert Storm. During this interval, President Bush assembled a coalition of nations to augment U.S. resources and isolate Iraq. War preparations were also aided by the lack of Iraqi interference with the large buildup of frontline forces and reserves. This six-month period of preparation in advance of the air campaign allowed the U.S. military planners to collect extensive intelligence about critical strategic targets and their locations. They were able to plot their initial actions thoroughly and in great detail, revising plans as necessary. In addition, the combat units had an opportunity to practice flying in a desert environment, honing their skills under conditions for which some had not been previously trained.

Early on the morning of 17 January 1991, Baghdad time, the U.S.-led coalition launched air attacks against Iraqi targets; it had become clear that Saddam would not withdraw, and Operation Desert Shield became Operation Desert Storm. On 24 February 1991, coalition ground forces began their attack. On 27 February 1991, Kuwait City was declared liberated and President George H. W. Bush and his advisers decided to halt the war. A cease-fire took effect at 8 A.M. the following morning. The overwhelming and speedy victory of the U.S.-led coalition was accompanied by minimal casualties.

Operation Desert Storm included four phases. Phase I was to gain air superiority by destroying Iraq's strategic capabilities. That strategic air campaign was accomplished within the first seven days. Phase II required the suppression of air defenses in the Kuwaiti theater of operations. During Phase III, the coalition airmen continued to service Phase I and II targets as needed, but also shifted emphasis to the field army in Kuwait. Finally, Phase IV entailed air support of ground operations.

During the military campaign, U.S. intelligence was expected to support the ground troops and the air force. Throughout the war, intelligence information was gathered from multiple sources. In regard to intelligence analysis, the results were mixed, though considered by and large successful. The U.S. intelligence community understood correctly that some key Iraqi antiair weapons were either quite old or limited in range and capability. Surface-to-air missile (SAMs) with the greatest range, SA-2s and SA-3s, had been deployed 30 years earlier, putting them at the end of their operational lifespan. Moreover, U.S. Air Force and other coalition air forces had long ago established countermeasures to these systems.

The most prominent analytical challenge of the intelligence effort, which was the assessment of battlefield damage, revealed the true intelligence failure of Operation Desert Storm. The count of dead Iraqi tanks, armored personnel carriers (APCs), and artillery pieces was not guided by any generally accepted methodology. The Defense Intelligence Agency (DIA) was supposed to provide battle damage assessment (BDA). However, BDA was performed on only 41 percent of the strategic targets in the Air Force's **Gulf War** Air Power Survey (GWAPS) Missions database. In some cases, DIA shortfalls resulted in a reduced level of success against certain target categories. The lack of sufficient or timely intelligence to conduct BDA led to additional costs and risks from possibly unnecessary restrikes, which were ordered to increase the probability that target objectives would be achieved. Insufficient intelligence on the existence and location of targets also inhibited the coalition's ability to perform necessary strikes and achieve campaign goals.

The DIA's analysis showed that more than 70 percent of the tanks in three Republican Guard divisions located in the Kuwaiti theater of operations remained intact at the start of the ground campaign and that large numbers were able to escape across the Euphrates River before the cease-fire. Moreover, no mobile Scud launchers were definitively known to have been located and destroyed despite the concerted campaign to do so.

Reconnaissance platforms provided support to combat aircraft by serving as airborne intelligence collection platforms, and they also provided communications and electronic and photographic intelligence on enemy targets. Intelligence from reconnaissance platforms was used to plan strike missions and for BDA purposes. The airborne surveillance and control platforms provided early-warning surveillance for navy aircraft carriers, command and control for Operation Desert Storm air defense forces, and airborne surveillance of ground targets.

Iraqi armed forces were not well equipped to effectively counter the coalition's offensive. After U.S. and coalition aircraft dominated early air encounters, the Iraqi Air Force essentially chose to avoid combat by fleeing to Iran and hiding its aircraft or putting them in the midst of civilian areas off-limits to attack by coalition aircraft. Except for the failed Iraqi action directed at the town of Khafji, the Iraqis did not take any ground offensive initiative throughout the air campaign, and the coalition was able to repeatedly attack targets, including those missed or insufficiently damaged on the first strike. As a result, when the ground war began, Iraqi ground forces had already been subjected to 38 days of nearly continuous bombardment. Intelligence analyses and prisoner-of-war interviews also indicated that many Iraqi frontline troops had low morale and were prone to heavy desertions even before the air bombardment started.

In regard to the search for weapons of mass destruction, the goal of the coalition was to eliminate Iraq's capabilities to build, deploy, or launch nuclear, biological, and chemical weapons (NBC). In the Central Intelligence Agency's (CIA) Report on Intelligence Related to **Gulf War** Illnesses, dated 2 August 1996, the number of sites suspected to have been connected to Iraq's chemical warfare program alone totaled 34. However, the intelligence community did not identify all weapons of mass destruction (biological, chemical, and nuclear) related facilities. The lack of target intelligence meant that Iraqi nuclear-related installations were neither identified nor targeted. The United Nations Special Commission (UNSCOM) that conducted chemical weapons–related inspections at over 60 locations found no evidence that chemical or biological weapons were present during the campaign. Postwar intelligence compiled by the CIA indicates some release of chemicals only at Muhammadiyat and al-Muthanna as a result of coalition bombing. However, both are in remote areas west of Baghdad, and each is over 400 kilometers north of the Saudi Arabian border and the nearest coalition base. *See also* IRAQI INTELLI-GENCE; U.S. PROPAGANDA IN IRAQ.

OPERATION EAGER GLACIER. This was the codename of a secret U.S. effort to spy on Iran with aircraft in 1987 and 1988. The information gathered became part of an intelligence exchange between U.S. military intelligence agencies and Iraq during the **Iran–Iraq War** (1980–1988). Operation Eager Glacier took place at the same time as other U.S. military operations in the Persian Gulf, including **Operation Earnest Will**, the naval escort of Kuwaiti-owned tankers; Operation Prime Chance, the secret attempt to prevent Iranian forces from attacking gulf shipping; and **Operation Praying Mantis**, the retaliation for mining the U.S. guided missile frigate USS *Samuel B. Roberts*.

OPERATION EAGLE CLAW. Known also as Operation Evening Light, this military operation was planned and organized by the Central Intelligence Agency (CIA) to rescue the 53 American diplomat hostages from the U.S. embassy in Tehran, Iran, on 24 April 1980. Under the command of Colonel Charles Beckwith, Delta Force moved to the embassy compound (while a Special Forces team went to the Foreign Ministry) with only 45 minutes to extract the hostages. The Americans faced a daunting task, as incomplete intelligence made the extraction process hit-or-miss. Good intelligence was hard to come by about forces inside the embassy and especially in Tehran, which is located far inside Iran and away from friendly countries.

All of the planning and training had to be carried out in complete secrecy. The operation was designed as a complex two-night mission. The first stage of the mission involved establishing a small staging site inside Iran itself. The site, known as Desert One, was to be used as a temporary airstrip for the C-130 Hercules transport planes and RH-53D Sea Stallion minesweeper helicopters that would undertake the actual rescue operation. After refueling the helicopters, the plan was for the ground troops to board the helicopters and fly to Desert Two near Tehran. After locating and extracting the hostages from Tehran, they would be transported by helicopter to Manzariyeh Air

Base outside Tehran, where C-130 aircrafts would take them out of the country under the protection of fighter aircraft.

An unforeseen low-level sandstorm caused two of eight helicopters to lose their way en route to Desert One, and a third helicopter suffered a mechanical failure and was incapable of continuing with the mission. Without enough helicopters to transport men and equipment to Desert Two, the mission was aborted. After the decision to abort the mission was made, one of the helicopters lost control while taking off and crashed into an aircraft. In the ensuing explosion and fire, eight U.S. servicemen were killed. During the evacuation, six intact RH-53 helicopters were left behind and now serve in the Iranian Navy. In their efforts to quickly evacuate the helicopters, the aircrews left behind classified plans that identified Central Intelligence Agency (CIA) agents within Iran. Wounded personnel, mostly with serious burns, returned with the rest of the Joint Task Force (JTF) to the launch base in Oman. Two C-141 Medivac aircraft from the rear staging base at Wadi Kena, Egypt, picked up the injured personnel, helicopter crews, and Delta Forces, and the injured personnel were transported to Ramstein Air Base, Germany.

Not long after the failure of the mission, the Iranian Embassy siege occurred in London. A second rescue mission was planned under the name Operation Credible Sport (also known as Operation Honey Badger), but was never put into action. On the political level, the failure of the operation had a severe impact on U.S. President Jimmy Carter's reelection prospects. The hostages were eventually released by diplomatic negotiations after 444 days of captivity on 20 January 1981, President Carter's last day in office.

On the military level, an official investigation was launched in 1980 under the leadership of retired chief of naval operations Admiral James L. Holloway III to explore the causes of the failure of the operation. The findings, which were published in the Holloway Report, primarily cited deficiencies in mission planning, command and control, and interservice operability, and provided a catalyst to reorganize the Department of Defense. The lack of cohesion among the various services led to the creation of a new multiservice organization, the U.S. Special Operations Command (USSOCOM), which became operational in 1988–1989. Each branch of the service subsequently established its own special operations forces under the overall control of USSOCOM. Furthermore, the lack of highly trained helicopter pilots who were capable of the low-level night flying needed for modern Special Forces missions prompted the creation of the U.S. Army 160th Special Operations Aviation Regiment (SOAR), known as the Night Stalkers. *See also* U.S. INTELLIGENCE IN IRAN.

OPERATION EARNEST WILL. In December 1986, at the height of the **Iran–Iraq War**, the government of Kuwait asked the Ronald Reagan administration to send the U.S. Navy to protect Kuwaiti tankers. On 28 February 1987, the crew of USS *Stark*, while anchoring in Djibouti, got an early warning from the intelligence officers of the U.S. Middle East Force assessing a significant danger in the Persian Gulf. The first American convoy operation commenced on 22 July 1987, when the crude oil tankers *Bridgeton* and *Gas Prince* got underway in the Gulf of Oman and set course for Kuwait.

On 24 July 1987, the Reagan administration agreed to register 11 Kuwaiti oil tankers under the U.S. flag and provide them with naval protection. Because of a lack of intelligence assessment, the United States did not anticipate the Iranian reaction to the American policy, which led to a number of violent naval actions and American retaliatory strikes on Iranian oil facilities.

Convoy operations resumed on 1 August 1987 when the *Gas Prince* departed Kuwait, escorted by the destroyer *Kidd* and frigate *Crommelin*. Inbound convoy operations resumed on 8 August 1987, *Kidd* and *Crommelin* escorting the crude oil tankers *Sea Isle City*, *Ocean City*, and *Gas King*. The U.S. convoy sailed despite intelligence indicating an Iranian minefield, taking the precaution of forming up farther south, a wise decision in light of the Panamanian-flagged tanker *Texaco Caribbean* striking a mine off Fujayrah in the Gulf of Oman on 10 August 1987.

By late September 1987, U.S. intelligence was alarmed by an Iranian buildup of small craft on Farsi and Kharg islands. On 30 September 1987, intelligence indicated a potential Iranian small-boat attack on Saudi and Kuwaiti offshore oil installations. On the night of 3 October 1987, a U.S. AWACS aircraft detected what was believed to be a formation of Iranian small craft on a course toward Kuwait. Aircraft and vessels were dispatched to intercept the Iranians, who failed to complete their attack. Many believe that the Iranian attack was a false alarm, the AWACS radar operators mistaking sea return as small attack craft.

In response to the *Bridgeton* mining, the Kuwaitis provided a converted oil support barge (*Hercules*) for use as a stationary sea base to allow small craft, Special Forces, and helicopters to patrol the shipping lanes west of Farsi Island. On the night of 8 October 1987, the *Hercules* conducted her first mission. Army special operations helicopters, reconnoitering an area off Farsi in which U.S. small craft were to establish a listening post, were startled to discover three Iranian patrol craft present. The Iranians fired unsuccessfully on the army helicopters and were destroyed when the aircraft returned fire. As *Hercules* was near completion in late September, intelligence operations closely monitored the massing of some 70 small boats near Blusher and Farsi islands following an Iranian exercise menacingly called "Martyrdom." Concern heightened when satellites imaged small boats massed along a 45-mile front, perhaps for an attack on the Saudi Khafji oil complex. The assault failed to materialize. However, U.S. forces still believed the Iranians were up to something in the northern gulf.

By April 1988, the United States achieved its main declared objectives, which were to secure the safe transit of Kuwaiti oil through the gulf and forestall the expansion of Soviet influence in the region. On 29 April 1988, however, the United States expanded the scope of the protection scheme, extending the U.S. Navy's protective umbrella to all neutral shipping in the Persian Gulf. This decision divorced the U.S. policy from its original limited objectives, increased the likelihood of further confrontation with Iran, and laid the groundwork for the destruction of an Iranian airliner by USS *Vincennes*.

Earnest Will overlapped with Operation Prime Chance, a largely secret effort to stop Iranian forces from attacking gulf shipping. Operation Earnest Will was officially ended on 26 September 1988 after Iran agreed to a cease-fire with Iraq on 20 August 1988. *See also* U.S. INTELLIGENCE IN IRAN.

OPERATION EL DORADO CANYON. This was the codename for the joint U.S. Air Force and Navy bombing against Libya on 15 April 1986. The bombing raid marked the conclusion of years of skirmishes over Libyan territorial claims to the Gulf of Sidra, a body of water extending far into international waters, and years of vulnerability to Libyan-supported **terrorism**. Following the Rome and Vienna airport attacks of 27 December 1985, the United States decided to send a message in response to international terrorism and sent a carrier task force to the region in March 1986. Libya responded with aggressive countermaneuvers on 24 March 1986 that led to the destruction of Libyan radar systems and missile attack boats. Less than two weeks later, on 5 April 1986, a bomb exploded in a West Berlin discotheque, La Belle, killing two American servicemen and a Turkish woman, and wounding 200 others. The United States claimed to have obtained cable transcripts from Libyan agents in East Germany involved in the attack. The U.S. National Security Agency (NSA) succeeded in intercepting a message from Libya's ruler, Colonel Muammar Qaddafi, ordering an attack on Americans "to cause maximum and indiscriminate casualties." Intelligence data from the Berlin disco bombing on 5 April clearly showed Libyan knowledge and support of the attack.

Ten days later, the United States launched a series of military air strikes against ground targets inside Libya. Dubbed Operation El Dorado Canyon, the action was defined as self-defense against Libya's state-sponsored terrorism. For achieving the aim of raiding Libya's bases of terror, the U.S. Air Forces in Europe (USAFE) initiated the Project Power Hunter intelligence network in December 1987. The wing first tested the Durandal runway-buster bombs during Exercise Red Flag in January and February 1988.

The raid was designed to strike directly at the heart of Qaddafi's ability to export terrorism, with five targets endorsed by the U.S. Joint Chiefs of Staff and secretary of defense and approved by President Ronald Reagan. All except one of these targets were chosen because of their direct connection to terrorist activity, including the command and control headquarters in Tripoli and other terrorist command posts used for storage of munitions and training grounds for terrorists in underwater sabotage. The single exception was the Benina military airfield, southeast of Benghazi, which was selected to ensure that its MiG fighter aircraft would not intercept or pursue U.S. strike forces.

As part of the effort to attain tactical surprise, mission planners decided to hit all five targets simultaneously. This decision had a crucial impact on nearly every aspect of the operation since it meant that the available U.S. Navy resources capable of conducting a precision night attack could not perform the mission unilaterally. Assistance was requested from Great Britain, which dramatically affected the scope and complexity of the operation. Planning was even further compounded when France and Spain refused to grant authority to fly over their territory, thereby greatly increasing the distance of the flight route from Great Britain to Tripoli, the hours of flight time for the pilots and crews, and the amount of refueling support required from tanker aircraft.

Concurrent with target selection, the nature and size of the strike force were considered. Concern for collateral casualties and risk to U.S. personnel, coupled with availability of assets, quickly narrowed the field to a strike by tactical aircraft. The size of the strike force's final configuration was immense and complex. Although joint in nature, the actual execution of the strike was operationally and geographically divided between the navy, which was assigned the target in the Benghazi area, and the air force, which hit the other three targets in the vicinity of Tripoli. This division of responsibility was done largely to simplify command and control of the operational aspects of the raid.

On 14 April 1986, approximately 100 aircraft were launched in direct support of the raid. Several helicopters were deployed for possible search-and-rescue operations, and more than 50 aircraft were airborne in the vicinity of the carriers some 150–200 miles offshore. The British Eighth Air Force's refueling support of the strike force made this the longest successful mission ever accomplished by tactical aircraft. The actual combat lasted less than 12 minutes and dropped 60 tons of munitions. Resistance outside the immediate area of attack was nonexistent, and Libyan air defense aircraft were never launched. One strike aircraft was lost during the operation. Although Libya anticipated retaliation for the Berlin disco bombing, for some unknown reason Libya's air defenses seemed almost wholly unprepared for the attack. Libya's air defense system was completely overwhelmed and it was reported that some Libyan soldiers abandoned their posts in fright and confusion. *See also* LIBYAN INTELLIGENCE.

OPERATION ENGULF. Engulf was a series of sophisticated operations conducted by the British agency MI5 from the mid-1950s to the mid-1960s in which Egyptian and French cipher transmissions were intercepted. The first and most successful Engulf operation was conducted during the Suez crisis of 1956, when an MI5 team, led by British spymaster Peter Wright, planted a bug in the cipher room of the Egyptian embassy in London.

The Suez Canal crisis began when President Gamal Abdel Nasser seized the Suez Canal, which had been controlled by Great Britain and France until July 1956. Nasser did so partially as an act of retaliation against the United States and Britain for their refusal to fund the construction of the Aswan High Dam but also as a means of raising money from the tolls imposed on ships during the Suez War. Great Britain and France occupied the Suez Canal zone and Israel occupied the Sinai Peninsula. Finally, pressures from the General Assembly of the United Nations and Soviet Union forced Great Britain and France to evacuate the Suez Canal and forced Israel to evacuate Sinai Peninsula.

MI5 managed to install the listening device in the Egyptian embassy with help from the British telephone service, which feigned problems with the embassy's phones. An MI5 undercover team disguised as repair operatives was then called in to "fix" the equipment. Interception of the Egyptian cipher transmissions enabled MI5 to listen in on discussions between the Egyptians and the Soviets, which revealed that the Soviet threats to intervene in Suez on behalf of the Egyptians were genuine. Even when the Soviets discovered the device planted by MI5, they opted to leave it in place without notifying the Egyptians, thus giving them an opportunity to convey to the British exactly where they stood on the Suez situation. *See also* BRITISH INTELLIGENCE IN EGYPT AND SUDAN; OPERATION MUSKETEER; SOVIET INTELLIGENCE IN EGYPT.

OPERATION ENTEBBE. On 27 June 1976, Air France Flight 139 was hijacked by four terrorists. Two of the terrorists belonged to the German Baader-Meinhof Gang. About 100 passengers on board the airplane were Israeli and Jews. The terrorists ordered the captain to fly to Benghazi, Libya. After six and a half hours in Benghazi airport, the airplane took off again and began flying eastward, as instructed. At 3 A.M. on 28 June, the airplane landed at Entebbe, Uganda.

Upon landing, the four terrorists joined the three others terrorists waiting in the Entebbe terminal, bringing the total up to seven. The passengers were kept on the aircraft until noon and then transported to the airport's old terminal building. Ugandan President Idi Amin visited the hostages in the terminal and told them he was working to achieve their release, and that Ugandan soldiers would remain at the terminal to ensure their safety. The next day at 3:30 P.M. the leader of the terrorists, a Palestine nicknamed "the Peruvian," released the specific demands the group of terrorists were seeking, namely that 53 terrorists—13 held in prisons in France, West Germany, Kenya, and Switzerland, and 40 in Israeli prisons—were to be released. If they were not, hostages would be executed starting on 1 July at 2 P.M.

Israeli Prime Minister Yitzhak Rabin convened a group of cabinet ministers, including the chief of the Israel Defense Forces (IDF) Lieutenant General Mordechai (Motta) Gur. There were serious complications in using military forces such a long distance from Israel.

On 30 June, the Israeli Military Intelligence and the **Mossad** obtained intelligence information according to which Idi Amin was not seeking the release of the hostages and was actually collaborating with the Popular Front for the Liberation of Palestine (PFLP). This made an early plan requiring marine commandos to rescue the hostages and then surrender to Ugandan soldiers undesirable. Motta Gur reported that the IDF had no viable plan to rescue the hostages. On 1 July, the Israeli government declared that it had adopted a resolution to release their Palestinian prisoners. As a result, the PFLP terrorists released the non-Jewish passengers, leaving only the flight crew and the Jewish passengers on the aircraft. Upon receiving word that Israel had agreed to the exchange deal, the terrorists moved the day of execution back to Sunday, 4 July 1976. Israeli Mossad case officers met with the released passenger in Paris. The released passengers gave them important details about the terminal in Entebbe. They said that the Ugandan soldiers were fully cooperating with the terrorists and that the Jewish passengers had been segregated from the rest. The real purpose of the hijacking was beginning to be made clear. Once again, the military was asked for options.

Yehonathan Netanyahu, commander of the IDF's elite unit Sayeret Matkal, was briefed on the roles and missions of the units in the plan that was then under development. Brigadier General Dan Shomron was appointed commander of the rescue unit.

The rescue mission took place on the night of 3 July and early morning of 4 July 1976. The mission succeeded, though Yehonathan Netanyahu was killed in action. The Entebbe operation serves as a classic example of a successful special operation based on excellent intelligence. The Israelis used surprise and superior training to overcome the terrorists and gain their objectives with a minimum loss of life. It was a logistically difficult mission. Thirty-five commandos in two Land Rovers and a Mercedes loaded with munitions had to be transported over 2,200 miles and back again with over 100 hostages. All the hijackers were killed by the Israeli forces.

OPERATION EVENING LIGHT. *See* OPERATION EAGLE CLAW.

OPERATION GAMMA. This covert Central Intelligence Agency (CIA) operation was initiated with the purpose of preventing war between Israel and Egypt and promoting peace in the Middle East in the mid-1950s. This was a period of tension in the Middle East, especially as a result of constant *fedayeen* ("freedom fighters") attacks on Israel and of Egypt's receipt of weapons from the Soviet Union.

Former senior U.S. Department of Defense expert Robert Anderson was secretly dispatched to Middle East capitals (in particular, Jerusalem and Cairo) to negotiate between Israel and Egypt and explore common ground for agreement. Anderson secretly met with Israeli Prime Minister David Ben Gurion and Egypt's leader Gamal Abdel Nasser in January 1956 and again in March 1956. During his negotiations, Anderson attempted to achieve any formula for peace, including the idea that Israel would cede parts of the Negev Desert in exchange for peace. However, Anderson's mission failed and by the spring of 1956, tension in the region was very high. Israel was reluctant to make any territorial concessions, especially in the Negev. Moreover, the Palestinian refugee problem looked like an unsolvable one. *See also* PEACE AND POLITICAL PROCESSES.

OPERATION HONEY BADGER. *See* OPERATION EAGLE CLAW.

OPERATION IRAQI FREEDOM. In November 2002, the United Nations Security Council adopted Resolution 1441 requiring Iraq to eliminate its weapons of mass destruction (WMDs). However, not all the members of the organization favored military intervention. As efforts to reach consensus in the UN continued, the United States and Great Britain formed a coalition of countries to forcibly overthrow the regime of Saddam Hussein in Iraq. The coalition knew that Iraqi forces were not strong enough to withstand such an attack, but there was serious concern about their possible use of unconventional weapons, since Iraq had used such weapons in the past against the Kurds and against Iranian forces during the **Iran–Iraq War** in the 1980s. In addition, there was concern that in case of military defeat, Iraqi agents would supply these weapons to terrorist organizations for use against Western targets outside Iraq.

In the fall of 2002, the U.S. intelligence community began to gather information and assess Iraqi weapons capabilities in preparation for the military operation. The coalition military forces assembled in February and March of 2003 for Operation Iraqi Freedom. On 17 March 2003, President George W. Bush appeared on worldwide television and gave Saddam Hussein an ultimatum of 48 hours to leave Iraq or face war. Saddam rejected the ultimatum, and the subsequent invasion received the most intensive media coverage in history. When the war started, U.S. General Tommy Ray Franks had a massive army of approximately 225,000 at his deposal, including the army, marines, navy, and air force, plus an additional British force of 25,000 soldiers.

The intelligence community worked closely with the U.S. Central Command (USCENTCOM) and provided its expertise and intelligence support to combat operations in Iraq throughout the operation. At the height of the combat, over 900 intelligence personnel were committed to assisting USCENTCOM. Various intelligence services and special operations units played an important role in target identification, including the use of electronic signature devices for directing the weapons to locate and zero in on targets. The CIA developed new intelligence methodologies for the analysis of Iraqi forces and created a sophisticated database that became the authoritative source on Iraqi military intelligence. The agency provided round-the-clock analytical support for military planning and rescue operations, including assessments of Iraqi force locations and defensive plans, as well as a digital map of Iraq with detailed geographical data and border crossings. The National Geospatial-Intelligence Agency (NGA) provided USCENTCOM with commercial imagery data for media release in order to demonstrate that battle damage from U.S. aircraft and missiles was restricted to government buildings and military targets. Medical facilities and civilian Iraqi infrastructure facilities were identified and added to the "No-Strike" list.

Although the coalition forces were not initially allowed to use Turkish soil as their military base for the fighting in northern Iraq, they were given limited use of Turkish airspace to strike Iraq once the hostilities started. The air arsenal included over 500 combat aircraft, including B-52s, F-117 stealth fighters, and B-2 stealth bombers. Moreover, there were inland bases in Qatar and Kuwait, as well as naval forces on five U.S. naval aircraft carriers and approximately 30 missile ships and submarines, located either in the Persian Gulf or the eastern Mediterranean within striking range of targets in Iraq.

The land invasion of Iraq began on 20 March 2003. American troops based in Kuwait advanced through the desert, while British forces surrounded and isolated the port city of Basra. Coalition forces took control over a huge amount of territory and the entire coastline of Iraq within three weeks. On 9 April 2003, coalition forces reached central Baghdad, where the Iraqi people celebrated by tearing down the statue of Saddam, an event that was broadcast live all over the world. On 15 April 2003, U.S. marines captured Tikrit, and the Pentagon announced that the main objective of the operation, toppling the regime of Saddam Hussein, had been achieved. Saddam, his sons, and other top officials were either captured or killed.

However, the rapid advancement of the forces left the country with no police or any other law enforcement, and intense looting ensued. Although the military victory was quick and decisive, pockets of terrorists have been operating there ever since, attacking both coalition forces and Iraqi security forces. These terrorists are supported by the ousted Sunnis and by several external terrorist organizations, which have succeeded in prolonging the internal struggle for more than five years. Due to increasing political pressure, the countries providing coalition forces are now reconsidering their present role in Iraq.

The failure to find large caches of biological or chemical weapons has resulted in an ongoing debate about whether reports of the Iraqi capabilities were exaggerated in order to justify launching the operation. The National Intelligence Estimate (NIE) Iraq's Continuing Programs for Weapons of Mass Destruction, based on intelligence acquired and evaluated over a 15-year period, detailed the intelligence community's knowledge and analysis of Iraq's WMD capabilities prior to the deployment of coalition forces to Iraq. Information acquired both during and after the major military operation has not changed the assessment that Iraq was intent on reconstituting its nuclear weapons program. However, prewar data and intelligence on the scope and status of Iraq's other WMD programs have proven to be less convincing than originally claimed. U.S. officials have raised the possibility that weapons and stockpiles may have been diverted to Syria, though Syria has denied those allegations. *See also* IRAQI NUCLEAR WEAPONS PROGRAM.

OPERATION MASS APPEAL. This covert propaganda campaign was launched in the late 1990s by the British Secret Intelligence Service (SIS) in order to gain public support for sanctions and the use of military force in Iraq. Stories about secret underground facilities in Iraq and ongoing programs to produce weapons of mass destruction were planted in newspapers in various countries, from which they were fed back to Great Britain and the United States. Poland, India, and South Africa were initially chosen as targets for the campaign because they were nonaligned United Nations countries that were not supporting the British and U.S. positions on sanctions. The aim was to convince the public that Iraq was a far greater threat than it actually was, and the campaign was judged to be having a successful effect on public opinion. Similar propaganda tactics were used by MI6 up until the time of the invasion of Iraq in 2003, ultimately raising the question of whether intelligence material was manipulated and misused in order to promote the case for going to war.

The British government confirmed that MI6 had organized Operation Mass Appeal but denied that MI6 had planted misinformation in the media about Saddam Hussein's weapons of mass destruction. The admission by the British government followed claims by Scott Ritter, a former U.S. military intelligence officer and senior United Nations weapons inspector in Iraq, that MI6 had recruited him in 1997 to help with the propaganda effort. David Kelly, a former United Nations weapons inspector and colleague of Scott Ritter, might also have been used by MI6 to pass information to the media. Kelly was in close touch with the Rockingham Cell, a group of weapons experts that received MI6 intelligence, and his involvement with the group was discovered by the press.

These developments were subsequently drawn to the attention of British parliamentarians, and a press conference was organized in the House of Commons for 21 November 2003. It was at that press conference that Ritter himself briefed British journalists on **Operation Rockingham** and also for the first time spoke about Operation Mass Appeal; he even started to name names. Ritter called for a full inquiry at which he was willing to testify under oath about both operations, and he called for relevant MI6 officers to be subpoenaed. Kelly testified to the parliamentary Intelligence and Security Committee (ISC) in a closed session on 26 July 2004, and the following day he committed suicide.

OPERATION MUSKETEER. This was the codename given to the 1956 Suez crisis, known also as Operation Sinai Campaign or Operation Kadesh by the Israelis. Operation Musketeer is the story of the 1956 British and French attempt to seize the Suez Canal from Egypt. Great Britain and, to a lesser extent, France, relied on the Suez Canal as the economic lifeline to the oil fields of the Middle East. The canal was administered by a British-dominated company for almost 75 years, until July 1956, when Egypt's President Gamal Abdel Nasser nationalized the canal.

The nationalization of the Suez Canal by Egypt was unacceptable to British Prime Minister Anthony Eden, who viewed Nasser as a threat to British influence in the Middle East. Likewise, French Premier Guy Mollet saw Nasser as the source of all trouble in Algeria. At the beginning of the Suez crisis, MI6 developed a plan to assassinate Nasser using nerve gas. Prime Minister Eden initially gave his approval for the operation but later rescinded it when he gained agreement from the French and Israelis to engage in joint military action. Their new rationale for seizing the canal evolved from one of regaining lost property to one of safeguarding a vital waterway from hostile neighbors.

The Central Intelligence Agency (CIA) warned that many in the Israeli leadership were committed to territorial expansion and would welcome a war that brought it about. U.S. intelligence officers continued to follow the Middle East situation as the pressure rose and as British radio propaganda against Nasser increased sharply. On 19 October 1956, the CIA expressed the belief that Britain and France would not resort to military action unless there was some new and violent provocation.

On 23 October 1956, a secret summit was held at Sevres, France, between the prime ministers, foreign ministers, and defense ministers of the three countries (France, Great Britain, and Israel). Over the course of two days, the three powers agreed on a schedule of events called Operation Musketeer. It was a political deception that involved the launching of an Israeli attack on Egypt in the Sinai Peninsula. An Israeli paratrooper drop would be interpreted by Britain and France as a threat to the Suez Canal. An ultimatum would then be addressed to Israel, requesting an immediate cease-fire and withdrawal of all military forces to a distance of 10 miles east of the canal. Britain and France would resolve to do all in their power to bring about the early cessation of hostilities between Israel and Egypt. The two governments would then demand that Egypt accept a temporary occupation by Anglo–French forces of key positions at Port Said, Ismailiya, and Suez in order to safeguard the freedom of navigation through the Suez Canal.

Prime Minister Eden insisted on one final provision: No copies of the accord would ever be made public. After the deal was made, the three parties returned to put it into action. On 26 October 1956, Israel launched its attack according to plan. However, the Israeli Army achieved its strategic objectives so rapidly that the threat to the canal had subsided before the allies were even ready to act. On 5 November, British and French paratroopers landed at key positions in Port Said, but by then their political collusion had been exposed by the efficiency of Operation Kadesh. British military success was severely limited by political failure, economic weakness, and intelligence short-sightedness. Britain's economy was collapsing and in order to gain American aid, the British government was forced to accept U.S. President Dwight D. Eisenhower's call for a cease-fire. France had no choice but to go along. Thus, only 44 hours after the first paratroopers landed, the war was over. At that point, the allies held only the northern end of the Suez Canal.

Prime Minister Eden's original political objective had been to depose Nasser. However, he so confused the objectives of his operation by attempting to find a plausible motive for it that he reduced the likelihood of achieving his original goal. By adding a military objective, he lowered his chances of eliminating the Egyptian Army, which constituted the base of Nasser's power. He placed himself in such a position that even though his real purpose remained the fall of Nasser, his stated cause was to achieve a cease-fire and to safeguard free passage on the Suez Canal.

It was obvious that Operation Musketeer would be unsuccessful in accomplishing its full political agenda. However, Operation Musketeer failed to achieve both its military and its political objectives. The principal architect for the disaster, Prime Minister Eden, failed to recognize that Great Britain's military was not structured to conduct rapid contingency operations. Once he decided on using the military option, Eden did not ensure that the political objective was supported by the military operation. The French shared in the disaster because they assumed the British were prepared to act quickly with military force and the goal was the removal of Nasser. However, as the crisis became prolonged and the Suez Canal became the military objective, the French failed to achieve their goals. It might be concluded that Operation Musketeer was a military success that ended in a political failure. *See also* NASSER'S ASSASSINATION ATTEMPTS.

OPERATION OPERA. The codename of the Israel Air Force (IAF) bombing of the Iraqi nuclear reactor Tammuz-1 at Osiraq on 7 June 1981. The raid surprised the Iraqis and the rest of the world; however, it had long been in the making by Israel and was executed only after failure on the diplomatic front and after consultation between Israeli Prime Minister Menahem Begin's cabinet and military and intelligence experts.

Israeli intelligence had confirmed Iraq's intentions to develop nuclear weapons at the Osiraq reactor since the late 1970s and recognized that the Iraqi threats against Israel were real. In October 1979, Begin asked the General Staff of the Israel Defense Forces to prepare plans to destroy the Iraqi reactor. In 1981, some estimates showed Iraq was 5–10 years away from a nuclear weapons capability, while other intelligence reports estimated that Iraq could have a bomb within a year or two. The Israeli intelligence community further estimated that the reactor was nearly operational and was ready to take in nuclear fuel. Once the fuel was inside the reactor, bombing it could lead to radiation that would endanger the population of Baghdad. Accordingly, Israeli intelligence assessed that the summer of 1981 would be the last chance to safely act against the reactor.

After Israel calculated that it had the capability to launch the attack, it did not immediately spring into action. Instead, in an unconventional move, Chief of the General Staff Rafael Eitan allowed the officers of the General Staff and Military Intelligence (MI) analysts to express their views on the pros and cons of such an attack. Supporters and opponents were evenly divided. MI director Major General Yehoshua Saguy believed that the Iraqi reactor was not an imminent threat. However, because of his absence abroad, his deputy, the head of the MI Research Division, Brigadier General Aviezer (Avik) Ya'ari, presented the threat in grim colors based on a rigorous study prepared in his division. This finally convinced the Israeli cabinet to adopt the decision to conduct the raid.

On 7 June 1981 at 4:01 P.M., eight F-16s and six F-15s took off from the Israeli Air Force (IAF) base at Etzion in the northern Sinai Desert. That day was chosen on the assumption that, being a Sunday, the French scientists and technicians would not be working in the reactor. The hour for approaching and leaving Tammuz-1 was to be last light so that the aircraft would be directly in front of the setting sun, making it more difficult for the Iraqi air defenses to see them. Flying time was estimated according to a route that minimized the chances of being detected by Jordanian, Saudi, or Iraqi radar. The bombing took place as planned, and all Israeli pilots and planes returned safely to base. *See also* IRAQI INTELLIGENCE; IRAQI NUCLEAR WEAPONS PROGRAM.

OPERATION PRAYING MANTIS. This operation was carried out on 18 April 1988 by U.S. naval forces in retaliation for the Iranian mining of a U.S. warship four days earlier. That mining nearly sank the guided missile frigate USS *Samuel B. Roberts* while sailing in the Persian Gulf as part of the **Operation Earnest Will** convoy escort missions conducted in 1987–1988. In this operation, U.S. warships escorted reflagged Kuwaiti oil tankers and other merchant ships in order to protect them from Iraqi and Iranian attacks during the **Iran–Iraq War**. After the mining, U.S. Navy divers recovered other mines in the area. By the time the *Samuel B. Roberts* was towed to Dubai on 15 April 1988, battered but saved and with no loss of life, U.S. planning for the retaliatory operation had already begun in earnest.

The one-day attack proved to be the largest engagement of surface warships since **World War II** and also marked the first surface-to-surface missile engagement in U.S. Navy history. The battle destroyed two Iranian warships and sank as many as six armed speedboats. One of the warships, the *Sabalan*, was repaired and upgraded and is still in service in the Iranian Navy. The U.S. fleet also damaged Iranian naval and intelligence facilities on two inoperable oil platforms in the Persian Gulf, which have since been repaired and are now back in service. The U.S. side sustained casualties of two pilots when their helicopter crashed while flying reconnaissance about 15 miles southwest of Abu Musa Island. Navy officials said that the wreckage showed no sign of battle damage, though the aircraft could have crashed while trying to evade Iranian fire. The attack helped pressure Iran to agree to a cease-fire with Iraq later that summer, ending their eight-year conflict.

The value of incorporating realistic intelligence into exercises was demonstrated during Operation Praying Mantis in 1988. The commander of a Special Purpose Marine Air-Ground Task Force (MAGTF) based his training scenarios on actual intelligence studies of potential raid sites in the Persian Gulf. For the execution of the operation, the MAGTF was directed to attack the "Sassan" gas-oil platform, a target the MAGTF had used in its training exercise. The use of realistic intelligence during training gave the MAGTF commander the necessary background knowledge and situational awareness to rapidly complete the plan.

OPERATION ROCKINGHAM. This was the codeword for Great Britain's involvement in inspections in Iraq following the war in

Kuwait in 1990–1991. The small group of members in this operation was known as the Rockingham Cell, which was responsible for briefing the United Nations Special Commission (UNSCOM) on Iraq and the International Atomic Energy Agency (IAEA) inspection teams. UNSCOM was established early in 1991 to oversee the disposal of Iraq's weapons of mass destruction (WMDs). The Rockingham Cell processed information received as a result of the inspections and acted as a central source of advice on continuing inspection activity.

The codename remained confidential for about a decade and was used only by those in support of inspections in Iraq. Each department of the British government directly involved in those support activities allocated staff to the Rockingham Cell. The codename became public after the invasion of Iraq in 2003, when allegations were made that Operation Rockingham was a British intelligence propaganda effort to manipulate sensitive intelligence information through a disinformation campaign.

In an interview with the Scottish *Sunday Herald* in June 2003, Scott Ritter, a former U.S. military intelligence officer and United Nations weapons inspector, claimed that Operation Rockingham was a secret British intelligence unit aimed at producing misleading intelligence on Iraq's weapons of mass destruction in order to justify action against Iraq. Ritter alleged that the Rockingham Cell was at the center of various British and U.S. intelligence organizations collecting information on Iraq's WMDs and that the unit dealt with intelligence obtained from a variety of sources, including Iraqi defectors and UNSCOM, which Rockingham had penetrated. According to Ritter, the unit used the evidence it had amassed selectively, with government backing, in order to promote a predetermined outcome. In an effort to create a public mind-set that Iraq was not in compliance with the inspections and still had WMDs, it presented only a small percentage of the facts, when most were ambiguous or even pointed to the absence of WMD. *See also* IRAQI NUCLEAR WEAPONS PROGRAM; OPERATION MASS APPEAL.

OPERATION SALAAM. Operation Salaam was a covert operation conducted in 1942 under the command of the Hungarian aristocrat and desert explorer **László Almásy** to insert two German agents deep into British-held Egypt. When Hungary had entered the war on the side of the Axis, Almásy was recruited by German military intelligence and given the rank of captain. From then on, he advised Field Marshal Erwin Rommel's Afrika Korps and the Seventh Panzer Division on desert warfare, while also leading military operations such as Salaam. In 1942, after numerous battles back and forth in the North African desert, German and Italian forces had pushed Commonwealth forces into a retreat that ended at the El Alamein battle. The Afrika Korps, which had been sent to support the Italians in North Africa, had demoralized the Allied forces with the fall of Tobruk and the **battle of Gazala**. Rommel had plans for capturing Egypt, which would have put the Allies in a very precarious situation with the Suez Canal under enemy control. The Germans had few agents in Egypt itself, and Operation Salaam would provide intelligence from Cairo, where the British were in a crisis over the Afrika Korps' advance.

To get into Egypt, a route was taken from the south where enormous expanses of desert would lessen the risks of being captured. Accompanied by commandos and Almásy himself, **Johannes Eppler** and Peter Stanstede were driven 4,200 kilometers in a convoy of captured American vehicles, starting from the Axis base in Libya. They passed many Allied vehicles during their journey and were waved through the few checkpoints and bases on the route, though little was known about the exact intentions of the group or their final destination. The entire round trip took two weeks, seven days there and seven days back.

Eppler went under the name of Hussein Gaffar. He had grown up in Alexandria and Cairo after his mother had remarried a wealthy Egyptian. Peter Stanstede posed as an American under the assumed name Peter Monkaster, since he had worked in the U.S. petroleum industry before the war and could pass as an American. Once the two spies were dropped off and on their way to Cairo, Operation Salaam became known as Operation Condor. Almásy and his convoy returned to Axis-held Libya, where he was awarded the Iron Cross (First Class) and promoted to the rank of major by Rommel.

After a rail journey to Cairo, the two spies rented a houseboat on the Nile River. Stanstede installed a radio set in the cocktail bar on the boat. They then proceeded to gather information on British troop and vehicle movements through the assistance of a belly dancer, Hekmat Fahmy, who was Eppler's friend from his younger days. Due to various leads picked up by Allied intelligence, the spies' hideout was discovered and their houseboat was boarded by British Field Security. Stanstede started to flood the vessel, but the two spies were quickly taken into custody. Both Eppler and Stanstede confessed but were spared execution. Hekmat Fahmy was caught and received a two-year prison sentence. *See also* OPERATION BERTRAM.

OPERATION SPHINX. This was the codename of a series of secret operations carried out by the Israeli **Mossad** in an attempt to disrupt Iraq's nuclear program. On 6 April 1979, three bombs exploded in the nuclear facility of the French firm of Constructions Navales et Industrielles de la Méditerranée in La Seyne-Sur-Mer near Marseilles. The reactor cores, which were about to be shipped to Iraq, were blown up. This operation set back **Iraq's nuclear weapon program** by at least half a year.

On 13 June 1980, Yahya al-Meshad, an Egyptian nuclear physicist working for Iraq's Atomic Energy Commission, was killed in his Paris hotel room. Meshad had been in France checking on highly enriched uranium that was about to be shipped as the first fuel for Iraq's reactor. On 2 August 1980, a series of bombs exploded at the offices or residences of officials of Iraq's key suppliers in Italy and France: SNIA-Techint, Ansaldo Mercanico Nucleare, and Techniatome. The three manufacturers were supplying Iraq with a reactor and hot-cell equipment. Their officials and workers were also harassed by threatening letters. *See also* OPERATION OPERA.

OPERATION STRAGGLE. *See* OPERATION WAPPEN.

OPERATION SUNRISE. This was the codename of the Israeli Security Agency (ISA) for protecting Prime Minister Yitzhak Rabin. The operation failed and on 4 November 1995 Yitzhak Rabin was assassinated by Yigal Amir. Amir wanted to kill the prime minister because of an agreement Rabin had signed with the Palestinians in September 1993 (the Oslo Accords). Prime Minister Rabin was one of the Israeli heroes of the 1967 Six Days' War. He was admired in Israel and in the world because of his attempts to reach a genuine peace agreement with the Palestinians. Because of the increased wave of suicide terrorists in Israel that followed the Oslo Accords, however, Rabin was hated by right-wing Israeli extremists.

On 4 November 1995, one of the biggest peace demonstration in Israeli history took place at the Malchei Yisrael Square in Tel-Aviv. More than 100,000 people who supported Rabin's peace initiative gathered in the square. Rabin and Foreign Minister Shimon Peres stood on the stage in the square. Rabin's limousine was parked in a blind side street.

Yigal Amir had planned to kill Yitzhak Rabin since January 1995. He tried twice, albeit without success. The first attempt was carried out when Prime Minister Rabin visited the Holocaust Memorial at Yad Vashem in June 1995, but because of a terrorist suicide attack committed by Jihad el Islami, Rabin postponed that visit. In September 1995, Rabin attended an official opening of a road in Kfar Smaryahu, but Amir was not able to break through the security measures.

On the eve of the peace vigil, the media published that Prime Minister Rabin and Foreign Minister Shimon Peres would attend the vigil. This leak of information made it easier for Yigal Amir to know exactly when and where the prime minister was supposed to be on the evening of 5 November 1995.

Yigal Amir loaded the magazine cartridge into his pistol, flipped on the safety lock, and tucked the gun inside his pants on his right side with his shirt covering it. Amir left his home at approximately 7:45 P.M. and used public transportation to reach the intersection of Ibn Gabirol and Arlozorov streets in Tel-Aviv. From there he walked toward Malchei Yisrael Square where the vigil was being held.

Amir removed his *kippa* (skullcap), wandered about the area, and decided to position himself in the parking lot next to City Hall, where the prime minister's and foreign minister's cars were parked. Amir stood in that spot for approximately 40 minutes and waited for the vigil to end. At 9:45 P.M. the prime minister left the dais escorted by his bodyguards and walked toward his car. One of them opened the car door and the prime minister prepared to step in. Amir approached the prime minister, and with the premeditated intention of murdering him, fired three bullets in his back at close range. Two bullets hit the prime minister, penetrating his body, and another bullet hit the left hand of bodyguard Yoram Rubin, who tried to protect the prime minister.

A regular bullet hit the bodyguard's hand, causing his six-day hospitalization at Ichilov Hospital in Tel-Aviv. The bullets that hit the prime minister were hollow-point bullets. One entered his back from the right side and went through his right lung. The second bullet penetrated his left hip from behind and passed through his spleen, diaphragm, and left lung. The prime minister was rushed to Ichilov Hospital in Tel-Aviv, where he died at 10:30 P.M. as a result of severe trauma to his lungs and spleen.

The Protective Security Department of the Israeli Security Agency (ISA) is responsible for protecting Israeli government ministers and buildings, Israeli embassies, defense industries, scientific installations, industrial plants, and the national airline. The failure to protect Prime Minister Yitzhak Rabin is regarded as the greatest failure since the 1973 **Yom Kippur War**. Rabin's assassination is regarded as a particularly serious failure in light of the facts the ISA was aware of cells of the religious right wing that opposed the prime minister's peace initiative with the Palestinian. Moreover, the ISA had a freelance informer, Avishai Raviv, a former member of the outlawed anti-Arab Kach movement. Raviv had been recruited by ISA in 1987 to inform on ultranationalist Israeli groups.

The ISA's reputation was compromised by its failure to prevent the assassination of Prime Minister Yitzhak Rabin. The director of the ISA, Carmi Gillon, resigned as a result of the assassination in early 1996. *See also* ISRAELI INTELLIGENCE.

OPERATION SUSANNAH. *See* LAVON AFFAIR.

OPERATION TPAJAX. Also known as TP-AJAX, this was a covert operation jointly carried out in 1953 by the United States and Great Britain to overthrow elected Iranian Prime Minister Muhammad Mossadeq and his cabinet and to bring to power Muhammad Reza Pahlavi as the shah of Iran. Fearful of Iran's plans to nationalize its oil industry, Britain initiated the plan for the coup in 1952 and pressured President S. Harry Truman to cooperate in a joint operation to remove the prime minister. However, it was only after Truman was succeeded by Dwight D. Eisenhower in 1953 that the British won

American approval for the operation. An important factor considered by the United States was Iran's border with the Soviet Union. A pro-American Iran under the shah would have given the United States a double strategic advantage in the Cold War, as the North Atlantic Treaty Organization (NATO) alliance was already in effect with the government of Turkey, also bordering the Soviet Union.

For the British, the operation was justified by Mossadeq's socialist political views and his nationalization, without compensation, of the oil industry, which had been operated by the Anglo–Iranian Oil Company (AIOC) under contracts disputed by the nationalists as unfair. A particular point of contention was the refusal of the AIOC to allow an audit of the accounts to determine whether the Iranian government had received its due royalties. Lack of cooperation on the part of the AIOC led the nationalist government to escalate its demands for an equal share in the oil revenues. The situation reached a final crisis when the oil company ceased its operations in Iran rather than accept the Iranian government's demands.

Following the takeover of the oil companies by the state, there was a marked drop in productivity and a shutdown of export markets. Nevertheless, royalties to the Iranian government were significantly higher than before nationalization. Without its own distribution network, it was denied access to markets by an international blockade intended to coerce Mossadeq into reprivatization. In addition, the appropriation of the companies resulted in Western allegations that Mossadeq was a communist and suspicions that Iran was in danger of succumbing to the influence of the Soviet Union. But Mossadeq refused to back down under international pressure.

In planning Operation TPAJAX, the Central Intelligence Agency (CIA) organized a guerrilla force in case the communist Tudeh Party seized power as a result of the chaos created by the operation. The CIA had reached an agreement with Qashqai tribal leaders in Southern Iran to establish a clandestine safe haven from which U.S.-funded guerrillas and intelligence agents could operate. The CIA and the British Secret Intelligence Service (SIS) handpicked General Fazlollah Zahedi to succeed Prime Minister Muhammad Mossadeq and covertly funneled $5 million to General Zahedi's regime two days after the coup was carried out. Iranians working for the CIA and posing as communists harassed religious leaders and staged the bombing of one cleric's home in a campaign to turn the country's Islamic religious community against Mossadeq's government.

Operation TPAJAX was the first time that the CIA was involved in a plot to overthrow a democratically elected government. The dissatisfaction of many Iranians with the regime of the shah, who was reinstalled in 1953, led to the 1979 Islamic Revolution in Iran. As a condition of restoring the AIOC, Washington was able to dictate that the AIOC's oil monopoly should lapse. *See also* IRANIAN INTELLIGENCE; ROOSEVELT, KERMIT; WILBER, DONALD N.

OPERATION WAPPEN. This was the codename for the U.S. covert operation against Syria in the 1950s. Over the course of a decade, from the mid-1940s until the late 1950s, U.S. involvement in Syria was punctuated by a series of coup d'états and covert operations. In late 1945, the Arabian American Oil Company (ARAMCO) announced plans to construct the Trans-Arabian Pipe Line (TAPLINE) from Saudi Arabia to the Mediterranean. With assistance from the United States, ARAMCO secured the right-of-way from Lebanon, Jordan, and Saudi Arabia. However, the Syrian right-of-way was stalled in Parliament.

A few years later, violent anti-American, anti-Israeli demonstrations in November 1948 forced Prime Minister Jamil Mardam to resign. He was succeeded by Khalid al-Azm. During this crisis, a Central Intelligence Agency (CIA) operative made contact with right-wing Syrian Army officers and met secretly with Syrian Army chief-of-staff Colonel Husni Zaim at least six times to discuss the possibility of an army-supported dictatorship. American officials realized that Zaim had a strong anti-Soviet attitude, and plans for the coup with Zaim were completed in early 1949. On 14 March 1949, Zaim requested that U.S. agents provoke internal disturbances as a catalyst for the coup. Nine days later, Zaim promised a "surprise" within several days with the assurance of U.S. support. Shortly thereafter, students protesting government corruption and mishandling of the war with Israel took to the streets.

On 30 March 1949, Zaim staged his coup and suspended the constitution. This was followed over the next two months by the arrest of hundreds of communists and left-wing dissidents and a ban of the Communist Party. Zaim's cooperation far exceeded Washington's expectations, including approval of ARAMCO's TAPLINE and plans to resume peace talks with Israel and resettle 250,000 Palestinian refugees in Syria. By July 1949, Zaim had signed a Syrian–Israeli armistice and was awaiting U.S. approval for $100 million in military and economic aid.

However, on 14 August 1949, Zaim was overthrown and executed by Colonel Sami Hinnawi. Elections in November 1949 produced a victory for Hinnawi's Populist Party, which announced plans for a Syrian union with Iraq's Hashemite dynasty. Hinnawi's victory was short-lived, though, as he was ousted on 19 December 1949 by Colonel Adib Shishakli in Syria's third coup in nine months. This was the first of what would become seven civilian cabinets in 23 months.

Resurfacing of the old tensions with Syria led the United States to again encourage a military quick fix, this time with Shishakli as the leader. Once it became clear that Shishakli was making friendly overtures to U.S. officials, they realized that Shishakli was one of the strongest anticommunist forces in the country. In November 1951, Shishakli dissolved Parliament and set up a military dictatorship. U.S. officials had been aware of Shishakli's plans in advance and welcomed his coup. Shortly thereafter, Syria renewed the TAPLINE concession. Shishakli was willing to consider a peace treaty with Israel and the resettlement of Palestinian refugees in Syria as long as substantial U.S. financial and military aid was forthcoming.

In 1952, the administration of Harry S. Truman pressed the World Bank to expedite Syria's request for a $200 million loan. Before they could reach a deal on an arms package, Shishakli was overthrown in an army-orchestrated coup on 25 February 1954. The Communist Party, whose membership had been cut in half and whose leaders had been driven underground by Shishakli, saw the coup as the first step toward a national front with the Ba'athists and others opposed to Western influence. When the Syrians went to the polls on 24 September, they favored the Ba'ath and other left-wing parties and voted Khalid Bakdash into Parliament as the first freely elected Communist Party deputy in the Arab world.

Operation Straggle differed from the earlier Zaim and Shishakli episodes because the United States had cooperation from Great Britain. In March 1956, CIA officials flew to London to work out the details for a coup with Britain's Secret Intelligence Service (SIS).

The original CIA-SIS plan was to trigger a pro-Western coup by indigenous anticommunist elements within Syria. However, London abandoned Operation Straggle to intervene in Egypt following Gamal Abdel Nasser's seizure of the Suez Canal on 26 July 1956. Nonetheless, Washington moved forward with plans for the coup and provided $150,000 to the conspirators. At the last minute, the SIS persuaded the CIA to postpone Operation Straggle for four days so that, unbeknownst to the United States, it would coincide with the British-backed Israeli invasion of the Sinai. Israel's strike on Egypt came as a complete surprise, as did the revelation that Syrian counterintelligence had uncovered Operation Straggle. In October 1956, it was decided that it would be a mistake to go ahead with the operation.

During an unprecedented New Year's Day meeting with key legislative leaders, President Dwight D. Eisenhower requested congressional authorization to use American troops to counter Soviet subversion in the Middle East. He cited Syrian developments as evidence of Russian intent. On 30 January 1957, the House of Representatives approved his proposal by 355 to 61, and the Eisenhower Doctrine went into effect. The Sixth Fleet was ordered to the eastern end of the Mediterranean, American jets were sent to a North Atlantic Treaty Organization (NATO) base in Turkey, and the Strategic Air Command was alerted. Eisenhower gradually edged away from the provocative scheme.

In August 1957, President Eisenhower apparently gave authorization for Operation Wappen, which was a CIA plot for a coup being planned with dissidents inside the Syrian army. The plan was to overthrow President Shukri Quwatly and install a pro-Western regime, reinstating Shishakli to power. However, Operation Wappen proved to be a clumsy CIA operation and was penetrated by **Syrian intelligence** after half a dozen Syrian officers approached by U.S. officials immediately reported back to the authorities. Syrian counterintelligence Chief Sarraj reacted swiftly, expelling three CIA agents, arresting dozens of officers, and placing the American embassy in Damascus under surveillance. *See also* SUEZ CRISIS.

OTTOMAN EMPIRE INTELLIGENCE. During **World War I**, **Aziz Bek** headed the intelligence of the entire Fourth Army. The principal unit of the Fourth Army was the **Eighth Corps**. The man in charge of finding, dealing with, and arresting enemy spies was Jihad Rifat. The commander of the military intelligence of the Eight Corps was Ahmed Dormesh, and his aids were Rashdi Bek and Abdel Rahman Elnatsuli. One of the secretive units within the intelligence department was the counterespionage unit commanded by Brahan al-Din Bek.

There were also specific intelligence units unconnected to the military intelligence of the Eighth Corps, such as a special intelligence service that conducted surveillance on Egypt, headed by Fuad al-Masri, a special intelligence unit that worked among the Bedouin tribes of the Syrian Desert, and another special unit that was responsible for surveillance of religious institutions, especially Christian institutions in Syria. In addition to the official intelligence units, every chief of police in each city was appointed by the authorities to seek out and catch spies in his jurisdiction. *See also* TURKISH INTELLIGENCE.

OUFKIR, MUHAMMAD (1920–1972). Muhammad Oufkir served for many years as the chief of intelligence in Morocco. In 1972, Muhammad Oufkir was accused of having made an abortive attempt to overthrow the Moroccan monarchy by convincing soldiers to fire at the royal plane conveying King Hassan home from an overseas trip. The coup was reported to have failed and General Oufkir was executed. *See also* BEN-BARKA AFFAIR; MOROCCAN INTELLIGENCE.

– P –

PAKISTANI INTELLIGENCE. The Directorate for Interservices Intelligence (ISI) was founded in 1948, a year following Pakistan's independence, and remains the country's top national security agency. The three main intelligence agencies in Pakistan are the ISI, the Military Intelligence (MI), and the Intelligence Bureau (IB). The ISI and MI are concerned with military matters, while the IB is more focused on domestic political affairs, with its monitoring of politicians, political activists, political operatives from countries it considers hostile to Pakistan's interests, suspected terrorists, and suspected foreign intelligence agents. Although there is some overlap in the activities of these three agencies, each agency has its own specific responsibilities.

Initially, the IB reported directly to the prime minister and the two military agencies (ISI and MI) reported to the commander-in-chief of the army. However, when martial law was imposed in 1958, all three intelligence agencies fell under the direct control of the president and chief martial law administrator, and they began competing to demonstrate their loyalty to the new government. Ayub Khan, the president of Pakistan from 1958 to 1969, expanded the role of the ISI in monitoring the regime's opponents and sustaining military rule in Pakistan. The importance of the ISI derives from the fact that the agency is charged with managing covert operations outside of Pakistan. The ISI is charged with the collection of foreign and domestic intelligence, the coordination of intelligence functions between the military services, the interception and monitoring of communications, the distribution of propaganda, the conduct of espionage and offensive intelligence operations in foreign countries, and the surveillance of foreigners, politically active segments of Pakistani society, diplomats of other countries serving in Pakistan, and Pakistani diplomats stationed abroad. With its headquarters in Islamabad, the ISI reportedly has a total of about 10,000 civilian and military officers and staff members and is organized into between six and eight divisions.

Critics of the ISI say that it has become a state within a state, answerable neither to the leadership of the army nor to the president or the prime minister. The result is that there has been no real supervision of the ISI, and its narcotics-based corruption has been used by the ISI to finance the war in Afghanistan as well as the ongoing war against India in Kashmir and Northeast India. Early in 1997, the Pakistani government initiated an accountability process aimed at identifying corruption in both the public and private sectors. The government established an Accountability and Coordination Cell to monitor and coordinate the accountability process, as well as a specialized police agency, the Federal Investigation Agency (FIA), to conduct investigations on reports of corruption received either through the Accountability and Coordination Cell or directly from the public. To date, more than 250 cases of corruption against senior civil servants, prominent politicians, judges, lawyers, bankers, bureaucrats, and business figures have been prosecuted, and 87 officials have been dismissed or arrested for fraud, kickbacks, and other financial irregularities.

The Military Intelligence is charged with monitoring activities of the leaders of political opposition groups. No known organized subversive groups currently threaten the government in any serious way. During the 1980s, Al Zulfiqar attempted to destabilize the government through terrorist activities, including the hijacking of an aircraft in 1981. In the early 1990s, the principal challenge in the form of civil unrest came from Sindh, Pakistan's second most populous province, where the indigenous population was under increasing pressure from non-Sindhis who had migrated there. The Sindhis formed several political movements, in particular the Jaye Sindh, which the government perceived as threatening to Pakistan's unity. The government also accused these groups of receiving help from India in their quest to establish a "Sindhudesh" or independent homeland for Sindhis. MI conducted operations in Sindh against Indian intelligence operatives, and army rule was imposed in 1992 following large numbers of kidnappings and bombings in Sindh.

Moreover, the ISI has covertly supported insurgents in India in their conduct of terrorist activities by supplying the Kashmiri mujahidin with weapons, training, and planning assistance. At least six major pro-Pakistani militant organizations, and several smaller ones, have been known to operate in Kashmir, with their forces variously estimated from 5,000 to 10,000. The oldest and most widely known militant organization, the Jammu and Kashmir Liberation Front (JKLF), spearheaded the movement for an independent Kashmir, but declared a cease-fire in 1994. Major pro-Pakistani groups include the Harakat-ul Ansar, Al Umar, Al Barq, Jaish-e-Muhammad, and Lashkar-e Toiba, and the most powerful of the groups is the Hizb ul-Mujahedin. Many of these militants were trained in Afghanistan, where several ISI agents were killed during U.S. air strikes in 1998 against terrorist training camps.

The Soviet invasion of Afghanistan made Pakistan a country of major strategic importance. In a matter of days, Washington declared Pakistan a "frontline state" against Soviet aggression and offered to reinstate aid and military assistance packages. William Casey, Director of the Central Intelligence Agency (CIA), made a secret visit to

Pakistan in 1986, when he made a commitment to cooperate with the ISI in their recruitment of radical Muslims for the Afghan war from other Muslim countries, including the Gulf States, Turkey, the Philippines, and China. The CIA provided hundreds of ISI officers with considerable espionage equipment and training in improved intelligence methods. The ISI themselves trained about 83,000 Afghan mujahidin from 1983 to 1997 and continued to actively participate in the Afghan Civil War until the terrorist attacks of 11 September 2001, when backing of the Taliban officially came to an end. However, there are suspicions that sympathetic elements of the ISI continue to aid Taliban fighters.

Since the defeat of the Taliban, militant training camps have moved to Pakistani Kashmir. The ISI has reportedly been operating terrorist training camps near the border of Bangladesh for members of separatist groups of the northeastern states, known as the United Liberation Front of Seven Sisters (ULFOSS). These groups include the National Security Council of Nagaland (NSCN), the People's Liberation Army (PLA), the United Liberation Front of Assam (ULFA), and the North East Students Organization (NESO).

Pakistan's military leader, General Pervez Musharraf, has attempted to rein in the ISI since the military coup in 1999. Since 11 September 2001, Islamic fundamentalists have been purged from leadership positions, including the head of the ISI. Additional reforms of the ISI have been made, most notably the decision to disband the Kashmir and Afghanistan units so as to curtail their promotion of Islamic fundamentalist militancy throughout South Asia. Some officials have been forced to retire and others have been transferred back to the military. In November 2007, President Musharraf stepped down as military leader and was sworn in for a third presidential term as a civilian president. Musharraf appointed General Ashfaq Kiyani, the head of the ISI, to be his successor in the position of military chief. On 7 July 2008, a suicide bomber attacked the Indian embassy in Kabul, Afghanistan. Claims that elements of the Pakistani intelligence services were behind the bomb attack were firmly refuted by the ISI, despite its admission that certain elements within the ISI were sympathetic to the insurgency in Iraq and Afghanistan.

PAKRAVAN, HASSAN (1911–1979). Hassan Pakravan was a well-known diplomat and minister in the Muhammad Reza Shah prerevolutionary government of Iran. Pakravan served as the second director of the Sazeman-e Ettelaat va Amniyat-e Keshvar (SAVAK; Organization for Intelligence and National Security), succeeding **Bakhtiar Taimour** in 1961. Pakravan was obliged to resign because he did not succeed in preventing the assassination of Prime Minister Hassan Ali Mansur on 21 January 1965. He was succeeded in 1965 by **Nematollah Nassiri**. After the 1979 Islamic Revolution, Pakravan was among the first of the shah's officials to be executed. *See also* IRANIAN INTELLIGENCE.

PALESTINIAN NATIONAL AUTHORITY INTELLIGENCE. The Palestinian National Authority, has several intelligence agencies. Each has different tasks and purposes. One of these agencies is the Special Security Force (SSF)/*al-Amn al-Khass*. Formed in January 1995 in order to monitor opposition groups in other countries, the organization was formed outside the primary command structure of the Palestinian security and intelligence forces—the General Security Service (GSS)—and remained under the direct supervision of Yasser Arafat. It is a relatively small organization, with perhaps a few dozen staff, under the command of General Abu Yusuf al-Wahidi. This is a very powerful organization in extreme disproportion to its size, because of its specific roles of gathering information on domestic opposition groups and conducting internal investigations on the other Palestinian security and intelligence services.

Another Palestinian intelligence agency is Presidential Security (*al-Amn al-Ri'asah*). The roots of this organization can be traced to an organization created by Fatah leaders in the 1970s, to provide security for Arafat and the Palestine Liberation Organization (PLO) leadership, Force 17, a unit that turned into an elite group engaged in intelligence activities and acts of terror against Israel and rival Palestinian groups, mostly during the 1980s.

Force 17 was officially disbanded upon the return of Arafat and the PLO to the Gaza Strip, but in fact, it was merged into the new Presidential Security. The organization was enlarged to a force of approximately 3,000 members commanded by Faisal Abu Sharah. Its primary task is the protection of the Palestinian president and other top

PLO officials and important institutions. Thus *al-Amn al-Ri'asah* works closely with the National Security Force (NSF)/*Quwat al-Amn al-Watani*. In addition to the above, the Intelligence Unit of *al-Amn al-Ri'asah* performs counter**terrorism** and antiopposition activities. The third organization is the General Security Service, subdivided into the following units: General Intelligence Service (GIS)/*Mudiriyat al-Amn al-Amma*; General Intelligence (GI)/*Mukhabarat al-Amma*; Military Intelligence (*Istkhabbarat al-Askariyya*); Coast Guard (Naval Police)/*Shurta Bahariyya*; Aerial Police (*Shurta al-Jawiya*); Civil Defense (*al-Difa'a al*-Madani); County Guard (*al-Amn al-Mahafza*); Public Security Rapid Response Teams and University Security Organ (*Jihaz Am el-Jamat*).

The GI was formed in 1994 as part of the Cairo agreement, and is now the main intelligence arm of the PNA. The organization is engaged in domestic and foreign intelligence-gathering, counterespionage operations, and deterring domestic subversion, as well as acting as liaison with foreign intelligence agencies. The organization was headed by **Amin al-Hindi**, until his resignation on July 2004, after a series of kidnappings that caused chaos in the Palestinian territories, but eventually led to reforms in the PNA. **Tareq Abu Rajab**, who replaced al-Hindi as head of the GI, escaped an assassination attempt in the Gaza Strip in August 2004. Abu Rajab was badly injured, one of his bodyguards was killed, and two others were also injured.

In 2004, the NSF was the PNA's largest security service although, officially, it falls under the umbrella of the GSS. The NSF contains about 14,000 troops, including ex-members of the Palestine Liberation Army (PLA), and is augmented by local recruitment. As the major military organization of the PNA, the NSF is responsible for maintaining security in Palestinian-controlled territories and protection against external threats. **Nasr Yousef**, the first head of the NSF, was succeeded by General Saeb Ajez, who was succeeded in turn by General Abdul Razek al-Majiada in the Gaza Strip, and Genral Hajj Ismail in the West Bank. Tawfic Tirawi was appointed commander of the General Intelligence Organization in the West Bank.

There were general expectations that the transfer of powers to the PNA would improve the situation for the people, but it did not. In fact, the situation deteriorated significantly. Palestinian security forces systematically tortured and mutilated detainees. The chief of the Palestinian Preventive Security Service (PSS) maintains strict censorship over the press. For example, the editor of *al-Quds* newspaper must get approval for all articles that could be construed as critical of the PNA

The PSS in the Gaza Strip, headed by Rashid Abu Shoubac and Samir Mashrahawi, that was formed to suppress terror, turned into an active terrorist organization, generating, initiating, backing, and giving protection to terrorists and terror attacks, both against Israeli armed forces and Israeli civilians. In April 2000, the PSS closed the office of the Civic Forum in Gaza, on the grounds that the office has no official permit.

In early 2002, PNA chair Arafat succeeded in removing **Jibril Rajoub** from the position of director of the PSS in the West Bank, however, his plan to replace him with Zuhair Manasreh, the governor of Jenin failed, when officers and troops in the service demanded that the next head of the PSS come from within the ranks.

A military operation conducted by the Israel Defense Force (IDF) and border police in Tel Al Hawa, a southern suburb of Gaza city, against the headquarters of the PSS, on 18 November 2002, revealed explosive and weapons making facilities within the PSS compound. They also found Qassam rockets, ammunition, and a significant stash of intelligence information. The aim of the IDF operation was the destruction of Palestinian weaponry.

Documents found by Israeli Intelligence in 2003 in the Gaza offices of the PSS exposed not only the corruption and mismanagement of the PNA, but also the channeling of PNA funds for the financing and implementation of terrorist operations. These documents found included hundreds of receipts, photocopies of checks, and other documentation related to the transfer of funds to operatives of all ranks. These funds, originating from the budgets of the PSS apparatus and its independent sources of income, were not used solely for preventive operations. In fact, much of the funds that were allocated to the PSS were used to finance and initiate **terrorism**. Funds were also transferred to financial interests of the PSS leadership, including special allocations to the heads of the Preventive Security apparatus, their cronies and those favored by the PSS, among them senior political figures. The payments were transferred directly by the Preventive Security apparatus, and occasionally by the Palestinian Ministry of Finance, sometimes with the personal approval of Arafat, and sometimes without. Funds were paid directly to beneficiaries or indirectly through intermediaries.

In August 2003, PNA State Security Minister **Muhammad Dahlan** announced that he had decided to merge the Preventive Security Service in the West Bank and Gaza under one command. Dahlan served as head of the PSS in Gaza until 2002, at the time when Jibril Rajoub, who was dismissed from the post in 2002, headed the West Bank force.

The Palestinian Civil Police (*al-Shurta Madaniyya*), like the National Security Force, the largest of the PNA's law enforcement agencies with over 10,000 officers, was also formed initially under the umbrella of GSS. The police perform traditional law enforcement and policing activities aimed to maintain everyday public order. But the Civil Police includes special units, such as the special rapid-deployment team of 700 officers trained to handle riots, execute counterterrorism operations, and perform rapid response to miscellaneous crises.

Ghazi al-Jabali, the head of the Palestinian police, has been criticized for corruption, suppressing the freedom of speech, and the detention of Palestinian civil rights activist, Eyad Sarraj, in 1996. In February 2004, there was an attempt to assassinate Jabali inside Police headquarters in Gaza. There was speculation regarding the culprits of the event, some officials claimed that armed militants conducted the assassination attempt, while others raised the suspicion that the attack was carried out by members of the Palestinian PSS, in the interests of his political rival, Muhammad Dahlan.

In July 2004, Jabali was kidnapped for a short while by militants and his humiliation was complete when he was dismissed by Arafat. The Jenin Martyrs Brigade, part of the Popular Resistance Committees, assumed responsibility for the abduction. Arafat replaced Jabali with his cousin, **Moussa Arafat**. A move that hardly promoted assurance that the PNA was really willing to reform and implement anticorruption measures.

On 25 January 2006, the Islamic militant group Hamas won a surprise victory in Palestinian parliamentary elections and took over the control in the Gaza Strip. The result was that the Gaza Strip and West Bank split apart. The PNA intelligence network has become almost useless and ineffective in the Gaza strip. Presently, the PLO and the

Hamas regimes in the West Bank and the Gaza Strip, respectively, are directing their part of the intelligence network against one another more than Israel. On the other hand, the PNA and Israel are cooperating against Hamas. After taking the control over the Gaza Strip, Hamas announced that it had found documents exposing a broad Fatah spy-ring working against Arab countries, including Egypt, Saudi Arabia, and the United Arab Emirates on behalf of the United States. *See also* PALESTINIAN NATIONAL AUTHORITY INTELLIGENCE LAW.

PALESTINIAN NATIONAL AUTHORITY INTELLIGENCE LAW. The Palestinian National Authority (PNA) Intelligence Law was adopted in 2005 and is composed of eight chapters detailing the official security body, which is subordinated to the Palestinian president and led by a chairman who is responsible for the organization's activities. The chairman of the intelligence organization is ranked as a minister and is appointed through a presidential decree for a term of three years, with an additional year as an option.

The organization's intelligence activities, both inside and outside the bounds of the PNA, are conducted in order to hinder incidents that might endanger Palestinian national security, including exposing outside threats, such as spying or sabotage. According to the law, the organization has the authority to collect intelligence information and to request cooperation with state institutions as well as with intelligence organizations of friendly countries. In regard to international agreements, the organization is authorized to activate interrogations and searches, including the confiscation of money and relevant documents when necessary in matters concerning people under arrest. If the person arrested is not a Palestinian citizen, then the organization has to help him contact the closest representative of his country.

The law stipulates that any person who wants to join the organization must have two Palestinian parents and no criminal offenses, must be healthy, cannot be married to a non-Arab, must be between the ages of 18 and 30, well-mannered, and educated to suit the position. Finally, after passing all the necessary tests for the position, the person must pledge allegiance to the nation and the Palestinian people in front of the head of the intelligence and the president, as well as sign the oath, which is kept in his personal file.

Every member of the organization must obey the organization's rules and regulations. In regard to forbidden activities, the law forbids workers in the intelligence organization from testifying in court (even if they are no longer affiliated with the organization) about things they saw during their duty that were not published in any legal way. The law does not allow anyone working in the organization to work in an additional job or to belong to any club or corporation. All workers are prohibited from being interviewed by the media or arranging a political or media event, regardless of whether or not they are still affiliated with the organization. The law forbids members of the organization from personally holding official documents even if they are related to an activity in which they were involved. Information about the intelligence organization, the organization's activities, its documents, and their whereabouts are all considered as part of the national security secrets of the Palestinian National Authority. It is forbidden to publish these documents, and whoever reveals such information is considered a traitor and will be punished accordingly. *See also* PALESTINIAN NATIONAL AUTHORITY INTELLIGENCE.

PEACE AND POLITICAL PROCESSES. Intelligence agencies of the countries in the Middle East as well as of foreign countries have been involved in the Middle East peace processes. Covert relations between Israel and Jordan started with the intelligence agencies of both countries, eventually paving the way for a full peace agreement in 1994. The **Mossad** started the covert relations with Jordan in the mid-1960s in a series of security cooperation agreements between Israel and Jordan against the threat to both countries from the Palestinian Liberation Organization (PLO). In 1965, the Central Intelligence Agency (CIA) of the United States set up a secret committee to coordinate Israeli and Jordanian antiterrorist activities and to serve as a channel for the flow of information about terrorist activities.

The CIA began maintaining a substantial presence in Egypt following the military coup in April 1954 when Colonel Gamal Abdel Nasser came to power as the ruler of Egypt. The CIA in Cairo worked together with Nasser to facilitate negotiations with Great Britain in 1954 on the withdrawal of British troops from Egyptian soil. Further, the CIA and the British MI6 were asked by their governments to assist in the peace initiatives between Israel and Egypt in an attempt to stabilize the volatile front and achieve a lasting peace agreement.

Britain initiated the idea of a territorial exchange among Israel, Egypt, and Jordan so as to promote political reconciliation among the three countries. According to the plan of the secret **Operation Alpha**, Israel would cede parts of the Negev Desert to Egypt and Jordan, and two triangular-shaped areas would be carved out of the Israeli Negev connecting Egypt and Jordan at their apex. The MI6 became the main conduit for political contact with Israel, and the plan was secretly submitted to the three governments. The plan was rejected by the Israeli government, which was reluctant to compromise the territorial integrity of the Negev, and it was rejected by the Egyptian government, which was not ready to be engaged in any political deal with Israel. Thus, Operation Alpha collapsed in 1955. Disappointed by the collapse of the Alpha plan, the U.S. administration secretly initiated **Operation Gamma** in March 1956 in an attempt to reach a political agreement among the three countries and thereby avoid a war in the region. Again the idea of territorial concessions was proposed, and again the operation failed.

During the War of Attrition between Egypt and Israel in the summer of 1970, the CIA proposed the Rogers II Plan, which called for imposing a 90-day cease-fire in the Sinai and freezing military deployment by either country within a 50-kilometer range of the Suez Canal. Both Egypt and Israel endorsed the plan. However, as soon as the plan went into motion, **Israeli intelligence** detected Egyptian efforts to move their surface-to-air missile batteries closer to the canal. Israeli intelligence provided a detailed report of Egypt's violations of the cease-fire agreement to the United States, which used its U-2 spy planes to verify the Israeli allegations.

After the Oslo Accords between Israel and the Palestinians in September 1993, the CIA intensified its contacts with **Amin al-Hindi**, Yasser Arafat's liaison officer to the CIA. The CIA was called upon to assist with the formation, training, and operation of the security services of the newly established Palestinian National Authority (PNA). Following the opening of the tunnel near the Wailing Wall in Jerusalem's Old City in September 1996, large-scale fighting broke out between Palestinian forces and the IDF. The tunnel crisis marked a watershed in Israeli–Palestinian relations and reinforced the role of the CIA as a peace facilitator.

Direct contact between Israel and the PNA was replaced with mediation by the CIA. The CIA mediation paved the way for further diplomatic efforts led by the American administration's special envoy Dennis Ross, whose goal was to get negotiations back on track. During the years 1996–1997, the CIA's role as facilitator was an informal one until an official endorsement by the Bill Clinton administration in the Wye River Memorandum (23 October 1998). The director of the CIA, George Tenet, played a key role behind the scenes in supporting the negotiations between the Israeli delegation and the Palestinian National Authority delegation. In the August 2000, Camp David negotiations between Israeli Prime Minister Ehud Barak and chair of the PNA Yasser Arafat, George Tenet participated with a team of CIA experts, though their contribution to those negotiations was marginal.

After the al-Aqsa Intifada broke out in September 2000, the CIA was again charged with the task of cooling the atmosphere between the Israelis and the Palestinians. Tenet was engaged in planning a cease-fire for the al-Aqsa Intifada, a plan known as the **Tenet Plan**. The CIA assumed a key role in mediating between the two sides, and in May 2001, CIA officers met with **Hamas** political activists to try to gain a better understanding of their position toward terror and politics. In January 2002, the CIA verified Israeli claims that the vessel *Karine-A*, which was captured by the Israeli Navy, was carrying arms for the PNA. As a result, President George W. Bush demanded reforms in the PNA.

During Operation Defensive Shield in spring 2002, the Israel Defense Forces surrounded the Church of the Nativity in Bethlehem, a holy Christian shrine. This move was made in response to the assassination of the Israeli minister of tourism, Rehavam Zeevi, in the fall of 2001. Israel demanded that Zeevi's assassins be turned over to Israel for trial and punishment. The CIA and the MI6 were tasked to negotiate the matter with both sides. After weeks of tense negotiations, the two intelligence agencies proposed a compromise in which the assassins would be imprisoned in a special jail in Jericho and guarded by British prison officers. The CIA officers transferred the convicted terrorists to the Jericho prison.

In summer 2002, the Egyptian General Intelligence Service joined the peacemaking efforts in an attempt to calm the volatile situation in the Palestinian territories. The chief of **Egyptian intelligence**, General **Omar Suleiman**, was dispatched by President Hosni Mubarak for several mediation missions between Israel and the Palestinians. In December 2003, Egyptian intelligence convened a series of meetings between all of the Palestinian factions in the Gaza Strip in an attempt to bring about a *hudna* (cease-fire) between Israel and the Palestinians. However, the negotiations failed in the absence of participation by Israel, the key player. *See also* PALESTINIAN NATIONAL AUTHORITY INTELLIGENCE.

PERIPHERY DOCTRINE. From the day of its establishment, Israel adopted a doctrine whereby it sought to counter its isolation by forming alliances with more remote, non-Arab neighbors—including Ethiopia, Iran, Sudan, Turkey, and to some degree even Morocco in the Maghreb—as well as non-Muslim minorities such as the Maronite Christians in Lebanon and the Kurds in Iraq. These relations were carried out as covert actions mainly by the **Mossad**.

Israel's relations with the Lebanese Maronites date back to 1920 with the first Treaty of Cooperation between the Zionist Organization and Maronite representatives. In the 1930s, the Maronite Church became actively involved in reinforcing relations with the Jewish community in Palestine in an attempt to form an alliance against Islam. Fear of loss of ethnic and religious identity in a "vast sea of Muslims" led to the concept of a natural alliance between ethnic and religious minorities. The Maronites remained in contact with Israel throughout the 1948 War of Independence; with the new power of Israeli statehood, plans for a Maronite revolt in conjunction with an Israeli invasion of Lebanon were mooted several times from 1948 to 1950. In the end, Israel decided against such action and instead confined itself to supporting the Maronite Kataib Party financially for the 1951 parliamentary elections. In 1956, Israeli Prime Minister David Ben Gurion appended to his Sinai Campaign the still unexecuted invasion of Lebanon to establish the Maronites in power and make Lebanon a Christian state. In 1958, during the first Lebanese civil war, Israel responded to the Maronites' appeal for help by providing arms via the border town of Metulla. From 1958 to 1975, Israeli–Maronite relations fell to an all-time low with only sporadic personal meetings, mostly abroad. Israel's relations with the Maronites had been conducted mainly by the Mossad.

Turkey was the first country with a Muslim majority to recognize Israel, although positive relations with Israel were not a general priority for much of that country's history. Only with the end of the Cold War and the subsequent geopolitical developments in the 1990s did Turkey and Israel move closer. In 1996 they formalized an accord cementing military ties between the two countries. Driven by common security interests, these states forged one of the most significant alliances in the Middle East. Both were regionally isolated, pro-Western, secular democracies fearful of the specter of radical Islamic groups, facing common enemies in Syria, Iran, and, at the time, Saddam Hussein's Iraq.

Elsewhere, under the premise of the Periphery Doctrine, where "the enemy of my enemy is my friend," Israel over the decades has helped southern Sudanese, Iraqi Kurds, Yemeni Royalists, Moroccans, Ethiopians, and the shah's regime in Iran, all with the goal of weakening the Arab mainstream. Relations with Iran especially were developed by the **Israeli intelligence** community, where **Ya'acov Nimrodi**, who represented the Mossad, contributed to the buildup of the Iranian Sazeman-e Ettelaat va Amniyat-e Keshvar (SAVAK; Organization for Intelligence and National Security)—a sound strategy in the time of Gamal Abdel Nasser's pan-Arab vision and all-out Arab wars against Israel. Israeli assistance to peoples on the Arab periphery who were themselves locked in a struggle with the Arab mainstream began in Ben Gurion's day in the late 1950s and also provided nonmilitary benefits: oil from Iran, as well as immigration to Israel of beleaguered Jewish minorities in Iraq and Ethiopia. And it corresponded closely with the U.S. strategic priority of opposing Soviet-influenced regimes in the greater Middle East.

But some drastic changes transformed the region during the late 1970s. Periphery friends such as the shah of Iran and Ethiopia's Haile Selassie were overthrown by radicals, while the Arab mainstream, led by Anwar Sadat, began to make peace with Israel. If Jerusalem had to choose between peace, however cold, with Egypt, and aid to Haile Mariam Mengistu's Ethiopia or the southern Sudanese—both seen by the Egyptians as potential threats to the sources of the Nile, its own paramount strategic interest—there was no contest.

In Lebanon, by contrast, with the first sign of trouble for the Maronites since the mid-1970s, the alliance was restored with even greater intensity. The 1982 Lebanon War, with its disastrous Israeli–Maronite, Israeli–Christian collaboration, sounded the death knell of the Periphery Doctrine. This was mainly due to the Mossad's failure to perceive the Maronites' incapacity to establish a state of their own in Lebanon—contrary to the Military Intelligence assessment that disparaged Maronite capabilities in this respect.

Since then, for better or for worse, Israel has played the Middle East strategic game by the local rules: an informal strategic alliance with non-Arab Turkey, but also with Arab Jordan; non-Arab Iran now tops the pile of Israel's enemies, while Arab Egypt is invited to help Israeli out in the Gaza Strip. *See also* IRANIAN INTELLIGENCE.

PHILBY, KIM (1912–1988). Born as Harold Adrian Russell Philby, only later did he become known as Kim Philby. For many years, Kim Philby was a Soviet spy within the British intelligence service. He came under suspicion when two of his associates, Donald Maclean and Guy Burgess, defected to the Soviet Union in 1951. After the defection of Burgess and Maclean, Philby was asked to resign from the Secret Intelligence Service (SIS), and he spent the next several years being questioned by MI5 and SIS. Since he did not break, he was finally cleared of being the "Third Man" by Foreign Secretary Harold Macmillan in the House of Commons. Eventually he was reemployed as an SIS agent, with the cover as a correspondent in Beirut for the *Observer* and the *Economist*. Philby's spying activities for the Soviet Union were not fully exposed until he himself defected in 1963. The case later received wide publicity.

PIRIE-GORDON, HARRY. Harry Pirie-Gordon was one of the British scholars who were active in the Levant during the years prior to the outbreak of **World War I**. He traveled widely in the Near East and was involved in a survey of the Syrian coastline around Alexandretta. He was then commissioned in the Royal Navy in 1914 and took part in the raid on Alexandretta by HMS *Doris*. Pirie-Gordon served in an intelligence capacity at Gallipoli before returning to Cairo to work with **David George Hogarth**. In 1916, he was involved in the occupation of Makronisi in the Gulf of Smyrna and later took charge of the Eastern Mediterranean Special Intelligence Bureau (EMSIB) operation at Salonika until early 1917. Pirie-Gordon subsequently returned to the **Arab Bureau in Cairo** and took part in the Palestine campaign. *See also* BATTLE OF GALLIPOLI; BRITISH INTELLIGENCE IN EGYPT AND SUDAN.

PRIMAKOV, YEVGENI (1929–). Born and raised in Georgia, Primakov graduated from Moscow's Institute of Oriental Studies in 1953 and went on to postgraduate studies at Moscow University. He speaks Georgian, Russian, Arabic, and English. In 1956, Primakov became a correspondent in the Middle East for the State Committee for Television and Radio. Since 1959 he has had close relations with the KGB foreign intelligence administration, and his KGB codename was Maxim. Primakov became the Middle East correspondent for *Pravda* during the 1960s and 1970. From 1970 to 1979, he served as director of the Institute for World Economy and International Relations (IMEMO) within the Central Committee's International Department. From 1979 to 1985, Primakov headed the Institute of Oriental Studies and then became the first chief chairman of the KGB foreign propaganda front organization, the Soviet Peace Committee. He returned as director of the IMEMO in 1985. From 1990 to 1991, Primakov served as Gorbachev's envoy to Baghdad during the **Gulf War**. He was appointed as head of the First Chief Directorate, later renamed the Foreign Intelligence Service (FIS) in 1991. In 1996, Boris Yeltsin appointed Primakov as foreign minister, and he later became Russia's prime minister. During the lead up to the 2003 **Iraq War,** Primakov made a diplomatic visit to Iraq, where he met with Saddam Hussein in an attempt to avert the war. *See also* SOVIET CONCEPT; SOVIET INTELLIGENCE AND THE PALESTINE LIBERATION ORGANIZATION.

– Q –

QAEDA, AL. Al Qaeda is an international alliance of Sunni Islamic militant organizations founded in 1988 by Abdullah Yusuf Azzam in order to finance, recruit, transport, and train Sunni Islamic extremists for the Afghan resistance against the Soviet Union. Azzam was later replaced by Osama bin-Laden and other veteran Afghan Arabs after the Soviet War in Afghanistan. Al Qaeda means "the base" in Arabic.

Its main aims are to put an end to foreign influence in Muslim countries and to create a pan-Islamic caliphate or Islamic militaristic state throughout the world. Al Qaeda seeks a global radicalization of existing Islamic groups, claiming that it is the duty of all Muslims to kill U.S. citizens, civilian or military, and their allies everywhere.

On 11 September 2001, 19 al Qaeda suicide attackers hijacked and crashed four U.S. commercial jets, two into the World Trade Center towers in New York City, one into the Pentagon near Washington, D.C., and a fourth into a field in Shanksville, Pennsylvania, leaving about 3,000 people dead or missing. This terrorist act marked the beginning of the U.S. administration's "war on terror." Although intelligence collection efforts on Osama bin-Laden and al Qaeda had already increased significantly and plans had been in the making to penetrate al Qaeda and to capture Osama bin-Laden in Afghanistan, a suitable strategic operation had not been executed in time for September 11.

In order to succeed in this kind of war, substantial intelligence efforts are required. On 15 September 2001, just four days after the attacks, U.S. intelligence analysts submitted their recommendations to President George W. Bush for covert operations against al Qaeda in the many countries around the world where al Qaeda was known to have active cells. Moreover, CIA director George Tenet described a plan to secretly dispatch CIA teams into Afghanistan jointly with the U.S. Army's elite units so as to work together with Afghan warlords in the fight against al Qaeda. After receiving approval for this proposal, the CIA geared up to take the lead in the attack on al Qaeda and the Taliban in Afghanistan. On 19 September 2001, the Northern Afghanistan Liaison Team (NALT) was formed, and on 26 September the team members entered Afghanistan. In addition, a new branch was added to the U.S. Counterterrorist Center (CTC), known as the CTC Special Operations (CTC/SO), which was assigned the task of dismantling al Qaeda's base of operations in Afghanistan. Although coalition forces were successful in removing the Taliban from power in Afghanistan in late 2001, Osama bin-Laden has not yet been tracked or captured.

Al Qaeda remains a multinational organization with a worldwide presence and members in numerous countries, with cells across Europe, Southeast Asia, and the Middle East. It serves as an umbrella organization for a worldwide network that includes many Sunni Islamic extremist groups, some members of **al-Gama'at al-Islamiyya**, the Islamic Movement of Uzbekistan, and the Harakat ul-Mujahidin. Senior leaders of al Qaeda are also senior leaders in other terrorist organizations, including those designated by the U.S. Department of State as foreign terrorist organizations, such as the Egyptian al-Gama'at al-Islamiyya and the **Egyptian Islamic Jihad**. Al Qaeda supports Muslim fighters in Afghanistan, Bosnia, Chechnya, Tajikistan, Somalia, Yemen, and Kosovo. It also trains members of terrorist organizations from such diverse countries as Algeria, Eritrea, and the Philippines.

During the years of its existence, al Qaeda has attacked civilian and military targets in many countries. Prior to the 11 September 2001 attacks, al Qaeda was accused of conducting many other bombings, including three in August 1998 of the U.S. embassies in Nairobi, Kenya, and Dar es Salaam, Tanzania, which killed at least 301 and injured more than 5,000 people. In 1999, al Qaeda was linked to a bomb set off at Los Angeles International Airport and to a plot to carry out terrorist operations against American and Israeli tourists visiting Jordan for millennial celebrations. On 12 October 2000, al Qaeda directed the attack on the destroyer USS *Cole* in the port of Aden, Yemen, killing 17 American sailors and injuring another 39.

In December 2001, suspected al Qaeda associate Richard Colvin Reid attempted to ignite a shoe bomb on a transatlantic flight from Paris to Miami. Al Qaeda was responsible for the firebombing of a synagogue in Tunisia on 11 April 2002 that killed 19 and injured 22 people; was linked to a nightclub bombing in Bali, Indonesia, on 12 October 2002 that killed about 180 people; and was behind the bombing of a hotel in Mombassa, Kenya, on 28 November 2002 that killed 15 and injured 40 people. It also perpetrated a suicide attack on the MV *Limburg* off the coast of Yemen on 6 October 2002, killing one and injuring four.

Al Qaeda carried out the bombing on 12 May 2003 of three expatriate housing complexes in Riyadh, Saudi Arabia, killing 20 and injuring 139 people. It assisted in carrying out the 16 May bombings in Casablanca, Morocco, of a Jewish center, restaurant, nightclub, and hotel, which killed 41 and injured 101 people. It was linked to the bombing on 5 August 2003 of the J. W. Marriott Hotel in Jakarta, Indonesia, that killed 17 and injured 137 people, and was responsible for the bombing on 9 November 2003 of a housing complex in Riyadh, Saudi Arabia, that killed 17 and injured 100 people. It conducted the 15 November bombings of two synagogues in Istanbul, Turkey, which killed 23 and injured 200 people, as well as the 20 November bombings of the British Consulate and HSBC Bank in Istanbul that resulted in 27 dead and 455 injured.

The arrests of senior-level al Qaeda operatives have interrupted other terrorist plots that were not carried out, including the assassinations of Pope John Paul II during his visit to Manila in late 1994 and of President Bill Clinton during a visit to the Philippines in early 1995, as well as the bombing in midair of a dozen U.S. transpacific flights in 1995. In November 2002, al Qaeda attempted to shoot down an Israeli chartered plane with a surface-to-air missile as it departed the Mombassa airport.

Al Qaeda continues to maintain moneymaking front businesses, solicits donations from like-minded supporters, and illicitly siphons funds from donations to Muslim charitable organizations. However, international efforts to block al Qaeda funding have hampered the organization's ability to obtain financial support. Osama bin-Laden has been stripped of his Saudi nationality and is sought by U.S. authorities, who are offering a reward of $5 million for any information leading to his arrest.

QATARI INTERNAL SECURITY. When Great Britain announced that it would withdraw its military forces from the Persian Gulf by 1971, Qatari leaders were forced to consider how to survive without British protection. Unable to support a large military establishment, Qatar has placed its reliance on small but mobile forces that can deter border incursions. In addition to seeking collective security through the Gulf Cooperation Council (GCC), which comprises the Persian Gulf States of Bahrain, Kuwait, Oman, Qatar, Saudi Arabia, and the United Arab Emirates, Qatar has formed close ties with Saudi Arabia through bilateral defense agreements.

Although the emirate has experienced little internal unrest, the large number of foreigners, who constitute 80 percent of the workforce, are regarded as possible sources of instability. Qatar is determined to maintain control over their activities and limit their influence. A significant number of resident Palestinians, some of whom include prominent businessmen and civil servants, were expelled after the Iraqi invasion of Kuwait. Iranian Shi'ites have not been a source of problems but are nevertheless viewed as potential subversives.

The Ministry of Interior has control over the police force, and the Mubahathat (secret police) is a nearly independent branch of the Ministry of Interior dealing with sedition and espionage. The police routinely monitor the communications of suspects and security risks. The army's mission does not include internal security, although it can be called upon in the event of serious civil disturbances. Nevertheless, a separate agency, the Mukhabarat, is under the armed forces' jurisdiction. Its function is to intercept and arrest terrorists and to maintain surveillance over political dissidents. Lacking permanent security courts, security-related cases are tried by specially established military courts, but such cases have been rare. Although warrants are usually required for searches, this does not apply in cases involving national security.

– R –

RAFIQDUST, MOSHEN. Moshen Rafiqdust served as head of the Iranian Revolutionary Guards Ministry when this institution existed from 1982 until 1989. He subsequently headed the Oppressed and Disabled Foundation, which funds Islamic Revolution Guards Corps (IRGC) activities through overseas enterprises that serve as fronts for IRGC operations. *See also* IRANIAN INTELLIGENCE.

RAHIM-SAFAVI, YAHYA (1958–). Yahya Rahim-Safavi served as the deputy head under **Moshen Rezai** in the Islamic Revolution Guards Corps (IRGC) and was subsequently appointed as head of the IRGC when Rezai left to serve on the Council for the Discernment of Expediency. *See also* IRANIAN INTELLIGENCE.

RAHMAN, ABDUL (1965–). General Abdul Rahman al-Duri was appointed as commander of **Iraq's Directorate of General Security** (DGS) by Saddam Hussein in 1987. He served in this position until the 1991 **Operation Desert Storm**, when Saddam Hussein decided to replace him with his stepbrother **Ibrahim Sabawi al-Tikriti**. *See also* IRAQI DIRECTORATE OF GENERAL MILITARY INTELLIGENCE; IRAQI INTELLIGENCE; IRAQI SPECIAL SECURITY ORGANIZATION.

RAJOUB, JIBRIL (1953–). Born to a prominent farming family in Dura, near Hebron, Jibril Rajoub served as Palestinian leader Yasser Arafat's national security advisor, with the rank of brigadier general, from August 2003 until Arafat's death in November 2004. He served as former head of the Palestinian Preventive Security Force (PSF) in the West Bank and was a member of **al-Fatah** Revolutionary Council, which is considered to be a politically moderate faction with long-standing close ties to the U.S. Central Intelligence Agency (CIA) and Israeli security officials. Rajoub was widely seen as one of the leading contenders to succeed Yasser Arafat because of his military base in the West Bank's PSF.

Rajoub had been sentenced to life in prison at the age of 15 for throwing a grenade at an Israel Defense Forces (IDF) convoy. He spent 17 years in an Israeli prison (1968–1985) and was released as part of a prisoner exchange in 1985. During the first *intifada* (1987–1991), he was expelled from the West Bank to Lebanon, and he then relocated to Tunis, where he served as Fatah deputy leader Khalil al-Wazir's advisor on the *intifada*. After **Abu Jihad**'s assassination, he became a close lieutenant of Arafat and spent seven years in exile with him.

Rajoub is viewed as a pragmatist concerning relations with Israel, and as such is deeply distrusted by **Hamas**. Although he spent years in Israeli prisons for **terrorism**, Rajoub now advocates a two-state solution and peaceful coexistence, warning that suicide bombs and violence will not serve the Palestinian cause. During the Oslo peace process, which began in the fall of 1993, he publicly criticized the rising influence of religious fundamentalism in Palestinian society and schools. Following the signing of the Oslo Accords, Rajoub returned to the West Bank in 1994 and was appointed as chief of the Palestinian National Authority (PNA) Preventative Security Force in the West Bank on 18 May 1994. The PSF, whose headquarters is in Jericho, was funded and trained by the CIA and works in close cooperation with the Israeli Security Agency (ISA).

Rajoub developed his own power base by becoming more closely allied with Fatah leaders in the PNA and by cultivating close ties with the West Bank Tanzim, a faction within the PNA. Rajoub was the subject of intense rumors that he was planning to take control of the West Bank in the event of Arafat's health failing. Some reports suggest that he was actually arrested and detained for five days by Arafat's Presidential Guard on suspicion of planning a coup with the support of the Israeli ISA and the approval of the CIA. He was suspended the following month from the al-Fatah Central Committee for unclear reasons. He was also criticized for profiting from the PNA's oil monopoly in the West Bank, though he was generally spared criticism whenever public anger was expressed at PNA corruption due to the personal price he had paid by spending almost 18 years in Israeli prisons.

When the al-Aqsa Intifada began in October 2000, Rajoub kept the PSF out of attacks on Israeli targets. It was therefore a cause of some surprise when he was wounded in an IDF tank and helicopter attack on his home on 20 May 2001. The Israeli government offered conflicting explanations for the attack, which was widely regarded as a shift in Israeli policy and a sign that Israel would not talk to anyone in the PNA, regardless of their past cooperation.

Rajoub's relationship with Arafat deteriorated in February 2002 when Arafat reportedly accused him of being an Israeli spy and CIA agent who was seeking to replace him. He was also widely condemned for betrayal when, following an April 2002 attack by the IDF on his headquarters, Rajoub himself escaped but surrendered up to 50 others to Israel in a CIA-brokered deal.

In May 2002, U.S. officials urged Arafat to unify the various PNA security agencies into a single organization under the control of Rajoub. Arafat responded on 2 July 2002 by firing Rajoub, who did not go quietly. He refused to go for two days, and protests were organized in his support in Hebron, but he eventually accepted the decision. He was restored to power in August 2003 when Arafat named him national security advisor and head of the new National Palestinian Security Council on which all the Palestinian security and intelligence chiefs were given seats. Arafat made these appointments largely as a means to counterbalance the attempts by **Muhammad Dahlan** to gain control of the PNA security apparatus after November 2004.

Rajoub was quickly effective in restoring some order to the armed factions in the PNA areas. He reactivated his armed supporters in the PSF, possibly as many as 20,000 men, and won back most of the West Bank Fatah and Tanzim members who had deserted Arafat during the period of the Abu Mazen government. He also had some success in healing his long-standing rift with Hamas and now apparently favors bringing them into the political process rather than allowing them to operate outside of PNA, where they can be restrained only by the use of force. *See also* PALESTINIAN NATIONAL AUTHORITY IN-TELLIGENCE; TENET PLAN.

RAYSHAHRI, MUHAMMAD. *See* MUHAMMADI-REYSHAHRI, HOJATOLESLAM MUHAMMAD.

RAZIEL MISSION. There are various accounts of what the David Raziel mission was and how it was initiated. According to one account, the idea for the mission was initiated by Zionist political executives and later approved by Prime Minister Winston Churchill. The British had been following the career of the Mufti Haj Amin al-Husseini with concern. In May 1940, the British Foreign Office allegedly refused a proposal from the Vaad Leumi (Jewish National Council in Palestine) to assassinate Husseini. However, in November, Churchill finally approved the plan.

According to a different account, it was David Raziel, the imprisoned leader of the Irgun (the underground militia of the Jewish community in Palestine), who proposed the plan, writing from his jail cell to the British commander in chief in Palestine, the government secretary of the mandate, and the British police commissioner. Eventually, the plan was changed to a mission of sabotage in Iraq. In May 1941, several members of the Irgun, including Raziel, were released from prison and flown to Iraq for this purpose.

The heads of **British intelligence in Egypt** requested that the Irgun dispatch a unit to blow up refineries in Baghdad, since the fuel reserves were so vital. Raziel immediately agreed and organized a four-man unit to execute the operation. His comrades tried, unsuccessfully, to dissuade him from taking part. On 17 May 1941, the four left for the military airfield at Tel Nof, where they boarded a Royal Air Force transport plane. After landing several hours later at Habanniya, it was explained to Raziel that the plan had been postponed and that, instead, the unit was to carry out intelligence missions in preparation for the capture of Faluga (en route to Baghdad). The next day, the unit set out and reached the river, which they were scheduled to cross. However, there was room for only two passengers in the sole available boat. Raziel ordered two of his comrades to cross the river and carry out the mission, while he made his way back to the car with the third partner and the British officer who had accompanied them. Suddenly a German plane swooped down and bombed the area, scoring a direct hit on the car and killing Raziel and the British officer instantly. The mission was abandoned after Raziel was killed by the German plane.

REZAI, MOSHEN. Moshen Rezai headed the Islamic Revolution Guards Corps (IRGC) from 1981–1997. He was then appointed to serve as secretary of the Council for the Discernment of Expediency. The IRGC worked closely with the Supreme Council for the Islamic Revolution in Iraq (SCIRI) during the **Iran–Iraq War** (1980–1988) and also sent personnel to Lebanon in the 1980s to work with **Hizballah**. *See also* IRANIAN INTELLIGENCE.

ROOSEVELT, KERMIT (1916–2000). Kermit (Kim) Roosevelt was the grandson of President Theodore Roosevelt and was born in Buenos Aires, Argentina. After graduating from Harvard University with a major in Middle East studies, he joined the Office of Strategic Services (OSS). He became the head of the Middle East Division of the Central Intelligence Agency (CIA) and traveled frequently to the Middle East on various secret missions.

On 3 August 1953, Roosevelt was dispatched to Iran, where he convinced the shah that there would have to be an insurrection in order to oust Prime Minister Muhammad Mossadeq, with the support of the army absolutely vital to success. Roosevelt became the mastermind of the ensuing CIA coup in Iran that restored the shah's regime and overthrew Mossadeq.

Roosevelt took all the necessary measures to ensure the success of the coup. However, after several days of rioting from crowds who remained loyal to Mossadeq, the shah escaped to Baghdad on 16 August 1953. Just three days later, the situation was under control and the shah was able to return triumphantly to Tehran, where he later expressed his heartfelt gratitude to the CIA and to Kermit Roosevelt. Mossadeq was sentenced to three years' imprisonment.

After retiring from the CIA in 1958, Kim Roosevelt worked for half a dozen years for Gulf Oil. Thereafter, he served as a consultant to U.S. corporations doing business in the Middle East and to Middle East governments in the United States. After retiring from consulting in 1979, he wrote a book about the CIA's role in the 1953 Iranian coup, entitled *Counter Coup: The Struggle for the Control of Iran*. In the book, he made it clear that he had no qualms about U.S. involvement or the chain reaction that the 1953 coup had triggered in Iran. *See also* OPERATION TPAJAX; WILBER, DONALD N.

– S –

SABAWI, IBRAHIM. Sabawi Ibrahim al-Tikriti, stepbrother of Iraqi President Saddam Hussein, was appointed by Hussein to command **Iraq's Directorate of General Security** (DGS) during the 1991 **Operation Desert Storm**. Sabawi served in this position until 1996, when he was replaced as commander of the DGS by General **Taha Abbas** al-Ahbabi. Sabawi then served in the position of presidential advisor to Saddam Hussein.

After the 2003 **Operation Iraqi Freedom**, Sabawi was accused of commanding a series of explosions and killings that took place after the collapse of the former regime. He was listed as wanted by U.S. forces for war crimes, and a $1 million reward was offered for information leading either to his capture or death. Sabawi secretly escaped Iraq and fled to Syria. He was captured in February 2005 and was turned over to Iraqi forces by Syria after his capture. On 9 December 2006, Sabawi was sentenced to life imprisonment. *See also* IRAQI DIRECTORATE OF GENERAL MILITARY INTELLIGENCE; IRAQI INTELLIGENCE; IRAQI SPECIAL SECURITY ORGANIZATION.

SADAT'S ASSASSINATION. Egyptian President Anwar Sadat was assassinated on 6 October 1981, while participating in a pass and review parade conducted by the Egyptian armed forces. The assassination was meticulously planned and was part of a wider plot to overthrow the Egyptian government. The policy adopted by Egypt's General Directorate for State Security Investigations (GDSSI) was to change the president's movements and itinerary 30 minutes before an event so as to ensure his safety. However, this was not done on the day that Sadat was killed. After Sadat's assassination, General **Fouad Allam**, the head of the Egyptian security service, argued with his chain of command for the need to infiltrate extremist Islamist organizations in order to gain the kind of quality human intelligence needed to uncover the military cells that had succeeded in killing Sadat. His ideas were not put into practice, and instead roundups were conducted on a regular basis. *See also* EGYPTIAN INTELLIGENCE; NASSER'S ASSASSINATION ATTEMPTS.

SAUDI ARABIAN INTELLIGENCE. Saudi Arabia is a huge country, dominating the Arabian Peninsula and thus strategically located. Its huge oil reserves turned it into one of the richest nation in the world, enabling it to maintain a large and highly sophisticated intelligence organization.

The unceasing influx of labor immigrants and refugees, some of whom were considered as a possible threat to the regime, provide plenty of work for the various intelligence and security agencies. Global concern over the Islamic terrorist network, and the suspicion that money and weapons were funneled to these organizations through Saudi Arabia, drove the Saudi government to reorganize and use sophisticated security and monitoring measures.

Saudi Arabia monitors closely its international border and coastlines. Its intelligence and security forces installed video, night vision, and thermal cameras for the purpose of surveillance, providing assistance to the police and other law enforcement organizations. In addition to the usage of high-tech electronic devices, the government offers incentives and significant prize money to citizens who aid the police and provide information that leads to the arrest of suspects or illegal aliens.

Saudi intelligence operates under the Ministry of the Interior and the Ministry of Interior Forces. The Intelligence Directorate conducts and coordinates intelligence operations considered civilian, and when the need arises, cooperates with the military intelligence. All incoming information, foreign and domestic, is gathered and processed by the directorate, which works with other Saudi law enforcement agencies. There are several special agencies in Saudi Arabia that participate in government efforts, and are in fact, parts of the intelligence community. The Directorate of Investigation conducts antiterrorism and anticrime surveillance and investigates all sorts of suspicious activity. It maintains operational units that take part in security operations and political espionage. The Committees for the Propagation of Virtue and the Prevention of Vice (religious police) enforce strict drug prevention and antitrafficking laws and also monitor social behavior laws such as the dress code of modesty and censorship on the media. The main law enforcement agency in Saudi Arabia is the Public Security Police. The police are responsible for law and order, and they monitor public safety and national security.

Saudi military has an intelligence force of its own. The main organization of military and foreign intelligence is the G-2 Intelligence Section. Military intelligence and security operations are conducted in extreme secrecy, and they are coordinated by the Ministry of Defense. Saudi military intelligence is equipped with state-of-the-art equipment for surveillance and espionage, enabling them to gather a wide range of intelligence information, by means of various signals and communication received and decoded. *See also* QAEDA, AL.

SAVAK. *See* IRANIAN INTELLIGENCE.

SAVAMA. *See* IRANIAN INTELLIGENCE.

SAYID, HAITHAM. Lieutenant Colonel Haitham Sayid served as deputy chief of Syrian Air Force Intelligence and its operations director in the 1980s and was second in command to Major General **Muhammad al-Khouli**. Sayid was involved in the **Syrian intelligence** attempted bombing of an Israeli airliner at London's Heathrow Airport in April 1986. The subsequent investigation revealed that the primary suspect, Nizar Hindawi, had tricked an unsuspecting woman into carrying explosives onto the aircraft and was operating in coordination with Haitham Sayid and Major General Muhammad al-Khouli. The two officials promised the Jordanian national Hindawi $250,000 in exchange for placing a bag of explosives on an El Al flight to Tel-Aviv and took part in the planning, financing, training, and recruiting for the operation. As a result of this incident, an international warrant for Sayid's arrest was issued and the British government severed diplomatic relations with Syria. *See also* HINDAWI AFFAIR.

SHARAF, SAMI (1929–?). President Gamal Abdel Nasser chose Sami Sharaf to work as his minister of information in Egyptian military intelligence, where he was entrusted with monitoring the dispatches of foreign correspondents. In effect, he was chief watchdog and did the government's dirty work. In later years, it became known that Sharaf had been recruited by the Komitet Gosudarstvennoy Bezopasnosti (KGB; Committee for State Security) to become their agent in Egypt. *See also* EGYPTIAN INTELLIGENCE; SOVIET CONCEPT; SOVIET INTELLIGENCE IN EGYPT.

SHAWKAT, ASSEF (1950–). Assef Shawkat is regarded as a mysterious figure who has emerged as one of Bashir al-Assad's top security chiefs. Born in Tartous, Shawkat moved to Damascus in 1968 to pursue his higher education in the field of law. He joined the Syrian Army in the late 1970s and rose through the ranks. By the mid-1980s, Shawkat had risen to prominence among officers of his generation, yet he still had no official status in the Syrian state. An ambitious man, he waited for the opportune moment to make his move, and this time came when he was introduced to Hafez al-Assad's daughter Bushra. However, her younger brother Basil strongly objected to the match, claiming that Shawkat was too old for her and too interested in her money. In order to prevent the couple from meeting, Basil had Shawkat arrested and put behind bars four times while he was courting Bushra. On 21 January 1994, Basil was killed in a car crash en route to the Damascus Airport, finally clearing the way for Shawkat to make his move.

In 1995, a year after Basil's death, Shawkat and Bushra eloped and then took up residence in Damascus. Although they did not immediately obtain her father's blessing, Hafez al-Assad summoned them to the palace to give them his blessing after news of their marriage began to spread. Shawkat became Assad's only son-in-law and was promoted in rank to major general.

In October 2000, a scandal rocked the Assad family when Shawkat was shot in the stomach by Maher, Assad's other son, during a family feud. Word of the feud spread all over Damascus and eventually reached the French newspaper *Libération*, which released a report claiming that Shawkat was in a Paris-based hospital being treated for his wounds. He eventually returned to Damascus, and under President Assad's mediation, made his peace with Maher. Shawkat was soon appointed deputy chief of military intelligence and is reportedly the de facto decision maker, while General Hassan Khalil remains the nominal head.

On 10 June 2000, Hafez Assad suddenly passed away. By that time, Shawkat was rumored to have become the strongest man in Syria behind the scenes. Those rumors were confirmed when he stood by Bashir's side at the funeral service, accepting condolences for the late president. He has since become very close to Bashir, who has relied heavily on Shawkat to strengthen the regime.

Ultimately, however, Shawkat's power is derived from the Assad family, as he has no power base of his own. Since he is not an Alawite notable, he cannot expect the larger Alawite community to support him. Indeed, there are no doubt some who resent his rapid advancement within the regime. Thus, his only chance for political survival is his alliance with Bashir and his position as the president's right-hand man.

In February 2008, Shawkat attempted to seize power by force while President Hafez al-Assad was hosting a meeting of the Arab League in Damascus. Shawkat was arrested after **Hizballah** military commander **Imad Mugniyah** informed Assad of the plot. *See also* SYRIAN INTELLIGENCE.

SIX DAYS' WAR. Events began leading up to war in November 1966 with the signing of an alliance between Egypt and Syria. An Egyptian mobilization of its military and announcement of combat readiness in the Sinai on 18 May 1967 was followed on 23 May 1967 by a closure of the Straits of Tiran, blockading the Israeli port of Eilat. Israel took these acts, particularly the blockade, to be cause for war. Further, **Israeli intelligence** was able to verify that Egypt had plans for an attack, codenamed Asad, on Eilat and other targets in the Negev on 27 May 1967. This revelation was passed to the United

States, which placed sufficient pressure on the Soviet Union and Egypt to force a cancellation of the attack. But when all further diplomatic efforts failed, the Israelis decided to make a preemptive strike.

A preemptive strike against the Arabs had always been a major part of the Israeli concept of operations, but it was the Israeli military intelligence, under the command of Major General Aharon Yariv, that proved decisive. In the two years before the Six Days' War, Yariv made it a priority to investigate the extent of Egypt's military capabilities and to infiltrate every air base. Israeli intelligence officers, often working as chefs or co-opting Egyptian soldiers, provided a complete picture of the Egyptian Air Force (EAF), including the whereabouts of every aircraft; personal data and schedules for every pilot, base commander, and radar controller; battle codes; and communication networks. As such, Israeli intelligence knew when the EAF would be most vulnerable, when the aircraft would be most exposed, when the pilots would be slowest in getting to their aircraft for flight operations, and when senior officials would be absent from their commands and unable to direct operations. Using this information as well as comparable intelligence on Egypt's land forces, Israeli officials were able to develop a precise targeting package.

This military operational intelligence was coupled with strategic and tactical intelligence provided by the Israeli **Mossad**. Prior to the war, the state intelligence agency had developed relationships with foreign governments and intelligence agencies, particularly with the United States. By making it clear to both the Central Intelligence Agency and the Pentagon that war was inevitable, Israel was able to get tacit approval for the plan. Knowing that the United States would not condemn the attack and armed with an exceptionally well-developed plan, Israeli leaders authorized the preemptive attack, thus seizing the initiative from their adversaries.

Israel was facing a monumental task. Despite the better training and superior leadership of Israeli forces, they were up against several Arab armed forces that, when combined, held an advantage of two to one in manpower, two to one in tanks, seven to one in artillery, three to one in aircraft, and four to one in warships. On its southern border, Israel had roughly 70,000 troops in the Sinai against Egypt's 100,000 and approximately 700 tanks against Egypt's 950, and it had to distribute its 200 aircraft across all fronts while facing Egypt's 430. Nor could Israel count on technological superiority to overcome the odds, as the Egyptian tanks and artillery were superior to Israel's. Israel faced a similar situation to the north, against Syria and Lebanon, and to the east, against Jordan.

However, the preemptive air strike proved decisive. The attack caught the EAF with its commander, General Sidqi Mahmud, out of contact with his forces. In his absence, the EAF was paralyzed. Without specific authorization, the vast majority of the EAF officers, from air sector commanders all the way down to pilots, were unwilling to implement even the most obvious emergency measures. Only eight MiGs got into the air to defend their airfields, and every one was shot down. The airfields that were undamaged in the initial strikes managed to get only 20 aircraft into the air, all of which were either shot down or crashed when they could find no undamaged airstrips to which to return. All told, three quarters of the EAF was destroyed in the first hours of the war. Intelligence had paved the way for the Israeli Air Force to win one of the most lopsided victories in history.

But credit for Israel's success cannot be explained by its intelligence alone; indicators and warnings should have prepared the Egyptians for what was to come. There was a massive failure of **Egyptian intelligence** services to provide the military with credible intelligence on Israel's order of battle, planned strategy, and location of troops. To the extent that Egyptian intelligence did have information, Israel's denial and deception campaign managed to cloud the picture enough that the reports issued to commanders changed daily and were often contradictory. As a result of these failings, Egypt was clearly at a significant disadvantage from the outset even if its military had been better trained and led. Once combat began, Egyptian forces had no understanding of where Israel would strike, with what force, in what manner, with what tactics or effect, over what duration, or with what objective.

Thus, Israeli intelligence on the eve of the Six Days' War demonstrates how strategic intelligence can be used in conjunction with operational intelligence to provide senior decision makers with the information necessary to make well-informed national security decisions. Yet, just as Israeli intelligence in this case can be viewed as an example of how intelligence operations should be conducted, Egypt's poor intelligence shows how it invited its own defeat. *See also* SOVIET CONCEPT; U.S. INTELLIGENCE DURING THE SIX DAYS' WAR.

SOVIET CONCEPT. The Soviet concept refers to the Soviet Union's incapacity to gather real intelligence about Israel and to their inflated notion of Egypt's military capability to overcome the Israeli Army prior to the Six Days' War of 5–10 June 1967. The direct involvement of Soviet personnel on Israeli soil, at least on a small scale, had already been in place well before 1967, when Israel had been targeted by the Foreign Intelligence Directorate of the Komitet Gosudarstvennoy Bezopasnosti (KGB; Committee for State Security) as a theater of operations. Preparations had been made there for parachuting *diversionnye razvedyvatelnye gruppy* (DRGs, sabotage-intelligence groups) in order to destroy Israeli targets.

Despite their sophisticated intelligence apparatus, the Soviet Union was not able to correctly assess the Israeli decision-making process prior to the Six Days' War or during the war because there were not enough Hebrew–Russian translators employed in the KGB's Foreign Intelligence Directorate. In Egypt, one of the agents that the KGB managed to recruit was **Sami Sharaf**, the minister of information in President Gamal Abdel Nasser's regime. In this position, Sharaf had access to classified conversations between Nasser and high-ranking Egyptian Army generals. Sharaf passed on top-secret information to his KGB connection, **Yevgeni Primakov**, who was working under cover as a Russian journalist in Cairo.

The Egyptian sources assured their Soviet handlers that Nasser's army would easily be able to defeat Israel. However, the Soviet military advisers who had been stationed in Egypt and Syria before the war were familiar with the armies on both sides and did not delude themselves into believing that this was in fact the case. Nevertheless, they were afraid to reveal the truth to their supervisors and instead regularly exaggerated in their reports to Moscow. The assessment of the Soviet intelligence analysts in Moscow was not based solely on the estimation of the Egyptian Army's capability but also on the reports of the strength of other Arab armies, as provided to them by the Soviet advisers stationed in those countries. Thus, the Arab sources and the Soviet military advisers spoke as one voice and promised the Kremlin a big victory over Israel.

In light of this optimistic, albeit false, information that reached the Soviet Union from various Arab countries, it is no wonder that during the first half of 1967, an assessment that those countries could easily strike Israel, even without the Soviet Army's interference, became popular in the Kremlin. In January 1967, the Soviet minister of defense, Andrei Antonovich Grechko, declared that the advanced weaponry being provided to the Arabs by the Soviets would allow them to achieve a historical victory over Israel and that they would owe that victory to the Soviet Union.

Based on this positive assessment, the decision makers in Moscow believed that an Arab victory over Israel was likely, and the Soviets missed all opportunities to prevent an escalation in the Middle East into war. In April 1967, the secretary of the Communist Party in Moscow, Nikolai Yegorchev, visited Egypt. The purpose of the visit was to personally examine and assess the reliability of the optimistic reports arriving from Cairo. As expected, Yegorchev was disappointed by his findings. In the beginning of May, he submitted a secret report to the Politburo in which he warned that, contrary to all previous assessments, Egypt was not prepared for a modern war at all. Yegorchev offered to increase the extent of the Soviet Union's military assistance to Egypt, and in parallel he cautioned Leonid Brezhnev that Egypt should not engage in war in the near future. However, Brezhnev and his ministers ignored Yegorchev's recommendations. The Soviet minister of defense, Andrei Grechko, told the members of the Politburo that Yegorchev's assessment was not professional and that it did not reflect the substantial work done by the Soviet advisors to improve the quality of the Arab armies.

The Arab countries were operating under the assumption that the Soviet Union had promised to always stand beside them in case of any aggression. In the eyes of the Soviets, this was a general expression of support, but the leaders of Egypt and Syria understood that the Soviet Union would provide them with practical assistance, not just moral or diplomatic support. When war broke out, the Soviets and the Arab countries were shocked by an Israeli Air Force (IAF) attack. The IAF dealt a harsh blow in the first hours of the war, when approximately 185 IAF aircraft attacked military bases and airports in Egypt, Syria, Jordan, and Iraq in an operation called Operation

Moked (*moked* in Hebrew means "focus") that neutralized all the runways on the airfields in those countries.

No one in the Kremlin imagined that the Egyptian Army, with its advanced military equipment from the Soviets, would collapse in a matter of days. The Soviet generals, who had repeatedly announced that the Soviet military advisors had built a strong army for President Gamal Abdel Nasser, realized that it was time to report the real truth. Nasser's militant declarations prior to the war regarding the Egyptian military's ability to strike heavily against Israel were thus exposed as being greatly inflated. *See also* SOVIET INTELLIGENCE IN EGYPT; SOVIET INTELLIGENCE IN ISRAEL.

SOVIET INTELLIGENCE AND THE PALESTINE LIBERATION ORGANIZATION. Since the establishment of the Palestinian Liberation Organization (PLO) in May 1964, the Soviets have been deeply involved in backing the organization and **terrorism**. Due to fear of discovery of their involvement in the PLO, the Soviets used to intervene in the PLO through their European satellite states or channel aid through Arab regimes. Wadi Haddad, deputy leader of the Popular Front for the Liberation of Palestine (PFLP), was a Soviet agent until his natural death in 1978. The Soviets supplied the PFLP with weapons, all of which were manufactured in other countries to conceal their supplier. A number of PFLP operations, including kidnappings and assassinations of American citizens, as well as attacks on Israel, were specifically approved in advance by Soviet leaders. The Komitet Gosudarstvennoy Bezopasnosti (KGB; Committee for State Security) had advance notice of all the main PFLP terrorist attacks.

The KGB's most important agent in the PLO, Hani al-Hasan, was a confidant of Yasser Arafat for four decades and, at the time of Arafat's death in 2004, was his national security advisor. His codename was Gidar. Moscow was suspicious of Arafat for several reasons, including his ideology, propensity to lie, and close ties with Romanian intelligence, which the KGB distrusted. The low quality of the trainees presented by the PLO made intelligence cooperation more difficult and made the Soviets disillusioned about dealing with Arafat at all.

SOVIET INTELLIGENCE IN EGYPT. The Soviet Union viewed the Middle East as its backyard and devoted considerable efforts to gaining influence there—efforts that ultimately ended in failure. Egypt, Iraq, Syria, and South Yemen were full of Soviet advisors, money, and weapons. The great Soviet hope in the Middle East was its relations with Egyptian President Gamal Abdel Nasser, who visited Moscow in 1958. Moscow supported Nasser's regime by every means.

By the end of the 1960s, Egypt seemed to offer a secure base for Soviet influence in the Middle East. In addition to the more than 20,000 Soviet advisers recruited in Egypt, the Komitet Gosudarstvennoy Bezopasnosti (KGB; Committee for State Security) had penetrated the Egyptian bureaucracy on an impressive scale. Its key agents included Nasser's chief intelligence advisor **Sami Sharaf**. In addition to reading Egyptian codes, the Soviets broke most Arab codes through cryptography or burglaries against their Moscow embassies.

In February 1967, following a sharp increase in border incidents between Israel and Syria, which was at that time linked with Egypt as part of the United Arab Republic (UAR), Nasser concentrated his forces in the Sinai in order to put pressure on Israel. A false warning came from Soviet intelligence sources on 15 May 1967 that Israel was massing troops on the Syrian border. On the eve of the 1967 Six Days' War, the Soviet Union's transfer of false information to Egypt about alleged prior Israeli troop concentrations facing Syria is still considered a major factor in the outbreak of the war. Soviet motivations and expectations, however, remain a topic of dispute.

Information on the circumstances and events during the period immediately before the 1967 war has been obtained primarily through interviews and memoirs, but also through the release of some important Soviet documents, including correspondence and reports of meetings between Soviet and Egyptian officials at the highest levels. A careful analysis substantiates the conclusion that Moscow did not initially expect or want war to break out between Israel and the Arabs. Soviet leaders had made efforts to moderate Egyptian actions and considered at least one proposal for averting war. By the first week of June 1967, as Egypt and Syria mobilized for an attack on Israel, the Soviet Union apparently expected a preemptive strike by the Israelis. Soviet actions during and immediately following the war indicated an interest in reducing the risks of the conflict, even in cooperation with the United States, although Soviet leaders seem to have held differing views about this matter.

After the June 1967 war, a weakened Nasser granted more concessions to the Soviets, and the Soviet Union poured aid into Egypt to replace lost military equipment and help rebuild the armed forces. However, by sending troops and advisers to Egypt, the Soviet Union took a calculated risk of a possible superpower confrontation over the Middle East, given that the United States under the administration of Richard Nixon was supplying Israel with military aid and regarded Israel as a bulwark against Soviet expansion in the area.

In 1970, during the War of Attrition, a 12,000-strong Soviet expeditionary air defense corps was sent to Egypt to help fight the Israeli Air Force. None of the officers or troops was told the ultimate destination before they docked in Alexandria, Egypt. The level of secrecy was such that generals, other officers, and troops were disguised as civilians and their transport ships were supposedly carrying "farming equipment." The ship captains were allowed to open an envelope containing information on their final destination only after they reached the eastern Mediterranean.

The tide began to turn against the Soviets after Nasser's successor, President Anwar Sadat, decided to switch to the American camp for support at a time when the Soviet side seemed to be winning. The vast structure of Soviet influence rapidly disintegrated as 17,000 Soviet advisers were expelled and contact was broken with many of the agents who had been recruited by Nasser. Sami Sharaf was arrested in 1972 and sentenced to life at hard labor. Because of the heavy surveillance by Egyptian security, meetings with the agents who remained usually took place outside Egypt in locations such as Cyprus and Beirut.

Sadat continued widening the contacts with the West, primarily with the United States. Sadat's director of intelligence, General **Ahmed Ismail**, was known to be in contact with the Central Intelligence Agency (CIA). However, the United States was reluctant in the period after the 1973 October War to assist Egypt financially to a level that was necessary in order to stabilize the Egyptian economy. At the same time, Sadat was unwilling to improve Egypt's relations with the Soviet Union. In March 1976, Sadat unilaterally denounced the Soviet–Egyptian friendship treaty.

Despite Moscow's anger at Sadat's betrayal, the oil crisis that followed the 1973 October War encouraged the revival of Soviet influence in the Middle East, albeit this time with the focus mainly on Iran and Turkey. By the mid-1970s, the Soviet Union had won the part of the Cold War being waged in the developing world. Of the Arab countries, only Saudi Arabia, the United Arab Emirates, Oman, and Morocco had managed to resist KGB penetration at the highest levels.

Although the Soviets spied effectively on Sadat's secret communications with the Americans, they chose not to actively support pro-Moscow Egyptians who were plotting a coup against Sadat. The KGB restricted itself to forging documents to persuade Sadat that the Americans were tricking him and portraying Egypt's leader in non-Egyptian Arab media as the dupe of Jewish bankers, a CIA agent, a sexual deviant, a drug addict, and mentally ill. However, some KGB officials were so infuriated by Sadat that they advocated his assassination. They knew that their contacts in **Syrian intelligence** and the Palestine Liberation Organization were involved in such a plan, which was ultimately carried out in 1981. *See also* EGYPTIAN INTELLIGENCE; SOVIET CONCEPT; SOVIET INTELLIGENCE IN IRAN.

SOVIET INTELLIGENCE IN IRAN. Following the 1953 pro-shah coup, the Soviets were left with little influence over Iran. They focused instead on undermining United States–Iran relations and made elaborate plans for sabotage inside Iran. Their forgeries of U.S. documents, ridiculing the shah or planning his overthrow, were so believable that they sometimes even fooled Iran's monarch. However, these schemes were aborted following the defection to the West by a key Komitet Gosudarstvennoy Bezopasnosti (KGB; Committee for State Security) officer who had been involved in their implementation. When the Central Intelligence Agency (CIA) passed information to Tehran, Soviet spies were expelled and 200 secret communists were arrested on charges of spying for the Soviet Union.

Following the disaffection of Egyptian President Anwar Sadat from the Soviet Union, General Vladimir Krychkov announced on 26 November 1975 that Iran and Turkey were designated as priority targets for intelligence work. However, heavy security in those two countries made intelligence operations extremely difficult. There was not a single Soviet intelligence agent working in Turkey at the time. The KGB's most important agent in Iran, General Ahmed Mogharabi, was arrested in September 1977 by the Iranian regime and later executed, leaving a Soviet intelligence vacuum there as well. The Soviets wrongly estimated that the shah was too strong to be toppled and, like others, discounted any chance of an Islamist revolution.

Although the Soviets had few intelligence assets in Islamist Iran, they continued their disinformation efforts, feeding forged documents—at times through Yasser Arafat—about U.S. and Israeli plots to overthrow or assassinate Ayatollah Ruhollah Khomeini. On one occasion, a tough anti-Soviet Iranian foreign minister was fired and then executed, along with 70 others, largely due to phony coup plans fabricated by the KGB. *See also* IRANIAN INTELLIGENCE; SOVIET INTELLIGENCE IN EGYPT.

SOVIET INTELLIGENCE IN IRAQ. In the early 1970s, Egypt was still the main focus of Soviet interest in the Arab world. The April 1972 Soviet Friendship Treaty with Iraq was one of the earliest of its kind. The initiative was taken by the Iraqis in February of that year when a Ba'ath Party delegation went to Moscow. However, after Anwar Sadat expelled 17,000 Soviet advisors from Egypt, Soviet attention in the area was divided between the two rival Ba'athist regimes: Saddam Hussein's in Iraq and Hafez Assad's in Syria.

In late 1973, Saddam Hussein personally negotiated the Iraqi–Soviet security and intelligence deals with Mikhail Gorbachev's mentor, Yuri Andropov, who was chief of the Komitet Gosudarstvennoy Bezopasnosti (KGB; Committee for State Security). Andropov and the Soviets played a major role in building up Saddam's security and intelligence services, which was the basis for his absolute power. In return, the Soviets were given the means to conduct relatively easy spying through Iraqi embassies in neighboring countries, notably Saudi Arabia.

Without the long stockpiling of Soviet arms, Saddam could never have attacked Iran or invaded Kuwait. Still, he was suspicious of everyone, including the Soviets; he also mistrusted the Iraqi communists, many of whom he executed. By 1982, however, the **Iran–Iraq War** pushed Saddam and the Soviets together in a joint effort to ensure that Iran did not win. The Soviets supplied Scud missiles, which Iraq fired at Iranian cities. Although the Soviet Union opposed Saddam's 1990 invasion of Kuwait, Soviet military experts showed him satellite pictures indicating accurately how the United States was going to attack him on the ground. Saddam viewed the Soviet overtures as a phony attempt to intimidate him and ignored their warnings. *See also* IRAQI INTELLIGENCE.

SOVIET INTELLIGENCE IN ISRAEL. Starting in the late 1940s, the Komitet Gosudarstvennoy Bezopasnosti (KGB; Committee for State Security) made strenuous efforts to place agents in Israel among Soviet-bloc Jewish emigrants. Many emigrating Jews promised to be Soviet agents—perhaps in order to get out—and later reneged on their promises. The Israeli Security Agency (ISA) considered every junior Soviet diplomat in Tel-Aviv as a potential senior spy.

By 1953, the Soviet regime had become so anti-Semitic that all Jews had been purged from the KGB. Forty years later, that ban was still in force. A major feature of KGB policy was its extreme obsession with "Zionist subversion." A 1982 KGB conference concluded that all the Soviet bloc's problems were traceable to Zionists. Soviet contempt for Israel was critical in such intelligence failures as the prediction that Israel would never be able to defeat Arab armies. In the end, Soviet efforts ended in failure, as Moscow faced an environment unfriendly to its ideology. Yet the KGB's efforts succeeded in another way, namely that many of its fabricated claims and arguments about the United States and Israel did gain wide acceptance, causing widespread suspicion of the West, general hatred of America and Israel in the Middle East, and entrenchment of radical ideologies. *See also* SOVIET CONCEPT.

SOVIET INTELLIGENCE IN SYRIA. Since the Ba'ath regime came to power in Syria in March 1963, Damascus was the favorite Arab dictatorship of the Komitet Gosudarstvennoy Bezopasnosti (KGB; Committee for State Security), as both cooperation and infiltration of agents to key posts flourished there. However, their efforts to prove that a small underdeveloped Arab country could be influenced by the slogans of scientific socialism were not successful. Moreover, some of the KGB tactics had tragic consequences, as false information planted in Damascus persuaded the Ba'ath regime to execute more than 200 officers.

SS 117: CAIRO, NEST OF SPIES. *See* ESPIONAGE MOVIES.

STEALING THE MIG-21. Soon after Meir Amit's appointment as director of the **Mossad** on 25 March 1963, he met many commanders in the Israel Defense Forces (IDF) to clarify the Mossad's objectives. Amit asked them what they thought could be the Mossad's most valuable contribution to Israeli security. Major General Ezer Weizman, then commander of the Israeli Air Force (IAF), remarked characteristically that bringing a Soviet-made MiG-21 to Israel would contribute the most to Israeli security. Israel would then have access to the secrets of the most advanced fighter planes the Arab states possessed, and according to the Russians, the most advanced strike aircraft in the world. The Soviet Union had begun to introduce the MiG-21 into the Middle East in 1961 under heavy secrecy, which was the Russian condition for any deal. By 1963, this aircraft had become the major aircraft of the air forces of Egypt, Syria, and Iraq. Few in the West knew much about the MiG-21, but all feared its capabilities. The Soviet Union was well aware of the risk it was taking by stationing MiGs outside its own borders in the service of foreign armies.

The Mossad had actually tried to acquire a MiG-21 twice before Weizman's request but had failed. Through the agency of an Egyptian-born Armenian named Jack Leon Thomas, the Israelis had tried in the early 1960s to pay an Egyptian Air Force pilot US$1 million to defect to Israel with his MiG-21. The pilot refused. Serving in a MiG-21 squadron was in the Arab air forces the highest honor that could be granted to a pilot. These pilots were not the kind of men who could be bribed easily. Jack Leon Thomas and a number of accomplices were caught. Thomas and two of his accomplices were hanged in December 1962. Another attempt to persuade two Iraqi pilots to defect to Israel also came to naught. But the third attempt succeeded. An unexpected source, with no prompting from **Israeli intelligence**, appeared when an Iraqi Jew called Yusuf (Joseph) contacted Mossad officers with the rather curious information that he might be able to arrange the theft of a MiG-21.

Yusuf had been born to an impoverished Jewish family and was indentured to an Iraqi Maronite Christian family at the age of 10. Although he never attended school and was illiterate, he, like the biblical Joseph, rose to prominence in this non-Jewish family's household. No decision was taken without his being consulted. He was present at all family meetings, and his was often the final word on any decision taken. He had risen to become a central figure in the family's affairs, one whom they all looked up to, admired, respected, and loved.

When he was almost 60, however, in a quarrel the actual head of the household told Yusuf that without the family he would have had nothing. Although the Maronite Christian soon apologized, Yusuf did not forget the barb. He decided then and there to explore his "otherness"—his Jewish identity, something he had hardly given a thought to before. He began to learn about Judaism and Israel. Although he maintained his loyalty to his adoptive family, he felt equally loyal to his newfound concern for Israel. In 1964, he contacted Israeli officials in Tehran (until 1979 Israel had sound relations with non-Arab Iran) and Europe. He had something important to tell them.

Through Yusuf, Israel made contact with a Maronite Christian pilot in the Iraqi Air Force. The family felt disaffected with their lot. The father was frustrated by the increasing pressures the Iraqi government was imposing on him and other Maronites. Some of his friends had even been imprisoned and he was finding it difficult to manage his business. He mentioned to Yusuf that he would like to leave the country.

After Yusuf first contacted the Israelis, many of the latter would have preferred to drop the issue as unrealistic. But not Meir Amit. Even when Yusuf began demanding more money, Meir Amit continued to support the plan. The Mossad had contacted a top agent in Baghdad, an American woman, and on Israeli orders or at her own initiative she decided to draw out Munir Redfa—an Iraqi Christian air force pilot and a member of Yusuf's adoptive family. The vivacious American woman, beautiful as well as intelligent, could mix easily in elite social circles wherever she went. She initiated the contact with Munir Redfa at a party, where the two immediately hit it off. He told her that he was a patriotic Iraqi, but he added that he had found himself in violent disagreement with the war waged by his government against the Kurdish minority in northern Iraq. He added that after accomplishing his training as a squadron commander, he had been stationed far from his home in Baghdad and was allowed to fly only with small fuel tanks because he was a Christian. In private conversation, he even admitted to his admiration of the Israelis: the few against so many Muslims.

The American woman listened and continued to meet him despite her being married with children. As relations between them developed, she even suggested that they take a holiday together in Europe in July 1966. After a couple of days there, she suggested to Munir that he fly to Israel with her; she added that she had friends in Israel who might assist him. Munir at once realized that this had obviously been planned from the start and that her attraction to him was not because of him personally, but he also recognized that she was making an offer that could be of great benefit to him. He arrived in Israel and was given VIP treatment. He was taken on tours and he met with Mossad officers as well as Israeli Air Force officers, and even the air force commander himself. They offered him US$1 million. The challenge was as attractive as it was dangerous. Munir insisted that the Mossad officers arrange for the escape of his family from Iraq as well: his wife, his children, and his parents, as well as the rest of his extended family. He received assurances on this but did not tell his family plainly that they were going to leave Iraq forever. It was decided that Munir would be granted Israeli citizenship, a job, and a home.

The new commander of the IAF since April 1966, Major General Mordechai Hod, met Munir himself to plan the MiG flight together. According to the plan, Munir was to fly a zigzag course to Israel to escape Iraqi and Jordanian radar. It was explained to Munir how dangerous the project was going to be. In a 900-kilometers flight his own colleagues, on realizing what he had done, might send aircraft to shoot him down. Hod suggested to him that he remain calm and follow the plan. All that remained for Munir was to fix the date for his flight, which he set for 16 August 1966.

Soon members of Redfa's family began leaving the country; one as a tourist, another for medical treatment. Israeli aircraft would be ready to escort him on the appointed date. On that day in August, Munir went about his business in Iraq as usual, as best he could with coworkers he would never see again. He asked the ground crew to fill his tanks to capacity, an order the Russian advisers generally had to countersign. But the Iraqis disliked the Russian advisers, who seemed to hold them in contempt, and this worked to Redfa's benefit. As a star pilot, they were happy to obey his orders rather than those of the Russians. After taking off, he headed out toward Baghdad, then veered off in the direction of Israel. The ground crew radar picked up a blip on the screen heading west and they frantically radioed him to turn around. He didn't. They warned him they would shoot him down. Hundreds of miles away Israeli radar picked up the blip on the screen. They sent up a squad of IAF Mirages to escort him. He went through his prearranged signals and they flew alongside him to a base deep in the Negev Desert.

On the same day, 16 August, Mossad agents in Iraq hired two large vans and picked up the remaining members of the pilot's family, who had left Baghdad ostensibly for a picnic. They were driven to the Iranian border and guided across by anti-Iraqi Kurdish guerrillas. Safely in Iran, a helicopter collected them and flew them to an airfield, from where an airplane took them to Israel. Newspapers all over the world carried the sensational story of an Iraqi pilot who had defected with his MiG-21 to Israel. But after a couple of days the story was almost forgotten. The Soviet Union demanded the return of the aircraft; Israel has never returned it. However, so as not to infuriate the Soviets too much, Israel did not share any information on the MiG-21 with the United States for a substantially long period. The whole story was not revealed by Israel for a relatively long time, beyond the fact that an Iraqi pilot had defected with his MiG-21 to Israel. It was no surprise when, during the Six Days' War in June 1967, the Israel Air Force demonstrated its superiority over the MiG-21 aircraft of the Arab air forces. Yusuf did not move to Israel, preferring to remain a Zionist abroad.

SUDANESE INTELLIGENCE. Little information about Sudanese intelligence is available. There is limited information about Sudanese intelligence agencies, the National Security Forces (NSF), which is subdivided into two major branches—Internal Security (Al Amn al-Dakhili) and External Security (Al Amn al-Khariji)—and the Military Intelligence Service, the Popular Police, the intelligence branch of the Special Police Force (SPF), the 144th Counterterrorist Unit (CTU), the Revolutionary Security Service (Amn al-Thawra), and the State Security Organization (SSO). The Internal Security reports to the minister of security, who brings the information to the president. The Internal Security office has several semi-independent departments, including political and economic sections. Ever since the peace agreement of 9 January 2005, many positions (over 25 percent) of Sudan's intelligence personnel have been given to former rebels, members of the Sudan People's Liberation Movement (SPLM).

The Popular Police is not part of the official police of Sudan. It is an unofficial security service of Islamic volunteers functioning as observers and informants of the NSF. They infiltrate and blend in, in refugee camps and in various groups, and gather information.

As Sudan has a unique position in the international war against **terrorism**, the functioning and orientations of its intelligence and security organizations, and their relations with other players in the field are of much more importance to the intelligence and security communities than those of other nations of inner Africa. Sudan went through a phase in which it willingly harbored terrorists, such as the infamous **al Qaeda** leader Osama bin-Laden (1991 to 1996). However, in 2001, Sudan chose to become a U.S. ally and to cooperate in the international efforts against Islamist terrorists. As a result of the Sudanese government's decision to prefer the Western camp, the administration of President George W. Bush reexamined relations between the two states. Since then, the U.S. and Sudanese intelligence communities have begun to share certain types of information. Sudan, for example, provided Washington information about suspected terrorists living in or having lived in Sudan in the past.

Most security issues in Sudan are of internal origin, as the unending civil war goes back to the 1950s. Sudan is a huge country, the largest in Africa. It contains two very distinct ethnic and cultural regions, the North, which is mainly Arabic and Muslim, is under government control, whereas the South is African and mostly non-Muslim (Christian or pagan). Much of southern Sudan was for many years under the SPLM and the Sudan People's Liberation Army (SPLA). However, government troops, especially unofficial bands, terrorize the civilian population, committing terrible war crimes that the government simply ignores. *See also* BRITISH INTELLIGENCE IN EGYPT AND SUDAN.

SUEZ CRISIS. *See* OPERATION MUSKETEER.

SULEIMAN, OMAR (1936–). In 1993, Omar Suleiman was appointed by Egyptian President Hosni Mubarak as the director of State

Security Investigations (GDSSI; Mubahath al-Dawla). In that position, Suleiman is considered to be the acting deputy to President Mubarak. He is in charge of representing the Egyptian government in the Israeli–Palestinian negotiations and frequently serves as mediator between both sides. In August 2008, he brokered a truce by **Hamas** and Israel. *See also* EGYPTIAN INTELLIGENCE.

SYRIAN INTELLIGENCE. Syria's intelligence services have been greatly influenced by the model of the French mandate that created the modern Syrian state. Before independence in 1945, the intelligence services in Syria were only responsible for internal security and counterespionage. After independence, the mission of these services gradually expanded to targeting opposition groups in Lebanon and to gathering intelligence against Israel. Lebanon was the location for numerous operations against political exiles and opponents as well as of *fedayeen* paramilitary and terrorist operations launched against northern Israel from south Lebanon.

The influence of the French is most striking in the intelligence branch of the Army General Staff, known until 1969 as the Deuxième Bureau. The dominant role of the military in politics was reflected in the rise of the Deuxième Bureau at the expense of the civilian Department of General Security (Sûreté Générale). Under the tenure of Abd al-Hamid Sarraj as head of the Deuxième Bureau, from 1955 to 1958, the Sûreté became no more than an executive arm of the Deuxième Bureau. During this period, Sarraj and the Deuxième Bureau pursued a generally anti-imperialist foreign policy. Even at this early stage, the military branch of Syrian intelligence displayed a high degree of independence in both the formulation and execution of policy.

In February 1958, the Syrian government merged with Egypt to form the United Arab Republic (UAR). The union lasted until September 1961. During the union, Syrian intelligence services came under the overall authority of the Egyptian Directorate of General Intelligence. The Deuxième Bureau was subordinated to Egypt's Directorate of Military Intelligence, while a new Special Bureau was set up under the Interior Ministry and became the prime intelligence service. During much of 1958 and 1959, the intelligence services of the UAR, and especially their Syrian elements, were kept busy controlling domestic dissent and executing a large-scale covert war in

Lebanon. After its secession from the UAR, the new Syrian government under President Nazim al-Qudsi had to defend itself against **Egyptian intelligence**, which was seeking to subvert it. The Deuxième Bureau and a reformed civilian intelligence, renamed the Internal Security Forces Command (ISFC), concentrated their activities on Lebanon. Their targets were pro-Egyptian Lebanese, Syrian exiles, and Egyptian agents.

Following the February 1966 coup within the Ba'ath Party, Salah Jadid emerged as the leader of Syria's regime, and he centralized control of all intelligence and security services under Colonel Abd al-Karim al-Jundi. From 1966 to 1969, Jundi further expanded the role and power of his agencies, both at home and abroad. These services were given an even freer hand in rooting out opponents, and it was during this period that their reputation for brutal ruthlessness was firmly established. Jundi's support for Jadid was so crucial that when Jundi died in March 1969, it was only a matter of time before Jadid fell.

In March 1969, Rifaat al-Assad, Hafez al-Assad's younger brother, used his paramilitary units in conjunction with military intelligence to crush Jundi's security force. In November 1970, Hafez al-Assad ousted Jadid in what he labeled as a "corrective coup." The Assad regime has proven to be Syria's most stable since independence, and there has been considerable continuity among the senior personnel in the intelligence community. This reflects the extent to which the top leadership and commanders of the main intelligence organs are drawn largely from the Alawite community and are linked to Assad by personal and family ties.

In the 1970s and 1980s, Syrian intelligence agencies were very active abroad and were heavily involved in guerrilla and terrorist operations. A major focus of this activity was on operations in the Golan Heights and northern Israel. Additionally, sabotage, assassination, and terrorist operations were carried out in Europe and elsewhere in the Arab world. Although Syria's exact role was murky, its intelligence and security networks were strongly implicated in the support of Middle Eastern and other international terrorist groups in Western Europe in order to achieve its diplomatic, military, and strategic objectives. In fact, Syria was one of the countries on the **terrorism** list issued by the U.S. government when it was first compiled in 1979.

The central importance to the regime of a disciplined and ruthless intelligence and security apparatus was demonstrated by the way in which Rifaat Assad's Special Forces crushed the insurgency in Hama led by the Muslim Brotherhood in 1982. The government was able to control the opposition only by bringing in armored units and shelling part of the town. During this period, the role and power of the intelligence agencies expanded even further, as they gained increased resources and personnel. Under President Hafez al-Assad, the regime has consolidated its grip on the intelligence agencies, and they have come to dominate all other political and military institutions, including the state itself. The Syrian intelligence agencies played and still play a leading role in shaping Syrian domestic and foreign policy.

Published sources show that Syria has 15 separate security and intelligence services. However, it is impossible to precisely analyze the exact structure of the country's intelligence apparatus, as personal relationships and loyalties matter much more than institutional divisions. The following are the most important Syrian intelligence agencies:

- The Presidential Security Council is responsible for supervising the other agencies and for resolving interservice disputes. The council also controls small intelligence and security organizations of its own, such as the Foreign Liaison Office, which monitors the activities of foreign diplomats in Damascus.
- Military Intelligence (MI), which was established in 1969, replaced the Deuxième Bureau and is now the dominant intelligence agency in Syria, appearing to control not only the military and internal security situations but also Syrian political policy. The MI's main role is to ensure the loyalty of the military. The MI controls the military police, which provide security for elements of the ruling elite, and the Office of the Chief of Reconnaissance, which is responsible for strategic and tactical military intelligence collection and analysis. It is also responsible for carrying out unconventional warfare operations. With their headquarters in the Defense Ministry complex in the center of Damascus, the Military Intelligence services (Mukhabarat) reputedly exercise immense authority from within the military establishment.
- Air Force Intelligence's (AFI) primary roles are to ensure the loyalty of the air force, to provide physical security arrangements for

official functions, and to carry out certain overseas operations. Within Syria's intelligence and security services, sponsorship of terrorism reportedly was conducted by Air Force Intelligence. Major General **Muhammad al-Khouli** served as its director from 1963 until 1987, when he was removed from the post after being linked to terrorist operations in Great Britain and West Germany. Air Force Intelligence operatives reportedly worked abroad in the offices of the Syrian national airline and also as military attaches in Syrian embassies.

- Special Forces (SF) was formed in the 1970s. This elite army unit has between 10,000 and 15,000 personnel and is equipped with heavy armaments. It has carried out operations against both the Muslim Brotherhood internally and the Israelis in Lebanon.

- The Presidential Guard (PG) was established in 1976; the role of the 10,000-strong guard is to guard the presidential palace and central Damascus.

- The General Intelligence Directorate (GID) was established in its present form in 1971 and controls civil intelligence. It has primary responsibility for overseeing the Ba'ath Party, the civil police, the border guards, the civilian bureaucracy, and the general populace.

- The Political Security Directorate (PSD) is the branch of the GID that handles political intelligence and security. It is divided into the Internal Security Department (ISD) and the External Security Department (ESD). The ESD appears to be divided into three units: Arab Affairs, Refugee Affairs, and Zionist and Jewish Affairs.

- Virtually every prominent personality in the regime has some sort of personal security unit. This may consist of a handful of bodyguards or may comprise an extensive intelligence apparatus. Most of these smaller units are only responsible for the security of their leader's personal entourage.

For more than three decades, Syria's intelligence network exerted considerable influence on Lebanese political and economic life. More than 5,000 Syrian intelligence operatives were deployed in Lebanon. When Bashir al-Assad became Syrian president, he did not change the Syrian intelligence apparatus except for reducing the Syrian intelligence presence in Lebanon. The assassination of former Lebanese Prime Minister Rafiq Hariri on 14 February triggered an international backlash that forced Syria to withdraw its military intelligence from Lebanon. Syria maintained that it closed its intelligence headquarters at the Beau Rivage Hotel, Beirut. However, according to Western intelligence agencies, Syria still has substantial influence on Lebanon. *See also* DOUBA, ALI; GHAZALI, RUSTUM; HARIRI'S ASSASSINATION; KANAAN, GHAZI; LEBANESE INTELLIGENCE; SYRIAN TERRORISM.

SYRIA'S INTELLIGENCE IN LEBANON. *See* DOUBA, ALI; GHAZALI, RUSTUM; KANAAN, GHAZI; LEBANESE INTELLIGENCE.

SYRIAN TERRORISM. Syria's role in **terrorism** has always remained murky, and Syria's intelligence and security networks were strongly implicated in the support of Middle Eastern and other international terrorist groups in Western Europe. The senior officials in the intelligence and security agencies involved in many terrorist attacks were headed by **Muhammad al-Khouli.** Their exposure did not harm their standing in the Syrian hierarchy; in fact, al-Khouli was promoted to commander of the Syrian Air Force. President Hafez al-Assad's supervision and control of Syria's intelligence and security apparatus involved in terrorist attacks was extremely close. It is therefore reasonable to assume that Assad was personally involved not only in creating the overall policy but also in making decisions regarding specific terrorist attacks. Indeed, many observers believe that Assad long used terrorism to further Syrian policy objectives in the Middle East. However, the regime has always denied having connections with any terrorist infrastructure.

– T –

TANNENBAUM, ELHANAN (1946–). Born in Israel as the son of Polish Holocaust survivors, Tannenbaum immigrated to Israel in 1949, together with his father, mother, and sister, after most of his relatives had perished in the Holocaust. The family settled in Holon (a small town near Tel-Aviv), where Tannenbaum spent his youth. He was an active organizer of the Boy Scout organization in Holon and later became a member of the Scout leadership in Israel, representing the Israeli Scout movement in the United States. At the age of 18, Tannenbaum enrolled in the Hebrew University of Jerusalem, studying economics and political science. During his academic studies, he began serving in the Israel Defense Forces (IDF). After graduation, he completed his army service as an officer in the artillery corps and continued to fulfill his reserve duties, where he achieved the rank of colonel. He continued his studies at the Tel-Aviv University School of Business Administration and went on to become a businessman, working both alone and with partners. Tannenbaum was also working with the Israeli Rafael Armament Development Authority as a consultant and weapons salesman and was thereby exposed to classified information.

It is unknown how the Obeid Kais contact was made, but Tannenbaum was befriended by Kais, an Israeli Arab who had ties with the Lebanese **Hizballah**. Kais was accused of playing a major role in the kidnapping of Tannenbaum by Hizballah in October 2000. Around the time of this kidnapping, Kais vanished from Israel. It is alleged that he succeeded in luring Tannenbaum into Abu Dhabi via Europe (possibly Switzerland). Suspicions are that Tannenbaum, who was reputedly an out-of-luck gambler with heavy debts, had followed in the hope of making a drug deal. Tannenbaum himself tried to clear his name by claiming to have followed on his own accord in search of clues about Ron Arad, the famous abducted Israeli navigator. Some reports claim that after reaching Abu Dhabi, Kais convinced Tannenbaum to accompany him on a flight back to Europe with a stopover in Lebanon, supposedly to pick up the drugs, and even provided Tannenbaum with a false passport for the trip. Other reports indicate that Kais called in **Iranian intelligence** agents, who captured Tannenbaum in Abu Dhabi and, after interrogating him, drugged him and shipped him in a crate to Lebanon.

Either way, immediately upon landing in Lebanon, Tannenbaum was captured by Hizballah operatives and taken to a safe hideout, where he was questioned. The Hizballah organization soon made it public that they were holding an IDF colonel who was also an Israeli **Mossad** agent (as Tannenbaum might have told Kais at one time, according to some reports). The facts were left obscure, leading **Israeli intelligence** to initially believe that Tannenbaum had been captured in Europe or had turned himself in there.

Upon his capture by the Hizballah, the Israeli security establishment was afraid that Tannenbaum would reveal information to which he had been exposed in his military service and in Rafael. Tannenbaum was kept in prison for over three years by the Hizballah until being returned in 2004, as part of a controversial prisoner exchange, along with the bodies of three IDF soldiers kidnapped several days before him. The extent of the damage caused by Tannenbaum has not been officially acknowledged by Israel, but considering his rank and role in the artillery corps of the IDF, it is potentially large.

TAWFIQ, WALID HAMID. Major General Walid Hamid Tawfiq replaced **Qusay Saddam Hussein** as the commander of **Iraq's Special Security Organization** (SSO), serving from June 2001 until September 2002. In contrast to Qusay, Tawfiq was an experienced army officer. Nevertheless, Tawfiq was ordered to report directly to Qusay about security matters. In September 2002, Tawfiq was reappointed to the position of governor of Basrah. *See also* IRAQI DIRECTORATE OF GENERAL MILITARY INTELLIGENCE; IRAQI DIRECTORATE OF GENERAL SECURITY; IRAQI INTELLIGENCE.

TENET PLAN. A vicious circle of violence by Palestinian terrorists started with the second *intifada* (uprising), known as the al-Aqsa Intifada, on 28 September 2000. George J. Tenet, the director of the Central Intelligence Agency (CIA), advanced a work plan for a cease-fire on 10 June 2001, which came to be known as the Tenet Plan. The objective of the plan was to bring the security organizations of Israel and the Palestinian National Authority to reaffirm their commitments to a cease-fire in line with the security agreements forged at Sharm al-Sheikh in October 2000. Those agreements were delineated in the Mitchell Report of April 2001, named after George J. Mitchell, who chaired an ad hoc commission to investigate the origins of the al-Aqsa Intifada and make recommendations for resolution of the conflict.

Although the Tenet Plan was not made public as a formal document, it was very detailed in its listing of key elements and specific steps for resuming security cooperation, enforcing strict adherence to the cease-fire, suppressing **terrorism**, and redeploying the Israel Defense Forces to their positions as of 28 September 2000. The plan called for an immediate cessation of hostilities, the arrest of terrorists by the Palestinians, and steps to stop anti-Israel incitement in the Palestinian media. This would be followed by the easing of travel restrictions and a withdrawal of Israeli troops from Palestinian population centers.

The Tenet Plan was scheduled to start on 13 June 2001. At the insistence of Prime Minister Ariel Sharon, the plan assumed a period of seven days without attacks as a precondition for implementation. Given that this condition was never satisfactorily met, the process never started. In early 2002, renewed severe violence by Palestinian terrorists led to stepped-up Israeli military operations in the territories, including the invasion of refugee camps to eliminate terrorist staging facilities. *See also* PEACE AND POLITICAL PROCESSES.

TERRORISM. The phenomenon of suicide terrorism first appeared in the Middle East in the 1980s in Lebanon and Kuwait. In the 1990s, the phenomenon spread to Algeria, Israel, Pakistan, and Turkey. After the end of the Cold War, Muslim terrorist groups set up infrastructures and increased their reach in Western Europe and North America as well. The main terrorist groups in the Middle East using the tactic of suicide bombers are the Islam Resistance Movement (**Hamas**) and the Palestinian Islamic Jihad (PIJ) of the Israeli-occupied territories; **Hizballah** of Lebanon; the **Egyptian Islamic Jihad** (EIJ) and Gama'at al-Islamiyya (IG; Islamic Group) of Egypt; the Armed Islamic Group (GIA) of Algeria; the Kurdistan Worker's Party (PKK) of Turkey; and the Osama bin-Laden network (**al Qaeda**) of Afghanistan. There were also four Syrian and Lebanese groups staging suicide terrorist operations alongside Hizballah in the 1980s, but they are no longer engaged in terrorist activities. These groups were the Natzersit Socialist Party of Syria, the Syrian Nationalist Party, the Lebanese Communist Party, and the Ba'ath Party of Lebanon.

Suicide groups may be motivated by religion, ethnic nationalism, or political aims and differ in form, size, orientation, goals, and support. The terrorist bombers are ready to sacrifice their own lives in order to kill civilians in buses, restaurants, malls, and other crowded places. Suicide bombers have also targeted political and military leaders. Examples of suicide operations include the attacks carried out in 1992 by Hizballah against the Israeli embassy in Argentina, as well as the embassy bombings in Pakistan and in East Africa perpetrated by Egyptian suicide bombers. All of the suicide terrorist groups have support infrastructures in Western Europe and in North America, with key figures distributing propaganda, raising funds, and in some instances procuring weapons.

There are six types of suicide improvised explosive devices (IEDs): those which are borne on the human body, also known as the suicide bodysuit; on a vehicle; on a motorcycle; on a naval craft; on a scuba diver; and in the air on a microlight, glider, or minihelicopter. All of these types have been used in the Middle East. The most frequently used suicide IED has been the suicide bodysuit, which has evolved to improve concealment and is becoming increasingly smaller. Initially, the device was a square block of explosives worn on the chest and abdominal area. As body searches for suicide devices are usually conducted around the abdomen, the device has gradually evolved into a heart-shaped block of explosives placed just above the navel. A suicide bodysuit can be made from commercial items, and most require no or little electronics, making it difficult for security agencies to develop countertechnologies to detect these devices. Moreover, several terrorist groups have used female suicide bombers because women are less suspicious and can easily hide a suicide device under their clothes, even appearing to be pregnant. In the conservative societies of the Middle East, there is a hesitation to body search women at all.

Organizing a suicide operation is extremely secretive, and the success of the mission depends on a number of elements: level of secrecy, thorough reconnaissance, and extensive rehearsals. Secrecy enables the preservation of the element of surprise; thorough reconnaissance enables the group to plan, often by building a scale model of the target; and extensive rehearsals allow bombers to gain stealth and speed. There are other elements involved as well, such as getting the bombers to the target zone and then to the target itself. The bombers are usually supported by an operational cell that is responsible for providing food, accommodations, transport, clothing, and security until the target destination is reached. Resident agents help generate intelligence for the operation, from target reconnaissance to surveillance. The cell members confirm the intelligence. Often, immediately before the attack, the bomber conducts the final reconnaissance. As comprehensive knowledge of the target is essential for the success of a suicide operation, terrorist groups depend on building solid resident-agent networks.

Some security and intelligence agencies have succeeded in penetrating the networks of various terrorist groups. This may be necessary when bombers infiltrate groups or even governments and gradually gain acceptance as trusted members, enabling them to reach and destroy valuable targets, whether human or infrastructure. In such cases, even the presence of bodyguards or guards assigned to protect sensitive installations cannot serve as an adequate countermeasure. As such, penetration of the terrorist group is the first line of defense, while hardening the vulnerable and likely targets is the last line of defense as a reactive measure.

The traditional concept of security is based on deterrence, where the perpetrator is either killed or captured. However, the success of a suicide terrorist operation is dependent on the death of the attacker. The suicide terrorist is not worried about capture, interrogation (including torture), trial, or imprisonment. Furthermore, in suicide attacks, the group does not have to concern itself with developing an escape route or providing a plan for the extraction of the attacker. As every prisoner has a breaking point under psychological or physical pressure, the certain death of the attacker enables the group to undertake operations while protecting itself against leaks of sensitive information. Terrorist groups learn from one another and share resources, intelligence, technology, expertise, and personnel.

The development of strategic and tactical countermeasures has led to a decline in the number of suicide attacks in recent years. In Israel, several rings of security prevent suicide bombers from reaching their intended targets. Due to the efficiency of the countermeasures adopted by Israeli police, military, intelligence, and security organizations, the number of fatalities and casualties caused by Hamas, the PIJ, and Hizballah suicide bombings has steadily declined since mid-2002. In deep-penetration operations, the Israeli Security Agency (ISA), the **Mossad**, has successfully removed key operatives of these groups. For example, the ISA assassinated Hamas suicide bomb maker **Yahya Ayash** by placing a microexplosive device in his mobile phone. *See also* JORDANIAN TERRORISM.

THOMPSON, EDWARD JOHN (1886–1946). Edward John Thompson, a British writer and poet, was a missionary in Bengal, India. He started his military career on 1916 as a military pastor. Later he participated in battles in Iraq, and from there was transferred to the Palestine front and focused his activities in Lebanon. He came to the area to learn the situation and invested effort in the building of spy networks to exchange information between Damascus, Hijaz, and other Arabic countries. It is believed that his activities caused the demise of several Arabs. *See also* BRITISH INTELLIGENCE IN MESOPOTAMIA; BRITISH INTELLIGENCE IN THE PALESTINE CAMPAIGN OF 1914–1918.

TILFAH, RAFI. Rafi Abd al-Latif Tilfah was the last commander of **Iraq's Directorate of General Security** (DGS), replacing **Tahir Jalil** in 1999. After the 2003 **Operation Iraqi Freedom**, Rafi Tilfah was listed as wanted by U.S. forces in Iraq. The DGS, like all of Saddam Hussein's intelligence agencies, was dismantled by U.S. forces. *See also* IRAQI DIRECTORATE OF GENERAL MILITARY INTELLIGENCE; IRAQI INTELLIGENCE; IRAQI SPECIAL SECURITY ORGANIZATION.

TRIDENT NETWORK. The Trident Network was the name given to the cooperation between the intelligence communities of Israel, Iran, and Turkey for collecting intelligence about the Egyptian government. The Trident framework was first mooted in the late 1950s, and in 1958 it came into being at the initiative of the Israeli **Mossad** under Isser Harel, with the cooperation of the intelligence communities of Turkey and Iran. Ethiopia joined Trident later.

The Trident member countries were supported or sponsored to some extent by some European and the U.S. intelligence communities, which were the driving forces behind its operation. Great Britain, which had lost the Suez Canal to Egypt's President Gamal Abdel Nasser in the 1956 Sinai Campaign, sought to maintain its influence and intelligence capabilities in the Middle East through the Trident Network. Conceptually Trident was based on the Israeli political **Periphery Doctrine** in the Middle East region. This posited that Arab nationalism was the main threat or chief cause of instability in the region; therefore, the non-Arab countries of the region should consolidate for closer cooperation. The aim of the Trident Network was accordingly to establish intelligence cooperation against the rising tide of Arab nationalism.

The Turkish and **Iranian intelligence** communities benefited from having close connections with their counterparts in several European countries, while the United States supported the Trident Network, hoping to exert influence in the region by such means. Trident was backed to some extent by the intelligence community of France, which at the time was embroiled in a civil war in Algeria, since the Algerian rebels were supplied and trained by Egypt and other Arab states. Trident institutionalized many aspects of the exchange of intelligence information among its member countries.

The Trident Network established the procedure of semiannual meetings of the directors of the intelligence communities of the member countries to coordinate policy and priorities, as well as day-to-day work, among the communities. They created standard forms of communications and appointed liaison officers, enabling officers of each intelligence community access to the others, including their technology and training facilities. Although its level of intensity fluctuated, intelligence cooperation within Trident Network was maintained until the 1979 Islamic Revolution in Iran and made a distinct contribution to closer security relations between the participating countries in the eastern Mediterranean. *See also* FRENCH INTELLIGENCE IN THE MIDDLE EAST; ISRAELI INTELLIGENCE; TURKISH INTELLIGENCE.

TUNISIAN INTELLIGENCE. Tunisia, formerly a French colony, became independent in June 1956. For 31 years after independence, Tunisia was dominated by Habib Bourguiba, who declared himself as president for life. In November 1987 Zine el-Abidine Ben-Ali succeeded in removing the aging ruler from office. Ben-Ali dramatically expanded Tunisia's internal security apparatus under the control of the Ministry of the Interior.

Tunisia's Ministry of the Interior controls effectively all of the security services and the civilian authorities in the country. Within the ministry, there are several law enforcement organizations, including the police, who have primary responsibility within the major cities. The National Guard is responsible for the security in smaller cities and in the countryside. The state security forces are tasked to monitor groups and individuals considered by the government as a threat to the regime. The media, Islamists, human rights activists, and opposition parties and leaders are included among these suspected groups. Tunisia's Ministry of the Interior monitors the communications of those groups and individuals, and there are a large number of plainclothes police throughout the country. In addition, Ben-Ali created a parallel security apparatus that runs directly from the presidential palace.

Tunisia's police share responsibility for internal security with the National Guard and other state security forces. All of Tunisia's security agencies are well organized and efficient. However, in several instances they were involved in petty corruption, including the solicitation of bribes by police at traffic stops and police brutality against individuals.

The Mukhabarat (the intelligence agency), which is under the control of the Ministry of the Interior, constitutes the state's advantaged institution serving as the bastion of elite privilege and guardian of regime interests. Tunisia's security apparatus, which before Ben-Ali was considered as relatively modest by Arab world standards, has ballooned under President Ben-Ali and become one of the most formidable in the Arab world.

During the age of the Internet, Tunisia's Ministry of Telecommunications formed the Tunisian Internet Agency (ATI), which monitors and censors all cyber dissidents. The ATI runs one of the world's most extensive Internet censorship operations. Tunisia's security apparatus is intended mainly for ensuring the internal security and to a certain extent to prevent Islamic infiltration from Algeria. *See also* FRENCH INTELLIGENCE IN THE MIDDLE EAST.

TURKISH HIZBALLAH (THB). The Turkish Hizballah (THB) is a Kurdish Islamic (Sunni) extremist organization that arose in the late 1980s in response to the Kurdistan Workers' Party (PKK) atrocities carried out against Muslims in southeastern Turkey, where the THB seeks to establish an independent Islamic state. The THB has a few hundred members and several thousand supporters and operates primarily in the Diyarbakir region of southeastern Turkey. The THB has been described as an organization in which every member is an intelligence agent with a codename, several identities, and a strict adherence to secrecy.

Beginning in the mid-1990s, the THB, which is unrelated to the Lebanese **Hizballah**, expanded its target base and modus operandi from killing PKK militants to conducting low-level bombings against liquor stores, bordellos, and other establishments that the organization considered anti-Islamic. In January 2000, Turkish security forces killed Huseyin Velioglu, the leader of the THB, in a shootout at a safe house in Istanbul. The incident sparked a yearlong series of counterterrorist operations against the group that resulted in the detention of some 2,000 individuals, of which authorities arrested several hundred on criminal charges. At the same time, police recovered nearly 70 bodies of Turkish and Kurdish businessmen and journalists whom the THB had tortured and brutally murdered during the mid to late 1990s. The group began targeting official Turkish interests in January 2001, when its operatives assassinated the Diyarbakir police chief in the group's most sophisticated operation to date. The THB did not conduct a major operation in 2002. The structure and practices of the THB have only come to light after years of successful operations by Turkish security and intelligence organizations.

Turkish security forces have conducted highly successful counterterrorism operations against the THB. Taking advantage of the cease-fire declared by PKK, the security forces focused their increased resources on an initial round of raids that netted significant pieces of information about the THB and its activities. The security forces then diligently took advantage of this new intelligence to conduct raids on a wider scale, thereby creating a snowball effect of gathering more intelligence followed by conducting wider and more devastating raids.

Milli Istihbarat Teskilati (MIT; the Turkish National Intelligence Organization) arrested thousands of terrorist suspects and THB operations subsequently dwindled. By late 2002, the THB had been effectively neutralized as a serious threat to Turkey. *See also* TURKISH INTELLIGENCE.

TURKISH INTELLIGENCE. The first Turkish intelligence organization was established in 1914 under the name of Teskilat-i Mahsusa (Special Organization) to undertake important missions and carry out military and paramilitary activities during **World War I**. It was dissolved at the end of the war and replaced by a new intelligence unit under the name of Karakol Cemiyeti (Police Guild) in 1918. This organization carried out many important missions during the National Liberation War, but was dissolved with the arrest of its members when Istanbul was occupied on 16 March 1920.

Between 1920 and 1926, a number of intelligence organizations were established and closed down. In July 1920, the Askeri Polis Teskilati (Military Police Organization) was founded to counter the enemy's espionage activities and propaganda infiltrating the army ranks. This organization, which carried out successful missions during the war, was dissolved in March 1921.

Two months later, in May 1921, another intelligence group named Mudafaa-i Milliye (MIM; National Defense) was founded by the Turkish Grand National Assembly in order to fill the intelligence vacuum left by the Askeri Polis Teskilaty. The MIM established an extensive network of spies and intelligence consisting of a large cadre of military and civilian officers. The MIM conducted vital activities during the National Liberation War, such as organizing the secret transfer of weapons and munitions to Anatolia and infiltrating enemy headquarters and groups collaborating with the enemy to get important information and documents. The organization was dissolved on 5 October 1923 following the liberation of Istanbul.

Present-day Turkey was created in 1923 from the Turkish remnants of the Ottoman Empire. During the period that followed the dissolution of various intelligence groups and the establishment of the Republic of Turkey, intelligence activities were carried out by the intelligence unit within the Turkish General Staff. At the beginning of 1926, Atatürk gave the order to form a modern intelligence organization having the same standards as those in the developed countries.

On 6 January 1927, the first intelligence organization of the Republic of Turkey was established under the name of Milli Emniyet Hizmeti (MEH; National Security Service), with the aim of putting an end to the chaos among the different intelligence organizations and to provide a systematic and centralized approach to carrying out intelligence activities. The MEH's objectives were to protect national security, prevent separatist activities, and follow the activities of foreign nations focused in particular on the Middle East.

The MEH survived until July 1965, when the Turkish Grand National Assembly passed Law 644, under which the name of the organization was changed to Milli Istihbarat Teskilati (MIT; National Intelligence Organization). The same law also provided for the control of the organization by an undersecretary who would be subordinate only to the prime minister in the fulfillment of duties defined under the law. Known as the MIT, the organization continued to carry out its duties for about 19 years under the provisions of Law 644.

However, rapidly changing conditions and new developments created the need for new legal arrangements. To that end, Law 2937 was passed on 1 November 1983 and put into effect as of 1 January 1984. In accordance with Law 2937, the MIT is in charge of collecting nationwide security intelligence from internal and external sources on existing and potential threats against territorial and national integrity, such as acts and movements of subversive or separatist elements, activities of foreign intelligence organizations in Turkey, and the proliferation of weapons of mass destruction, either for terrorist or ideological purposes. The MIT is also in charge of counterintelligence and signals intelligence (SIGINT) activities. In addition, intelligence is collected about organized crime, such as drug trafficking and money laundering.

The Ministry of Interior directs the National Police and several special commando units, including the Gendarmerie, a special commando unit of the police. This is the main counterterrorist unit, and it is particularly concerned with activities of Kurdish separatist organizations. It has three Special Forces companies and is specialized in antiterrorist operations, hostage rescue, and antihijacking, as well as riot control. In times of war, the Gendarmerie falls under military command with separate military intelligence units of the army, navy, and air force. *See also* ARAB SPIES IN OTTOMAN SERVICE; BEK, AZIZ; ÖCALAN'S CAPTURE;OTTOMAN EMPIRE INTELLIGENCE; TURKISH HIZBALLAH; TURKISH SPY SATELLITES.

TURKISH SPY SATELLITES. Turkey's air force has plans to spend at least $200 million to buy an electro-optical reconnaissance satellite and launch it into orbit by 2011. Turkey is a North Atlantic Treaty Organization member and has some access to information from U.S. satellites. Moreover, Turkey can also buy imagery on the open market from Spot Image, DigitalGlobe, or other suppliers. Nevertheless, the Turkish government decided that it would acquire its own satellite so as to be able to keep track of activities throughout the region. Space-based observation is one important way that it can keep track of activities in places like Armenia, Iraq, or the Aegean Sea, where Turkey's national security interests are at stake.

Western intelligence agencies assess that for $200 million it is impossible to buy sophisticated pointing, maneuvering, and field-of-view technology. Effective space-based reconnaissance, even for a medium-sized power, depends on a minimum level of space situational awareness. Not only do they need to know exactly where their satellite is at all times, they also need to be able to precisely control where its sensors are pointing. These specifications require much larger budgets and one or more large ground stations. However, because Turkey needs to use the satellites only for regional monitoring, it does not require the expensive relay systems used by the United States and (probably) other global powers.

Turksat, the government-owned civilian corporation, owns and operates three Alcatel-built satellites and has a fourth under construction. The satellites provide direct broadcast and other communications services to Turkey and Central Asia, where Turkey has significant interests. These communication services have given the Turkish-speaking people in Central Asia access to the Turkish media and have helped Ankara compete for cultural, economic, and political influence against the other major regional powers, such as Russia, Iran, Pakistan, India, and China.

The military reconnaissance program, as defined by the Turkish Ministry of Defense, will probably not contribute much, if anything, to achieving information from these countries but will instead concentrate on taking pictures of neighboring states that directly border on Turkey. For this purpose of legitimate espionage, Turkey needs experienced teams of imagery interpreters, without whom the most expensive satellite information is useless. With this goal in mind, the Turkish government has been dispatching Turkish experts since the turn of the 21st century to the European Union Satellite Centre (EUSC) in Torrejón,

Spain. There they receive training in satellite imagery interpretation and management, with the expectation that Turkey will have a good-sized cadre of experts by the time the first Turkish imaging satellite is launched in 2011. Turkey is already buying imagery from commercial sources and building the imagery archive that is indispensable to making real use of satellite reconnaissance.

In addition, the British Surrey Satellite Technology Ltd. (SSTL) developed an enhanced microsatellite for Turkey, called the BILSAT-1, during a know-how and technology transfer program for the Information Technologies and Electronics Research Institute (BILTEN) of Turkey. BILTENs main goals for the BILSAT-1 program are to acquire the knowledge and expertise necessary for manufacturing small satellites. The BILSAT-1 program includes the satellite, a mission control station in Ankara, and hands-on training in Surrey for a team of BILTEN engineers. SSTL also acted as prime contractor in Ankara for the design and construction of a satellite manufacturing facility, laboratories, and clean rooms. The BILSAT spacecraft carries payloads for Earth remote sensing and spacecraft technology demonstration. *See also* TURKISH INTELLIGENCE.

– U –

U.S. INTELLIGENCE DURING THE SIX DAYS' WAR. The Central Intelligence Agency (CIA) played a critical role in analyzing the crisis in Arab–Israeli relations both before and during the 1967 Six Days' War. On the morning of 23 May 1967, President Lyndon B. Johnson assigned the Director of the Central Intelligence Agency (DCI) Richard McGarrah Helms the task of assessing the increasingly volatile Middle East situation. This took place the day after Egypt closed the Gulf of Aqaba, which is Israel's only access to the Red Sea. By lunchtime of 23 May, the DCI had submitted two memoranda—"United States Knowledge of Egyptian Alert" and "Overall Arab and Israeli Military Capabilities"—and added a Situation Report (SITREP) to President Johnson. The second memorandum was the crucial one, predicting that Israel could successfully defend itself against simultaneous Arab attacks on all fronts or at least hold its own on three fronts while mounting a major offensive on the fourth.

Two days later, Tel-Aviv confused this clear intelligence picture by submitting a **Mossad** assessment to Washington, claiming that the Israeli forces were poorly equipped to take on the Soviet-backed Arab military. The Office of National Estimates was instructed by Helms to prepare an appraisal of the Mossad assessment, which was subsequently not judged to be a serious estimate of the sort they would submit to their own high officials. Rather, it was considered to be a political maneuver designed to sway American foreign policy toward providing more military supplies, making more public commitments to Israel, and exerting more pressure on Egyptian President Gamal Abdel Nasser. They further concluded in this appraisal that the Soviets were bent on avoiding their own military involvement while attempting to give the United States a bad name among the Arabs by identifying it with Israel. Indeed, the Soviet Union probably lacked the ability to openly help the Arabs and likely would not have done so in any case for fear of retribution from the United States.

At Helms's request, the CIA issued a paper on 24 May 1967 entitled "Military Capabilities of Israel and the Arab States" that predicted the outcome of the war in detail, even as far as the day it would end. In another memorandum issued the same day, the Office of National Estimates concluded that Moscow would not intervene with its own forces to save the Arabs from defeat. One senior CIA analyst who helped write these papers later remarked that the intelligence community had rarely spoken with such clarity and unanimity.

Based on these assessments, President Johnson decided against airlifting special military supplies to Israel or even publicly supporting the war effort. Having answered the crucial question of how the war would end, Helms was also able to warn the president about when it would begin. According to several published accounts, Helms met on 1 June with a senior Israeli official who hinted that Israel could no longer afford to exercise restraint in response to pressure from the United States at the expense of preserving the element of surprise. The following day, Helms wrote a confidential letter to President Johnson warning that Israel was expected to start a war in the coming few days. In addition, it was clearly understood that although Israel expected U.S. diplomatic backing and the delivery of weapons already agreed upon, it would request no additional support and did not expect to receive any.

On 5 June 1967, when Israel launched its attack, President Johnson was gratified that the CIA analyses and the warning from Helms allowed him to inform congressional leaders that he had been expecting Israel's move. The war was brief. On 10 June 1967, as an Israeli victory was on the horizon, the White House received a message from the Kremlin that necessary actions would have to be taken if the Israelis did not halt their advance across the Golan Heights. In an attempt to avoid a confrontation of the two superpowers, President Johnson dispatched the Sixth Fleet to the eastern Mediterranean, thereby conveying American resolve without backing the Soviets into a corner. Moscow got the message, and the announcement of a cease-fire later that day restored a semblance of peace to the region.

The CIA's timely and accurate intelligence prior to and during the 1967 war was considered a triumph, and its analytical achievement brought short-term political benefits for both Helms and the agency. The evidence had been on the CIA's side, as Israel could not prove its case that it would be overcome by the Arab armies. The CIA had presented information and assessments regarding the likely outcome of the conflict if the United States were to stay out of it. Analysts did not have to present vague medium- or long-term predictions that could go wrong because of unforeseen events. Rather, they had hard data with which to work, including military statistics and reliable information on weapons systems. In this way, Helms fulfilled what he regarded as perhaps his greatest responsibility as director of the CIA, namely to present the facts objectively and stay out of policy discussions. *See also* SOVIET CONCEPT.

U.S. INTELLIGENCE IN IRAN. Since the days of the Iranian Revolution in 1979 and under the ayatollah's regime, the U.S. intelligence community has had difficulty obtaining sufficient intelligence about Iran. The Central Intelligence Agency and other intelligence services do not have the ability to gather essential information in order to be able to make judgments regarding Iran's intentions, its nuclear program, and its involvement with **terrorism**. This lack of ability places the United States time and again in a compromising position in the region.

The U.S. intelligence community failed to provide the nation's leadership with adequate information about **Iran's nuclear weapons program**, and its potential chemical and biological weapon programs, thus, forcing the government to make decisions based on assumptions and surmise. All they know is that Iran openly supports and sponsors the **Hizballah** in Lebanon, and to a lesser extent, certain components within the Palestinian National Authority. There is also some evidence of Iranian involvement in Chechnya, but that is a Russian problem.

The reason for the enormous difficulty to obtain such information lies in the fact that since the Khomeini revolution and cessation of the diplomatic relations between Iran and several Western countries, and the strict inner monitoring of Iranian citizens, the West—and the United States in particular—has been unable to activate local agents in Iran, and all they can rely on is information obtained by spy satellites.

The limited human intelligence the United States has access to comes from exile Iranians residing in the United States, mainly in California; Iranian opposition circles; and friendly foreign intelligence communities, such as Israeli and German intelligence sources. The inspectors of the International Atomic Energy Agency may have been another source but all the above-mentioned are by far insufficient to learn about inner moves and developments in Iran. The question is, how reliable is the official information presented by Iran's media and representatives abroad? For the time being, it is difficult to assess. *See also* IRANIAN BIOLOGICAL WEAPONS PROGRAM; IRANIAN CHEMICAL WEAPONS PROGRAM; IRANIAN INTELLIGENCE; OPERATION EAGLE CLAW; OPERATION TPAJAX; ROOSEVELT, KERMIT.

U.S. PROPAGANDA IN IRAQ. The use of psychological warfare in Iraq by the United States came into its own during **Operation Desert Storm** in January 1991. This propaganda campaign started earlier, in December 1990, when pairs of leaflets—one warning of an impending raid and the second warning of further destruction following a bombing campaign—were prepared to threaten specific Iraqi frontline infantry divisions. The Fourth Psychological Warfare Group, based in Fort Bragg, North Carolina, designed more than 100 leaflets during the months of buildup and ground battle, with many images transmitted via satellite to be printed in Saudi Arabia or Turkey. Starting with black-and-white line drawings, they progressed to more impressive and effective four-color leaflets carrying a message of soldiers surrendering with pride, without raising their hands. Roughly a dozen styles of surrender leaflets are thought to have influenced some of the 85,000 surrendering Iraqi soldiers who fled southward to surrender due to the bombing. Thus, the propaganda campaign had the intended impact during the first **Gulf War**.

In 1998, Operation Desert Fox, a four-day attack on Iraq, was conducted by the United States and Great Britain after its refusal to allow United Nations inspectors to search for evidence of weapons of mass destruction. Four leaflets depicted scenes of destruction from Operation Desert Storm, such as destroyed vehicles left along the "highway of death," while the message warned against resisting the allied forces.

In December 2002, a new psychological warfare operation was started, using the same EC-130 aircraft to drop hundreds of thousands of leaflets advertising new radio broadcasts identified as Information Radio. Initially the station was broadcasting for five hours every evening, with programming including both Arabic and English pop music. In the beginning of March 2003, the broadcast hours of Information Radio were expanded by using mobile transmitters on the ground and others on board naval ships.

At the same time, a significant change of emphasis took place in the broadcasts of Information Radio. Until that time, the messages transmitted by the station had been aimed primarily at members of the Iraqi military and government officials. Now the leaflets dropped on Iraq urged ordinary Iraqis to tune in to Information Radio for important news and information about the coalition's support for the Iraqi people, as well as reactions of the international community to actions taken by Saddam Hussein's regime. The leaflets emphasized that the coalition wished no harm to fall on innocent Iraqi civilians and warned them to stay in their homes away from military targets for their own safety.

On 21 March 2003, two days after the United States imposed a 48-hour deadline for Saddam Hussein to exile himself from Iraq, the coalition launched **Operation Iraqi Freedom** with a "shock and awe" attack. Aircrews targeted Baghdad, Mosul, Basra, Tikrit, and Kirkuk with 1,500 bombs and more than two million propaganda leaflets. The messages were a mix of warnings urging Iraqi soldiers to surrender and instructions about how to do so, alongside offers of rewards to Iraqi families for helping downed coalition pilots. When the coalition aircraft dropped more leaflets on 23 March 2003, the messages were more threatening, promising destruction to the Medina Republican Guard Division.

These leaflet themes—safe-conduct passes, rewards, threats—have all been used repeatedly since **World War II** in wartime and peacetime psychological operations, though the content of most leaflets remained classified until the conflicts had ended. During Operation Iraqi Freedom, however, the U.S. Army amazed observers by posting half of its new leaflets (in Arabic and English) on the Central Command Website, giving the public unprecedented access to American propaganda.

On 10 April 2003, the day after the fall of Baghdad, the press office of 10 Downing Street announced that a new television service, Towards Freedom Television, would be launched that day and would operate five hours a day on the former Iraqi television frequencies, with four hours a day originating in the United States and one hour contributed by Great Britain. The production team was set up and the first program produced in just eight days. Starting with messages to the Iraqi people from President George W. Bush and British Prime Minister Tony Blair, the first broadcast was said to include an interview with an opposition group, a report on humanitarian aid, and a feature on Iraqi arts. The content of the new television service was agreed upon following discussions by Iraqi journalists with the Iraqi exile community in London. The service was initially available to people in central Iraq, including Baghdad, before being transmitted nationwide on frequencies previously used by Iraqi television. Leaflets were dropped to inform Iraqis of the new station, and it was also publicized on Information Radio. According to a British foreign office spokesman, the service will last until free and open media can be established.

U.S. INTELLIGENCE IN SYRIA. *See* OPERATION WAPPEN.

U.S.–RUSSIAN COOPERATION IN AFGHANISTAN. On 11 September 2001, about three hours after the terrorist attacks in New York and in Washington, Russian President Vladimir Putin called Air Force 1, which was flying President George W. Bush from Louisiana to Omaha, Nebraska, and suggested that it was time the two countries and their two main spying organizations cease their intelligence war and begin to cooperate in the war against terror. George Bush accepted the offer and for the first time, the Russians and Americans agreed to put their intelligence war of over half a century behind them and open a new page in their relationship. As part of this historical conversation, Putin offered to make available all their files about Muslim **terrorism** as well as all the information in their possession about Osama bin-Laden's electronic systems and codes. Two days after a second phone conversation between Bush and Putin on 23 September 2001, General Sergei Nikolaevich Lebedev arrived in Washington at the head of a large Russian delegation of spying, communication, and code systems experts.

Since then, Lebedev's men have been operating a big part of the electronic spying systems for the Americans inside and outside Afghanistan and the countries in Central Asia. The first main political intelligence directorate of the Sluzhba Vneshney Razvedki (SVR; Foreign Intelligence Service), which is the successor of the Komitet Gosudarstvennoy Bezopasnosti (KGB), now has two electronic spying bases in Afghanistan, with one in the capital of Kabul.

UNITED ARAB EMIRATES INTERNAL SECURITY. The United Arab Emirates (UAE) is a federation of seven emirates established in 1971, with Abu Dhabi as the largest. The two emirates with the biggest petroleum production enterprises are Abu Dhabi and Dubai, in addition to being growing financial and commercial centers in the Persian Gulf. The UAE has a free-market economy based on oil and gas production, trade, and light manufacturing. The economy is heavily dependent on foreign workers, who constitute at least 80 percent of the general population.

None of the emirates has any democratically elected institutions or political leaders. Traditional rule in the emirates generally has been patriarchal, with political allegiance defined in terms of loyalty to the tribal leaders. In accordance with the 1971 constitution, the seven emirate rulers constitute a Federal Supreme Council, the highest legislative and executive body, which selects a president and vice president. The president in turn appoints the prime minister and cabinet, which manages the federation on a day-to-day basis.

While all internal security organs of the emirates are theoretically branches of one federal organization, in practice they operate with substantial independence. Each emirate maintains its own independent police force and in effect retains control over its own internal security. The federal government asserts primacy in matters of foreign and defense policy, as well as some aspects of internal security. The judiciary generally is independent, but its decisions are subject to review by the political leadership.

USS *LIBERTY* ATTACK. The events that led to the Israeli Air Force (IAF) attack on the intelligence ship USS *Liberty* on 8 June 1967 have never been fully explained. The attack on the *Liberty* occurred during the days of tension just prior to the outbreak of the Six Days' War. Official reports by both the Israelis and the U.S. Navy declared it accidental as a case of mistaken identity. The navy ship was attacked with rockets, cannon fire, and torpedoes while in international waters off the town of El Arish in the Sinai Desert. Of its 295 crewmen, 34 were killed and 171 injured. The *Liberty* was a converted former **World War II** ship that was supposedly being used for scientific investigation, but was actually an offshore electronic eavesdropper. The mission of the USS *Liberty* was highly secret because spying on other nations by intercepting radio signals (SIGINT) was strictly forbidden at that time. Despite its thousands of employees, the SIGINT-handling National Security Agency (NSA) was so secret in 1967 that officially it did not exist. In the intelligence community, its initials were said to stand for No Such Agency.

On 23 May 1967, the ship was ordered to the eastern Mediterranean to monitor the deteriorating relations between Israel and Egypt. However, while the *Liberty* was still on its way, Israel launched its air force against Egyptian airfields, destroying almost all of its air power in about 80 minutes on 5 June 1967. When informed that war had broken out, the U.S. Navy ordered all its vessels to stay at least 100 miles from the war zone. The NSA and the Joint Chiefs of Staff followed that up with at least five similar orders directed specifically to the *Liberty* in order to inform them that they were in a war zone. However, the messages were delayed for 16 hours and never received.

The *Liberty* took station just outside Egypt's 12-mile territorial limit off the Gaza Strip at dawn on 8 June 1967. Israeli planes circled the ship several times at close range. Then, shortly before 2 P.M., a flight of Israeli Mirage jets approached the ship in a typical attack pattern. The officer on duty on board shouted a warning, but before he could sound the ship's general alarm, the planes attacked the ship with rockets and cannon fire. The attack shattered virtually all of the ship's 45 communications antennae, and it took technicians more than 10 minutes to send an SOS to the U.S. Sixth Fleet stationed 500 miles to the north. A radio operator on the USS *Saratoga* heard the message that the *Liberty* was under attack but demanded an authentication code, which had been destroyed by the first shots.

Israeli officials maintained that they had investigated the *Liberty* earlier and that a plotting error had convinced them that the ship was traveling at the rate of a serious warship. The Israeli Navy then summoned the air force to intercept the mysterious vessel. When the U.S. Navy finally heard that the *Liberty* was under attack, it was assumed that the attackers were Egyptian. Strike aircraft were launched from the carrier *Saratoga* and elsewhere. There is much debate about whether the *Liberty*'s U.S. flag was visible, whether the Israeli jets were unmarked, and whether the Israeli pilots could have mistaken the *Liberty* for the Egyptian *El Quseir*. The debates will probably never be resolved.

The ship's casualties were vastly underreported initially. The Pentagon censored all reports, and survivors were threatened with court-martial or prison if they discussed the incident. Israel eventually paid $6 million in restitution to the survivors of those killed and another $6 million to the U.S. government to end litigation.

– W –

WAVELL, ARCHIBALD PERCIVAL (1883–1950). Following his father's career choice, Field Marshal Archibald Percival Wavell was an officer in the British Army and one of Great Britain's great military leaders. He joined the Black Watch in 1900 and fought in the second Boer War. In 1903, he was transferred to India. In 1911, Wavell spent a year as a military observer with the Russian Army.

Wavell was working as a staff officer when **World War I** broke out. He was transferred to a combat unit and was wounded in the Battle of Ypres in 1915, losing an eye. Following his recovery, he was assigned as a liaison officer to the Russian Army in 1916, this time stationed in Turkey. In 1918, he was transferred to Field Marshal Edmund Allenby's staff in Palestine. In August 1939, 56-year-old Wavell was appointed commander of the newly created Middle East Command, where he served with great distinction in the Middle East, Africa, and Asia. However, "the Chief," as he was popularly known, faced colossal difficulties in controlling simultaneous campaigns that eventually encompassed nine countries on three continents. In January 1941, Wavell created a unit called **A Force**, which was dedicated to counterintelligence and strategic deception, and had a number of achievements in North African campaigns. *See also* CAMILLA PLAN; CLARKE, DUDLEY WRANGEL.

WILBER, DONALD N. In 1953, Donald N. Wilber was one of the key planners of **Operation TPAJAX**, the Central Intelligence Agency's (CIA) operation overthrowing Iran's Prime Minister Muhammad Mossadeq in 1953. According to his background, Wilber was an expert in Persian architecture. As one of the leading planners, he asserted in his memoirs (published in 1986) that the Iran coup was different from later CIA efforts. The CIA planners of Operation TPAJAX stirred up considerable unrest in Iran, giving the Iranians a clear choice between instability and supporting the shah. The move to oust Prime Minister Mossadeq gained substantial popular support in the inner circles of the U.S. administration and in the CIA.

Wilber's memoirs were heavily censored by the CIA, but in one way or another he succeeded in describing his role, together with **Kermit Roosevelt**, in planning the 1953 coup in Iran.

WILENSKY, NAHUM. *See* JEWISH AGENCY IN EGYPT.

WINGATE, FRANCIS REGINALD (1861–1953). Born at Broadfield, Renfrewshire (Scotland), Sir Francis Reginald Wingate was the British general and imperial administrator, principal founder, and governor-general (1899–1916) of the Anglo–Egyptian Sudan. In 1880, Wingate was commissioned in the British artillery. In 1883, he was assigned to the Egyptian Army. In 1889 Sir Francis became director of British military intelligence in Egypt.

Francis Wingate mastered the Arabic language and as an intelligence officer in Egypt he was engaged in interrogating prisoners of war and refugees from Sudan. He also analyzed documents captured from the Sudanese dervishes. This gave the British army an advantage in the **battle of Omdurman** (2 September 1898). In 1899 Wingate succeeded Horatio Kitchener as governor-general of Sudan and *sirdar* (commander in chief) of the Egyptian Army. He served in this position until 1916 and then he was appointed as the British high-commissioner in Egypt.

WINGATE, ORD CHARLES (1903–1944). He was born in India and educated at Charterhouse School and the Royal Military Academy at Woolwich. Wingate served in the Sudan from 1928 to 1933 and then was dispatched as special adviser to the Jewish community police in Palestine. During the **Great Arab Revolt** (1935–1939) Wingate, as an intelligence officer, trained the Special Night Squads of the Jewish community in Palestine. These special squads were known later as Palmach. In 1940, Ord Wingate was sent to advise the Ethiopian patriots to form Gideon Force and became the trusted adviser to Emperor Haile Selassie.

WORLD WAR I. *See* ALMÁSY, LÁSZLÓ; *ARAB BULLETIN*; ARAB LEGION; ARAB REVOLT; BATTLE OF BEERSHEBA; BATTLE OF GALLIPOLI; BATTLE OF MEGIDDO II; BATTLE OF RO-MANI; BATTLES OF GAZA; BEK, AZIZ; BELL, GERTRUDE MARGARET LOWTHIAN; BRITISH INTELLIGENCE IN EGYPT AND SUDAN; BRITISH INTELLIGENCE IN MESOPOTAMIA; BRITISH INTELLIGENCE IN THE PALESTINE CAMPAIGN OF 1914–1918; CLAYTON, GILBERT; EIGHTH CORPS; GERMAN INTELLIGENCE IN THE MIDDLE EAST; HIJAZ OPERATION; HOGARTH, DAVID GEORGE; *INTELLIGENCE AND ESPIONAGE IN LEBANON, SYRIA, AND PALESTINE DURING THE WORLD WAR*; ISRAELI INTELLIGENCE; ITALIAN INTELLIGENCE IN PALESTINE; JEWISH INTELLIGENCE IN PALESTINE; LAWRENCE, THOMAS EDWARD; MEINERTZHAGEN, RICHARD; NILI; OTTOMAN EMPIRE INTELLIGENCE; PIRIE-GORDON, HARRY; TURKISH INTELLIGENCE; WAVELL, ARCHIBALD PERCIVAL; WYMAN, BURY GEORGE.

WORLD WAR II. *See* A FORCE; ALMÁSY, LÁSZLÓ; BATTLE OF CAPE MATAPAN; BATTLE OF GAZALA; BRITISH INTELLI-

GENCE IN EGYPT AND SUDAN; BRITISH INTELLIGENCE IN WESTERN DESERT BATTLES; CAMILLA PLAN; CICERO AFFAIR; CLARKE, DUDLEY WRANGEL; EPPLER, JOHANNES; FRENCH INTELLIGENCE IN THE MIDDLE EAST; GERMAN INTELLIGENCE IN PALESTINE; GERMAN INTELLIGENCE IN THE MIDDLE EAST; GLUBB PASHA; GREAT ARAB REVOLT; HIJAZ OPERATION; HORESH, JOSHUA; *INTELLIGENCE AND ESPIONAGE IN LEBANON, SYRIA, AND PALESTINE DURING THE WORLD WAR*; ISMAIL, ALI AHMAD; ISRAELI INTELLIGENCE; JEWISH INTELLIGENCE IN PALESTINE; MASKELYNE, JASPER; MEINERTZHAGEN, RICHARD; OPERATION BERTRAM; OPERATION COMPASS; OPERATION PRAYING MANTIS; U.S. PROPAGANDA IN IRAQ.

WYMAN, BURY GEORGE (1874–1920). Bury George Wyman began his scientific and intelligence career on 1895, when he joined one of the rebellious tribes in Morocco. A year later he arrived in the southern part of the Arabian Peninsula and served in the British protectorate of Aden, combining his archeological work with an intelligence survey of the area. He was a member of the Ottoman–British committee that determined the borders of the region. He served in Aden for a couple of years, then went to Somalia for a zoological survey of the area, and returned to Aden, from where he conducted a series of journeys in parts no European had ever been to before disguised as a Bedouin.

On 1912, Wyman went to Yemen, and traveled all over the country presenting himself as a British scholar, interested in the flora and fauna of the land. In reality he was working for British interests. When **World War I** broke out, he went to Cairo and joined British intelligence. He was a member in the team that was set up to fight the Islamic propaganda promoted by the Ottomans, and later was appointed as political officer of the Royal Navy squadron that sailed on the Red Sea, and participated in the preliminary contacts with Sharif Hussein bin-Ali. Toward the end of 1916, he was sent to Damascus. His method was similar to the one he used in the Arabian Peninsula; he spoke the language and could disguise himself as a local sheik.

The Turks were chasing him, and once even managed to kill him—or so they thought. Apparently, they killed someone else, as Wyman lived until 1920, and wrote a book on Pan Islam in 1919. The interesting information in this book refers to Ahmed Jamal Pasha's resentment of the Germans, who were Turkey's alleys. The book describes the events that led to the German pressure on Istanbul to remove the governor of Syria, Ahmed Jamal Pasha.

– Y –

YEMEN CIVIL WAR. During the Yemen Civil War (1962–1965), Great Britain was engaged in covert operations in support of the Royalist forces that were fighting the Egyptian-backed Republican regime, which had seized power in Yemen in September 1962. Covert action was regarded by the British as a legitimate tool for protecting the newly formed South Arabian Federation against the aggression of President Gamal Abdel Nasser. The British involvement in the Yemen Civil War was mainly in providing cash and equipment for Royalist forces, with the aim of keeping the Republican government and its Egyptian backers so preoccupied with a civil war of attrition that Nasser in particular would be frustrated in his attempts to take over southern Arabia. The Royalists were supported not only through supplies of arms and cash but also through officially sanctioned cross-border counterterrorist operations and through the activities of mercenaries, some of whom were British.

The Foreign Office and Sir Dick White, then "C" of SIS, were very reluctant to be dragged into the conflict. White felt that the SIS should avoid entanglements beyond the arena of Cold War competition in Europe, while the Foreign Office favored the approach of proactive cooperation with President Nasser in the hope of facilitating Britain's achievement of peaceful decolonization in southern Arabia. As part of this strategy, the Foreign Office strongly supported giving early recognition to the Republican regime in Yemen. Despite this pressure, British covert action in the Yemen Civil War prevailed and was successful in imposing a war of attrition upon Nasser while securing the future stability of the Federation of South Arabia.

YOM KIPPUR WAR DECEPTION. The 1973 Yom Kippur War, also known as the October War, started on 6 October 1973, when Egyptian and Syrian forces launched a surprise joint attack on Israel. The Egyptian forces surprised the Israeli forces by attacking across the Suez Canal, allowing them to gain a significant foothold in the Sinai Desert. At the same time, the Syrian forces penetrated the Golan Heights and came within 10 kilometers of securing a key bridge that would have left northern Israel vulnerable to attack. These offensive campaigns caught the Israelis off guard and achieved strategic as well as tactical surprise before the IDF could fully mobilize. The conflict raged for almost three weeks before the United Nations intervened, imposing a cease-fire on 24 October 1973 prior to any clear-cut military resolution on the battlefield.

Despite Israel's sophisticated and renowned intelligence-gathering apparatus, the Arab forces achieved total surprise on the Suez front and near complete surprise on the Golan front. Their deception operation was a shrewd combination of political and military maneuvering, directly contributing to their initial successes. The success of the Arab deception plan was due in large part to incorrect analysis rather than failure in intelligence gathering by the Israelis. The elaborate deception plan convinced senior Israeli officers, including Major General Eliyahu Zeira, the chief of **Israeli intelligence**, that Egypt and Syria would not attack and were only conducting routine defensive training exercises.

Israeli intelligence gathered many indications in the spring of 1973 that war was probable, including brigade-size movements up to the canal and extensive modifications and improvements to defensive works and roads on the West Bank. Major General Eliyahu Zeira disagreed with the analysis but briefed Lieutenant General Elazar, who concurred with the assessment of war and recommended preparatory measures to the Golda Meir government. Mobilization was ordered in May, but this judgment turned out to be incorrect and costly, both financially and politically. Over the next four months, the Arabs stepped up their deception operation with monthly movements of men, equipment, and supplies up to the borders in combat formations as large as divisions. Their exercises portraying the intent to cross the canal were repeated until the Israelis became conditioned to them. In September alone, the Egyptian formations moved up to the canal six times and then withdrew. Thus, preparations for defensive operations continued as normal and were heavily emphasized in military radio traffic. False reports of faulty missile systems and the like were exchanged on open radio in order to deceive Israeli signals intelligence operatives. The Egyptian Navy made open arrangements for two submarines to receive repairs in Pakistan so as to deceive the Israelis into believing they were operationally unready. Egypt also made public announcements that naval forces had performed poorly during exercises and would undergo further training in laying mines. In fact, the mines laid during this subsequent exercise were real and actually used as part of the blockade. A flood of reports on Egypt's economic instability and its inability to afford another war were also made public, stressing the importance of a political solution to regaining the Sinai. Articles were planted in newspapers quoting Anwar Sadat and Hafez al-Assad, alternating between strong condemnation and conciliatory speeches to keep the Israelis off balance.

Despite the deception operations, tactical observers reported with increasing urgency that the Egyptian buildup and activity were significant, with elite commando units detected along the front. Their reports caused concern but no action. Egyptian forces exploited these vulnerabilities and timed the attack to occur on Yom Kippur, the Jewish Day of Atonement, when only a skeletal Israeli force would be deployed and any response would be slower. The Arab deception plan was so successful that as late as the morning of 5 October 1973, Major General Zeira advised Lieutenant General Elazar that the risk of attack was low. Not until the morning of 6 October 1973, the day of the attack, did the general headquarters of the Israel Defense Forces inform its reserve commanders that war was imminent and give orders to begin mobilization. Even after Israeli troops were belatedly placed on high alert, Prime Minister Meir made the decision not to preemptively attack the Arab forces.

Coordination between Egypt and Syria had been established for a long time prior to the attack, with a well-practiced mobilization of reserves ensuring that the maximum number of forces would be ready for zero hour. The Arabs conducted extraordinary operations security, with no more than a dozen people on each side aware of the exact plans. Most troops and officers were informed no more than two hours before the attack was launched. As a result of their deception efforts, the Arab forces quickly and decisively overwhelmed Israeli forces in the early stages of the war. Although the Arab forces won an initial advantage, the Israelis managed to recover, fighting in two separate theaters of operation. The Israelis eventually scored a tactical victory against the Syrians and the Egyptians, but the victory came at a very high cost in the loss of men and equipment. *See also* ASHRAF, MARWAN; EGYPTIAN INTELLIGENCE; SYRIAN INTELLIGENCE.

– Z –

ZADMA, ABDALLAH SALEM. Zadma is number three in the Libyan External Security Organization (ESO). In September 1998, a French court issued an international warrant for the arrest of Zadma for his role in the air sabotage of the French DC-10 aircraft en route from Brazzaville, Congo, to Paris via Chad. The aircraft was blown up over Niger. All 171 passengers were killed. *See also* LIBYAN INTELLIGENCE.

ZIBIN, FANNAR. Fannar Zibin al-Hasan served as the commander of **Iraq's Special Security Organization** (SSO) during the 1991 **Operation Desert Storm**. He is Saddam Hussein's cousin. **Qusay Saddam Hussein** served as Zibin's deputy. *See also* IRAQI DIRECTORATE OF GENERAL MILITARY INTELLIGENCE; IRAQI DIRECTORATE OF GENERAL SECURITY; IRAQI INTELLIGENCE.

Bibliography

I. INTRODUCTION

Most of the countries in the Middle East are not democracies and one of our first assumptions was that not much has been published about the intelligence issues of the countries in this region. However, after we began the study and the writing of this book, we discovered that there are a lot of printed and electronic publications about intelligence issues of the Middle East. Most of the publications are in English, although there are publications published in Hebrew and in Arabic as well.

Because of the numerous publications, it became easier to arrange the titles according to geographic areas in the region and according to specific countries and specific issues.

Many of the intelligence communities of the Middle East have websites. Links to their websites can be found in the third part of this bibliography.

II. PRINTED RESOURCES

1. General Survey of Arab Intelligence

Caroz, Ya'akov. *The Arab Secret Service.* London: Corgi, 1978.

Eickelman, D. "Intelligence in an Arab State." In *Comparing Foreign Intelligence: The U.S., the USSR, the U.K., and the Third World,* ed. Roy Godson, 89–114. Washington, D.C.: Pergamon-Brassey's International Defense, 1988.

Richelson, Jeffrey T. *Foreign Intelligence Organizations.* Cambridge, Mass.: Ballinger, 1988.

Tauber, Eliezer. *Secret Societies and Resistance Movements in the Fertile Crescent 1875–1920.* Ramat-Gan: Bar Ilan University, 1994. (Hebrew)

2. Foreign Intelligence in the Middle East

2.1. British Intelligence in the Middle East

2.1.1. World War I

Bidwell, Robin, ed. *The* Arab Bulletin: *Bulletin of the Arab Bureau in Cairo, 1916–1919.* Oxford: Archive Editions reprint, 1986.

Capstick, Peter Hathaway. *Warrior: The Legend of Colonel Richard Meinertzhagen.* New York: St. Martin's Press, 1997.

Cocker, Mark. *Richard Meinertzhagen: Soldier, Scientist and Spy.* London: Secker & Warburg, 1989.

Engle, Anita. *The NILI Spies.* Jerusalem: Phoenix Publications, 1989

Garfield, Brian. *The Meinertzhagen Mystery: The Life and Legend of a Colossal Fraud.* Dulles, Va.: Potomac Books, 2007.

Hopkirk, Peter. *On Secret Service East of Constantinople.* London: John Murray, 1994.

Lawrence, T. E. *Seven Pillars of Wisdom.* London: Jonathan Cape, 1935.

Lockman, J. N. *Meinertzhagen's Diary Ruse: False Entries on T. E. Lawrence.* Grand Rapids, Mich.: Cornerstone, 1995.

Lord, John. *Duty, Honor, Empire: The Life and Times of Colonel Richard Meinertzhagen.* New York: Random House, 1970. London: Hutchinson, 1971

Meinertzhagen, Richard. *Middle East Diary, 1917–1956.* New York: Thomas Yoseloff, 1960.

Mockaitis, Thomas R. *British Counterinsurgency 1919–60.* London: Macmillan. 1990.

Mohs, Paula. *British Intelligence and the Arab Revolt: The First Modern Intelligence War.* Series in Intelligence. London: Routledge, 2006.

Presland, John. *Deedes Bey: A Study of Sir Wyndham Deedes, 1883–1923.* London: Macmillan, 1942.

Popplewell, Richard J. "British Intelligence in Mesopotamia 1914–16." *Intelligence and National Security* 5, no. 2 (April 1990): 139–72.

Sheffy, Yigal. "British Intelligence and the Middle East, 1900–1918: How Much Do We Know?" *Intelligence and National Security* 17, no. 1 (Spring 2002): 33–52.

———. *British Intelligence in the Palestine Campaign, 1914–1918.* London: Frank Cass, 1997.

———. "Institutionalized Deception and Perception Reinforcement: Allenby's Campaigns in Palestine." *Intelligence and National Security* 5, no. 2 (April 1990): 173–236.

Thomas, Martin. *Empires of Intelligence: Security Services and Colonial Disorder after 1914.* Berkeley: University of California, 2007.

Verrier, Anthony. *Agents of Empire: Anglo–Zionist Intelligence Operations, 1915–1919; Brigadier Walter Gribbon, Aaron Aaronsohn and the NILI Ring.* Washington, D.C.: Brassey's, 1995.

Wallach, Janet, *Desert Queen: The Extraordinary Life of Gertrude Bell: Adventurer, Adviser to Kings, Ally of Lawrence of Arabia.* New York: Anchor/Doubleday, 1996

Weldon, L. B. *Hard Lying: Eastern Mediterranean, 1914–1919.* London: Herbert Jenkins, 1925.

Westrate, Bruce. *The Arab Bureau: British Policy in the Middle East, 1916–1920.* University Park: Pennsylvania State University Press, 1992.

Winstone, H. V. F. *Gertrude Bell.* London: Barzan, 2004.

———. *The Illicit Adventure: The Story of Political and Military Intelligence in the Middle East from 1898 to 1926.* London: Jonathan Cape, 1982.

2.1.2. Battles of World War I
2.1.2.1. Battle of Gallipoli

Haythornthwaite, Philip J. *Gallipoli 1915: Frontal Assault on Turkey.* Westport, Conn.: Praeger, 2004.
Travers, Timothy. *Gallipoli, 1915.* Stroud, Gloucestershire: Tempus, 2001.

2.1.2.2. Battles of Gaza

Grainger, John D. *The Battle for Palestine, 1917.* Warfare in History. Rochester, N.Y.: Boydell Press, 2006.

2.2. World War II

Aldrich, Richard J. "Soviet Intelligence, British Security and the End of the Red Orchestra: The Fate of Alexander Rado." *Intelligence and National Security* 6, no. 1 (January 1991): 196–218.
Arbogast, E. R. *Contribution of Intelligence to the Battles of Alam Halfa and El Alamein: August–November 1942, Final Report.* Newport, R.I.: Naval War College, 1993.
Atherton, Louise. *SOE Operations in Africa and the Middle East: A Guide to Newly Released Records in the Public Record Office.* London: PRO Publications, 1994.
Barkas, Geoffrey, and Natalie Barkas. *The Camouflage Story: From Aintree to Alamein.* London: Cassell, 1952.
Barkas, Geoffrey, and John Hutton. "Camouflage of Airfields in the Middle East, 1941–42." *R.A.F. Quarterly* 5, no. 2 (April 1953): 112–20.
———. "Camouflage of Middle East Airfields." *Military Review* 33, no. 10 (January 1954): 99–107.
Bazna, Elyesa, with Hans Nogly. *I Was Cicero.* New York: Harper & Row, 1962.
Chappell, F. R. *Wellington Wings: An RAF Intelligence Officer in the Western Desert.* Somerton, Somerset: Crecy Books, 1992.
Clarke, Dudley. *Seven Assignments.* London: Jonathan Cape, 1948.
Cox, Sebastian. "'The Difference between Black and White': Churchill, Imperial Politics, and Intelligence before the 1941 Crusader Offensive." *Intelligence and National Security* 9, no. 3 (July 1994): 405–47.
Denniston, Robin. *Churchill's Secret War: Diplomatic Decrypts, the Foreign Office and Turkey 1942–44.* London: Sutton, 1997.
Dovey, H. O. "Cheese." *Intelligence and National Security* 5, no. 3 (July 1990): 176–85.

——. "The Eighth Assignment, 1941–1942." *Intelligence and National Security* 11, no. 4 (October 1996): 672–95.

——. "The Eighth Assignment, 1943–1945." *Intelligence and National Security* 12, no. 2 (April 1997): 69–90.

——. "The False Going Map at Alam Halfa." *Intelligence and National Security* 4, no. 1 (January 1989): 165–68.

——. "The Intelligence War in Turkey. *Intelligence and National Security* 9, no. 1 (January 1994): 59–87.

——. "Maunsell and Mure." *Intelligence and National Security* 8, no. 1 (January 1993): 60–77.

——. "The Middle East Intelligence Centre." *Intelligence and National Security* 4, no. 4 (October 1989): 800–812.

——. "Operation Condor." *Intelligence and National Security* 4, no. 2 (April 1989): 357–73.

——. "Security in Syria, 1941–45." *Intelligence and National Security* 6, no. 2 (April 1991): 418–46.

Elliott, Nicholas. *Never Judge a Man by His Umbrella*. Salisbury: Michael Russell, 1991.

Eppler, John. *Operation Condor: Rommel's Spy*. London: Macdonald & Jane's, 1977.

Everett, H. W. "The Secret War in the Desert." *British Army Review* (December 1978): 66–68.

Ferris, John. "The British Army, Signals and Security in the Desert Campaign, 1940–42." *Intelligence and National Security* 5, no. 2 (April 1990): 255–91.

——. "The 'Usual Source': Signals Intelligence and Planning for the Eighth Army 'Crusader' Offensive, 1941." *Intelligence and National Security* 14, no. 1 (Spring 1999): 84–118.

Flicke, Wilhelm F. "The Lost Keys to El Alamein." *Studies in Intelligence* 3, no. 4 (Fall 1959): 73–80.

Funk, Arthur Layton. "The OSS in Algiers." In *The Secrets War: The Office of Strategic Services in World War II*, ed. George C. Chalou. Washington, D.C.: National Archives, 1992.

Gladman, Brad K. "Air Power and Intelligence in the Western Desert Campaign, 1940–43." *Intelligence and National Security* 13, no. 4 (Winter 1998): 144–62.

Gordon, John W. *The Other Desert War: British Special Forces in North Africa, 1940–1943*. Westport, Conn.: Greenwood, 1987.

Gossett, Renee P. *Conspiracy in Algiers, 1942–1943*. New York: Nation, 1945.

James, Malcolm. *Born of the Desert: With the SAS in North Africa*. London: Greenhill Books. 2001.

Keatts, Dorothy. "Footnote to Cicero." *Studies in Intelligence* 1, no. 4 (Fall 1957): 47–53.

Kelly, Saul. *The Lost Oasis: The Desert War and the Hunt for Zerzura*. New York: Westview, 2003.

———. "A Succession of Crises: SOE in the Middle East, 1940–45." *Intelligence and National Security* 20, no 1 (March 2005): 121–46.

Kennedy Shaw, W. B. *Long Range Desert Group*. Rev. ed. London: Greenhill, 2000.

Lloyd Owen, David. *Providence Their Guide: The Long Range Desert Group, 1940–1945*. Rev. ed. Barnsley, U.K.: Leo Cooper, 2000.

McKee, Alexander. *El Alamein: ULTRA and the Three Battles*. London: Souvenir Press, 1991.

Morgan, Mike. *Sting of the Scorpion: The Inside Story of the Long-Range Desert Group*. London: Sutton, 2004.

Mosley, Leonard. *The Cat and the Mice*. London: Barker, 1958.

Moyzisch, L. C. *Operation Cicero*. New York: Coward-McCann, 1950.

Mure, David. *Master of Deception: Tangled Webs in London and the Middle East*. London: Kimber, 1980.

———. *Practise to Deceive*. London: Kimber, 1977.

Piekalkiewicz, Janusz. *Rommel and the Secret War in North Africa 1941–1943: Secret Intelligence in the North African Campaign*. Trans. Fred Clemens. West Chester, Pa.: Schiffer, 1992.

Sansom, A. W. *I Spied Spies*. London: Harrap, 1965.

Slowikowski, Rygor. *In the Secret Service: The Lighting of the Torch*. London: Windrush, 1988.

Smith, Kevin D. "Coming into Its Own: The Contribution of Intelligence at the Battle of Alma Halfa." *Military Review* 82, no. 4 (July–August, 2002): 74–77.

Smyth, Denis. "Screening 'Torch': Allied Counter-Intelligence and the Spanish Threat to the Secrecy of the Allied Invasion of French North Africa in November 1942." *Intelligence and National Security* 4, no. 2 (April 1989): 335–56.

Thomas, Martin. "The Massingham Mission: SOE in French North Africa, 1941–1944." *Intelligence and National Security* 11, no. 4 (October 1996): 696–721.

Timpson, Alastair, and Andrew Gibson-Watt. *In Rommel's Backyard: A Memoir of the Long-Range Desert Group*. Barnsley, U.K.: Pen and Sword, 2000.

Vaughan, Hal. *FDR's 12 Apostles: The Spies Who Paved the Way for the Invasion of North Africa.* Guilford, Conn.: Lyons, 2006.

Wharton-Tigar, Edward, with A. J. Wilson. *Burning Bright: The Autobiography of Edward Wharton-Tigar.* Worcester Park, U.K.: Metal Bulletin Books, 1987.

Wires, Richard. *The Cicero Spy Affair: German Access to British Secrets in World War II.* Westport, Conn.: Praeger, 1999.

2.3. Superpowers' Intelligence in the Middle East during the Cold War

Aldrich, Richard J. "Intelligence, Anglo–American Relations and the Suez Crisis, 1956." *Intelligence and National Security* 9, no. 3 (July 1994): 544–54.

Caplan, Neil. *Futile Diplomacy: Operation Alpha and the Failure of Anglo–American Coercive Diplomacy in the Arab–Israeli Conflict 1954–1956.* Portland, Ore.: Frank Cass, 1997.

2.4. Italian Intelligence in the Middle East

Williams, Manueal. *Mussolini's Propaganda Abroad: Subversion in the Mediterranean and the Middle East, 1935–1940.* Studies in Intelligence. London: Routledge, 2006.

2.5. U.S. Intelligence in the Middle East

Cogan, Charles G. "From the Politics of Lying to the Farce at Suez: What the U.S. Knew. *Intelligence and National Security* 13 (Summer 1998): 100–122.

Riordan, Barrett J. "The Plowshare Program and Copeland's Suez Energy Deception." *International Journal of Intelligence and CounterIntelligence* 17, no. 1 (2004): 124–43.

3. Gulf States' Intelligence

3.1. General

Cordesman, Anthony H. *The Gulf and the Search for Strategic Stability: Saudi Arabia, the Military Balance in the Gulf, and Trends in the Arab-Israeli Military Balance.* Boulder, Colo.: Westview Press, 1984.

3.2. Bahraini Intelligence

Allen, Robin. "Bahrain Spy Chief Replaced." *Financial Times*, 20 February 1998, 8.

3.3. Omani Intelligence

Eickelman, Dale F., and M. G. Dennison, "Arabizing the Omani Intelligence Services: Clash of Cultures?" *International Journal of Intelligence and CounterIntelligence* 7, no. 1 (Spring 1994): 1–28.

4. Egyptian Intelligence

Bar-Joseph, Uri. "Israel Caught Unawares: Egypt's Sinai Surprise of 1960." *International Journal of Intelligence and CounterIntelligence* 8, no. 2 (Summer 1995): 203–19.
Rathmell, Andrew. "Brotherly Enemies: The Rise and Fall of the Syrian–Egyptian Intelligence Axis, 1954–1967." *Intelligence and National Security* 13, no. 1 (Spring 1998): 230–53.
Sheffy, Yigal. "Unconcern at Dawn, Surprise at Sunset: Egyptian Intelligence Appreciation before the Sinai Campaign, 1956." *Intelligence and National Security* 5, no. 3 (July 1990): 7–56.

5. Iranian Intelligence

5.1. The Shah's Regime

Abrahamson, Everand. *Iran between Two Revolutions.* Princeton, N.J.: Princeton University Press, 1982.
Dareini, Ali Akbar, ed. *The Rise and Fall of the Pahlavi Dynasty: Memoirs of Former General Hussein Fardust.* New Delhi: Motilal Babarsisass, 1999.
Hoopes, John M. "Iranian Intelligence under the Shah." *Naval Intelligence Professionals Quarterly* 14, no. 1 (January 1998): 7–9.
Ledeen, Michael, and William Lewis. *Debacle: The American Failure in Iran.* New York: Knopf, 1981.
Rubin, Michael. "The Telegraph, Espionage, and Cryptology in Nineteenth Century Iran." *Cryptologia* 25, no. 1 (January 2001): 18–36.
Samii, Abbas William. "The Shah's Lebanon Policy: The Role of SAVAK." *Middle Eastern Studies* 33, no. 1 (January 1997): 66–91.

5.2. The Ayatollah's Regime

Barber, Ben. "Iran Increases Funds for Terrorist Activities." *Washington Times*, 18 August 1999.

Coughlin, Con. "Iran Sends More Spies to Europe." *Electronic Telegraph*, 4 May 1997.

Miller, Greg. "CIA Believes It Can See into Tehran from L.A.: Agency Seeking Help from Many Iranians in Area." *Los Angeles Times*, 16 June 2002.

"New Evidence Ties Iran to Terrorism." *Newsweek*, 15 November 1999.

Omestad, Thomas. "A Stunning Admission: Iran's Secret Agency Confesses to Murder." *U.S. News & World Report*, 18 January 1999, 36.

Sherwell, Philip. "Teheran 'Executed CIA's Spy Network 10 Years Ago.'" *Electronic Telegraph*, 13 February 2005.

Wege, Carl Anthony. "Iranian Intelligence Organizations." *International Journal of Intelligence and CounterIntelligence* 10, no. 3 (Fall 1997): 287–98.

6. Iraqi Intelligence

Al-Marashi, Ibrahim. "The Family, Clan, and Tribal Dynamics of Saddam's Security and Intelligence Network." *International Journal of Intelligence and CounterIntelligence* 16, no. 2 (Summer 2003): 202–11.

———. "An Insight into the Mindset of Iraq's Security Apparatus." *Intelligence and National Security* 18, no. 3 (Autumn 2003): 1–23.

———. "Saddam's Security Apparatus during the Invasion of Kuwait and the Kuwaiti Resistance." *Journal of Intelligence History* 3, no. 2 (Winter 2003): 61–86.

Coughlin, Con. "Iraq Executes Espionage Chief." *Electronic Telegraph*, 17 October 1999.

———. "Russian Space Pictures Enable Saddam to Target Gulf States." *Electronic Telegraph*, 10 October 1999.

Francona, Rick. *Ally to Adversary: An Eyewitness Account of Iraq's Fall from Grace.* Annapolis, Md.: U.S. Naval Institute Press, 1999.

Masri, Ibrahim al-. "The Family, Clan, and Tribal Dynamics of Saddam's Security and Intelligence Network." *International Journal of Intelligence and CounterIntelligence* 16, no. 2 (April 2003): 202–11.

Myers, Steven Lee. "U.S. to Aid Iraqi Opposition to Develop a Military Cadre." *New York Times*, 28 October 1999.

Smith, Michael. "Fate of Iraqi Mole Led to Spy Clash." *Electronic Telegraph*, 4 February 1999.

Sumaida, Hussein Ali, with Carole Jerome. *Circle of Fear: From the Mossad to Iraq's Secret Service.* [U.S. Title: *Circle of Fear: My Life as an Israeli and Iraqi Spy.*] Toronto: Stoddart, 1991.

United States Information Agency. *Iraqi Disinformation: Allegations and Facts (Fact Sheet).* Washington, D.C.: USIA, 4 February 1991.

Wren, Christopher S. "U.S. Gives Its Backing, and Cash, to Anti-Hussein Groups." *New York Times*, 2 November 1999.

7. Israeli Intelligence

7.1 Prestate Intelligence

Charters, David A. "Eyes of the Underground: Jewish Insurgent Intelligence in Palestine, 1945–47." *Intelligence and National Security* 13, no. 4 (Winter 1998): 163–77.

Engle, Anita. *The NILI Spies.* Jerusalem: Phoenix Publications, 1989.

Lavenberg, Haim, *Military Perceptions of the Arab Community in Palestine 1945–1948.* London: Frank Cass, 1993.

7.2. State of Israeli Intelligence

Black, Ian, and Benny Morris. *Israel's Secret Wars: A History of Israel's Intelligence Services.* New York: Grove Weidenfeld, 1991.

Deacon, Richard. *The Israeli Secret Service.* London: Hamish Hamilton, 1977.

Eisenberg, Dennis, Uri Dan, and Eli Landau. *The Mossad.* New York: Paddington Press, 1978.

Jones, Clive. "'Reach Greater than the Grasp': Israeli Intelligence and the Conflict in South Lebanon 1990–2000." *Intelligence and National Security* 16, no. 3 (Autumn 2001): 1–26.

Kahana, Ephraim. *Historical Dictionary of Israeli Intelligence.* Lanham, Md.: Scarecrow Press, 2006.

Payne, Ronald. *Mossad: Israel's Most Secret Service.* London: Bantam Press, 1978.

7.3. Surprise Attacks

Cohen, Raymond. "Threat Assessment in Military Intelligence: The Case of Israel and Syria, 1985–86." *Intelligence and National Security* 4, no. 4 (October 1989): 735–64.

Handel, Michael I. "Crisis and Surprise in Three Arab Israeli Wars." In *Strategic Military Surprise: Incentives and Opportunities*, ed. Klaus Knorr and Patrick Morgan, 111–22. New Brunswick, N.J.: Transaction Books, 1984.

Kahana, Ephraim. "Analyzing Israel's Intelligence Failures." *International Journal of Intelligence and CounterIntelligence* 18, no. 2 (Summer 2005): 262–79.

7.4. Suez Crisis

Handel, Michael I. "Crisis and Surprise in Three Arab Israeli Wars." In *Strategic Military Surprise: Incentives and Opportunities*, ed. Klaus Knorr and Patrick Morgan, 111–22. New Brunswick, N.J.: Transaction Books, 1984.

Sheffy, Yigal. "Unconcern at Dawn, Surprise at Sunset: Egyptian Intelligence Appreciation before the Sinai Campaign, 1956." *Intelligence and National Security* 5, no. 3 (July 1990): 7–56.

7.5. Rotem Affair

Bar-Joseph, Uri. "Israel Caught Unawares: Egypt's Sinai Surprise of 1960." *International Journal of Intelligence and CounterIntelligence* 8, no. 2 (Summer 1995): 203–19.

7.6. War of Attrition (1969–1970)

Adamsky, Dima, and Uri Bar-Joseph. "'The Russians Are Not Coming': Israel's Intelligence Failure and Soviet Military Intervention in the 'War of Attrition.'" *Intelligence and National Security* 21, no. 1 (February 2006): 1–25.

8. Jordanian Intelligence

Yitzhak, Ronen, "The Beginning of Transjordan Military Intelligence: A Neglected Aspect of the 1948 War." *Middle East Journal* 57, no. 3 (Summer 2003): 449–68.

9. Lebanese Intelligence

Aburish, Said K. *Beirut Spy: International Intrigue at the St. George Hotel Bar*. London: Bloomsbury, 1990.

Harnden, Toby. "CIA Gets the Go-ahead to Take on Hizbollah." *Daily Telegraph* (London), 10 January 2007.

Kennedy, David, and Leslie Brunetta. "Lebanon and the Intelligence Community: A Case Study." *Studies in Intelligence* 37, no. 5 (1994): 37–51.

Nasif, Nicholas. "Tenet Given Assurances That No al-Qa'ida Cells Infiltrated Lebanon." *al-Nahar* (Beirut), 28 November 2002. (Arabic)

Phares, Walid. "The Intelligence Services in Lebanon during the War of 1975–1990." *International Journal of Intelligence and CounterIntelligence* 7, no. 3 (Fall 1994): 363–81.

10. Palestinian Intelligence

Pacepa, Ion Mihai. "The Arafat I Know." *Wall Street Journal*, 10 January 2002.

Weiner, Tim. "C.I.A. Is Teaching Tricks of the Trade to the Palestinians." *New York Times*, 5 March 1998.

11. Sudanese Intelligence

Shane, Scott. "C.I.A. Role in Visit of Sudan Intelligence Chief Causes Dispute within Administration." *New York Times*, 18 June 2005.

12. Syrian Intelligence

Cambill, Gary C., "The Military-Intelligence Shakeup in Syria." *Middle East Intelligence Bulletin*, February 2002.

Rathmell, Andrew. "Brotherly Enemies: The Rise and Fall of the Syrian-Egyptian Intelligence Axis, 1954–1967." *Intelligence and National Security* 13, no. 1 (Spring 1998): 230–53.

———. "Syria's Intelligence Services: Origins and Development." *Journal of Conflict Studies* 16, no. 2 (Fall 1996): 75–89.

Thomas, Martin. "Crisis Management in Colonial States: Intelligence and Counter-Insurgency in Morocco and Syria after the First World War." *Intelligence and National Security* 21, no. 5 (October 2006): 697–716.

Wege, Carl Anthony. "Assad's Legions: The Syrian Intelligence Services." *International Journal of Intelligence and CounterIntelligence* 4, no. 1 (Spring 1990): 91–100.

———. "The Syrian Socialist Party: An Intelligence Asset?" *International Journal of Intelligence and CounterIntelligence* 7, no. 3 (Fall 1994): 339–51.

13. Turkish Intelligence

Bek, Aziz. *Intelligence and Espionage in Lebanon, Syria, and Palestine (1913–1918)*. Bar-Ilan: University Press, 1991. (Hebrew)

Gunter, Michael M. "Susurluk: The Connection between Turkey's Intelligence Community and Organized Crime." *International Journal of Intelligence and CounterIntelligence* 11, no. 2 (Summer 1998): 119–41.

———. "United States–Turkish Intelligence Liaison since World War II." *Journal of Intelligence History* 3, no. 1 (Summer 2003): 33–46.

Hacaoglu, Selcan. "Turkish Spy Agency Raises Profile." *Associated Press*, 7 August 1999.

Komisar, Lucy. "Turkey's Terrorists: A CIA Legacy Lives On." *Progressive* (April 1997): 24–27.

Lefebvre, Stéphane. "Turkey's Intelligence Community in Changing Times." *International Journal* 51, no. 1 (Winter 2005–2006): 105–24.

Macfie, A. L. "British Intelligence and the Turkish National Movement, 1919–22." *Middle Eastern Studies* 37, no. 1 (January 2001): 1–16.

Miller, James E., ed. *Foreign Relations of the United States, 1964–1968*. Vol. 16: *Cyprus; Greece; Turkey*. Washington, D.C.: U.S. Department of State, Office of the Historian, Government Printing Office, 2000.

Patterson, David S., ed. *Foreign Relations of the United States, 1964–1968*. Washington, D.C.: U.S. Department of State, Office of the Historian, Government Printing Office, 2000.

Tauber, Eliezer. "The Capture of the NILI Spies: The Turkish Version." *Intelligence and National Security* 6, no. 4 (October 1991): 701–10.

Weiner, Tim. "U.S. Played Key Role in Capture of Kurd Rebel, Officials Say." *New York Times*, 20 February 1999.

14. Yemeni Intelligence

Jones, Clive. *Britain and the Yemen Civil War, 1962–1965: Ministers, Mercenaries and Mandarins: Foreign Policy and the Limits of Covert Action*. Brighton, U.K.: Sussex Academic Press, 2004.

15. Covert Action

15.1. U.S. Covert Action

Bearden, Milt, and James Risen. *The Main Enemy: The Inside Story of the CIA's Final Showdown with the KGB*. New York: Random House, 2003.

Cooley, John K. *Payback: America's Long War in the Middle East*. New York: Brassey's, 1991.

Copeland, Miles. *The Game of Nations: The Amorality of Power Politics*. London: Weidenfeld & Nicolson, 1969.

———. *The Game Player: Confessions of the CIA's Original Political Operative*. London: Aurum, 1989.

Eveland, Wilbur Crane. *Ropes of Sand: America's Failure in the Middle East*. New York: Norton, 1980.

Wilber, Donald N. *Adventures in the Middle East: Excursions and Incursions*. Princeton, N.J.: Darwin, 1986.

Wroe, Ann. *Lives, Lies and the Iran–Contra Affair*. London: I. B. Tauris, 1991.

15.2. U.S. Covert Action in Afghanistan

Calabresi, Massimo. "The bin Laden Capture That Never Was." *Time*, 20 March 2000, 24.

Cogan, Charles G. "Partners in Time: The CIA and Afghanistan." *World Policy Journal* 10, no. 2 (Summer 1993).76–79.

Coll, Steve. "Anatomy of a Victory: CIA's Covert Afghan War." Part 1. *Washington Post*, 19 July 1992, 1, 24.

———. "In CIA's Covert Afghan War, Where to Draw the Line Was Key." Part 2. *Washington Post*, 20 July 1992, 1, 12.

———. "Flawed Ally Was Hunt's Best Hope: Afghan Guerrilla, U.S. Shared Enemy." Part 2. *Washington Post*, 23 February 2004, A1.

———. *Ghost Wars: The Secret History of the CIA, Afghanistan, and bin Laden, from the Soviet Invasion to September 10, 2001*. New York: Penguin, 2005.

———. "Legal Disputes over Hunt Paralyzed Clinton's Aides." *Washington Post*, 22 February 2004, A17.

———."The Other Battle for Afghanistan." *Washington Post National Weekly Edition*, 31 August–6 September 1992, 10–11.

———. "A Secret Hunt Unravels in Afghanistan: Mission to Capture or Kill al Qaeda Leader Frustrated by Near Misses, Political Disputes." *Washington Post*, 22 February 2004, Part 1.

Cooley, John K. *Unholy Wars: Afghanistan, America and International Terrorism*. Sterling, Va.: Pluto Press, 1999.

Cordovez, Diego, and Selig S. Harrison. *Out of Afghanistan: The Inside Story of the Soviet Withdrawal*. New York: Oxford University Press, 1995.

Crile, George. *Charlie Wilson's War: The Extraordinary Story of the Largest Covert Operation in History.* New York: Atlantic Monthly, 2003.

Farr, Grant M., and John G. Merriam. *Afghan Resistance: The Politics of Survival.* Boulder, Colo.: Westview, 1987.

Mcgrory, Daniel. "CIA Stung by Its Stingers." *Electronic Telegraph*, 3 November 1996.

Lohbeck, Kurt. *Holy War, Unholy Victory: Eyewitness to the CIA's Secret War in Afghanistan.* Washington, D.C.: Regnery Gateway, 1993.

Prados, John. "Notes on the CIA's Secret War in Afghanistan." *Journal of American History* 89, no. 2 (September 2002): 466–71.

Weinbaum, Marvin G. "War and Peace in Afghanistan: The Pakistani Role." *Middle East Journal* 45, no. 1 (Winter 1991): 71–85.

Weiner, Tim. "Blowback from the Afghan Battlefield." *New York Times*, 13 March 1994.

Yousaf, Mohammed, and Mark Adkin. *Afghanistan the Bear Trap: The Defeat of a Superpower.* Havertown, Pa.: Casemate, 2001.

15.3. U.S. Covert Action in Iran

Abrahamian, Ervand. "The 1953 Coup in Iran." *State & Society* 66, no. 2 (Summer 2001): 182–215.

Barber, Ben. "Iran Increases Funds for Terrorist Activities." *Washington Times*, 18 August 1999.

Ledeen, Michael, and William Lewis. *Debacle: The American Failure in Iran.* New York: Knopf, 1981.

Samii, Abbas William. "The Shah's Lebanon Policy: The Role of SAVAK." *Middle Eastern Studies* 33, no. 1 (January 1997): 66–91.

Weiner, Tim. "U.S. Plan to Oust Iran's Government Is an Open Secret." *New York Times*, 26 January 1996, A1, A5.

15.4. U.S. Covert Action in Iraq

Ahrens, Frank. "Radio Free Iraq's Strong Signal: U.S. News Service Heats Up for First Time since Cold War." *Washington Post*, 18 December 1998, D2.

Burgess, John, and David B. Ottaway. "Iraqi Opposition Unable to Mount Viable Challenge." *Washington Post*, 12 February 1998.

Colvin, Marie. "Revealed: CIA's Bungled Iraqi Coup." *Sunday Times* (London), 2 April 2000.

Fedarko, Kevin. "Saddam's CIA Coup." *U.S. News and World Report*, 21 September 1996, 42–44.

Gunter, Michael. "The Iraqi National Congress (INC) and the Future of the Iraqi Opposition." *Journal of South Asian and Middle Eastern Studies* 19 (Spring 1996): 1–20.

———. "The Iraqi Opposition and the Failure of U.S. Intelligence." *International Journal of Intelligence and CounterIntelligence* 12, no. 2 (Summer 1999): 135–67.

———. "Mulla Mustafa Barzani and the Kurdish Rebellion in Iraq: The Intelligence Factor." *International Journal of Intelligence and CounterIntelligence* 7, no. 4 (Winter 1994): 465–74.

Hoagland, Jim. "How CIA's Secret War on Saddam Collapsed." *Washington Post*, 26 June 1997, A21, A28–29.

"James Bond vs. Saddam Hussein." Editorial. *New York Times*, 27 February 1998, A20.

Kitfield, James. "The Trouble with Iraq." *National Journal*, 28 February 1998, 446–49.

Lancaster, John, and David B. Ottaway. "With CIA's Help, Group in Jordan Targets Saddam." *Washington Post*, 23 June 1996.

Lippman, Thomas W. "A Blueprint to Overturn Iraq." *Washington Post National Weekly Edition*, 10 August 1998, 14.

Loeb, Vernon. "Congress Stokes Visions of War to Oust Saddam: White House Fears Fiasco in Aid to Rebels." *Washington Post*, 12 August 1998, A1.

———. "Saddam's Iraqi Foes Heartened by Clinton: No Immediate Plan for Overthrow Seen." *Washington Post*, 16 November 1998, A17.

Oberdorfer, Don. "A Carefully Covert Plan to Oust Hussein." *Washington Post National Weekly Edition*, 25–31 January 1993, 19.

Pincus, Walter. "Justice Asked to Investigate Leaks by CIA Ex-Officials." *Washington Post*, 19 July 1997, A16.

Randal, Jonathan C. "Iraqi Opposition Describes Mass Execution near Irbil." *Washington Post*, 2 September 1996, A20.

———. "Linked to the CIA, Their Lives Now Are on the Line." *Washington Post National Weekly Edition*, 16–22 September 1996, 8–9.

Sciolino, Elaine. "C.I.A; Asks Congress for $19 Million to Undermine Iraq's Rulers and Rein in Iran." *New York Times*, 12 April 1995, A4.

Smith, R. Jeffrey, and David B. Ottaway. "Anti-Saddam Operation Cost CIA $100 Million." *Washington Post*, 15 September 1996, A1, A29–30.

———. "The CIA's Most Wanted Man: The Agency Has Spent $100 million Trying to Catch Saddam Hussein, but Has Little to Show for the Effort." *Washington Post National Weekly Edition*, 23–29 September 1996, 14–15.

Weiner, Tim. "C.I.A. Drafts Covert Plan to Topple Hussein." *New York Times*, 26 February 1998, A11.

———. "Crisis with Iraq: Baghdad's Foes." *New York Times*, 16 November 1998.

———. "Iraqi Offensive into Kurdish Zone Disrupts U.S. Plot to Oust Hussein." *New York Times*, 7 September 1996, A1, A4.

Wise, David. "Another C.I.A. Disaster." *New York Times*, 13 September 1996, A23.

Woodward, Bob. "President Broadens Anti-Hussein Order: CIA Gets More Tools to Oust Iraqi Leader." *Washington Post*, 16 June 2002, A1.

15.5. U.S. Covert Action in Syria

Rathmell, Andrew. "Secret War in the Middle East: The Covert Struggle for Syria 1949–1961." *Journal of Conflict Studies*: 97–103.

15.6. British Covert Action in Iran

Bamberg, J. H. *The History of the British Petroleum Company*, Vol. 2: *The Anglo–Iranian Years, 1928–54*. Cambridge: Cambridge University Press, 1994.

Gasiorowski, Mark J. "The 1953 Coup d'état in Iran." *International Journal of Middle East Studies* 19, no. 3 (1987): 261–86.

Gasiorowski, Mark J., and Malcolm Byrne, eds. *Mohammad Mosaddeq and the 1953 Coup in Iran*. Syracuse, N.Y.: Syracuse University Press, 2004.

Gavin, Francis J. "Politics, Power, and U.S. Policy in Iran, 1950–1953." *Journal of Cold War Studies* 1, no. 1 (Winter 1999): 56–89.

Heiss, Mary Ann. *Empire and Nationhood: The United States, Great Britain, and Iranian Oil, 1950–1954*. New York: Columbia University Press, 1997.

"How Our Man in Tehran Brought Down a Demagogue: The CIA vs. Mohammed Mossedegh." *Esquire* 91 (June 1975).

Karabell, Zachary. *Architects of Intervention: The United States, the Third World, and the Cold War, 1946–1962*. Baton Rouge: Louisiana State University Press, 1999.

Kinzer, Stephen. *All the Shah's Men: The Hidden Story of the CIA's Coup in Iran*. New York: Wiley, 2003

Kisatsky, Deborah. "Donald Wilber: 'Gentleman Spy' at Helm." *New York Times*, 16 April 2000.

———. "Voice of America and Iran, 1949–1953: US Liberal Developmentalism, Propaganda and the Cold War." *Intelligence and National Security* 14, no. 3 (Autumn 1999): 160–85.

Risen, James. "C.I.A. Tried, with Little Success, to Use U.S. Press in Coup." *New York Times,* 16 April 2000.

———. "How a Plot Convulsed Iran in 1953 (and in 1979)." *New York Times,* 16 April 2000.

———. "Secrets of History: The CIA in Iran." *New York Times,* 16 April 2000.

Roosevelt, Kermit. *Countercoup: The Struggle for the Control of Iran.* New York: McGraw-Hill, 1979.

Ruehsen, Moyara de Moraes. "Operation 'Ajax' Revisited: Iran, 1953." *Middle Eastern Studies* 29, no. 3 (July 1993): 467–86.

Sciolino, Elaine. "Mohammed Mossadegh: Eccentric Nationalist Begets Strange History." *New York Times,* 16 April 2000.

Wilber, Donald N. *Adventures in the Middle East: Excursions and Incursions.* Princeton, NJ: Darwin, 1986.

15.7. The Iran Hostage Crisis of 1979–1981

Armstrong, Scott. "Carter Held Hope Even after Shah Had Lost His." *Washington Post,* 25 October 1980, A12.

———. *The Chronology: The Documented Day-to-Day Account of the Secret Military Assistance to Iran and the Contras.* New York: Warner, 1987.

Bani-Sadr, Abol Hassan. *My Turn to Speak: Iran, the Revolution and Secret Deals with the U.S.* Washington, D.C.: Brassey's, 1991.

Bill, James A. *The Eagle and the Lion: The Tragedy of American–Iranian Relations.* New Haven, Conn.: Yale University Press, 1988.

Bowden, Mark. *Guests of the Ayatollah: The First Battle in America's War with Militant Islam.* New York: Atlantic Monthly Press, 2006.

Brzezinski, Zbigniew. *Power and Principle: Memoirs of the National Security Advisor, 1977–1981.* New York: Farrar, Straus, & Giroux, 1983.

Buhite, Russell D. *Lives at Risk: Hostages and Victims in American Foreign Policy.* Wilmington, Del.: Scholarly Resources, 1995.

Carter, Jimmy. *Keeping Faith: Memoirs of a President.* 3rd ed. Fayetteville: University of Arkansas Press, 1995.

Christopher, Warren. *American Hostages in Iran: Conduct of a Crisis.* New Haven, Conn.: Yale University Press, 1985.

Currie, James T. "Iran–Contra and Congressional Oversight of the CIA." *International Journal of Intelligence and CounterIntelligence* 11, no. 2 (Summer 1998): 185–210.

Daugherty, William J. "Behind the Intelligence Failure in Iran." *International Journal of Intelligence and CounterIntelligence* 14, no. 4 (Winter 2001–2002): 449–84.

———. "A First Tour Like No Other." *Studies in Intelligence* (Spring 1998): 1–45.

———. *In the Shadow of the Ayatollah: A CIA Hostage in Iran.* Annapolis, Md.: Naval Institute Press, 2001.

Donovan, Michael. "National Intelligence and the Iranian Revolution." *Intelligence and National Security* 12, no. 1 (January 1997): 143–63.

Draper, Theodore. *A Very Thin Line: The Iran–Contra Affair.* New York: Hill & Wang, 1991.

Farber, David. *Taken Hostage: The Iran Hostage Crisis and America's First Encounter with Radical Islam.* Princeton, N.J.: Princeton University Press, 2004.

Feldman, Daniel L. "Constitutional Dimensions of the Iran–Contra Affair." *International Journal of Intelligence and CounterIntelligence* 2, no. 3 (Fall 1988): 381–97.

Fisher, Louis. "Review Essay: How to Avoid Iran–Contras." *California Law Review* 76 (1993): 919–29.

Gwertzman, Bernard. "Government in Iran Vows Help in Siege; U.S. Uncertain despite Promise by Tehran to Do Its Best." *New York Times*, 5 November 1979, A1.

Koh, Harold Hongju. *The National Security Constitution: Sharing Power after the Iran–Contra Affair.* New Haven, Conn.: Yale University Press, 1990.

Rhee, Will. "Comparing U.S. Operations Kingpin (1970) and Eagle Claw (1980)." *International Journal of Intelligence and CounterIntelligence* 6, no. 4 (Winter 1993): 489–506.

Rivers, Gayle, and James Hudson. *The Tehran Contract.* New York: Doubleday, 1981.

Ryan, Paul B. *The Iranian Rescue Mission: Why It Failed.* Annapolis, Md.: Naval Institute Press, 1984.

Salinger, Pierre. *America Held Hostage: The Secret Negotiations.* Garden City, N.Y.: Doubleday, 1981.

Schemmer, Benjamin F., and John T. Carney Jr. *No Room for Error: The Covert Operations of America's Special Tactics Units from Iran to Afghanistan.* New York: Ballantine, 2002.

Southworth, Samuel A., ed. *Great Raids in History: From Drake to Desert One*. New York: Sarpedon, 1997.

Turner, Stansfield. *Terrorism and Democracy*. Boston: Houghton Mifflin, 1991.

U.S. Department of Defense. *Rescue Mission Report*. Washington, D.C.: Government Printing Office, 23 August 1980.

15.8. Operation Eagle Claw: The Hostage Rescue Mission in 1980

Barnard, Richard. "Bad Luck behind Chopper Failures Prior to Iran Rescue Mission, but Did They Listen?" *Defense Week*, 28 July 1980, 6–7.

Beckwith, Charlie A., and Donald Knox. *Delta Force: The Army's Elite Counterterrorist Unit*. New York: Harcourt, 1983.

Ben-Menashe, Ari. *Profits of War: Inside the Secret U.S.–Israeli Arms Network*. Lanham, Md.: Sheridan Square Press, 1992.

Burt, Richard. "Many Questions, Few Answers on Iran Missions." *New York Times*, 11 May 1980, E3.

Domanski, Walter. "The Raid That Failed." *Combat Illustrated* 5 (October 1980).

Felton, John. "Eight Americans Killed: Congress Rallies behind Carter after Abortive Rescue Mission." *Congressional Quarterly Weekly Report*, 26 April 1980: 1067–68.

Fink, D. E. "Rescue Helicopters Drawn from Fleet." *Aviation Week & Space Technology*, 5 May 1980, 24–25.

Griffiths, David R. "Report Reviews Iran Rescue Mission Flaws." *Aviation Week & Space Technology*, 1 September 1980, 44–46.

Harris, David. *The Crisis: The President, the Prophet, and the Shah—1979 and the Coming of Militant Islam*. New York: Little, Brown, 2004.

Harwood, Richard. "Series of Mishaps Defeated Rescue in Iran." *Washington Post*, 2 May 1980, A1.

Herz, Martin F., ed. *Contacts with the Opposition: A Symposium*. Washington, D.C,: Institute for the Study of Diplomacy, Georgetown University, 1979.

Hilzenrath, David S. "Encounter with Global Con Artist Left Reston Firm Reeling." *Washington Post*, 23 January 1999, E1.

Honegger, Barbara. *October Surprise*. New York: Tudor, 1989.

Hosenball, Mark. "What October Surprise?" *Washington Post National Weekly Edition*, 29 April–5 May 1991, 24–25.

Houghton, Patrick David. *U.S. Foreign Policy and the Iran Hostage Crisis*. New York: Cambridge University Press, 2001.

Huyser, Robert E. *Mission to Tehran*. New York: Harper & Row, 1986.

Karabell, Zachary. "'Inside the US Espionage Den': The US Embassy and the Fall of the Shah." *Intelligence and National Security* 8, no. 1 (January 1993): 44–59.

Koehl, Stuart L., and Stephen P. Glick. "Why the Rescue Failed." *American Spectator*, July 1980, 23–25.

Koskinas, Gianni "Desert One and Air Force Special Operations Command: A 25-Year Retrospective." *Air & Space Power Journal* 19, no. 1 (Spring 2005).

Kyle, James H., and John Robert Eidson. *The Guts to Try: The Untold Story of the Iran Hostage Rescue Mission by the On-Scene Desert Commander*. New York: Crown, 1990.

Ledeen, Michael, and William Lewis. *Debacle: The American Failure in Iran*. New York: Knopf, 1981.

Lenahan, Rod. *Crippled Eagle: A Historical Perspective of U.S. Special Operations, 1976–1996*. Charleston, S.C.: Narwhal Press, 1998.

Levin, Bob, et al. "A Grim Pentagon Critique." *Newsweek*, 1 September 1980, 20–21.

Martin, David C. "New Light on the Rescue Mission." *Newsweek*, 30 June 1980, 18–20.

Mendez, Antonio J. "A Classic Case of Deception." *Studies in Intelligence* (Winter 1999–2000): 1–16.

Middleton, Drew. "Failed Rescue Attempt Raises Doubt about U.S. Maintenance and Planning." *New York Times*, 26 April 1980, 9.

Moss, Robert. "Who's Meddling in Iran?" *New Republic*, 2 December 1978, 15–18.

Parry, Robert. *Trick or Treason: The October Surprise Mystery*. New York: Sheridan Square Press, 1993.

Pelletier, Jean, and Claude Adams. *The Canadian Caper*. New York: Morrow, 1981.

Rhee, Will. "Comparing U.S. Operations Kingpin (1970) and Eagle Claw (1980)." *International Journal of Intelligence and CounterIntelligence* 6, no. 4 (Winter 1993): 489–506.

Rivers, Gayle, and James Hudson. *The Tehran Contract*. New York: Doubleday, 1981.

Rubin, Barry. *Paved with Good Intentions: The American Experience in Iran*. New York: Oxford University Press, 1980.

Ryan, Paul B. *The Iranian Rescue Mission: Why It Failed*. Annapolis, Md.: Naval Institute Press, 1984.

Salinger, Pierre. *America Held Hostage: The Secret Negotiations*. Garden City, N.Y.: Doubleday, 1981.

Schemmer, Benjamin F., and John T. Carney Jr. *No Room for Error: The Covert Operations of America's Special Tactics Units from Iran to Afghanistan*. New York: Ballantine, 2002.

Sick, Gary. *All Fall Down: America's Tragic Encounter with Iran*. New York: Random House, 1985.

———. *October Surprise: America's Hostages in Iran and the Election of Ronald Reagan*. New York: Random House–New York Times Books, 1991.

Smith, Hedrick. "U.S. Aides Say Loss of Post in Iran Impairs Missile-Monitoring Ability." *New York Times*, 2 March 1979, A1, A8.

Southworth, Samuel A., ed. *Great Raids in History: From Drake to Desert One*. New York: Sarpedon, 1997.

Stemple, John D. *Inside the Iranian Revolution*. Bloomington: Indiana University Press, 1981.

Sullivan, William H. *Mission to Iran*. New York: Norton, 1981.

Taheri, Amir. *Nest of Spies*. London: Hutchinson, 1988.

Turner, Stansfield. *Secrecy and Democracy: The CIA in Transition*. Boston: Houghton Mifflin, 1985.

———. *Terrorism and Democracy*. Boston: Houghton Mifflin, 1991.

U.S. Congress. House Subcommittee on Evaluation, Permanent Select Committee on Intelligence. *Iran: Evaluation of U.S. Intelligence Performance Prior to November 1978*. 96th Cong., 1st sess., 1979. Committee Print.

U.S. Department of Defense. *Rescue Mission Report*. Washington, D.C.: Government Printing Office, 23 August 1980.

Vance, Cyrus. *Hard Choices: Critical Years in American Foreign Policy*. New York: Simon & Schuster, 1983.

Vandenbroucke, Lucien S. *Perilous Options: Special Operations as an Instrument of U.S. Foreign Policy*. New York: Oxford University, 1993.

Wilton, Terry L. "My View of Operation Eagle Claw." *Naval Intelligence Professionals Quarterly* 23, no. 4 (September 2007): 26–27.

15.9. British and U.S. Covert Action in Syria

Blackwell, Stephen. "Britain, the United States and the Syrian Crisis, 1957." *Diplomacy and Statecraft* 11, no. 3 (2000): 139–58.

Gorst, Anthony, and W. Scott Lucas. "The Other Collusion: Operation Straggle and Anglo-American Intervention in Syria, 1955–1956." *Intelligence and National Security* 4, no. 3 (July 1989): 576–95.

Jones, Matthew. "The 'Preferred Plan': The Anglo–American Working Group Report on Covert Action in Syria, 1957." *Intelligence and National Security* 19, no. 3 (Autumn 2004): 401–15.

Lesch, D. "The United States and Syria, 1953–1957: The Cold War in the Middle East." PhD diss., Harvard University, 1990.

Little, Douglas. "Cold War and Covert Action: The United States and Syria 1945–1958." *Middle East Journal* 44, no. 1 (Winter 1990): 51–75.

Rathmell, Andrew. "Copeland and Za'im: Re-evaluating the Evidence." *Intelligence and National Security* 11, no. 1 (January 1996): 89–105.

———. *Secret War in the Middle East: The Covert Struggle for Syria, 1949–1961*. New York: I. B. Tauris, 1995.

Seale, Patrick. *The Struggle for Syria*. Oxford: Oxford University Press, 1986.

15.10. U.S. Covert Action in Jordan

Woodward, Bob. "CIA Paid Millions to Jordan's King Hussein." *Washington Post*, 18 February 1977, A1.

15.11. Covert Action in Lebanon

Alin, Erika. *The United States and the 1958 Lebanon Crisis*. Lanham, Md.: University Press of America, 1994.

Fry, Michael Graham. "The Uses of Intelligence: The United Nations Confronts the United States in the Lebanon Crisis, 1958." *Intelligence and National Security* 10, no. 1 (January 1995): 59–91.

Harnden, Toby. "CIA Gets the Go-ahead to Take on Hizbollah." *Daily Telegraph* (London), 10 January 2007.

Karabell, Zachary. *Architects of Intervention: The United States, the Third World, and the Cold War, 1946–1962*. Baton Rouge: Louisiana State University Press, 1999.

16. Operations Desert Shield and Desert Storm, 1990–1991

Anderson, G. S. *Charting the Storm: DMA's Role in Operation Desert Shield and Desert Storm, Final Report 10 Feb 92–21 Feb 93*. Newport, R.I.: Naval War College, 1993.

Armstrong, Douglas G. "The Gulf War's Patched-Together Air Intelligence." *U.S. Naval Institute Proceedings* 118, no. 11 (November 1992): 109–11.

Ball, Desmond J. *Intelligence in the Gulf War*. Canberra: Australian National University, 1991.

Campen, Alan D., ed. *The First Information War*. Fairfax, Va.: AFCEA International Press, 1992.

Centner, Christopher M. "Intelligence, Gulf War Illnesses and Public Perceptions of Conspiracies." *American Intelligence Journal* 21, nos. 1–2 (Spring 2002): 37–45.

Covault, Craig. "Recon Satellites Lead Allied Intelligence Effort." *Aviation Week and Space Technology*, 4 February 1991, 25–26.

Drachman, Edward R., and Alan Shank. *Presidents and Foreign Policy: Countdown to Ten Controversial Decisions*. Ithaca, N.Y.: SUNY Press, 1997.

Estavanik, R. D. *Intelligence and the Commander: Desert Shield/Storm Case Study*. Newport, R.I.: Naval War College, 1992.

Francona, Rick. *Ally to Adversary: An Eyewitness Account of Iraq's Fall from Grace*. Annapolis, Md.: U.S. Naval Institute Press, 1999.

Fredericks, Brian, and Richard Wiersema. "Battlefield TECHINT: Support of Operations." *Military Intelligence* 18, no. 2 (April–June 1992): 13–19.

Fulghum, David A. "Key Military Officials Criticize Intelligence Handling in Gulf War." *Aviation Week & Space Technology*, 24 June 1991, 83.

Goodman, A. Sue, comp. *Persian Gulf War, 1990–1991: Desert Shield/Desert Storm*. Special Bibliography no. 297a. Maxwell Air Force Base, Ala.: Air University Library, November 1991.

Gordon, Michael R., and Bernard E. Trainor. *The Generals' War*. Boston: Little, Brown, 1995.

Gregory, Shaun. *Command, Control, Communications and Intelligence in the Gulf War*. Working Paper no. 238. Canberra: Strategic and Defence Studies Centre, Australian National University, 1991.

Hammer, Joshua, and Douglas Waller. "Special Ops: The Top-Secret War." *Newsweek*, 18 March 1991, 32.

Haselkorn, Avigdor. *The Continuing Storm: Iraq, Poisonous Weapons, and Deterrence*. New Haven, Conn.: Yale University Press, 1999.

Hoffman, Daniel M. "A Beltway Warrior Looks at Gulf War Intelligence." *U.S. Naval Institute Proceedings* (January 1993): 86–89.

"Intelligence Successes and Failures in Operations Desert Shield/Desert Storm." *Foreign Intelligence Literary Scene* 12, no. 5:1–3.

Johnson, Richard D. *PSYOP, the Gulf Paper War: Psychological Warfare Operations against the Iraqi Military and Civilian Establishments between November 1990 and February 1991*. Titusville, Fla.: R. D. Johnson, 1992.

Jones, Jeffrey B. "Psychological Operations in Desert Shield, Desert Storm and Urban Freedom." *Special Warfare* 7, no. 3 (July 1994): 22–29.

Leadbetter, Wyland F., Jr., and Stephen J. Bury. "Prelude to Desert Storm: The Politicization of Intelligence." *International Journal of Intelligence and CounterIntelligence* 6, no. 1 (Spring 1993): 43–54.

Nash, Douglas E. "Civil Affairs in the Gulf War: Administration of an Occupied Town." *Special Warfare* 7 (October 1994): 18–27.

Rip, Michael Russell, and David P. Lusch. "The Navstar Global Positioning System in Operation Desert Storm." *Intelligence and National Security* 10, no. 2 (April 1995): 327–35.

———. "The Precision Revolution: The Navstar Global Positioning System in the Second Gulf War." *Intelligence and National Security* 9, no. 2 (April 1994): 167–241.

Russell, Richard L. "CIA's Strategic Intelligence in Iraq." *Political Science Quarterly* 117, no. 2 (Summer 2002): 191–207.

Smith, Bruce A. "U-2/TR-1s Provided Critical Data to Theater Commanders." *Aviation Week & Space Technology*, 19 August 1991, 60–61.

"Spacecraft Played Vital Role in Gulf War Victory." *Aviation Week & Space Technology*, 22 April 1991, 91.

Summe, Jack N. "PSYOP Support to Operation Desert Storm." *Special Warfare* 5 (October 1992): 6–9.

Towell, Pat. "Schwarzkopf Points Out Flaws in Wartime Intelligence." *Congressional Quarterly Weekly Report*, 15 June 1991, 1603.

U.S. Central Intelligence Agency. *CIA Support to the US Military during the Persian Gulf War*. Washington, D.C.: Government Printing Office, 16 June 1997.

Waller, Douglas. "Exclusive—Behind Enemy Lines: The First Combat Photos of Green Beret Commandos on a Secret Mission Deep inside Iraq." *Newsweek*, 28 October 1991, 34.

Wickham, John A., Jr. "The Intelligence Role in Desert Storm." *Signal* (April 1991): 12ff.

17. United Nations Intelligence in Iraq

Gellman, Barton. "Annan Suspicious of UNSCOM Role: U.N. Official Believes Evidence Shows Inspectors Helped U.S. Eavesdrop on Iraq." *Washington Post*, 6 January 1999, A1.

———. "Did the UNSCOM Inspectors Eavesdrop?" *Washington Post National Weekly Edition*, 11 January 1999, 15.

————. "There's Information-Gathering and There's Spying." *Washington Post National Weekly Edition*, 8 March 1999, 16–17.

————. "U.S. Spied on Iraqi Military via U.N." *Washington Post*, 2 March 1999, A1.

Hersh, Seymour M. "Saddam's Best Friend: How the C.I.A. Made It a Lot Easier for the Iraqi Leader to Rearm." *New Yorker*, 5 April 1999, 32ff.

Lippman, Thomas W., and Barton Gellman. "U.S. Says It Collected Iraq Intelligence via UNSCOM." *Washington Post*, 8 January 1999, A1.

Lippman, Thomas W., and John M. Goshko. "'Spying' by UNSCOM Denied." *Washington Post*, 7 January 1999, A18.

Miller, Judith. "Arms Aide Who Quit Assails U.N. on Iraq." *New York Times*, 1 August 1999.

Nelan, Bruce W. "Bugging Saddam." *Time*, 18 January 1999.

Riley, Mark. "UN Chief Spied on Arms Team: Butler." *Sydney Morning Herald*, 5 August 1999.

Ritter, Scott. *Endgame: Solving the Iraq Problem Once and for All*. New York: Simon & Schuster, 1999.

————. *Iraq Confidential: The Untold Story of the Intelligence Conspiracy to Undermine the UN and Overthrow Saddam Hussein*. New York: Nation Books, 2005.

Shenon, Philip. "C.I.A. Was with U.N. in Iraq for Years, Ex-Inspector Says." *New York Times*, 23 February 1999.

————. "Former U.N. Arms Inspector Is Criticized by State Dept." *New York Times*, 24 February 1999.

Vest, Jason, and Wayne Madsen. "A Most Unusual Collection Agency: How the U.S. Undid UNSCOM through Its Empire of Electronic Ears." *Village Voice*, 2 March 1999, 46–48, 52.

Weiner, Tim. "The Case of the Spies without a Country." *New York Times*, 17 January 1999.

————. "U.S. Aides Say U.N. Team Helped to Install Spy Device in Iraq." *New York Times*, 8 January 1999.

————. "U.S. Spied on Iraq under U.N. Cover, Officials Now Say." *New York Times*, 7 January 1999.

18. Operation Iraqi Freedom 2003

Balano, Randy Carol. "Operation Iraqi Freedom: The Role of the Office of Naval Intelligence." *Naval Intelligence Professionals Quarterly* 19, no. 3 (September 2003): 9–10.

Barton, Gellman. "Lessons Learned from OIF: An SF [Special Forces] Battalion S2's Perspective." *Military Intelligence* 30 (April–June 2004): 35–42.

Barton, Gellman, and Dana Priest. "CIA Had Fix on Hussein: Intelligence Revealed 'Target of Opportunity.'" *Washington Post*, 20 March 2003, A1.

Bowers, Faye. "Secret Weapon in US War against Iraq: The CIA." *Christian Science Monitor*, 25 March 2003.

Brinkley, Joel. "Ex-C.I.A. Aides Say Iraq Leader Helped Agency in 90's Attacks." *New York Times*, 9 June 2004.

Burns, John F. "Al Qaeda Leader in Iraq Killed by U.S. Bombs." *New York Times*, 9 June 2006.

Clapper, James R., Jr. "Desert War Was Crucible for Intelligence Systems." *Signal* (September 1991): 77ff.

Coll, Steve. "Seized Intelligence Files Spur U.S. Investigations." *Washington Post*, 3 November 2003, A15.

DeYoung, Karen, and Walter Pincus. "Satellite Images, Communications Intercepts and Defectors' Briefings." *Washington Post*, 6 February 2003, A1.

Drechsler, Donald R. "Reconstructing the Interagency Process after Iraq." *Journal of Strategic Studies* 28, no. 1 (2005): 3–30.

Efron, Sonni, and Greg Miller. "Intelligence Veteran Faults Iraq Arms Data." *Los Angeles Times*, 29 October 2003.

Ensor, David, Jonathan Karl, and Steve Turnham. "CIA under Fire in Iraqi Intelligence Flap." *CNN*, 11 July 2003.

Fainaru, Steve, and Alec Klein. "In Iraq, a Private Realm of Intelligence-Gathering: Firm Extends U.S. Government's Reach." *Washington Post*, 1 July 2007, A1.

Ferris, John. "Netcentric Warfare, C4ISR and Information Operations: Toward a Revolution in Military Intelligence?" *Intelligence and National Security* 19, no. 2 (Summer 2004): 199–225.

Filkins, Dexter. "Exile with Ties to C.I.A. Is Named Premier of Iraq." *New York Times*, 29 May 2004.

Fitzgerald, Michael, and Richard Ned Lebow. "Iraq: The Mother of All Intelligence Failures." *Intelligence and National Security* 21, no. 5 (October 2006): 884–909.

Freedman, Lawrence. "War in Iraq: Selling the Threat." *Survival* 46, no. 2 (Summer 2004): 7–50.

Fulghum, David A. "Shooting Images." *Aviation Week & Space Technology*, 23 May 2005, 53–54.

Gerth, Jeff. "Military's Information War Is Vast and Often Secretive." *New York Times*, 11 December 2005.

Hastedt, Glenn. "Public Intelligence: Leaks as Policy Instruments—The Case of the Iraq War." *Intelligence and National Security* 20, no. 3 (September 2005): 419–39.

Hulse, Carl, and David E. Sanger. "New Criticism on Prewar Use of Intelligence." *New York Times*, 29 September 2003.

Ignatius, David. "When the CIA Got It Right." *Washington Post*, 23 September 2007, B7.

Iraq Study Group. *The Iraq Study Group Report: The Way Forward—A New Approach*. Washington, D.C.: Government Printing Office, 6 December 2006.

Jehl, Douglas. "Spy Agencies Vindicated after String of Setbacks." *New York Times*, 15 December 2003.

Kessler, Glenn, and Dana Priest. "Iraq Data Not Old, Bush Aides Insist." *Washington Post*, 29 September 2003, A15.

Levin, Carl. "Press Release: Levin Releases Newly Declassified Pentagon Inspector General Report on Intelligence Assessment Activities of the Office of Under Secretary of Defense Doug Feith." Washington, D.C.: Government Printing Office, 5 April 2007.

Nolte, William. "Keeping Pace with the Revolution in Military Affairs: Operation Iraqi Freedom and the Challenge to Intelligence." *Studies in Intelligence* 48, no. 1 (2004): 1–10.

O'Connell, Ed, and Cheryl Benard. "A New IO Strategy: Prevention and Disengagement." *Strategic Insights* 5, no. 5 (May 2006).

Pillar, Paul R. "Inside Track: Sometimes the CIA Is Right." *National Interest*, 6 June 2007.

———. "Intelligence, Policy, and the War in Iraq." *Foreign Affairs* 85, no. 2 (March–April 2006): 15–27.

———. "The Right Stuff." *National Interest*, 29 August 2007.

Pincus, Walter. "Intelligence Agencies 'Must Do Better': Panel Faults Quality of Information on Insurgency, Militias." *Washington Post*, 8 December 2006, A31.

———. "Spy Agencies Warned of Iraq Resistance." *Washington Post*, 9 September 2003, A1.

———. "U.S.–British Differences Show Iraq Intelligence Gap." *Washington Post*, 30 September 2003, A12.

Pincus, Walter, and Karen DeYoung. "Analysts' Warnings of Iraq Chaos Detailed: Senate Panel Releases Assessments From 2003." *Washington Post*, 26 May 2007, A1.

Pincus, Walter, and R. Jeffrey Smith. "Official's Key Report on Iraq Is Faulted: 'Dubious' Intelligence Fueled Push for War." *Washington Post*, 9 February 2007, A1.

Pound, Edward T. "The Iran Connection." *U.S. News & World Report*, 22 November 2004, 32–48.

Priest, Dana. "House Probers Conclude Iraq War Data Was Weak." *Washington Post*, 28 September 2003, A1.

———. "Telling Secrets: Not Just What, but How; Speech Is Revealing on Gathering Intelligence." *Washington Post*, 6 February 2003, A23.

———. "Violence, Turnover Blunt CIA Effort in Iraq." *Washington Post*, 4 March 2004, A1.

Priest, Dana, and Thomas E. Ricks. "Focus Shifts from Military Police to Intelligence." *Washington Post*, 11 May 2004, A15.

Rayment, Sean. "Top Secret Army Cell Breaks Terrorists." *Sunday Telegraph* (London), 5 February 2007.

Ricks, Thomas E. "Intelligence Problems in Iraq Are Detailed." *Washington Post*, 25 October 2003, A1.

Robinson, Linda. "The Propaganda War." *U.S. News & World Report*, 29 May 2006, 29–31.

Scarborough, Rowan. "U.S. Search for bin Laden Intensifies." *Washington Times*, 23 February 2004.

Schmitt, Eric. "U.S. Drones Crowding the Skies to Fight Insurgents in Iraq." *New York Times*, 5 April 2005.

Shane, Scott, and Mark Mazzetti. "Ex-C.I.A. Chief, in Book, Assails Cheney on Iraq." *New York Times*, 27 April 2007.

———. "Senate Democrats Say Bush Ignored Spy Agencies' Prewar Warnings of Iraq Perils." *New York Times*, 26 May 2007.

Shanker, Thom, and Eric Schmitt. "Firing Leaflets and Electrons, U.S. Wages Information War." *New York Times*, 24 February 2003.

———. "Pentagon Says a Covert Force Hunts Hussein." *New York Times*, 7 November 2003.

Sherwell, Philip. "Teheran 'Executed CIA's Spy Network 10 Years Ago.'" *Electronic Telegraph*, 13 February 2005.

Vanden Brook, Tom. "Drones' Supply Short of Demand." *USA Today*, 28 March 2007.

Waller, Douglas. "The CIA's Secret Army." *Time*, 3 February 2003, 22.

Ware, Michael. "The Secret Collaborators." *Time*, 11 October 2003.

Waterman, Shaun. "Baker-Hamilton Report Slams U.S. Intel on Iraq, Says Violence Under-Counted." *United Press International*, 7 December 2006.

White, Rebecca N. "Inside Track: The Facts of the Matter." *National Interest*, 21 September 2007.

Wilson, Scott. "Chalabi Aides Suspected of Spying for Iran; Raid at Leader's Home Targeted His Associates." *Washington Post*, 22 May 2004, A20.

Wong, Edward. "New Iraq Agency to Hunt Rebels." *New York Times*, 31 January 2004.

Woodward, Bob. "Attack Was 48 Hours Old When It 'Began.'" *Washington Post*, 23 March 2003, A1.

19. Terrorism

Anderson, Sean K., and S. Sloan. *Historical Dictionary of Terrorism*. 3rd ed. Lanham Md.: Scarecrow Press, 2009.

Cooper, H. H. A., and Lawrence J. Redlinger. *Terrorism and Espionage in the Middle East: Deception, Displacement and Denial*. Lewiston, N.Y.: Edwin Mellen Press, 2005.

Pipes, Daniel. "Why Assad's Terror Works and Qadhafi's Doesn't." *ORBIS* 33, no. 4 (Fall 1989): 501–8.

Pritchett, Diane Tueller. "The Syrian Strategy on Terrorism: 1971–1977." *Conflict Quarterly* 8, no. 3 (Summer 1988): 27–48.

Rubin, Barry, and Judith Colp Rubin. *Anti-American Terrorism and the Middle East: Understanding the Violence*. New York: Oxford University Press, 2002.

Shibley, Telhami, and Michael Barnett, eds. *Identity and Foreign Policy in the Middle East*. Ithaca, N.Y.: Cornell University Press, 2002.

———. *The Stakes: America and the Middle East*. Denver, Colo.: Westview Press, 2002.

20. Satellites in the Middle East

Rip, Michael Russell, and David P. Lusch. "The Precision Revolution: The Navstar Global Positioning System in the Second Gulf War. *Intelligence and Nationals Security* 9, no. 2 (April 1984): 167–241.

21. Weapons of Mass Destruction

Butler, Richard, and James C. Roy. *The Greatest Threat: Iraq, Weapons of Mass Destruction, and the Crisis of Global Security*, New York: Public Affairs, 2001

Eddington, Patrick G. *Gassed in the Gulf: The Inside Story of the Pentagon–CIA Cover-Up of the Gulf War Syndrome.* Washington, D.C.: Insignia, 1997.

Phelps, Timothy M., and Knut Royce. "Columnist Blows CIA Agent's Cover." *Newsday*, 22 July 2003.

Pincus, Walter. "CIA Did Not Share Doubt on Iraq Data." *Washington Post*, 12 June 2003, A1.

———. "CIA Director George J. Tenet Discusses the National Intelligence Estimate." *Washington Post*, 10 August 2003, A10.

———. "CIA Says It Cabled Key Data to White House." *Washington Post*, 13 June 2003, A16.

———. "Panel to See Prewar CIA Memos on Iraq: White House Agrees on Release." *Washington Post*, 5 November 2003, A24.

———. "Tenet Says He Didn't Know about Claim." *Washington Post*, 17 July 2003, A1.

Pincus, Walter, and Mike Allen. "CIA Got Uranium Reference Cut in October; Why Bush Cited It in Jan. Is Unclear." *Washington Post*, 13 July. 2003, A1.

Pincus, Walters, and Dana Priest. "U.S. Had Uranium Papers Earlier: Officials Say Forgeries on Iraqi Efforts Reached State Dept. before Speech." *Washington Post*, 18 July 2003, A1.

Priest, Dana, and Thomas E. Ricks. "CIA Poised to Quiz Hussein; Rumsfeld Says Agency to Control Interrogations." *Washington Post*, 17 December 2003, A1.

Priest, Dana, and Robin Wright. "Iraq Spy Service Planned by U.S. to Stem Attacks; CIA Said to Be Enlisting Hussein Agents." *Washington Post*, 11 December 2003, A41.

Risen, James, and Thom Shanker. "Hussein Enters Post-9/11 Web of U.S. Prisons." *New York Times*, 18 December 2003.

Sanger, David E. "A Shifting Spotlight on Uranium Sales." *New York Times*, 15 July 2003.

Sanger, David E., with Judith Miller. "National Security Aide Says He's to Blame for Speech Error." *New York Times*, 23 July 2003.

Sanger, David E., and James Risen. "C.I.A. Chief Takes Blame in Assertion on Iraqi Uranium." *New York Times*, 12 July 2003.

Shadid, Anthony, and Daniel Williams. "U.S. Recruiting Hussein's Spies." *Washington Post*, 24 August 2003, A1.

Shenon, Philip. "C.I.A. Is Unfairly Blamed in Chemical Blast, Panel Is Told." *New York Times*, 17 April 1997, A14.

———. "C.I.A. Report Says It Failed to Share Data on Iraq Arms." *New York Times*, 10 April 1997, A1, A12.

———. "Powell Says C.I.A. Failed to Warn of Chemical Arms." *New York Times*, 18 April 1997, A11.

Shoham, Dany. "The Anthrax Evidence Points to Iraq." *International Journal of Intelligence and CounterIntelligence* 20, no. 4 (December 2007): 755–59

———. "An Antithesis on the Fate of Iraq's Chemical and Biological Weapons." *International Journal of Intelligence and CounterIntelligence* 19, no. 1 (January 2005): 59–83.

———."Image vs. Reality of Iranian Chemical and Biological Weapons." *International Journal of Intelligence and CounterIntelligence* 18, no. 1 (December 2004): 89–141.

———. "Technical Intelligence in Retrospect: The 2001 Anthrax Letters Powder." *International Journal of Intelligence and CounterIntelligence* 20, no. 1 (March 2007): 79–105.

22. Peace Processes in the Middle East

Shapiro, Shlomo. "The CIA as Middle East Peace-Broker." *Survival* 45, no. 2 (Summer 2003).

———. "Intelligence, Peacekeeping and Peacemaking in the Middle East." In *Peacekeeping Intelligence: Emerging Concepts for the Future*, ed. Wies Platje, Dame Pauline Neville-Jones, and Ben de Jong. Oakton, Va.: OSS International Press, 2003.

———. "Intelligence Services and Political Transformation in the Middle East." *International Journal of Intelligence and CounterIntelligence* 17, no. 4 (October–December 2004): 575–600.

III. INTERNET SOURCES

Al-Ahram Centre for Political and Strategic Studies (ACPSS): http://www.ahram.org.eg/acpss/Eng/index.asp

Jordanian General Intelligence Department: http://www.gid.gov.jo

MEMRI: The Middle East Media Research Institute: http://www.memri.org

SANA—Syria News Agency: http://www.sana.org/index_eng.html

About the Authors

Ephraim Kahana holds a PhD in international politics. He chairs the National Security Program in the Department of Political Science at Western Galilee College in Israel. He also taught international relations in the National Security Program at the University of Haifa and the Israeli Technion, where he was elected as outstanding lecturer. Dr. Kahana is a member of the Board of Editors of the *International Journal of Intelligence and CounterIntelligence*. He is also a member of the executive committee of the Israeli International Studies Association (IISA).

Dr. Kahana has written numerous papers on intelligence and national security issues. Some publications are "Covert Action: The Israeli Experience," *Strategic Intelligence* 3 (2007); "Analyzing Israeli Intelligence Failures," *International Journal of Intelligence and CounterIntelligence* (2005); "Early Warning versus Concept: The Case of the Yom Kippur War 1973," *Intelligence and National Security* (2002); "Reorganizing Israel's Intelligence Community," *International Journal of Intelligence and CounterIntelligence* (2002); "Mossad–CIA Cooperation," *International Journal of Intelligence and CounterIntelligence* (2001). In addition, he authored the *Historical Dictionary of Israeli Intelligence* (2006).

In 2004, Dr. Kahana was the academic director for a conference on "The War in Iraq and the New International Order," held on 29 November at Western Galilee College. He regularly presents papers at conferences of the International Studies Association (ISA) and serves on panels in intelligence studies. Dr. Kahana received his early and secondary education in Haifa. He obtained his BA degree from Hebrew University in Jerusalem and his PhD from the University of South Africa, Pretoria.

Muhammad Suwaed holds a PhD in Middle Eastern Studies from the University of Bar Ilan and graduated with distinction. He is a faculty member of the National Security Program in the Western Galilee College and the Kinneret College in Israel. In his doctorate dissertation, he researched the relations between the Bedouins and Israel since the days of the British mandate in Palestine. Dr. Suwaed teaches courses about the national security of the Arab states and the Arab–Israeli conflict.